ELMER ISELER
Choral Visionary

Walter Pitman

DUNDURN PRESS
TORONTO

Copy-editor: Jennifer Gallant
Design: Erin Mallory
Printer: Transcontinental

Except where indicated, photos arte courtesy of the Iseler family archives.

Library and Archives Canada Cataloguing in Publication

Pitman, Walter
    Elmer Iseler : choral visionary / Walter Pitman.

Includes bibliographical references and index.
ISBN 978-1-55002-815-7

    1. Iseler, Elmer, 1927-1998. 2. Choral conductors--Canada--Biography.
I. Title.

ML422.I785P68 2008   782.5'092   C2008-900692-5

1   2   3   4   5   12   11   10   09   08

We acknowledge the support of the **Canada Council for the Arts** and the **Ontario Arts Council** for our publishing program. We also acknowledge the financial support of the **Government of Canada** through the **Book Publishing Industry Development Program** and **The Association for the Export of Canadian Books**, and the **Government of Ontario** through the **Ontario Book Publishers Tax Credit program**, and the **Ontario Media Development Corporation**.

Care has been taken to trace the ownership of copyright material used in this book. The author and the publisher welcome any information enabling them to rectify any references or credits in subsequent editions.

                                                                                    J. Kirk Howard, President

Printed and bound in Canada.
Printed on recycled paper.

www.dundurn.com

Dundurn Press
3 Church Street, Suite 500
Toronto, Ontario, Canada
M5E 1M2

Gazelle Book Services Limited
White Cross Mills
High Town, Lancaster, England
LA1 4XS

Dundurn Press
2250 Military Road
Tonawanda, NY
U.S.A. 14150

Elmer and Jessie attend an Order of Ontario gala evening, circa late 1990s.

Elmer and Jessie on vacation by the sea at Ocean City, New Jersey.

Table of Contents

Foreword by Jessie Iseler

"You're taking on a genius, but I think you can handle it!"
— my father, John Balsillie, as he advised
me when I was about to marry Elmer Iseler

"BEND AND STRETCH, REACH FOR THE STARS.
Here comes Jupiter, there goes Mars." Together, Elmer and I always
looked up to the heavens for solace and guidance, always looking towards
the future. Elmer even endeared himself to the Hale-Bopp comet to take
away his cancerous tumour!

I am so pleased that Walter Pitman has completed this first biography
of Elmer Iseler and that Dundurn Press has seen to its publication. I hope
that this will be the first of several. These pages do not purport to explore
the dozen volumes of handwritten diaries that Elmer wrote about our
exquisite times on the Severn River, nor is it a memoir of our family life,
our love story, or his photography, but rather it's Elmer's journey as he
followed his heart in pursuing choral music in Canada.

Walter Pitman has been tireless in his dedication to search for accuracy
in detail and to expound on the incredible impact that Elmer's life's work
had in advancing and elevating the appreciation of and performance in
singing. Elmer was a pioneer in the development of professionalism in
choral music in Canada. Together with the support of many colleagues

and institutions, sponsors, and individuals who believed in his mission, Elmer Iseler's energy and vision touched thousands of choral performers in every city, town, and hamlet in Canada — indeed around the world!

It's no secret that I coiffed his wonderful white hair before concerts as an immense aura of energy gathered from within his persona. He sought quiet and solitude prior to a performance. The downbeat mattered. Although I may not agree with every word of his interpretation, I believe that Walter Pitman has captured the essence, importance, and impact of an extraordinary conducting career through choral concert performance, repertoire presentations, and a history that changed the lives of people forever.

Composer Derek Holman referred to Elmer as the "Wizard" because of his magic with a score. Colleague John Reeves called him a "Renaissance man." Many thought he was superhuman. For me, I had in the dance of life one perfect partner. We were connected in a magical way.

The story must be told. This is not a book that Elmer would have written himself — some days being too painful to recount, others being such glorious peak experiences but with no time to revel in success.

I am still in love with the man I married; his glasses stay by the bed. The only regret I have is that Elmer didn't get to see Vanessa and Juzzelle grow up. Our two grandchildren never say goodbye — they say "la-lu," which is short for "love you" — sincere and affectionate. Elmer would approve! "We rise again in the faces of our children."

To all who ever sang with Elmer across this country, this book is dedicated. It's your story too!

Jessie Iseler
Jessie Iseler
From our cedar log home, Caledon, Ontario
A beautiful sunny fall day
October 14, 2007 — Elmer's eightieth birthday

With all good wishes

Preface

THE NAME ELMER ISELER CONJURES UP JUST
one visual image — that of a tall, imposing figure with arms and hands
extended, with eyes and facial expression intent upon encouraging the
sound of voices addressing the great choral repertoire of the ages —
Handel's *Messiah*, J.S. Bach's *St. Matthew Passion*, or the Mass in B Minor.
For Canadians, he was the dean of choral conductors and in the last half
of the twentieth century his choral musical reach seemed infinite.

Often a strong and talented musician can bring into focus a new
enthusiasm for a particular musical form, but rarely does a single person
enhance the full spectrum of a musical genre across the breadth of an
entire country as Elmer Iseler did in his relentless pursuit of excellence in
choral presentation during the last decades of the twentieth century.

There is no parallel to Elmer Iseler's role in challenging and changing
the context of choral music in Canada. Before his arrival on the scene such
performance was essentially to be found in two areas — both drawn from
the dominance of the United Kingdom over its far-flung colony. One
was the church choir stall, from which music was produced every Sunday
morning to enhance the quality and intensity of divine worship. The
liturgy that encouraged choral expression was and remains a major source
of inspiration in both the Protestant and Roman Catholic traditions found
thriving in the frigid climes of the North American continent. Indeed,
the paragon of High Anglican musical composition was the Canadian
composer Healey Willan, whose work was internationally recognized and
regularly performed. Unfortunately, along with commendable pride there

was often the sense that singing to the glory of God legitimized the most abysmal standards of musical expression and performance. Elmer Iseler was to change that perception in his own lifetime.

The second major influence was the nineteenth-century British oratorio choir movement brought across the Atlantic by immigrants to Canada from the old country. Their delight in singing in large choral ensembles inspired replication in their new homeland. The *Messiah* choral presence was and still is very basic to the United Kingdom music scene. These massive gatherings of singers, sometimes measured in the thousands, addressed the monumental offerings of Handel, Haydn, Mozart, and Mendelssohn, to which were wedded in the late nineteenth century and throughout the twentieth the mountaintop compositions of Johann Sebastian Bach.

Elmer Iseler drew strength from both of these traditions. Through his high expectations of a distinctive quality of tone, balance, and blend, the standards of choral music performance in every province of Canada were perceptibly changed. He transformed the quality of music expression in both the choir stall and the concert hall, raising the expectations of parishioners and the concertgoing public alike. Through his commitment to workshops directed at both choristers and choral conductors, both small choirs and eventually larger choral ensembles were influenced. Canadian choral music was never to be the same again.

From this transformation in the sound and competency of choral ensembles came the understanding that singers were indeed musicians who deserved recompense for their efforts. The concept of a truly professional choir working year after year to improve itself consistently and to address new repertoire constantly was Elmer's dream that eventually became reality, not only in Toronto, but under other conductors in Montreal and Vancouver and beyond. It fulfilled his vision that truly great music deserves the skill, time, energy, and commitment that symphony orchestras, string quartets, and instrumental chamber ensembles give to the performances that move their listeners.

Elmer's determination and single-mindedness sometimes aroused strong antipathy. Even in moments of triumph Elmer was critically appraised. Perhaps every conductor faces a degree of unpopularity, as by definition the conductor's role is to push singers, in most cases amateurs, to reach heights they had never considered possible. In 1975, on presenting him with the Canadian Music Council Citation for his contribution to his country, his friend and colleague Keith MacMillan referred to him as an "exasperating" man.[1] That adjective, along with "difficult," followed him down the decades. It was part of the cost of working on the frontier. There would be two major explosions involving his forced resignation from the leadership of both the Festival Singers, his first chamber ensemble, and the Toronto Mendelssohn Choir, his large "oratorio" choir. There were those in positions of power in both organizations who failed to understand his vision and who initiated a process that brought about his downfall as conductor of both these prestigious choral institutions.

Elmer has been described as a Renaissance man. He depended on an extraordinary library containing the collective wisdom of his generation, but the term "Renaissance," with its glance backward, quite fails to capture the rich quality of his mind and spirit. He articulated no overarching understanding of the heights of human wisdom in areas of history, philosophy, language, mathematics, science, or theology of civilizations of the past, but rather he lived out an extraordinary style of daily activity that revealed his curiosity and understanding, his wonder and his enthusiastic appreciation of the world around him.

More accurately, Elmer could be described as a twenty-first-century man. The new millennium has already been described as the era that will demand the attention of the holistic individual, one for whom the twentieth century, with its emphasis on specialization and information gathering from profound research, no longer holds the solutions for human development. Elmer was not given to sociological meanderings about his unusual lifestyle — he just lived differently. Besides a passion for great music, he gardened avidly; pursued form, colour, and texture through his photography; searched, in awe, the skies with his telescope; watched, identified, and fed birds and sundry animals; gloried in the beauty of countryside and waterway; and reached out to a family that included his beloved wife, Jessie, and their two children but was inclusive as well of Jessie's entire Balsillie clan. He spent time collecting objects of beauty and antique significance, all in the name of living a horizontal life that brooked no discontinuities from one activity to another. The above proclivities were not hobbies pursued to fill in available time between conducting engagements. These were all building blocks, segments of a life well lived, one that eschewed competition and conflict and was supported by cultural values that were communicated by such a lifestyle.

There is no mystery behind Elmer's confrontation with others in places of power in the arts. It was more than the usual resentment of the conductor's dominant role. He could not accept values that undermined his vision of a world of compassionate human relationships and total environmental responsiveness that he knew must dominate a new century if it was to be sustainable. It was not just the arguments about repertoire, soloists, and venues that normally beset choral governing bodies and can be accommodated with diplomatic interventions — but profound differences over the deeper commitments to great music and its performance that arose from a kind of understanding about the human condition that is in defiant contrast to the values revealed in the more dominant economic interpretations of success that so often confront the artist and his craft.

In the context of such a lifelong philosophy, Elmer Iseler realized that musical expression must speak to the lives of men and women facing the challenges of the century in which they lived. He fully understood that J.S. Bach's Chorales and Passions addressed the great questions facing humankind beyond the particular Christian biblical texts on which they were based. He realized that if music was to be a vital, dynamic influence on people's beliefs and behaviours, there must be compositions in the repertoire of every chorus written by contemporary composers who shared the mysteries of living in a modern age with both choristers and their audiences. He encouraged creators of music to address these issues of human alienation, injustice and inequality, peace and war, into their choral efforts. They would do so in the knowledge that their work would be superbly performed by the Festival Singers or, later, the Elmer Iseler Singers, and if demanding larger choral forces, the Toronto Mendelssohn Choir. The work of these three choral bodies consumed the entire mature life of Elmer Iseler. Indeed, I decided to organize the latter chapters of this biography not in the traditional chronological format but rather to trace his work first with the smaller chamber choirs and then to provide an account of his efforts with the much larger chorus, the Toronto Mendelssohn Choir.

He left a legacy of many great choral works composed as a result of his efforts with both kinds of choirs, and in doing so he created a Canadian tradition that choral performance audiences deserve the very best repertoire and quality of performance and that those who devote their lives to ensemble singing deserve to be treated as true professionals. Canada is now recognized abroad as a "singing nation." Even more astonishingly, now, almost a decade after his death, there is a choir bearing his name, superbly conducted by Lydia Adams, still managed with care and sensitivity by Elmer's widow, Jessie, still following the path he set in terms of choral excellence and repertoire development, but, as he would have had it, taking new paths that stretch beyond any single man's lifelong reach.

No introduction to the life and work of Elmer Iseler could approach accuracy without the recognition of the role that his wife played in his success. Jessie understood and supported Elmer's vision of the place of choral music and the means by which he would enhance the choral art in Canada. More importantly, she realized that all his enthusiasm beyond the rehearsal hall and the performance venue was essential in a lifestyle that exhibited the kind of society and country that demanded a choral response of cultural significance. Elmer and Jessie were united intellectually and spiritually in a crusade that was directed towards changing a nation and its people.

Acknowledgements

A BIOGRAPHY OF AN ELMER ISELER DEMANDS
the attention of an enormous number of people who were his friends
and associates. It is significant that more than a hundred people have made
some contribution to the examination of this man's life and influence.

From the outset, it was evident that the most important individual
in his life was his wife and life partner, Jessie. She carefully stored all of
Elmer's papers and records and most generously made them available for
my perusal and study. However, as the collection has not been formally
archived, the normal referencing was not possible. As well, she has given
me her time for extensive interviewing.

Jessie's Balsillie family became a valuable source, particularly her
brother David and her sister-in-law Darlow. It was David and Darlow
who hosted my visit to Copp Bay on the Severn River to meet the members of that extraordinary community, in particular Paul Singleton and his
wife, Barbara, and Martie Strayer Russel and her husband, Philip. From
them I discovered a totally different Elmer in a totally different culture.

However, Jessie and Elmer's own daughter, Jessie Jr., who will be
identified as "Buffy" as she is called by all who know the family, was most
expressive of her knowledge of Elmer's lifestyle as a family man, as was
her oldest daughter, Vanessa.

The most numerous category of friends and colleagues of Elmer's,
was, as would be expected, the choristers, past and present, from Elmer's
three choirs and the choral conductors with whom he worked. Their
astute judgments were, in themselves, a proof of his educational role. Don

Bartle was in Elmer's Festival Singers from its beginning, and his wife-to-be, Jean Ashworth Gam, joined him in the Toronto Mendelssohn Choir some years later, though I perceived her most clearly as the founder and conductor of the Toronto Children's Chorus and as a colleague among a host of admiring choral conductors — such as Lydia Adams, Doreen Rao, Linda Beaupré, Donna Colley, Melva Graham, Robert Cooper, Howard Dyck, Douglas Elliott, Ted Moroney, David Fallis, Gerald Fagan, Fred Graham, Wayne Strongman, and Giles Bryant, with all of whom I spoke.

There were many choristers from the early years who had splendid memories — Joanne Eaton, Elizabeth Elliott, Mary Morrison, Jean Edwards, Jean Patterson, Stephen Clarke, Clair Pace, Malcolm Russell, and Frank Taylor — and others who came later and were most helpful were Ed Wiens, David King (also now a conductor), Peter Fisher, Judith Young, Carolyn Frank, Mary Lou Fallis, Jane Darling, Chuck Butler, Robert Missen, Alison Roy, and Alex Jozefacki. Also in this category must be added now choral conductor Brad Ratzlaff, who once sang in the Elmer Iseler Singers with his conductor wife-to-be, Carol Woodward Ratzlaff.

I was particularly interested in spending some time on Elmer's career as a teacher in the public schooling system of Ontario. Judy Kennedy, principal of Northview Heights Collegiate Institute at the time when the school's auditorium was named after Elmer Iseler a few years after his death, advised me to contact Baird Knechtel, who was most helpful in providing names of other teachers and students who were contemporary with Elmer's presence, such as David Smith, Nancy Thomson, Bert Mitchell, and a host of students — Linda Sword, Susan Silverberg, Barbara Myers, Jean McKay, and Pat Hartman. It was more difficult to find associates, either teachers or students, from Elmer's first school — York Memorial Secondary School. However, students Ken Dyck, Jim Copeland, Ken Thomson, and especially Margaret McCoy all remembered him well.

It was in the Waterloo area that many of Elmer's most important decisions were made about the career he might choose to follow. Paul Fischer not only provided insights but also led me to Dr. Delton Glebe, to Ulrich Leupold's widow, Gertrude, and to Fr. Erich Schultz, all of whom knew Elmer from these days a half-century ago. Most important of the Waterloo area influences was his first wife, Trudie Mosig, a member of the Mosig family of New Hamburg who all played a part in Elmer's initiation as a choral conductor. Trudie Iseler, now Cochrane, was a most willing interviewee and provided generous verbal snapshots of her life with Elmer during these significant years as he completed his academic and professional preparation.

There were long-term friends whose influence stretched across many decades of Elmer's life. Richard Shibley fits this description completely and was most generous with his time. John Bird's time as mentor began in Elmer's university days, and though Vern and Elfrieda Heinrichs' closeness came later, they all participated in the process of completing this volume. Gabriella and Harry Currie, intimate friends of both Jessie and Elmer for many years, agreed to be interviewed and provided fascinating insights.

Choirs demand much more than just choristers and conductors — accompanists play a central role in the making of fine choral music, if not in concert, most certainly in rehearsal. Ruth Watson Henderson and Lydia Adams were both thoughtful and expressive observers of many hours of Elmer's conducting magic. Eugene Watts of the Canadian Brass was most helpful in analyzing Elmer's interaction with one of the instrumental ensembles that accompanied his choirs.

Choirs also need a board of directors drawn from the community to give assurance to the public that their contributions and volunteer activities are being appropriately utilized. John Fenton was Elmer's financial confidant and a valuable board appointee to his choirs. George Pennie, as well as being a brother-in-law, could also be counted upon to serve Elmer's needs for support. Others consulted include Irene Bailey, Lorna Butler, Hans Schade, and the extraordinary John Lawson, who, as a chorister as well as seasoned board chair and TMC president, gave inestimable assistance to my efforts, as did Dr. Don Kramer, also a chorister in several choirs but one who finally found his way on to the board of the Elmer Iseler Singers.

Choirs also need audiences, and from the earliest days, the CBC, Canada's national public broadcaster, hired Elmer's Festival Singers and subsequent choirs. I was able to interview John Reeves, not just a broadcaster but also an athlete, a writer, and a composer, who along with a bevy of splendid CBC producers and executives supported Elmer's efforts.

As well, John Peter Lee Roberts, a stellar broadcaster and advocate for music at the CBC, was a source of valuable insight. Of course, considerable on-air attention was given to Elmer's choirs by *Choral Concert* host Howard Dyck and producer Robert Cooper. Their assistance was essential.

There were so many who rode several horses through their journey with Elmer. As well as the John Birds, the John Lawsons, and the Richard Shibleys, there was Mary McKellar (now Coutts), who played a major role in Elmer's musical development in his high school days and remained to serve him as a board member and who along with her husband, John, was a friend of the entire Iseler family. Indeed, it was John Coutts who put me in touch with both Chuck Miller, a valued municipal employee of Port Colborne, Elmer's beloved birthplace, and John Freeman-Shaw, the present vice-principal of Elmer's hometown high school.

Even institutions become involved in such an enterprise of discovery and I am indebted to Carol Nagel, the archivist for the Lutheran Church of Canada, who provided information I could not have gained in any other way. The Toronto Mendelssohn Choir maintains an archive, and Sylvia Winder, the archivist, was most helpful. She was assisted by Susan Wilson, another TMC chorister. One cannot thank sufficiently Patti Tompkins, the manager of the TMC over so many of Elmer's years, for her thoughtful responses to often difficult questions. I am always thankful for the presence of our public broadcaster, the CBC, which keeps several splendid archival collections on all the various functions that frame the Corporation's work. The names of Vivian Moenes, Laurie Nemetz, Gail Donald, and Lillian Hunkeler come to mind. A special thanks goes to Alan Morriss, who searched out references that were most valuable.

There are those who read every page of this manuscript and whose advice was treasured. First and foremost was, once again, my patient wife, Ida. Indeed the volume reached out to our entire family. My daughter, Anne, who did not know the Iselers, acted as an editor and could utilize that distance as well as her perspective from another generation to give the author a unique response to his search for meaning. My sons, Wade and Mark, as in the past, saved the author from any technological disaster that might have otherwise lengthened the process exponentially. A special appreciation must be directed to Paul Schafer, a close friend and colleague whose work in Canada's cultural history is unparalleled, who also read the entire work with a critical eye. As well, I am indebted to Robert Cooper, who read selected passages from the viewpoint of a choral conductor and as a friend of Elmer's without having any part in the portrayal of his personal role in the story. A similar appreciation is due to Vern Heinrichs, who provided information that was essential to the understanding of Elmer's last days. Pauline Couture led me through the labyrinth of the World Wide Web as an introduction to yet another research tool.

Once again, I cannot express sufficiently my appreciation for the professionalism of my publisher, The Dundurn Group, particularly CEO Kirk Howard and his colleague Beth Bruder and the efforts of Jennifer Scott, designer, and Jennifer Gallant and Barry Jowett, editors.

The errors and misinterpretations are entirely my own.

Chapter 1
An Incredible Beginning

CANADA'S MOST FAMOUS CHORAL CONDUCTOR, Elmer Walter Iseler, was born on October 14, 1927, in the humble community of Humberstone, soon to become part of the municipality of Port Colborne. This border town on the shores of Lake Erie in the area of Southwestern Ontario known as the Niagara Peninsula is recognized by many as mainly a gateway to the United States. He was the third offspring of Lydia and Theodore Iseler, a couple who had been called to serve the First Lutheran Church in that community the very year of Elmer's birth. He remained in Port Colborne for almost two decades and the community had an enormous effect on his career.

His father, Theodore Iseler, had arrived in Canada in 1916, a date of some significance in the life of the nation that he had chosen to live in and serve. The Great War, with its unparalleled savagery, was at its height, and Canada's role was central to the struggle on the Western Front. Ultimately, Canada won its sovereignty as a nation and a seat in the League of Nations from the magnificent effort of Canadian soldiers in those horrific trenches. From this point the cultural life of the nation and its expression would be of increasing interest to the entire English- and French-speaking world.

The Reverend Theodore A. Iseler, originally an American Lutheran from Michigan, had experienced a sojourn in rural Quebec, and then a pastorate in Williamsburg, Ontario, in the 1920s, before accepting the call to lead the First Lutheran Church on Elm Street in Port Colborne. Though he was a young American Lutheran pastor with German roots, he had begun his work in St. Paul's Lutheran Church in Poltimore, Quebec, north of Ottawa. There he had served a largely German community from 1916 to 1918. Preaching in the German language throughout these years in most parts of Canada might have been a questionable practice, but hardly in rural Quebec where British jingoism was modified in the presence of a less motivated French-Canadian Catholic population feeling that it was inexorably caught up in a British imperialist war. The German settlers in that region were able to avoid the kind of pressures faced by fellow German immigrants in a prominent Ontario community whose early settlers had named the urban area in their midst "Berlin" and woke one morning to find that it had been renamed "Kitchener" in honour of a British military hero.

Reverend Theodore Iseler spent two years in Quebec on this missionary charge that had included two other small churches besides St. Paul's and also demanded that he teach all week in the one-room schoolhouse beside that church. It was exhausting and challenging. As impossibly strenuous as this schedule was, there was a lively social life in the community that ultimately decided that an Iseler family would be established and would have a distinguished future in Canada.[1]

It was in those two years that Theodore met, courted, and married Lydia Paesler and thereby inherited a family of Paeslers in nearby Val-des-Bois who included Lydia's brother, Elmer (who was to be honoured by his sister's naming of her first son), and his wife, Evelyn. Throughout his life, Elmer Iseler returned at least every other year to rural Quebec in order to keep warm that relationship with his mother's and his namesake uncle's extended families — as well as to engage enthusiastically and successfully in fishing the abundant lakes near their homes.

Theodore and Lydia were known both within family ranks and beyond as a "hot couple" who had engaged in a whirlwind love affair and had become married within a few short months. It was a passionate description of his parents that son Elmer found quite appealing. He never lost his own trust in spontaneous responses to opportunities that presented themselves in both his work and daily life.

The next few years at St. Peter's Lutheran Church in Williamsburg, Ontario, a largely English-speaking community, were valuable preparation for the calling to Port Colborne. The First Lutheran Church on Elm Street, Port Colborne, was in need of a vigorous pastor and Theodore was a perfect choice. He arrived with his two young girls and a Lydia ready to provide a third offspring. It was a difficult birth for Elmer on a hard kitchen table at 57 Union Street, the only home that he was to know until he left Port Colborne to study at university. The labour of childbirth went on for an astonishing four days. Elmer was caught in the birth canal, unable to emerge through those many hours. The experience was one that neither mother nor son forgot. Many years later, Elmer suffered recurring claustrophobic nightmares and a psychologist advised him to speak to his mother about his birth. He did so, discovered the trauma of his birthing process, and the nightmares ceased.

Yet this event was to affect his life in another way. Elmer was fascinated by airplanes — indeed, as a boy, he was constantly building models of them — but hated to travel by air. The constrained and constricting nature of the narrow cabin left him nervous and uncomfortable. Whenever he could, he drove his car to the places where he was conducting or shared the bus with his choristers. Inevitably, he had to overcome his fears and accompany his choirs around the world by air. Yet it was shorter trips to smaller communities rather than flights to the cultural centres of Europe that Elmer most enjoyed.[2]

Elmer never ceased to brag about his birthplace. The municipality was in an expansionist phase both geographically and industrially before he became an inhabitant. However, this municipality did not stand out as a particularly delightful destination for all those who insisted upon making the nearby Niagara Falls the major tourist attraction in North America in the nineteenth and most of the twentieth century. It was mainly known as a very busy crossing point for people wishing to visit the United States or come back to Canada. It was and is today a major centre for the export of goods back and forth across the international border. However, though Port Colborne has an exciting Lake Erie waterfront, it is not an architecturally memorable community and the people that one meets are seemingly always going somewhere else.

A border town rarely reveals the best impression of the cultures of either the country in which it is to be found or the nearby foreign land. The overwhelming presence of at least a few Americans and their worst features confronted Elmer from the outset. The image of the "ugly American," loud, demanding, and uncouth, those characteristics of the tourist "on the loose," that has been exploited in both literature and film became a part of the ongoing life experience of the young Elmer Iseler. When the Second World War began and the United States delayed in joining the Allied cause, American tourists seemed to be enjoying all the North American luxuries while Canadians were facing limits on their consumption through a stringent rationing process. It was an unpleasant contrast to behold and attracted much negative comment.

Throughout his life Elmer enjoyed visiting his father's relatives in Michigan and, as a tourist, he explored the warmer climes and exotic flora and fauna of Florida and the delights of the New Jersey shores. Yet he rejected all offers of employment south of the border, and at one point there were as many as eighteen American universities seeking his services, any of which would have allowed him to move to a more lucrative position and thereby to accept invitations to perform in the more prestigious performing venues in the many cultural centres of that country. Elmer became the ultimate Canadian nationalist who sometimes embarrassed himself by his exaggerated and vociferous patriotism.

Only a handful of the people of Port Colborne of that time had any notion that there was amidst them a young musical genius who would change the cultural life of an entire nation, transforming the genre of choral music performance and even the quantity and quality of Canadian choral music composition. Elmer attended the Elm Street Public School and distinguished himself as a young scholar who could cope with the demands of the Ontario elementary school curriculum. Significantly, although there was no music program that can be identified as having set Elmer on the path towards a lifetime pursuit of music excellence, at least nothing transpired that reduced his interest in an enthusiasm nurtured both in his home and in his father's church.

Lydia's Paesler family had established a reputation, not only as a bulwark of the Lutheran faith in the province of Quebec, but as lively contributors to the social life of the entire area. Indeed, Lydia, who was now to take on the role of a pastor's wife, had been identified as the "best dancer in Quebec" — no small feat in a community in which dancing was as important as praying. Her musical son was attracted to the lively nature of a mother for whom rhythm and physical movement were ingrained and celebrated as thoroughly as the more intellectual attributes of devout followers of the Lutheran Christian faith!

Elmer has described his childhood in Port Colborne in almost idyllic terms. He was a typical boy finding delight in being the first each spring to swim in the Welland Canal, the most obvious man-made feature in the community, observing and chasing girls, biking and hiking about the escarpment, and enjoying the open spaces beyond the town's settled areas.

The most intense aspect of Elmer's warm nostalgia is the love his parents bore for the countryside. His father, in particular, worshipped the land and the luxuriant variety that is characteristic of the Niagara Region. For Elmer it was a gift he appreciated beyond all measure. As well, during Elmer's childhood, Theodore developed the practice of visiting his relatives in Michigan in one summer and Lydia's folks in Quebec the following July. In both situations, the Iseler family was accommodated in a semi-wilderness setting. Camping out was the order of the day. It was during these yearly recreational times that Theodore taught his eldest son to appreciate his natural surroundings, their variety and beauty. As well, it was Theo who taught Elmer to fish, a skill that he celebrated and was, in turn, to teach Jessie and his own children. This early intimacy with nature led to a love affair with the Caledon Hills, the wilds of Quebec and Michigan, the beaches and marshlands of Florida, and the New Jersey coast — all inherited from his parents, particularly his father.

Elmer, from the earliest age, was captivated by the phenomenon of music performance. His father played the church organ and Elmer's enforced presence at Sunday services and weekly prayer meetings brought the mysteries of the keyboard to his attention. While he certainly experimented with the living room piano, he also made efforts to access the church's more intricate instrument and was occasionally rebuffed by the committee of the church responsible for the pipe organ's health and maintenance. He received informal, offhand instruction from a father who saw in these interests the possibility of a son who would follow in his footsteps. Theodore not only preached but also led the choir in the absence of a trained choirmaster and soon realized that his son might accept a role that would relieve him of some of the pressure that the musical portions of the service presented. Indeed, Elmer did take on the leadership of the handful of congregants who had become a choral ensemble and led it in the important aspect of hymn singing that was central to worship in the Lutheran church service. At the age of ten, his parents became aware of the degree of musicality their son was exhibiting and contacted a music teacher. After three weeks, the deflated instructor appeared before Elmer's parents to inform them that he could teach Elmer nothing. He had already picked up enough on his own to make a teacher's ministrations quite pointless![3]

Another aspect of the family environment was the German language and traditions that were recognized as very much a part of normal life. Although Elmer never achieved familiarity with his father's native tongue, his exposure to German culture did make it easier for him to open doors to an unparalleled musical cultural tradition — the Chorales and Passions of J.S. Bach and his contemporaries. From the outset this repertoire was in Elmer's blood. The sound he learned to create from the efforts of his choristers was important but it was also his incredible acquisition of a baroque repertoire that had been little known and even less heard in Canada that amazed his early audiences. Here, familiarity with the German language was at the centre of his success in broadening his experience of the range of performable choral music in his early years.[4]

There is a stereotype that children from the manse have a propensity to become the hellions in the community. Elmer did not achieve that reputation but conceded it to one of his older sisters, Lucy. Elmer had early found that skills on the keyboard and an enlarged appreciation of music was a better strategy for assuring attention both at home and in the community. He was the third child to be spawned by Theodore and Lydia. Two daughters, Lucy and Edna, had preceded Elmer, and a fourth child, Leonard, was to follow a few years after Elmer's birth. The Iseler family was complete long before the family moved to Galt (now Cambridge) after Elmer's decision to leave the homestead in Port Colborne and head for Waterloo, Ontario, to seek a university education.

The 1920s brought a decade of prosperity and expansion to Port Colborne in the Niagara Region, situated as it was close to cheap electric power and on a major thoroughfare that would take goods to more populous communities in northern New York State. Industries settled in the booming city — Algoma Steel and Robin Hood Mills were examples. By far the most dominant participant in the economy of the municipality was the giant International Nickel Corporation (INCO), a company that had come in 1918 and was to dominate the community and that decades later was to become connected to controversial health issues that beset Port Colborne and, in particular, members of the Iseler family.

Within a couple of years of Elmer's birth, the future economic context of the Niagara Peninsula had dramatically changed. Small businesses and the surrounding farming communities faced the bewildering reality of the Great Depression that brought near collapse to so many Canadian urban centres. Being close to the United States was of no advantage, as it too was paralyzed by this phenomenon. Suddenly, Theodore's congregants saw their incomes diminish or, in some cases, disappear. The local Lutheran church became a support system, providing food and clothing for people now on relief, and Theodore's own family income diminished as the congregation's collective capacity to support its minister increasingly became a problem. The Lutheran Church of Canada in the early decades of the twentieth century was limited in terms of its membership and number of adherents. In comparison to the large numbers of Methodists and Anglicans who dominated the major Protestant faith communities in post–First World War Canada, the Lutherans represented but 3 percent of the total, drawn mainly from middle- and lower-income Canadians. There was no extra money for luxuries in a family dependent on such a small and desperate religious community.

This lack led a young Elmer to acquire an extensive newspaper delivery empire in Port Colborne, one that provided not only resources to support the Iseler family but also gave him the purchasing power so that when economic pressure lessened, he could reach beyond the immediate community for inspiration and insight to the recordings of great music that would be marketed in larger centres.

The coming of radio broadcasting and especially the establishment of the CBC, which began its broadcasting life in the mid–1930s, changed the lives of rural and small community dwellers forever. Elmer could be said to have been a phenomenon of a new era in the cultural history of the continent. Traditionally, musicians had been born in urban communities and had, to large degree, followed the lead of older family members. Only such urban centres could support the public concerts or theatrical offerings that are basic to the health of a musical culture. However, the mid–twentieth century was to make possible the emergence of young people from rural areas that would be considered cultural wastelands. Port Colborne, in spite of its Niagara Peninsula location not that many miles from Buffalo and New York State, most certainly fitted that description. But now, because of the CBC, young people could emerge from such a hinterland armed with memorable moments of listening to good music often accompanied by intelligent commentary from knowledgeable cultural figures. Indeed, young people gathered round the radio with their families and could experience, at least in part, the sounds of great drama and music from most recognized cultural centres of the English-speaking world.

Robert Cooper, an experienced producer of music at the CBC, makes the point that the 1920s, '30s, and '40s, the years of Elmer's childhood and youth, were those of the emergence of radio as the paramount communication technology around the western world, but particularly in Canada with its small population and enormous distances between those who had gathered in urban spaces. It is not surprising that Elmer would come to see radio signals as a major factor in the transmission of great music.

The Canadian Broadcasting Corporation, upon its creation by the Bennett Government in 1935, had taken on a national educational and cultural role. It was not just about the provision of entertainment. The mandate of the Corporation in its legislative creation explicitly expressed the expectation that its programming should be directed towards keeping the country together by exhibiting the ideas and talents of Canadians from coast to coast. Only this intervention could save the nation from being culturally diluted by the countless American stations flooding the country with the news and the talents of artists living in another country. One may read the *CBC Times* during these early days with utter astonishment at the high quality of content expected from the new network and its affiliates. Not-for-profit broadcasting was considered a missionary activity by those inside the Corporation. For the first time in history a child in Port Colborne could listen and become a culturally aware citizen. Indeed, it is surprising how many Canadian choral conductors, like Howard Dyck, the host of CBC's unique program *Choral Concert*, and Wayne Strongman, a devoted Toronto-based choral and operatic conductor, emerged unexpectedly from farm communities and rural villages to grace the podiums of major choruses in the latter decades of the twentieth century.

It was of this new age that Elmer took advantage. Another development had an equally dramatic impact — the invention of the record player and the availability of commercially available 78-rpm recordings after the First World War. By the 1920s, the opportunity to hear great music on easily available discs was realized. Recordings of full symphonies began to appear along with the array of shorter compositions that together made an excellent concert repertoire available to the average citizen. As a youth, Elmer heard a performance of Schubert's *Unfinished Symphony* played by Serge Koussevitzky and the Boston Symphony and was, in his own words, "blown away." He had to hear it again — and his purchase of recordings began. In prosperous times, in spite of personal economic limitations, his collection reached considerable proportions. His greatest enjoyment came from listening to these selections on a rather battered record player — but one that brought at least some of the excitement of live performance to his ear.

Thus it was that these influences — the continuing presence of a musically inspired parent and the access to electronically created sound — that provided the ground on which the seeds of Elmer's future personal musical development would be planted. The lack of live theatre and musical performance in his town could not divert, diminish, erode, or destroy the ultimate flowering of musical genius that was to follow.

Elmer's sense of self-confidence had to be developed in the context of a childhood and youth that was very much family oriented. As a minister's son, he was an object of curiosity on the part of every inhabitant he encountered. Indeed, the entire family of a pastor in the early twentieth century was a source of potential rumour and fantasy, particularly in small communities. Both Lydia and Theodore were intense personalities. Theodore most certainly had propensities towards dominance but Lydia was also strong-willed and articulate. The most innocent differences of opinion aroused suspicions that their marriage was in jeopardy. A young boy in such a home became the victim of unexpressed foreboding. The fear of family breakup may have been illusory, but to Elmer it was real and was only increased by normal adolescent tensions that abound in these difficult years. Elmer developed a strong need for a family life that was inclusive, communal, and supportive.

Growing up in Port Colborne along with his home and school influences somewhat narrowed Elmer's social contacts and encouraged a tendency to exhibit a shyness he never quite overcame. Elmer never felt comfortable among the rich and powerful who came into his life as an artist dependent on the generosity of the well-to-do. In order to create and maintain as expensive an instrument as a professional choir, he had no choice but to seek the interest and support of corporate donors. He could not resolve that internal dilemma. Elmer was most delighted when his choral ensembles were invited to small towns and villages where the rich were unlikely to be present. Yet he realized that even large audiences in major centres would not pay the bills. He had to be a reluctant part of promoting himself and his choir to the private sector. He loved the making of music but found little excitement or fulfillment in the finding of wealthy donors to support the art of choral performance.

An event in his Port Colborne elementary school placed another burden on his shoulders. Elmer never conveyed the confidence of a public orator in advancing his own causes. In later life, when preparing a response to expected complimentary comments directed to him on the receipt of yet another award for his contribution to the country's musical life, he described his reluctance to speak formally before an audience:

> I am not a speaker; I fancy myself a conductor. The
> reason I am not a speaker may be truly laid at the door

of a terrifying experience in my childhood. Reciting in front of the class (with my teacher, Mr. Arthur, behind me) the scene is imprinted on my mind in surrealistically agonizing bold strokes … I was reciting in front of the class "The Night Before Christmas." I had hardly reached the "mouse" when giggling, tittering, and smirking rolled in nauseating waves across the room.

Following the direction of many glances I looked down to see my trousers open at the front. In shame and remorse I crept back to my seat. The crowning blow was dealt by a girl with whom I was in love at the time — Arleen. At recess she said disdainfully — "You sissy, you cried."[5]

"Except for comments at conferences and workshops," Elmer continued, "I have made no speeches." This incident in front of his classmates had enormous ramifications for a future in which verbal communication was to be so important in revealing both his philosophy of music making and justifying the resources that were necessary.

The early years of life are now recognized as supremely significant in the development of an individual's learning style and feelings of self-confidence. A sense of place and the impact of that place is also central to the psychological well-being of every human being, particularly one engaged in the world of musical performance who must always appear filled with self-assurance. Howard Dyck, the aforementioned host of CBC Radio's popular programs *Choral Concert* and *Saturday Afternoon at the Opera*, developed a relationship with the twentieth-century icon of orchestral conducting, Herbert von Karajan. Dyck speaks of the influence on Karajan's personality of growing up in a small, isolated village in the mountains of Austria. Karajan, even at the height of his fame, was a shy, withdrawn, unapproachable individual (often accused of being "cold" and "arrogant") who came to trust others only after a lengthy acquaintance and a history of positive interaction. Port Colborne is a long distance from such a dramatic landscape, though its presence near an escarpment and the rushing waters of the Niagara River gives it a geographic prominence in the northeastern reaches of the continent. Yet Elmer, like Karajan, was not a social animal, given to chatter and easy familiarity. He too was called "arrogant" when the word "restrained" might have been more appropriately applied. Like Karajan, he made lifelong friends who were his treasures in this world but had but a few prosperous and influential followers who could provide magnanimous financial support. He never felt comfortable rallying his supporters to his vision when engaged in any debate that would reveal the intensity of his beliefs.

Unfortunately, it meant there were those to whom Elmer presented himself as conceited, distant, or unfriendly. These critics never experienced his acceptance, inclusiveness, jocularity, and warmth. For them, Elmer was a problem for the choral community rather than a solution to its needs. They thought he received too much attention and, more seriously, too many resources from the CBC, the Ontario Arts Council, and the Canada Council. There were choristers who resented his moments of petulance and impatience on the podium and his occasional acid response to their differing views. The role of the choral conductor, by definition, is not one that encourages warmth and acceptance. At times all conductors become the enemy of comfortable choristers unwilling to be challenged, and Elmer did not escape the unkind barbs that exposed the distance between their expectations and his vision.

Elmer was often seen as naive and unsophisticated. Perhaps it had something to do with his Lutheran faith. The strength and courage that comes from being a part of a loyal minority of believers had much to do with the integrity and commitment that Elmer displayed in his music making. But perhaps as a member of a smaller faith community one may develop a lack of flexibility with those who have a different vision and belief system. Elmer was not to escape the charge of being stubborn and uncooperative in the presence of those who differed with him or failed to understand his vision. Often he could not see a middle ground — an intransigence that seemed at times irrational and foolhardy and made amicable resolution of conflict impossible. Combined with his lack of persuasive articulation, it was an explosive mixture.

There was an aspect of Port Colborne's influence that seriously affected Elmer and the entire Iseler family: Edna, Lucy, Leonard, and

Elmer himself all died of cancer before the average age of mortality. The issue of Port Colborne's unhealthy environment stands out in dramatic fashion.[6] INCO had been charged with contaminating the community with its polluted emissions for many decades, a charge that had never been sustained — evidence could not be accumulated effectively, particularly in a municipality with a comparatively small population.

Elmer's untimely death at age seventy had major ramifications in the choral world. Every community depends on the mature presence of those whose influence has shaped its artistic life. Our times look desperately for those who will enlarge our visions and arouse our compassion. As in no other age, we live in the shadow of enormous weaponry on a planet facing severe deterioration in the affairs of humankind, developments that threaten the very existence of the human species. Society craves creative and visionary figures. In a midst of a war on terror that seems to have multiple agendas that promise continuing violence and conflict for decades, we are perplexed by the lack of restraint and compassion the human species seems to be able to muster. The presence of military and economic competition and conflict appears to be the everlasting order of the day.

Elmer Iseler was a person who saw in music a cure for the destructive and death-dealing preoccupations of humanity. The role of choral music may seem very insignificant in the shadow of the monumental problems that beset the human race. Yet, in the absence of any overwhelming alternative solution, it may be through the presence of a cultural context in which great musical sound, dramatic expression, visual beauty, and the physical grace of dance abound that any salvation for the human race is possible.

Increasingly, we are becoming even more aware that life experiences produce a wisdom that humankind ignores or trivializes at its peril. Gone are the assumptions that deterioration of the brain begins at middle age and continues with savage impact until at the age of sixty or seventy Alzheimer's or some comparable incapacity becomes inevitable and makes people by the age of eighty or ninety intellectually paralyzed. Society, now spurred on to recognize that early enforced retirement has a financial cost that is unsupportable, is also recognizing that the loss of experience and wisdom in its commercial and industrial enterprise can be detrimental to every society's well-being. That can also be said about the arts. It is not an argument for either rejecting early retirement as a social advantage or seeking technological support systems to achieve everlasting life on earth but rather a base of consideration and appreciation for an appropriate nurturing of an active maturity and making better use of the skills retained by those who do survive to be octogenarians.

To his dying day, Elmer spoke lovingly of Port Colborne, with its waterfront and surrounded by the farmlands and the rural communities he worshipped. After he was recognized as an icon of choral conducting, he brought his Singers back to Port Colborne for a gala occasion at which he could express through music the love he had for his childhood and adolescent home community. For years, Elmer carried on a good-natured jousting with Lydia Adams, his Singers' pianist, who wrong-headedly believed Glace Bay in the Maritimes deserved greater attention and accolades. Elmer realized small communities could be limiting, but he never lost his faith in a Port Colborne that he believed had provided both confidence and vision that preceded his contribution. He believed that growing up in such a place focused his attention on the important by warding off the clamour and continuous distraction that beset those dwelling in a large urban community. Put simply, Port Colborne, its schools, its churches, its surroundings, and most of all its people, was his route to what was significant and lasting.

That perception was one that Elmer Iseler took with him to his grave.

Chapter 2

The Muse Beckons — A Partner Emerges

BY THE TIME ELMER ARRIVED AT PORT COLBORNE
High School, he had gained considerable confidence in himself. He had
conquered the vicissitudes of elementary school with ease. Even though
some of his time and energy was taken up with delivering newspapers
and helping at his father's church, he had graduated from Grade 8 to
Grade 9, or first form in this secondary school, when such elevation was
not automatic.

By this time the world around him had, once again, changed.
Throughout his childhood years he had watched the economic prospects
of his father's flock decline. He had been too young to understand much
about the Depression, but throughout his childhood he had become
an avid radio listener and carefully read the accounts of human pain in
the daily newspaper he delivered. However, he was also aware that news
reports from abroad indicated the situation in Europe was deteriorating.
With roots in the German nation and the sounds of the language very
often in his ears, he had been aware that an evil force had taken over the
nation of his ancestors. By the first years of his secondary school career,
Canada was at war with Germany. Though his family roots had not put
him at risk of harassment in the considerable population of German stock
in the Niagara Peninsula as they might have in other communities in
Canada, he knew he had to make clear his allegiance to the country his
parents had chosen.

It was easy to do. Elmer had developed his skill as a marksman with
a rifle and his sure eye and steady hand placed him well ahead of his

schoolmates. It also led directly to his assumption of the captaincy of the school's cadet corps, a role that brought out leadership qualities that he had never exhibited before. As the platoon of student cadets marched proudly around the school's neighbourhood, the sight of Elmer Iseler giving orders and making motions with his officer's baton was one that surprised even his sisters and mother. Indeed, Richard Shibley[1] noted many years later that Elmer's comfortable use of the conductor's baton could have had its beginnings in the easy manipulations of an officer's stick he had observed during periods of military drill in the streets of Port Colborne. As for his precision with a rifle, it became one of his passions later in life to shoot rabbits that insisted upon feasting in his garden. As with so many of his enthusiasms, his marksmanship never failed him. However, his role as a hunter of small game halted when his young daughter, Buffy, cried uncontrollably upon seeing the victims of his skill on the kitchen table. Elmer never took up the rifle again. The tears of his little girl ended his relationship with firearms forever.

There were other attractions at the secondary school level. Elmer had no interest in playing the team games that captured attention of so many of his fellow students — neither football nor basketball was his thing, even though by this point he had grown into a strong, tall, lean young man. He did excel at track and field. In his first year at Port Colborne High School (PCHS), the school newspapers, the *Tattler*, recorded that in the midget age classification Elmer had come first in the hurdles, the broad jump, and the shot put and second in the hundred-yard sprint. These athletic accomplishments illustrate the quality of his physique by the time he reached high school. He was quick and lithe, with long, muscular legs. But as well he had strength and power in his upper body that allowed him to propel a ten-pound metal ball some 28 feet 11 inches in the air. However, in spite of this initial display of physical prowess, it could not be said that sports were at the centre of his life at Port Colborne High School.

By the early years of secondary school, Elmer had discovered another enthusiasm — photography. The universally available production of images through simple, easily operated, hand-carried box cameras had come into its own in the first decades of the twentieth century. By this time, almost every middle-class family was taking black and white pictures of its children and the places visited on holidays to show friends and relatives. In typical Elmer fashion, this tradition was expanded to new heights by a young man who realized that his delight in the beauty of landscape and the human body could be accommodated by this invention, and he became the informal photographer of almost every school event he attended.

The skills he acquired served him throughout his life: his delight in creating attractive visual images was honed in the gymnasium, the auditorium, and the corridors of PCHS. His capacity to pose the human figure was particularly noticed by the more physically attractive young women who shared his school life. He was forever taking their pictures, carrying out all the darkroom processes of film development, enlargement, and cropping necessary to move the results of his efforts to a level of aesthetic appreciation that heralded the fact that a visual artist was being born. He became a prominent figure in his school, with a special attraction to the female half of the student body. Needless to say, this predilection, not music, became his greatest asset as a young man seeking popularity and recognition.

The science of biology captured Elmer while he was studying at Port Colborne High School. He had brought to his classroom his father's passion for nature and his interest flowered throughout his adolescent years. This focus was more than a mere short-lived hobby. There were several activities that were to sustain him throughout his lifetime but an intimate connection with nature was paramount. Even as a teenager, he watched and fed birds. He learned to garden, growing not only flowers but also a broad range of vegetables and fruits. He experimented even with various grains. Though his academic focus was on English literature, his curiosity led him to delight in the sciences, and within a few years he himself was teaching in the laboratory as well as in the music room and the typical classroom.

Many years later, Elmer was asked in a program aired by Vision Television what the most important things were in his life. First, he replied — his family. Anyone who had experienced the close, warm relationship that he and his wife, Jessie, displayed and the caring love they extended to both their children, Buffy and Noel, was not surprised by that response. With the ever-present support of Jessie's family much in evidence, this choice could have been expected. But his second most important preoccupation was not music, as all expected, but nature. Even Elmer's friends and associates were surprised by his response. However, by "nature" he meant that totality of beauty that had been the inspiration to be found every day of his life, from the time he rode his bicycle on country roads and walked the fields and forests of nearby rural areas on the Niagara Peninsula. He rarely used the word "environment," loaded as it was with all the scientific interaction and problematic human behaviour that term came to represent. By "nature" Elmer meant the full spectrum of divine creation he experienced from the moment he rose in the morning to his last look at the skies before retiring. And, of course, Elmer concluded the interview by identifying his third priority, the one that everyone expected — music. The pattern of priority of family, natural world, and musical presence had been established when he was a teenager and was never abandoned throughout the decades of his maturity.

Elmer's love of literature and particularly poetry that had emerged during his elementary school days was enlarged during his secondary school years, and that was most certainly a factor in his later decision to pursue choral music with its emphasis on text rather than the more prominent field of orchestral sound. The tradition of depending upon textual interpretation and expression that became the Iseler trademark with his choirs was honed in the English literature classrooms of Port Colborne High School.

One looks in vain for Elmer's source of musical inspiration at the Port Colborne High School. It was certainly a step above the elementary institution from which he had graduated, but to say there was a music program would be an exaggeration. However, teacher Douglas Rowe taught an introductory course essentially devoted to the appreciation of fine music. He also put on a musical presentation each year for parents and the community — inevitably Gilbert and Sullivan — and Elmer did sing in the chorus. Indeed, with a voice at least trained in the choir stall of his father's church he was something of a find, but he was not distinguished enough to be considered for even the minor solo roles that abound in the music theatre of G. and S.

The principal of Port Colborne High School did come to recognize that there was an extraordinary student for whom music was central in his life and for whom its performance was an obsession. He allowed Elmer to play records over the public address system in the morning, establishing legitimacy for a young man seeking to convert his colleagues to the delights of musical presentation.

The most important role of PCHS was that it was the context in which he eventually found allies in his determination to know more about the world of music. He had begun a very modest collection of recordings — indeed, with little money to spare they were a luxury he could not afford. However, miraculously, with the coming of the war, the Canadian economy improved and by the 1940s not all his earnings from his paper route were needed at home. He was now able to buy a few 78-rpm recordings. At this point, it was not to choral music that he was turning his attention. Indeed, few choral works were available on record in these early years. It was the enlarging orchestral and symphonic repertoire of RCA Victor and Columbia Records that captured his enthusiasm.

One day, when Elmer was in Grade 10, he was playing on an upright piano that was stored behind protective mesh in the gymnasium. A new melody recorded by Glenn Miller had caught his ear. Called "Elmer's Tune," it was catchy and Elmer was delighted with it. He could find the theme easily and provide chords that would improve its presentation as well as the words that would, over the years, become his theme song on birthdays and other celebratory occasions. In the gym on that occasion a Grade 9 student, Richard Shibley, appeared, totally mesmerized by the musical talent of this slightly older fellow student. They greeted each other and Elmer discovered that Richard played the violin. Like Elmer, Richard had been made aware that there was no source of adequate instrumental instruction in Port Colborne. Here were two young teenagers sharing the same interest — and the same frustrations. A friendship was born that lasted throughout Elmer's entire lifetime. Richard Shibley was there for Elmer throughout his career and, indeed, provided a moving eulogy at his funeral in Toronto's St. James Cathedral in April 1998.

No longer was Elmer isolated in his loneliness as the single enthusiast, as he believed, for what was termed classical music. He and Richard discovered the thrill of making music together. They had no scores to guide their efforts: there were none available at any store nearby. In any case, they did not have money to invest in sheet music for all they wished to play. Both did have access to recordings from which, by ear, they could draw musical themes and could play well enough to provide acceptable entertainment for both themselves and others. This they proceeded to do, and with the lack of any alternative performers in town they were invited to play in every church basement of every denominational stripe in Port Colborne and beyond. It was exciting. The plaudits were many and they even found that there were people prepared to provide a small honorarium. The duo also became rather famous at their school, playing regularly at the weekly assembly in the spacious auditorium. Most importantly, they found performing for other people was fun. They became inseparable, meeting each day precisely halfway between their homes at the railway tracks that bisected the town. They rode to school together and schemed to extend their musical hegemony even further.[2]

The most infamous venture initiated by the pair was a madcap notion of how they could transform Port Colborne overnight into a cultural centre. The plan was an example of adolescent insanity but reveals the extent of their commitment. Richard and Elmer wanted to transport an electric record turntable by canoe out to the harbour breakwater along with speakers they believed sufficiently strong enough to envelop the town with the sound of Beethoven's Choral Symphony. This, they believed, would be a defining moment. Crowds would gather on the shore. There would be wild enthusiasm and the pair not only would find themselves instant heroes but would be invited to convert this deadly dull and pedestrian community into a world-class musical showplace.

The equipment was assembled on the cement breakwater — the moment had arrived. Suddenly reality intruded. There was no place to plug in the record player and amplification devices! Understandably, the builders of this major harbour structure dominating the Port Colborne waterfront had provided no electrical outlets. The boys were devastated. Their great plot to bring instant appreciation of great music to the world around them had failed miserably. Embarrassed and frustrated, they reloaded the canoe and paddled disconsolately back to shore, sobered by the fact that the absence of a mere electrical outlet had frustrated their grand plans. Many years later, Richard became a prominent lawyer and found himself involved in a case opposing the actions of Ontario Hydro. His intense preparation and eloquent presentation was seen to hark back to this event when his youthful efforts to improve society had come to naught as a result of Ontario Hydro's failure to provide basic power services to the Port Colborne harbour operation.

They were a strange couple. Elmer was the son of the town's most prominent Lutheran minister. Richard was an altar boy in Port Colborne's Roman Catholic church. No one believed they could continue to be a duo, either as musicians or as friends. Port Colborne was no more ecumenical in its attitudes than the rest of Ontario in the 1940s. Protestant and Catholic were expected to be enemies to the core and most of their friends thought their relationship would be short term and end in disappointment and mutual recrimination.

However, Elmer exhibited not an iota of religious superiority and Richard was equally devoid of the animosity and prejudice that poisoned the lives of those around them. Often when performing with Elmer, Richard found himself in Theodore's Lutheran church at a Sunday evening service. On one occasion, a young man preparing himself for the Lutheran ministry was the preacher and, sensing a bigotry that he could tweak to his advantage, proceeded to rail against the papacy as the Antichrist incarnate. As they were leaving the sanctuary at the end of the service, Theodore Iseler sensed Richard's embarrassment, put his arm around him, and whispered, "Don't take offence, these young potential ministers are full of piss and vinegar — they eventually mellow."[3]

The intervention revealed a side of Elmer's father that Richard had not previously experienced. Theodore had to play the role of the Lutheran patriarch, not only in his church and before his flock, but in the family setting as well. It had led to a mental rigidity that Elmer came to resent and impacted particularly on Theodore's wife, Lydia, who had refused to become a typical pastor's wife, withdrawn and subservient. On the other hand, there was an entrepreneurial energy to Theodore's role as a pastor that Elmer came in later years to realize was the source of his own dynamism. In Port Colborne and later in the Galt (Cambridge) pastorate of St. Paul's Lutheran Church on Grand Avenue North, Theodore was responsible for dramatic growth in both numbers and activity in the churches he served. The energy and drive that characterized Elmer's career had a genetic source that was quite evident to all observers who had known both father and son.

As he passed through his high school grades with evident success, Elmer saw a wonderful future looming beyond the town of Port Colborne. However, in spite of the changing economic times that the 1940s had heralded, he could see no reason to believe there was family support for his ambitions to pursue a university education. Certainly his older sisters had not been encouraged to pursue higher education. A younger brother, Leonard, might well want to imitate Elmer's ambitions, but that would not be for some years. Indeed, with that possibility of another son at university, the financial stakes were even more reason for Theodore and Lydia to dampen Elmer's ambitions.

As he completed his high school years, Elmer saw his hopes for university diminishing and realized that his desire to explore a world beyond the confines of Port Colborne might well be unattainable. This led him to a disappointment in his parents' lack of approval for his choice of future and a later appreciation of an extended family setting that promised only acceptance and support. These were the assets that his relationship with Jessie Balsillie was to offer him and included unlimited enthusiasm for his work and the provision of a household in which he could always find warmth and recognition.

As his high school days came to an end teenage frustrations at the perceived disinterest of his family had infected Elmer. He wanted to go on to a university where he could achieve the education needed to become a teacher himself — but could see no path. The thoughts of being a professional musician had not entered his mind. There were no examples of this phenomenon to be observed in Port Colborne. In terms of appropriate preparation for such a career, he had little formal training to offer. His love of literature had made him into a voracious reader and being a teacher of English literature was becoming a possibility in his mind. Endless conversations around a possible future certainly took place with Richard Shibley, and from these interchanges plans began to be formed. Indeed, there were even occasions when another figure joined them. Lyle Walker, an older town character who had an intellectual strength and curiosity, attracted both Richard and Elmer. They met him on the steps of the post office for extended conversations. He lent them Will Durant's *Story of Philosophy*, and for two young men brought up in the narrow confines of the Lutheran and Roman Catholic belief systems, such a window on a comprehensive account of human wisdom was heady stuff.

There was another high school acquaintance who was to be a central figure in Elmer's life. Her name was Mary McKellar. She was two grades ahead of Elmer at PCHS, and to the astonishment of both Richard and Elmer she played the violin and played it well. (Indeed, some years later she would study with Elie Spivak, the concertmaster of the Toronto Symphony Orchestra.) Her father, Captain John O. McKellar, was a leading figure in the community, a marine engineer who not only had sailed ships on the Great Lakes but had created a prosperous shipping company. Most important he was a highly visible cultural figure. Both he and Mary's mother sang and the Captain played both the mandolin and the ukulele.[4] He was determined that his daughter Mary would enjoy the delights of a musical education. With a grand piano gracing the living room he set about finding proper instruction. After an initial disaster whereby she had suffered at the hands of a piano instructor who hit her hands with a ruler when she played a wrong note, he accepted her desired shift to the violin as her chosen instrument. She was adventurous and athletically inclined, aware of the excitement accessible to children in a port city. She thought nothing of venturing in her skiff beyond the breakwater to feel the power of a sudden summer storm. She was also very attractive and talented, but too shy to exhibit her musicality publicly. Mary heard Elmer and Richard play, discovered their delight in the music of the masters, struck up a friendship, and invited them over to her home where there was a splendid gramophone and a fine collection of records. They enthusiastically accepted her invitation.

Elmer and Richard experienced the richness of a prosperous home where the arts were evidently central to the way of life of a warm and supportive family. From listening to the splendid collection of the latest recordings played on the most technically up-to-date equipment (complete with woofers and tweeters), they moved to playing trios, with Elmer immediately assuming the role of artistic director as well as ensemble pianist. From the themes Richard and Elmer had played by ear as a duet, there was a significant elevation to the actual scores of major compositions for instrumental trios. It was not too long before Richard and Mary were attempting J.S. Bach's Concerto for Two Violins with Elmer contributing the orchestral accompaniment on the keyboard.

This friendship with Mary and her father was to have an enormous influence on Elmer's career. Some years later, after high school graduation and an initial effort to prepare himself to be an English teacher by attending Waterloo College — a fine post-secondary institution under the aegis of the Lutheran Church at which offspring of Lutheran clergy could receive support for their academic costs — Elmer realized that his overwhelming ambition was to become a musician, or at least a teacher of music. To prepare himself he had to attend the University of Toronto's Faculty of Music for a new degree program for potential music teachers before attending the Ontario College of Education, where he could secure a certificate that would allow him to teach at the secondary level in Ontario schools. The costs would be prohibitive and he knew his family would have neither the resources nor any enthusiasm for his change of academic plans.

With great reluctance Elmer approached the only person he knew would understand his dilemma. He was anxious to become a wage-earner. The costs of the years at Waterloo College had already put him into debt. As well, he had become attracted to Trudie Mosig and they had married a few months after meeting. Elmer now needed money even more desperately. Captain McKellar had welcomed him into his home over many years and had shown interest in his musical talent. Would he loan him the money? It was his only hope!

Captain McKellar agreed without argument. In fact, he gave Elmer the money that enabled him to survive in Toronto over the years it would take to complete both the Bachelor of Music and the qualifications for a teaching certificate. Elmer was embarrassed by his generosity, assuring him that he would eventually pay him back. McKellar's response was "You help someone else when you have the resources." Elmer accepted the loan and did indeed set up a scholarship in Captain McKellar's name at the University of Toronto. Captain McKellar died in 1951 and never lived to see Elmer make his mark as a choral conductor. (The Festival Singers did not come into existence until 1954.) However, years later his daughter Mary wrote Elmer her only fan letter ever in which she commented that "he was the best investment her father had ever made."[5]

As Elmer was moving through elementary school and preparing to take his place in a Grade 9 class at Port Colborne High School, a child was born to an extraordinary couple, John and Elizabeth Balsillie, living in central Toronto. They called her Jessie Greenshields Sloan and she quickly became the centre of their lives. Both parents were examples of the flood of immigration that had descended on Canada from the United Kingdom in the years after the First World War. Elizabeth had come to Canada with her parents, the Prentices, whose lives in Scotland had been changed when the mining industry had been destroyed. In Toronto she had met John Balsillie, a now demobilized soldier of Her Majesty's Forces, whose life in Scotland had been interrupted by war and who had returned home like so many servicemen to find that his fiancée, during his absence at the front, had decided to marry another. John and Elizabeth fell in love, married, and Jessie was the first result of their union. John's efforts to establish himself in the dry goods department at Simpson's, one of Toronto's greatest department stores during these decades, was successful, if not fully satisfying.

The entire family moved to a house they had found on Chicora Avenue, just off Avenue Road, a major thoroughfare in an expanding city. Besides John, Elizabeth, and Jessie, the household now included Elizabeth's sister, Mary, and Elizabeth's parents, the Prentices — all part of an extended family that remained a unit throughout the decades after the Second World War. The clan Balsillie could be described as a "commune" decades before the word had common usage in North America. This family unit was completed when Jessie's younger brother, David, was born a few years later. It was this second family that Elmer joined in the mid and late 1950s and of which he remained an appreciative member throughout the first years of his intimate relationship with Jessie, the birth of their children, and the initial stages of his career.[6]

Jessie began her elementary school career at Brown School on Avenue Road, but after two years, Kindergarten and Grade 1, John found a new job as an inspector, which suited his skills more fully than selling dry goods, at the Canadian Acme Screw and Gear Company operating in West Toronto. It meant that by the end of the 1940s the entire Balsillie family had moved to lodgings in another house on Bartonville Avenue not too far distant from John's workplace. Jessie transferred from Brown School to Bala Avenue Public School, where she thrived, obviously a student of some capacity in spite of spells of sickness that interrupted her early studies. Years later she was joined there by her brother, David, who shared the warmth of his older sister's love and concern not just at home but in the school they now shared.

It was a unique arrangement. Jessie had the advantage of constant stimulation from an ongoing interchange of articulate and caring parents, grandparents, and an aunt — all devoted to her well-being. Grandfather Prentice took her for long walks past a little park at St. Clair and Avenue Road that, years later, was to be named after Glenn Gould, Canada's most internationally recognized classical musical superstar, who worked in an undistinguished apartment building nearby. The Balsillie family eschewed rigidity and patriarchy. Indeed, the entire Balsillie-Prentice clan was the epitome of deep affection and comfortable informality. Jessie observes, of her mother and father's love for each other, "I watched the benefits of tenderness." Judgment and subsequent guilt were not built into the family values. Openness and respect abounded. Jessie believes she was the product of, and saw the importance of, a "loving, caring, heartfelt, emotionally satisfying environment." It became her gift to her chosen life companion, Elmer Iseler.

The church and music were central to the life of the Balsillie family. Both John and Elizabeth sang, initially at Chalmers United Church, where John carried the load as clerk of session, even filling in as a lay preacher in the newly created union of Methodist, Presbyterian, and Congregational churches that made up the United Church of Canada, the largest Protestant denomination in the land. The Balsillie family was at home in a religious community that tolerated unorthodox lifestyles and where a commitment to the unique and experimental was more celebrated than in any other sector of the Protestant community in Canada.

Indeed, young Jessie throughout her childhood and youth found her family circle more interesting than her school chums, all seemingly caught up in their frantic efforts to be accepted by their peers. Her hero in adolescence was very much her father. The height of her delight came in joining him in the many chores of daily family life, like washing the car on Saturday afternoon. His sympathetic support became even more central to her happiness when tonsillitis struck and took a full year of her academic life, depriving her of the close friends who were so important to a young girl.

The delight of extended family intimacy was balanced by the serious reality that age was diminishing the lives of her grandparents. Grandmother Prentice, who had suffered a serious stroke, survived as a home patient dependent on Jessie's mother's and aunt's nursing for four years, and then died, followed by a similar process that brought to an end Grandfather Prentice's life a few years later. It was in the service of family well-being that Jessie learned home nursing skills alongside her mother that were to be essential later in her own life. In spite of these troubles, a classmate of Jessie's termed the togetherness and mutual support of this family quite unique. Her friend Margaret McCoy agreed with Jessie's idealistic perception of her father's personal strengths and added her own judgment that "he was the loveliest man I ever met."[7] Jessie advanced through elementary school with very little interest in boys: "None of them could measure up to the quality of character I found in my father."

Jessie knew she was interested in languages, but she had also come to enjoy music in her home and in her church. As well, she had sung in the Bala Avenue Public School choir. She knew she wanted to play in an orchestra when she reached high school. Elmer, who by 1952 was in his first year of teaching at York Memorial Collegiate Institute, was auditioning players for his school orchestra. Examining Jessie's hands, observing the strength of her arms and legs, he perceived she had all the attributes of a fine cellist. She took her new role seriously, eventually in the mid–1950s taking private lessons from Charles Mathé, a splendid cellist in the Toronto Symphony Orchestra, and developed considerable skill even though she had no intention of becoming a professional musician.

She found playing in Elmer's orchestra a sensational experience. There were music teachers in other secondary schools who wondered why Elmer refused to have his orchestra or choir compete in the Kiwanis Festival, where they openly declared he would "clean up." But he wanted to have his ensemble engaged in playing the best music possible for their own pleasure of performance rather than practising test pieces for an afternoon appearance in an annual competition. Jessie agreed with these values and played in the cello section for the next four years until her graduation in 1956.

Having now entered her teens, Jessie was unaware she had matured into a beautiful, slim, sylphlike creature who captured the attention of Festival Singer observers when she appeared with her school colleagues at the rehearsals on Elmer's invitation. Even more amazing, she did not realize at first that the conductor had any more interest in her person than in the other forty or fifty students bowing and blowing away, week after week, month after month, year after year. But Elmer had been struck by the quiet, thoughtful demeanour along with the evident physical beauty of the Balsillie girl who now shared his obsession with the sound of great music. Over those five years, the intensity of that relationship of student and teacher grew exponentially, and before she left York Memorial their lives were inextricably intertwined.

Jessie graduated from secondary school without difficulty, continuing her role as a nurse to an ailing Aunt Mary. She supported the family fortunes by assisting her mother, who now managed and operated a telephone answering service from a downtown office. Jessie had spent her summer holidays working the phones and now simply joined the business as a full-time employee. However, she had also graduated into a world of life with a man whom she now loved with all her being. In the midst of a growing close relationship she had turned to her father for advice and he had not failed her: "You have chosen a man who is a genius. It will be a difficult journey. But I think you are up to it." Nothing could have given her more confidence in her choice — no matter the cost![8]

Chapter 3

The Wider World

AS AN HONOUR GRADUATE OF PORT COLBORNE
High School, it was time for Elmer Iseler to leave his home and
community. He had a developed a number of strengths. His high school
career had revealed a scholarly affinity for studies in English literature and
the natural sciences and these, along with an amazing capacity to engage
in musical performance, gave every reason for confidence in pursuing a
university degree. Though his formal studies in music were sparse, indeed,
almost non-existent, the Shibley-Iseler duo had proven that in terms of
showmanship, Elmer had the goods. As well, he had taken advantage of
his role as a Lutheran pastor's son to give leadership to his father's church
choir and in doing so had conquered a small part of a choral repertoire
that would form the base of his church and concert hall choral programs
for years to come.

Through recordings and radio broadcasts, Elmer had become
familiar with some of the great compositions of the ages, including the
works of the twentieth century. As well as the works of Bach, Mozart,
Schubert, Beethoven, and Brahms, he was familiar with the compositions
of Richard Strauss and Igor Stravinsky, and that could not be said of the
vast majority of his secondary school contemporaries. Most of all, he
had learned to listen to music with intensity and purpose. He actually
heard music with all the beauty of line and complex harmonies that gave
depth and force to its performance. Elmer's admirers never ceased to
comment on his listening skills and these had been partially developed
before leaving Port Colborne.

Elmer had also made some decisions about what he did not wish to do. His father had hoped that the Lutheran ministry might be a vocation that would attract his oldest son. However, already there were indications that Elmer was losing the faith that had been so much a part of his religious experience in his father's church. Although the first years of his post-secondary learning career were within the familiar structures of a Lutheran church institution, he was looking for something beyond theological studies.

Though music was his obsession, he was aware of his limitations. After hearing Stravinsky's *Petrouchka,* he had tested himself as a composer — and had found himself wanting. "I was just not good enough," he told Richard Shibley. "Everything I wrote down sounded like something I had just heard."[1] His interest in music was to this point quite universal, including the popular music that excited his schoolmates. Yet he realized he was drawn more powerfully to what he termed "classical" forms of composition. At that time, baroque to renaissance and romantic — all were encompassed by this designation.

Though he had conducted a church choir, choral music had not yet become his preoccupation. Indeed, he was more knowledgeable of the orchestral repertoire at this time in his life. He had come to realize that at his advanced age there was no chance that a keyboard career could now be an option. The lack of any instruction except from his father on piano and organ had ensured that by the time he was a late teenager, this window had been closed forever. Within months of leaving Port Colborne, he discovered that he could sing well enough to be part of a choral ensemble of some merit. Even more important, he had come to realize that the role of conductor offered him the best chance for a career in music performance.

Rarely does one find an individual who can be truly identified as "self-made." Individuals who claim this distinction have usually deluded themselves as well as those about them. However, those who knew Elmer in these early days of high school attendance speak of a musical genius who arrived full blown at the Iseler household, an unexplainable phenomenon of extraordinary power and presence. Other members of the family did not share this excessive talent or intense enthusiasm for musical expression. His younger brother, Leonard, was a splendid dancer and had an extraordinary sense of rhythm no doubt acquired from his mother, but had no desire to exploit that particular aptitude professionally. Edna, his more flamboyant older sister, was dating a young man who was an opera lover, and although she shared his interest in that form of music theatre, this connection had no ongoing influence on the direction of her life. Though every form of music fascinated him, Elmer had no great interest in exploring that particular genre — nor did opera ever attract his commitment even later in life when so many of his choral associates were heavily engaged in the beginnings of the Canadian Opera Company in Toronto.

There can be an advantage in pursuing a career largely identified through initiatives and techniques that are truly one's own. It encourages self-reliance and independence. Such figures reach beyond the expected traditional boundaries of a particular discipline more easily. They are often not confined by the walls of constraint that demand subservience to the tried and true directions of the past, the well-worn paths that have been trodden down through the ages and in some cases have become comfortable ruts! These individuals find their own way and in so doing often advance exponentially, in the case of music, the variety and quality of its performance. It was in the context of exploring the fringes and the lesser known that Elmer was to make his unique contribution to Canadian choral music.

On the other hand, it scarcely needs to be stated that self-taught geniuses can be difficult artists for others to appreciate and accommodate. Often these unconventional figures fail to understand why others with lesser talents do not display the same excitement for the endowment that they have unearthed within themselves. In Elmer's case, this failing was partly corrected by his training as a teacher and his several years in that profession. He developed a capacity to be patient with those who did not share his innate musical intelligence. However, as a choir leader he could also be infuriated by what he regarded as an inadequate commitment of musicians, both amateur and professional, to the performance of music at the quality level he desired to produce, one that, with his genius, he could "hear" in his head and wanted to inspire his singers to replicate.

There is another danger faced by those who have found their own way little assisted by others. These are the rebels who rarely acquire the formal educational qualifications that are the norm for those who are their colleagues and have worked their way through the established processes of degrees and certificates that ensure the coverage of a body of knowledge or the acquisition of a particular skill. They often emerge from their individual and unique learning process with a degree of insecurity that diminishes their confidence in themselves when confronted by the presence of the conventionally trained and paper qualified. Sometimes it results in overcompensation — the appearance of an inflated ego that manifests itself in a seemingly arrogant style. On other occasions it supports a rigidity and inability to make accommodations to the views and behaviours of others. These were the challenges that Elmer faced. He had to struggle against that perception at every stage of his career. It accounts as well for his appreciation for the honours bestowed upon him by universities and various levels of government as his career matured and his contributions were more widely recognized.

Graduation from PCHS had given the teenage Elmer the opportunity to discover the wider world. However, there was a major obstacle. He had virtually no money and could not rely on his family to support him for the three or four years of undergraduate learning that would earn him a first degree, followed by a further year at the Ontario College of Education in Toronto that would finally produce a teacher's certificate and eventually a regular paycheque. However, he did find an option that would reduce his costs at the outset and, to some extent, reduced the fears of his parents that he might fall among atheists and sinners. He could attend Waterloo College in Western Ontario, not too far from home and a Lutheran place of learning that was gathering respect as a post-secondary institution in his home province.

The Evangelical Lutheran Synod had established the Waterloo Lutheran Seminary in 1911. It had been founded as an institution that would serve young people who were being prepared to enter the Lutheran ministry. Free land had been generously offered by a benefactor in Waterloo County that would provide a venue close to the large concentration of German-speaking Lutherans settled in the Kitchener-Waterloo area.

However, it was soon perceived essential to provide a broader preparatory liberal arts experience for those pursuing the ministry, and by 1918 academic courses were being offered that led to a bachelor's degree over three years of attendance. By 1924, a Faculty of Arts had been established, and in that same year, Waterloo College was put in place for young people who had no ambitions to pursue the credentials for working as a pastor but wanted further study in the arts and sciences within in the context of the Lutheran faith. In that year, there were only twenty-four students, but the college had grown in both numbers of students and academic prestige, in part through negotiations that had led to an affiliation with the University of Western Ontario.[2]

By 1945 it was a perfect destination for a young Lutheran like Elmer Iseler desiring a degree he could use to enter a teacher's college and pursue a career that would lead to financial independence. There was the added advantage that being the son of a Lutheran pastor his fees would be subsidized and his overall costs of being away from home reduced. In Elmer's case it was also a step that would not intimidate his parents, who could assume that his Lutheran principles would be strengthened by the presence of the Waterloo Lutheran Seminary nearby.

Elmer had met, in his first few months at Waterloo College, Trudie Mosig, the daughter of Reverend Richard Mosig, the pastor of Trinity Lutheran Church in New Hamburg, Ontario, and his wife, Melinda. The town and its Lutheran church were only a few short miles from the college. Trudie was in her final year and was preparing to go on to the Ontario College of Education. She was a member of this prominent family that included five daughters — Elsa, Trudie, Frieda, Rosemary, and Gretel. All but Trudie had pursued studies in music. She had chosen to study elocution, a sensible option for a woman with an enthusiasm for language and visual arts and who was preparing to enter the teaching profession. Ironically, on visiting the church and meeting the family, it was Trudie who captured Elmer's interest and affection.

It was the fabled and familiar love at first contact. Elmer was a handsome, lively first-year student with red bushy hair and a slim, athletic physique that was truly eye-catching. Trudie commented, "My life began when I met Elmer. He had enormous energy and enthusiasm for life."[3]

She, in turn, was a small, dark, quite attractive, highly intelligent, and articulate woman. They seemed a perfect match and a normal but intense college romance developed very quickly. They had both been reared in a Lutheran parsonage, had experienced an identical faith experience to match their similar educational backgrounds and future goals.

During the first year of Waterloo College, Elmer was in rapture over his find and Trudie was delighted to have an admirer she could take back to New Hamburg with her on weekends. Proper decorum demanded that Elmer would camp on nearby parkland until, by his second year at Waterloo College, they decided to become man and wife. A simple ceremony in Theodore's parsonage in Galt, involving both Lutheran pastor fathers, concluded the courtship and the couple began to plan the complicated lives of being married while Elmer remained a university student and Trudie was just launching her teaching career. It would be a difficult beginning for two young people not yet established in terms of employment that both would find challenging.

Trudie's mother, Melinda, was not only pastor Richard's wife but was as well the organist and choir leader in her husband's church. She had organized a youth choir made up of several young girls, including Trudie and most of her sisters. Elmer, with all the confidence of youth, suggested to Melinda that he would take over the youth choir with a special emphasis on bringing in boys, who had until that point been uninvolved. In what became a typical initiative, Elmer attracted a number of young males playing street hockey and football in the church parking lot and soon had a chorus capable of four-part harmony. Within a few weeks there were about twenty young people rehearsing on Sunday afternoons and performing Bach chorales at the subsequent morning service at the New Hamburg Lutheran Church.

At the beginning, he had a collection of teenagers of whom few could read music or sing with any evident capacity. They had been led to believe that singing loudly was singing well and he soon convinced them that effective choral performance had to do with purity of tone, not volume. Those who were unfamiliar with a musical score were fed the proper notes at the appropriate time. With sufficient rehearsal they were able to memorize the music. He insisted on singing a cappella when even his more able choristers' experience had previously been with organ accompaniment. Elmer displayed an obsession with the sound of the choir and insisted that it be in tune and with the four-part harmony completely blended. Members of the choir remember Elmer's constant admonition: "Martha, you're flat, I'll have to slap you," followed by words of encouragement and appreciation when her voice joined the others in the sound he coveted. Even at this time, Elmer, with limited keyboard skills, could read choral scores like a book. "I can hear it all in my head" was his familiar response to doubting observers. His impact on these young and impressionable singers was dramatic.

Just two months before his death in 1998, Elmer received a note from Trudie, now his estranged former wife of some decades, containing the most generous and thoughtful response to her learning of his predicted demise.

> I don't want to miss the opportunity to tell you how much you have influenced my life, my sisters' lives and that small group of choristers in New Hamburg. Whenever any of us are together our conversation invariably turns to Elmer, and how he opened our ears and eyes — taught us to really listen to music, to hear the structure of the composition, to be critical of the performance, but above all, to realize the power it has to bring joy.[4]

Elmer made the point on many occasions that there was no sudden moment of revelation when he decided on choral music as his path to fame and fortune. Indeed, there was little "fortune" or "fame" to be found in the ranks of Ontario choir directors that could attract an ambitious and highly energetic young man. This New Hamburg initiative was nothing more than a modest response to the need for musical leadership in a Lutheran congregation near Waterloo College whose pastor had a daughter with whom Elmer had fallen in love. Elmer was pleased to accept the challenge of creating a youth ensemble capable of contributing to each Sunday morning service. He had found an eager group of young people and very quickly he was ministering to them in a way that would be experienced by the choirs he served over the next half-century.

The New Hamburg Youth Choir became Elmer's pride and joy during the years at Waterloo College, years when he was still preparing himself to become a secondary school teacher of English literature. Working with teenage and young adults with whom he could share some knowledge of the choral art and his enthusiasm for its expression was truly a gift at this point in his life. It provided an opportunity for Elmer to take charge as a recognized choral conductor, and soon he began to seek out repertoire that went beyond the Lutheran Hymnary. The weekend, with first a romantic interest, then a fiancé, and finally a new bride, along with an exciting choral experience, became the focal point of Elmer's life.

There were moments of triumph. He continued to conduct that choir even after he had moved to Toronto in pursuit of a university degree and a teacher's certificate. Indeed, he spent a year teaching his New Hamburg Youth Choir the Bach *St. Luke Passion* and mounted a performance of the work to which he brought colleague instrumentalists from the Toronto Conservatory of Music. His efforts received positive comment from all sides, including the adulatory attention of the local press. The presentation also received the attention of Sir Ernest MacMillan, the Conservatory's principal, and was one factor in Sir Ernest's decision to appoint Elmer as a rehearsal conductor of his Toronto Mendelssohn Choir a few years after this performance. *St. Luke Passion* was a work he would repeat with other choirs he conducted in later years.

On one Christmas Eve he took the entire New Hamburg Youth Choir on to the streets to sing carols for congregational shut-ins. At one home, they were given $50 to buy music by an appreciative listener who happened to be the wife of the town's medical doctor. Well into the evening of tramping his chorus about the town, Elmer realized that the Toronto to Stratford train would arrive at the New Hamburg station in a few minutes. He gathered his choristers on the platform beside the tracks, and as the train came to a stop, they carolled the astonished passengers. The train delayed its departure time, the windows were thrown open, and passengers were thrilled by the sounds of Elmer's chorus. Days later, a letter from an obviously knowledgeable choral aficionado arrived at the New Hamburg parsonage that spoke of "the wonderful choir" and its "unbelievable sound." It was a response that choir members and their young conductor never forgot.[5]

Elmer's choice of Waterloo College brought a major influence into his life in the person of Dr. Ulrich ("Rick") Leupold, who was the music director at Waterloo College.[6] As well, Leupold taught church music at the nearby Waterloo Lutheran Seminary where he also gave courses in New Testament theology. Here was a figure of considerable academic distinction, having a doctorate in musicology from a European university and having completed most of his preparatory academic work toward a theology degree. His intention was to qualify as a Lutheran pastor. Gentle and humble, he was a man whom Elmer could admire without reservation.

Even more impressive was Leupold's non-academic background. He had been living in Germany at the time of the rise of the Nazi Party. Very early he recognized the evil intentions of its leadership. The seminary in which he was studying was closed down by the Nazis and he acted as a contact with students who wanted to continue their work in that institution. The coordinating role soon became too dangerous to continue. His apartment was searched, and though no incriminating evidence was found he realized that he was at considerable threat, as his mother's maiden name, Igel, was Jewish in origin. Leupold left Germany on the pretense that he was visiting his sister in England — but knew he would never return. His mother would be hounded by the Nazis throughout the Second World War and escaped the concentration camp by constantly moving from place to place in Germany throughout the several years of the conflict. Though she survived, her younger sister was indeed executed in a concentration camp.

The fact that Leupold was intent upon becoming a Lutheran pastor, a fine musician, and a musicologist automatically commanded Elmer's confidence and trust.[7] Elmer took advantage of every opportunity to learn all he could from this illustrious figure. Leupold obviously knew something of the musical heritage and the state of choral music in Europe. One of Elmer's early attributes was an extraordinary command of baroque repertoire and an appreciation of the improved choral singing standards in Europe. There is little doubt that Dr. Leupold had a hand in that substantial acquisition.[8]

Elmer was entranced with Dr. Leupold and his wife, Gertrude, who lived in a house very close to the college. As Gertrude puts it, "They were always together, always talking music." Leupold's father had played the largest organ in Berlin and gave concerts that a distinguished American musician had attended and appreciated and from this contact was forged a personal relationship that brought his son Ulrich to the United States shortly before the 1941 Pearl Harbor attack. From there it was a short leap to Canada and the Kitchener area. Thus by this circuitous route had Rick Leupold reached the North American continent and finally settled in Waterloo, Ontario. Gertrude was a schoolteacher in Kitchener — another reason for Elmer's determination to become Leupold's star pupil. Eventually, Elmer took both piano and organ lessons from his university mentor — the only formal musical training he had received to that point.

It was during these years that Elmer established a questionable reputation on the Waterloo College campus. Living in the modest residence, he had the habit of opening his window during the day, placing a recording on his turntable, and turning up the volume full blast, ensuring his fellow scholars were made aware of the great music that should enliven their academic pursuits. It was not a procedure that was universally appreciated.[9]

Dr. Leupold had a choir of male undergraduates at the seminary who travelled about Ontario, visiting, on invitation, Lutheran churches desiring to extend the musical education of their congregants. Elmer became a member of this ensemble, contributing his tenor voice to all the rehearsals and concerts that Professor Leupold was able to organize. Thus came another link with the world of choral music presentation. As well, it was from these years of membership in Leupold's Waterloo Seminary Choir that Elmer learned something of the joys and frustrations of touring a group of performing singers.

Elmer had no hesitation in conceding the debt he owed to those he met in the years at the University of Toronto and the Ontario College of Education. He spoke warmly and often of Healey Willan and Sir Ernest MacMillan as his most valuable mentors in these years. Less is known of Leupold's influence, but it was while in his orbit and under his influence that Elmer made one of the most important decisions of his life — to leave Waterloo College, to regard music in general and choral music in particular (rather than English literature) as his main teaching focus. It forced his attendance at the University of Toronto's Faculty of Arts to make up sufficient academic credits to allow acceptance into a newly developed special program for prospective teachers of music offered by that university's Faculty of Music. A further year at the Ontario College of Education would provide him the teaching certificate he required to be hired by a board of education to instruct in a secondary school in his province. As well, he would become familiar with the Royal Conservatory of Music as another place of lively interchange of students and faculty.

In Ulrich Leupold, Elmer was happily under the influence of a man of significant ability and accomplishment. Even more fortunately, Leupold was a man of stature who could see past the pathetic limitations of Elmer's formal training to a musical intelligence that must be released and allowed to soar. Dr. Leupold and his wife, Gertrude, made more than one trip to converse with Elmer's parents in an effort to convince them that Elmer's transfer to Toronto's musical education opportunities was essential, in spite of their fears over the costs this change would represent and the distance that such a venture might take him from his Lutheran past.

It could be said that Waterloo College was both the pinnacle and the conclusion of Elmer's intimacy with his father's denomination. But it was not the end of his interest in theological concerns, though there is evidence that Elmer had lost any uncritical faith of childhood days. It was a process that so often transpires in the transition between youth and maturity, particularly when it is accompanied by absence from the well-known venues of religious experience of the past. Elmer, in his studies, was journeying through an understanding of the universe that Martin Luther could never have imagined. It was no mystery that Elmer's simple Lutheran faith was seriously being eroded. Trudie and Elmer found that they had both moved on. Elmer in later years admitted his distance from any conventional religious affiliation that would expose his faith, but always accompanied this admission of a falling from grace with an intense assurance that through his music he could reach the Divine.

Rev. Charles Cooley contributed his memories of Elmer to the *Canadian Lutheran* in May 1998. He spoke of meeting Elmer in 1979 at

Val-des-Bois, Quebec, "his mother's congregation," when he himself was a minister in that area. "I was privileged to be his [Elmer's] long-term and long-distance pastor and friend." When Elmer visited his church, Cooley appreciated that "Elmer encouraged us to keep singing in the Lutheran tradition," and the reverend commented that during Lent in 1980 Elmer had been involved in a splendid broadcast from CBC Toronto on Lutheran liturgy. "It was the best of continuing education courses and something I needed after four years as a missionary pastor in Quebec," he said of Elmer's efforts.[10] His Lutheran faith might have been eroded, but Elmer never completely abandoned the strong precepts that had surrounded him in his childhood and adolescence.

After a third year of Arts at Waterloo College, with an emphasis on English literature, Elmer transferred to the University of Toronto for a year in the Faculty of Arts in order to qualify for a special program of undergraduate studies in music that would enable him to teach music at the secondary school level. However, the transfer was not decided before he had appeared at St. Michael's College, where Richard Shibley had begun the studies that would eventually take him to Osgoode Hall and a distinguished legal career. It was Elmer's belief that they should both find their futures in music — but Richard declined. "I had to find a profession that would ensure that I could support myself and my future family," he said. Elmer responded that he would "follow his heart" and make his way into some aspect of music making.[11] With the resources of his Port Colborne mentor Captain McKellar and the earnings of his wife, Trudie, Elmer was able to complete his studies at the University of Toronto, spend a year at the Ontario College of Education, and emerge with a Bachelor of Music degree and an Ontario Teaching Certificate.

The next years in Toronto can only be described as a whirlwind of activity — all focused on the excitement of performing music in a city becoming fully aware of its cultural possibilities for the first time in its history. Ezra Schabas and others have commented on the excitement of the late 1940s and 1950s at the Toronto Conservatory (soon to be the Royal Conservatory) and the University of Toronto's Faculty of Music.[12] It was as though the Depression and the war had damned up a flood of musical talent that was suddenly released and appeared on site shortly after 1945 and remained to give a sense of a special future for those interested in composing or performing great music. It resulted in the emergence of an extraordinary bevy of outstanding singers. These were the years that saw Lois Marshall, Jon Vickers, Teresa Stratas, Mary Morrison, Jimmy Shields, Edmund Hockridge, Louise Roy, James Milligan, Andrew MacMillan, and many more become national and international figures as vocal soloists. It was also a time that saw the presence of a significant number of outstanding voice teachers, some of whom had fled the Nazi takeover in Europe. The names of Diament, Simmie, Lambert, Vinci, Goldshmidt, and Walter leap out of the publications of both the Faculty of Music and the Conservatory.

Elmer had missed joining the war by only a few months (the war was ending in the very year he graduated from high school). He was fortunate to benefit from the presence of these gifted colleagues and instructors in Toronto who represented this postwar flowering of Canadian musical intelligence and creativity that was to change the face of Canadian culture forever. No longer could Canada and particularly Ontario and Toronto be considered culturally deprived. Elmer was aware of the significance of this extraordinary moment in time that had brought together new opportunities for making music, particularly choral music. He was to exploit these circumstances to the fullest extent by the mid-1950s.

Elmer himself most certainly took advantage of the lectures (fortunately, at that time, few were offered) that constituted the program offered by the Faculty of Music. In particular, he never missed a presentation given by Healey Willan. Though Elmer had not lost his interest in the great literature of the English language he was determined to connect this passion with his love of music. His delight in literature, both prose and poetry, shared by his new young wife, Trudie, played a large part in the fact that he was veering in the direction of choral rather than orchestral performance as he prepared himself for a career teaching music.[13]

In spite of the obvious relevance of his formal studies in Toronto, his main interest could be found elsewhere. He continued to return to New Hamburg most weekends to rehearse and conduct his New Hamburg Youth Choir. It also meant that both he and Trudie could spend time with the Mosig family in the warm context of the Lutheran community that they both loved despite all their theological doubts. When they had moved to Toronto, Trudie had already begun teaching but rejected the idea of employment in a large secondary school, knowing that it demanded the onerous policing of students. Instead she took a job in the Toronto offices of Manufacturer's Life Insurance Company with no loss of salary in order to help Elmer complete his education and qualify for a position in a Toronto secondary school.

In order to carry out his responsibilities to the choir his presence was obviously required in New Hamburg on some weekends. His absence from the campus tended to include Fridays and often he did not return until the following Tuesday. One of his professors became upset with his frequent absences and threatened to deny him the marks that would ensure his graduation. Elmer became sufficiently concerned that he decided he must appeal to the dean of the faculty — at that time Sir Ernest MacMillan. His response could not have been more helpful: "What you are doing in New Hamburg will teach you more about the making of music than all we can tell you around here." It was a statement of confidence in self-learning from a man who had fully discovered his own genius in a German civilian detention camp during the First World War.

On a New Hamburg Trinity Lutheran Church anniversary in the 1980s, Elmer brought his Elmer Iseler Singers for a concert that became a memorable nostalgic celebration, with now "old" youth choir members with their children and grandchildren present to watch this legendary figure conducting the chorales of J.S. Bach and playing favourite Lutheran hymns on the piano. All this with his aging mother, Lydia, smiling with pride at the presence of her beloved son, whom she still constantly admonished should not "get above himself."

As his academic work in Toronto proceeded, it was becoming more likely that choral music was to be the focus of Elmer's interest. However, it did not prevent him from participating in the ranks of the University of Toronto Symphony Orchestra. This ensemble, like the All-Varsity Mixed Chorus in which he also participated and which became another of his passions, was also not associated with the Faculty of Music. It was rather a campus-oriented recreational music-making organization devoted to the proposition that there were students to be found in all the faculties of the university who might wish to continue playing orchestral music but whose main interest would not be to achieve a highly professional standard of performance. It was open to all kinds of students whose level of competence might be rather modest but whose enthusiasm would carry the day.

Elmer, with no area of instrumental training at his fingertips, but realizing his desire for some kind of orchestral experience, chose to play in the percussion section of the University of Toronto Symphony Orchestra, where even a minimal acquaintance with the keyboard would allow him to make some contribution. Eventually he became the orchestra's timpanist. John Bird, who was to be one of his closest friends and mentors over the next fifty years, played the euphonium in the brass section close by.[14] He teased Elmer mercilessly about the fact that the tympani were never in tune. It meant that Elmer spent a great deal of his time bent low over the drumheads desperately trying to tighten or loosen their tension in order to satisfy John's supposed preoccupation with proper percussion sound. Over the many decades of professional and social association, this Iseler–Bird clowning and joking that began in the back row of the University of Toronto's Symphony Orchestra never ceased.

It is indicative of the still unresolved determination about the course of his future in music that Elmer had joined the All-Varsity Mixed Chorus. It, too, was modest in its performing commitment and more interested in the sheer joy of singing. Elmer's role in both of these ensembles soon changed somewhat dramatically. Before he had finished his training for a teacher's certificate, he was conducting them both, as well as, for a short time, the Victoria College Chorus, and in the case of the latter he was able to involve Trudie as a chorister.

Perhaps the most significant "extracurricular" activity that imposed itself on Elmer's time and attention during these important years was his decision to join Healey Willan's senior choir at the Church of St. Mary Magdalene. Elmer had a pleasant tenor voice and would have been an asset to any choir. However, he had not been trained as a singer and never had any pretensions about the limited volume and quality of his voice. Throughout his career as a conductor, he never demonstrated before his choristers what he wanted in terms of tone, rhythm, or volume. It is another example of Elmer's feeling of inadequacy in the presence of those who had received proper instruction, in this case, in voice production and presentation. He was not prepared to expose his untrained voice in any demonstration of technique to be replicated, even though, by this time, he had sung with some of the best choristers in Toronto's burgeoning force of fine vocal performers.

Without reservation, Elmer credits Healey Willan with being his most important guide and mentor. Giles Bryant, Canada's most prestigious performer of the master's work and Canada's pre-eminent Willan scholar, agrees with Elmer's assessment. He knew both men well. Bryant had sung in both Willan's St. Mary Magdalene Choir and in Iseler's Festival Singers; indeed, Bryant assumed the music directorship of the Church of St. Mary Magdalene after Willan's death.[15] At the time Elmer had met Willan he was the country's most illustrious composer and performer of church music. (There are some who would say that he remains the paragon.) Bryant credits Willan as the towering figure who provided Elmer with the essential skills needed by a choral conductor in Canada's mid-1950s and 1960s. Willan himself had composed music quite prolifically and, even more important for Elmer's purposes, also had a total command of the repertoire of the High Anglican and Roman Catholic churches.

As well, Willan was a demanding choirmaster who became a model for the young Iseler. He enforced a discipline that became the style for Elmer in his first years as a young conductor. Elmer recounted the fact that during these years, he was "terrified" of Willan. Just a critical look from the master reduced him to tears. There were those who accused Elmer of seeking to replicate these aspects of Willan's example to his own detriment. There are others who would say it was merely a base upon which he built in order to raise the standards of Canadian choral music performance significantly higher.

Perhaps even more pointed was Willan's influence on the sound of voices making choral music. It was an English tradition he passed on to Elmer. Willan remained a Victorian Englishman throughout his life and most of his contemporaries would say that he never really became a Canadian — either in terms of lifestyle or nature of composition. But Elmer learned from him something of the English, as opposed to the hard vowel and more aggressive consonant sounds of the European and American schools, in the singing of the baroque repertoire. Willan had a profound respect for text, an attribute that Elmer Iseler was pleased to emulate. Even the conducting technique that encouraged a more collegial atmosphere for performance was found, on occasion, in Bryant's view, in the choir stalls of St. Mary Magdalene. Bryant, in the spirit of respect and goodwill records that Iseler was, in these years, a "highly intelligent sponge," and the Canadian choral scene eventually became the much better for it.

One advantage that Elmer had over Willan was a working knowledge of the German language. It meant that he could explore information about repertoire beyond that to be found in North American choral collections.[16] Indeed, Elmer discovered works of composers whose very names had disappeared from the choral experience of the continent but became prominent items in his own concert repertoire.

It seems unbelievable, but Elmer found yet another commitment during these special years of attendance at the University of Toronto and Ontario College of Education. No doubt as a result of his positive relationship with Sir Ernest MacMillan, Elmer decided he would like to join Sir Ernest's Toronto Mendelssohn Choir (TMC). At the time it did not mean a major commitment. The choir rehearsed on Monday evenings and performed only three or four times a year, essentially when the Toronto Symphony Orchestra (TSO) wished to play a composition that demanded choral forces, such as Beethoven's Choral Symphony, or particularly when the programming of the TSO would benefit from a presentation of Handel's *Messiah* or Bach's *St. Matthew Passion*.

Certainly there was no indication that Elmer had any notion that this prestigious choral organization would have any part in his future. The TMC had been organized in a previous century and was historically the oldest musical organization in the country. It had been established to build in Canada the kind of large oratorio choir (up to two hundred singers) that had become so popular in the United Kingdom. Such choirs had, to some extent, been the result of the industrial revolution in Great Britain. Much more in the United Kingdom than in Canada these massive forces of vocal power were social institutions, often supported by the local mining or manufacturing enterprises, and they provided a form of motivational excitement that people much appreciated in these depressing new industrial cities. Their performances were highly prized by the populace and now that the arts had left the salon and had moved to the large auditorium, huge audiences could be accommodated.

The presence of these choral behemoths had encouraged English composers such as Stanford, Parry, Elgar, Holst, and later Vaughan Williams and Britten to write major choral works and would indeed influence the composing lives of Canadian counterparts such as John Beckwith, Derek Holman, Imant Raminsh, R. Murray Schafer, Srul Irving Glick, and Christos Hatzis, to name but a few. Elmer knew little of this corner of the music repertoire and no doubt realized that he could benefit from being a part of this prestigious institution at least for a short period of time. His enthusiasm for singing in TMC ranks was so pronounced that his fellow choristers found it necessary to advise him to modify the animated shaking of his head in the more dramatic bars of the score with the admonition that he "should let Sir Ernest decide the tempo." Largely as a result of his New Hamburg accomplishments, he soon received recognition from Sir Ernest, who surprisingly appointed him a rehearsal assistant.

The appointment was both short and controversial. The young Elmer Iseler, scarcely out of his teenage years, took his duties very seriously. When called upon to replace Sir Ernest at a rehearsal, he was ecstatic and determined to get the immediate attention of his choral colleagues. In the first fifteen minutes, Elmer admits to pointing out some fourteen mistakes in tone, tempo, and articulation. Veteran Mendelssohn Choir members were outraged, and even though he did reduce his critical approach to their efforts in subsequent appearances, it was decided that after one year he should be dismissed from the position. It was hurtful and humiliating for him. Not only did he not return to his place in the tenor section, he soon became a major critic of the Mendelssohn Choir and its often lacklustre performances. Even Sir Ernest, for all his accomplishments, did not escape Elmer's nostalgic negative comments: "He was not a great conductor. Often we were not adequately prepared." However, Elmer conceded, "Sir Ernest always came through." It was one of the ironic moments in his life when, a decade and a half later, he was asked to take over the TMC as its musical director, thereby replacing an aging Sir Ernest and his less illustrious successors.

Elmer looked back on these frantic days of the late 1940s and early 1950s with a fondness that swept aside the horrendous pressures he felt. After a decade-long depression and five years of war, the country was developing a consciousness of its strengths and possibilities. Nowhere was this more the case than in the halls of the Faculty of Music and the Toronto's Conservatory of Music. The list of figures that Elmer met in those days would become the names of the cultural giants of his nation for the next fifty years. As well as the aforementioned Marshall, Vickers, Morrison, Stratas, and Sheilds, there were singers Patricia Rideout, Jan Rubes, Elizabeth Elliott, and Glen Gardiner, the piano virtuoso Glenn Gould, organist Douglas Elliott, composers Harry Somers, R. Murray Schafer, Harry Freedman, John Beckwith, and Louis Applebaum — a veritable array of individuals of talent and presence who would provide leadership at every level in a country swiftly throwing off its reputation as a primitive frontier to don the cloak of a truly exciting artistic cultural revolution.

During his years at the university, Elmer's colleagues were appearing on radio and the most prominent choir was most certainly the all-female Leslie Bell Singers. However, on occasion when he needed male voices Bell would hire a group called Comrades in Arms, an ensemble in which Elmer sometimes appeared. Thus as a performer Elmer also met an impressive selection of fine singers. Indeed, he marginally became one of their number. It was at a broadcast session of this ensemble that Elmer first met Howard Cable, who was to become Canada's pre-eminent radio and television conductor, composer, arranger, and producer and, as well, Elmer's colleague and friend.

In the euphoria of an expansive postwar Canada, there were performers needed everywhere. Each year, at the Canadian National Exhibition (still the world's largest annual agricultural fair), there was a grandstand show written by Howard Cable sometimes demanding a huge cast of hundreds to support the big names from the U.S. entertainment industry (a Danny Kaye or a Bob Hope) who could attract a huge audience. An orchestra of sixty-five and a chorus of thirty or more singers were occasionally needed.

Elmer, with his modest tenor voice, was hired for the three-week late summer gig and met Conservatory and Faculty singers all around him, all being paid $65 a week and revelling in their relative wealth. Even at this stage, Howard Cable, frantic for the time to write the script and organize the various segments of the show, saw in a bright and extrovert Elmer the trainer and conductor of this pick-up chorus and was impressed by his efficiency and effectiveness.[17]

The CBC at that time presented a generous spectrum of choral music in its programming, attracting singers both on a regular and a single performance basis. There was the aforementioned Leslie Bell Singers, led by this music teacher at Parkdale Collegiate who had gathered his female alumni and trained this able ensemble to present a weekly program of light popular and folk songs. Elmer's relatives and in-laws even walked up the street to see a television store front set that would let them watch him singing for Leslie Bell when, occasionally, males were required. The Carl Tapscott Singers was another fine group presenting popular fare, sometimes including music from the nations from whose shores people were arriving in Toronto and other Canadian urban centres. Don Wright also had a bevy of singers performing on the Westinghouse broadcast in the 1950s, a chorus particularly adept at providing a musical background of jingles for broadcast advertisement breaks. There were variety shows on CBC that required one-night appearances and Elmer discovered that these might even involve dancing — not an attribute he exposed with any enthusiasm.

In the University of Toronto and Ontario College of Education years, Elmer, desperate to add to Trudie's income and Captain McKellar's contribution to his maintenance, became a part of the Toronto cultural scene. In these years he came to know the choristers who would form his first ensemble, the Festival Singers. There were typical examples at hand. Elizabeth Elliott had met her future husband, Douglas, in the armed forces. They had married six months after demobilization and both were making use of their educational credits accumulated through years of service. Elizabeth had been a soprano soloist at Donlands United Church before the war and as a member of a family struggling to survive the Depression could not afford to buy sheet music. She visited music stores in order to memorize the music score for the selection she had to perform the next day.

Another was tenor Don Bartle, who simply turned up in Toronto because his father had been moved there during the war. He had been well trained in Windsor and discovered he had a fine voice and soon sought out a church in Toronto that could prepare him as a chorister and ultimately as a soloist. He had been advised to choose from the choirs of three churches — St. Michael's Cathedral, St. James Cathedral, or St. Simon-the-Apostle. After a year at St. James, he moved to St. Simon's and remained for ten years before moving on to other church ensembles.

Both Elizabeth and Don were perfect examples of Elmer's attention to the kind of fine performer he might invite to join any choir he would wish to lead. There were many such individuals in the chorus that became the Festival Singers by the mid-1950s.

It was these kinds of musicians, not yet household names, but now focused and ambitious, who realized there was no choir of excellent quality unattached to any religious institution that was capable of singing the finest choral music of the ages. It was this phalanx of splendid enthusiasts who were confident that someone in Canada should be doing so. They believed that Canadians had a special reason to be the first, with a harvest of talent, a radio broadcaster, the CBC, filled with entrepreneurs such as Terrence Gibbs, Geoffrey Waddington, John Peter Lee Roberts, and John Reeves and later Srul Irving Glick and, for a short time, Louis Applebaum, all ready and willing to present such jewels to a loyal broadcasting audience. There was enormous optimism that was infectious.

Elmer came to realize he had dropped into a unique concentration of extraordinarily motivated and gifted young people — not unlike himself. It would be the basis of the career in the arts that would come to astonish those who considered creativity the monopoly of those who were rich and well placed. The highest priority was to climb out of the pit of penury he had dug for himself by finding regular employment. It was to the public educational system at the secondary level he turned, knowing that he could then pursue his literary interests as a teacher and, more importantly, find an opportunity to conduct choirs.

Chapter 4

The Ultimate Pedagogue

"ELMER ISELER WAS THE SUPREME PEDAGOGUE," concluded Brad Ratzlaff, a choral conductor and a one-time member of the Elmer Iseler Singers.[1] Yet the Iseler name has only one association in the minds of most Canadians — that of a conductor of choirs. The fact is that Elmer spent a dozen years in the classrooms of two sizeable and academically significant secondary schools, York Memorial Collegiate Institute and Northview Heights Secondary School, both still very much in operation within the boundaries of what is now the City of Toronto.

For his last academic year, 1951–52, on the University of Toronto campus, Elmer had been enrolled in the Ontario College of Education, "OCE" as it was called by its attendees and graduates. In the 1950s it was the only institution in which a prospective Ontario secondary school teacher could secure provincial certification. It was not a popular place. The opinion of many educators was that the single year at OCE was a pathetic attempt to train graduates of the provincial university system to occupy the classrooms in such a way as not to embarrass the potential teacher, the welcoming school, or the profession as a whole. Attending OCE was not a very inspiring experience. Little time was allocated to dispense profound knowledge of the schooling system and even less to understand the complex issues surrounding the transmission of either information or skill. Almost unanimously, it was defined as a considerable waste of time unless one included in the evaluation the weeks of "practice teaching." These were days spent in the classrooms of Toronto secondary schools in the presence and under the tutelage of outstanding teachers in the field. Most important, these weeks provided opportunities to teach actual lessons to real students.

For Elmer, the reduction in intellectual expectation that OCE represented had been a decided relief. With his involvement in the All-Varsity Mixed Chorus and the University of Toronto Symphony Orchestra, singing in Healey Willan's St. Mary Magdalene Choir, and providing artistic leadership to his New Hamburg Youth Choir, he had no time to contemplate the inadequacies of teacher preparation in Ontario. The success of all these activities, along with a record of stellar performance in the practice lessons in classroom settings, led him to become the envy of his OCE colleagues in torture. As the school year went by he was gaining confidence that he would not only receive a job offer but it would be one that enabled him to remain in the Toronto area. He and Trudie were in the early years of married life and still excited by hopes for a satisfying future together, and Elmer's acquisition of a teaching position was crucial.

Every year, during the week of Easter holidays and the Annual Convention of the Ontario Educational Association, there was in place a hiring process resented by teachers and deprecatingly called the "meat market." It was centred in a well-known hotel, the Park Plaza, in downtown Toronto. School boards rented rooms and organized panels of principals and educational administrators to review job applicants. Hopeful teachers were scheduled for interviews every quarter-hour. In these few minutes, principals and superintendents were expected to make a judgment on the host of applicants awaiting their decision and the prospective teachers had to make instantaneous responses to job offers that might decide the course of their entire career.

Elmer was fortunate. In the spring of 1952, he was offered a position by the Board of Education of the Borough of York in a long-established secondary school in its system, York Memorial Collegiate Institute (YMCI). The principal offering the position was Roy Rutherford, an able and popular administrator who had a daughter, Mary (now Mary Gardiner), who was to become a nationally recognized composer, well respected and admired, as well as a leading figure in the work of the Canadian Music Centre in the 1990s and the early years of the new century.

The vice-principal of the school was to have an even greater relevance to the future plans of the young musician-conductor, Elmer Iseler. His name was Lt. Col. James W. Singleton and he was to be one of Elmer's closest friends and advisers amidst the numerous teaching colleagues he attracted during these years in the classroom. Rutherford and Singleton together formed a fine administration that was capable of recognizing the treasure it had acquired but was also capable of handling the fallout that would come from coping with a troublesome and yet inspired teacher-colleague.

Fortunately his predecessor at YMCI had been Jack McAlistair, a successful but unorthodox English literature and drama instructor who had, after an adventurous and flamboyant interlude abroad, become the founder of the Theatre School at Ryerson Polytechnical Institute, now Ryerson University. At first glance, Elmer appeared to be a replacement for another now absent colourful colleague. It was soon discovered that Elmer was very much one of a kind, and though he was similar to McAlistair in that he had a comparable lack of respect for rules and regulations that had no learning legitimacy it was soon clear that he had his own unique style of apparent disdain for traditional teacher behavioural expectation.

Elmer had been hired (at a yearly salary of $2,400) not only to teach orchestral music performance and to lead the school choir on an extracurricular basis, but also to take on a schedule filled with English and, oddly, science classes. His timetable was, by all standards, impossibly frantic as he began his first job as an Ontario secondary school teacher in the 1952–53 academic year.

It was soon evident that Elmer was determined to do far more than simply carry out the functions of covering curriculum and keeping order in the classroom. He was one of those learning missionaries who wanted to make a difference in the lives of his students and for whom the formal schedule of classes and outline of courses was merely a launching pad for a program of pedagogical interventions that captured the attention and came to thrill his students, baffle their parents, and, in some cases, shock his colleagues.

Ken Thomson, who spent a year in his English class, describes Elmer as a staff "rebel" who found unusual ways of interesting students in aspects of literature all designed to fire their imaginations. The teaching of Shakespeare was too often a process that turned young people away from the excitement of the stage, but Elmer was determined to enhance Shakespeare's *The Merchant of Venice* by bringing in recordings of music inspired by the drama. Thomson came to see him as a teacher who challenged the norm and who had quickly became a favourite with both many students and some of his colleagues. There was that element of the daring and radical in each class. Iseler, for example, was prepared to confront sexual references in prose and poetry rather than simply ignoring or trivializing the text in question.[2] Though Thomson had to transfer after only one year at YMCI, he never forgot those months under Elmer's influence.

Margaret McCoy was one of Elmer's students at York Memorial for nearly four years in the mid-1950s. She was in his orchestra and his school choir as well as his English classes. She describes him as an "outstanding teacher." When there was a choice, he judiciously selected the novels, plays, and poetry that would reach out to his students, inspire them, and lead them to treasure their study of literature as lasting moments of beauty and meaning. For these urban students who almost all came from working-class homes, he added Stephen Leacock's *Sunshine Sketches of a Little Town* to the curriculum. The book amused them and portrayed a world they knew little of. Never was there any hint of condescension or discounting of their inadequate response or impatience at their lack of comprehension.[3]

McCoy tells a very moving story of Elmer's caring style. She had arrived at YMCI mid-term — always a traumatic experience for a shy youth now consigned to be the "new kid" by the rest of the class whose loyalties to each other had already been formed. One of the compulsory elements in the English course was an introduction to public speaking. She claims to have been "pathologically reticent" and, indeed, terrified to the core at the thought of standing in front of assembled students and baring her soul. Inevitably, when her turn came she broke down in tears, thoroughly humiliated and deeply concerned that her tenuous relationships with members of the class were now in tatters. Elmer quietly, unobtrusively, took her aside, listened to her fears, and helped her deal with the situation in her own way. He stayed with her after class until her composure was restored and the causes of her terror were understood. But he scheduled her to speak the next day. She not only recovered her pride but went on to the finals of the public-speaking competition in the school. It was a response of a man who had found his own confidence only with special effort and realized that only "tough love" would enable her to overcome the terror she faced.

It is little wonder that half a century later, McCoy can state that Elmer Iseler "liberated" her. He had spanned that chasm between teacher and student, treated her as a person, and listened to her in her moment of pain. He was careful not to be arbitrary and judgmental when it would bring only hurt. From this interaction came a strong, able, and confident young woman who was eventually to give valuable leadership to choral music as an administrator of the Ottawa Choral Society.

As a member of Elmer's York Memorial Choir, McCoy remembers vividly the experience of singing Bach's *St. Luke Passion*, the now familiar work he had introduced previously to his New Hamburg Youth Choir. This time it was for performance on a CBC Radio Good Friday program — the first time a public secondary school choir had been invited to sing on air. Elmer treated his choir members as professionals and taught them what that term meant. They were to be at every rehearsal. If they missed one, they would not be allowed to perform. All were to arrive at rehearsals on time, indeed, to be in their places some fifteen minutes ahead of the designated hour. In short, he made the point that each one had a commitment to a radio audience that he or she must honour. As a result of this discipline, the York Memorial Choir became a regular feature on CBC. Its members could be counted upon to be present and prepared whenever a broadcast was scheduled.

Even more striking was his commitment to the choral life of each individual singer. When Healey Willan expressed a need for an expanded choir at St. Mary Magdalene Church, Elmer drove members of his school choir miles into the centre of the city to Thursday night rehearsals and returned them individually to their homes and anxious parents. On Sunday evenings, he went through the same drill, often remaining to sing with them both at rehearsal and at evensong. Another York Memorial chorister, Ken Dyck, remembers these precious evenings when he realized that he was singing in a famous church choir led by Canada's foremost composer and standing beside an Elmer Iseler who alone could have made this happen.[4]

Elmer enhanced the life of the school by staging an array of special performances of musical skits and tuneful musical comedy that involved both his orchestra and his choir. He knew he had no capacity for authoring librettos or composing scores. Rather, he engaged his close friends to write the texts of skits for school assembly programs, in particular, Keith MacMillan, the son of Sir Ernest and a musical figure in his own right with Hallmark Recordings, the CBC, and eventually the Canadian Music Centre along with a score of other cultural initiatives. Other colleagues, T.L. Roy and especially John Bird, his companion from University of Toronto days, together often provided him with the basic material. The themes of these mini-dramas were contemporary and frequently hilariously irreverent. He wanted music to be seen as fun as well as hard work and students appreciated his extensive commitment to their enjoyment.

On other occasions, he would take the entire choir to other cities, like neighbouring Hamilton, for example, when there was an opportunity to perform for a music teachers' conference. However, he had no interest in preparing either choirs or orchestras for Kiwanis Festivals. He did not agree with the competitive nature of these events built around compulsory test pieces he felt were invariably inferior to the very best music he wished to place before students at this very impressionable age. He also wanted students to realize that performances were not for judgment but for inspiration and that the highest standards were expected on every occasion, not just when judges were sitting before them.

In the 1950s Ontario educational system, the Grade 13 examination was the ultimate academic determinant of what students could do with their lives. The results decided whether pursuing further studies at a university was appropriate or whether seeking employment would be the next step. He wanted to give his students an advantage by securing a music credit, not by normal classwork but by taking the Grade 7 Royal Conservatory examination privately and thereby adding an additional mark to their final standings in achieving an Ontario Secondary School Honours Graduation Diploma. Elmer arrived an hour early in the morning to instruct the young people with the will, ability, and stamina to make the extra effort that would bring this quest to a successful conclusion.

One of Elmer's seemingly unexplainable passions was ice hockey. He could not skate and had no interest in bodily contact sports that seemed to encourage aggressive behaviour, but he was entranced with the speed, the cleverness, and the spontaneity of the game. It was Canada's sport and that fact gave legitimacy to his excitement. As well, in Port Colborne he had shared his school days with a youngster by the name of Kennedy who, though no great scholar, was a marvel on the local skating rink. Significantly he was also a most pleasant, friendly figure in Elmer's life who was to become the renowned "Teeder" Kennedy of the Toronto Maple Leafs, a professional hockey player with the same reputation for tough, relentless performance on ice as Elmer displayed on the choral podium.

Whenever he could convince John Bird to acquire tickets, it was off to Maple Leaf Gardens. A night of wild gyration and lusty exclamation sometimes ended with John's hat on the ice and gone forever. At this stage, Elmer could not afford to buy a television set, but at NHL playoff time Elmer would rent one for a week or two and he and Trudie would invite both orchestral students and choristers over for an evening in their living room. These were magic moments for young people who came to see teachers as normal human beings who could share their enthusiasm without the usual distance and seemly proper restraint. It was at an exciting time when the Toronto Maple Leafs actually achieved Stanley Cup champion status on occasion.

Elmer discovered that his love of photography could serve many supportive roles in his efforts to be an effective teacher. He took pictures of his orchestra members, both male and female, incessantly, and they were delighted to see their images as instrumentalists on the walls of his classroom. It was another example of crossing the gaps between expressions of beauty of sound and image that made Elmer's work as a teacher memorable for so many of his students at YMCI. It was also another strategy to make their roles as musicians pleasurable. He realized that most of his students came from homes in which the sounds of "serious" music were not to be heard and enjoyed. He was determined to share with them the special feelings he had for both music and literature.

Some, he was sure, would discover the fire of his commitment and be changed forever.

During the years at York Memorial Elmer himself made life-changing decisions that resulted in the extraordinary role he was ultimately to play in his country's cultural history. Just two years after his arrival he felt called upon to become the founding conductor of the Festival Singers, eventually the most prestigious choral ensemble in Canadian musical history. He accepted that responsibility and from that point his life took on a direction that was irreversible.

The second decision was equally momentous and came to be very much connected to the first. A very intelligent, well-spoken, mature-beyond-her-years, attractive young woman called Jessie Balsillie had appeared for an audition to play a cello in his York Memorial instrumental ensemble. Very quickly she had developed the musicality and tenacity that enabled her to become a valuable member of Elmer's orchestra. They were attracted to one another and what began as a student-teacher relationship developed over the years into a union that immeasurably enhanced both their lives.

In these initial years at York Memorial, Elmer realized that his marriage to Trudie was not going well. She had expected to be the wife of a classroom teacher, not the companion of a superman of infinite enthusiasms capable of a multiplicity of directions that left her breathless and feeling less than competent. As well, she had a career of her own. The year at the Ontario College of Education and experiences in a continuation school in Delaware (a community near London, Ontario) had revealed that she too was an outstanding teacher. As an office worker in an insurance company she was obviously not now fulfilling her potential.

Then there was the question of producing a family. Both had married in expectation that within a year or two there would be an offspring to brighten their lives. None came. In the early 1950s they sought medical advice and were informed that they could not have children. This announcement disappointed both. The adoption of a child was seen to be the solution. Linda, a full-blooded Chippewa girl, very spirited, intelligent, and attractive, became Trudie's delight. It did not, however, do much to assuage Elmer's disappointment.

Ultimately, the answer to the very different expectations of the troubled couple was separation, with Trudie resignedly spending some time in Nova Scotia with her sister. The next step for Trudie was to take a teacher's position, moving to Dundas, near Hamilton, where she taught secondary school for a while, and then on to Burlington, Ontario, to assume a similar position. Soon after her divorce from Elmer she met Joe Cochrane. They married, and when he was transferred to British Columbia she and Linda happily accompanied him. Even though both Elmer and Trudie realized their union was doomed, the divorce proceedings involved money that neither could spare and were by definition time consuming. In the end, Elmer secured his rights to visit Linda throughout these years of separation, but it was only while Trudie was in Ontario that it was possible. Her move to British Columbia made visitation impractical, leading to a chasm in the relation of father and adopted child that inevitably ended in estrangement and an understandable resentment that Linda was to carry into her adult life.

During the mid-1950s, Elmer became increasingly attracted to the beautiful young cellist, Jessie, who had become an extremely welcome companion. In the 1950s a divorce was not perceived as a respectable and legitimate solution to marital incompatibility. Nothing at this time could speed the process involving interminable legalities that frustrated all involved — but Elmer's new relationship with Jessie and her Balsillie family was filled with understanding and healing. Surprisingly, the Mosig daughters and their spouses, though sensitive to Trudie's disappointment, attended Festival Singers concerts and followed Elmer's exploits closely. Indeed, George Pennie, who had married Trudie's youngest sister, Frieda, continued to see Elmer, accompanying him in his efforts to strengthen his ties with his mother Lydia's family near High Falls, Quebec, and joining him on fishing expeditions to the lakes nearby. Indeed, in the years to come, George and Frieda picnicked with Elmer and Jessie and their children on the Caledon Hills property that was ultimately to become Elmer and Jessie's home. Eventually, George became the chair of the board of the Elmer Iseler Singers, the successors to the Festival Singers. Just weeks before his death, knowing that his former brother-in-law had recently visited Leipzig, Elmer phoned to learn more about the Bach legacy in that city.

It was not until 1961 that the final step in the divorce settlement had been taken. However, even before that date the delays and inevitably unpleasant events around the breakup had scarred Elmer, and the disruption of his sense of well-being was finally having its effect on his health. In the wake of his perceived abandonment of Trudie and Linda, Elmer, his Lutheran conscience shattered, suffered deeply. In the midst of this trauma, his relationship with the bright young cellist in his orchestra took on even deeper meaning. It turned out that Jessie was exactly the person Elmer needed to share his life and hopes for the future, an opinion remarkably shared by Trudie. "Jessie was perfect for him," she concluded, after nearly half a century of observation.[5] By the mid-1950s, Elmer was living contentedly in a basement apartment with Jessie in the Thistletown home of the Balsillie family.

Elmer had come to realize that fate had directed Jessie to his English class as well as to his orchestra, where he found her response to great ideas and their expression in forceful language most engaging. When confronted by Elmer as a teacher rather than conductor she displayed both mind and spirit. At one point he asked her while analyzing a particular passage in a novel whether she had ever read a certain relevant comic strip. Her reply, "No, I don't read comics," brought a response from Elmer that aroused her ire: "You haven't lived." Her rejoinder, "Oh yes I have," left Elmer speechless.[6] She was to become the supreme love of his life. He came to be totally bewitched by this lovely young woman who exhibited all the personal qualities he desperately desired in a life partner — one who would share his vision for a country's cultural possibilities and the role of choral music in that quest. Fortunately she had both the courage and the will to be a part of that vision. She became the mother of his children, his constant companion, his completely dedicated supporter, the manager of his personal finances, and by the late 1970s the administrator of his Elmer Iseler Singers, his compassionate nurse in his final illness, and, on his death, the guardian of his legacy.

Changing schools is not a dramatic event in the careers of most teachers in the public sector. It happens often. However, Elmer's shift to a new school, Northview Heights, opening in the fall of 1957, could have been predicted. Jim Singleton had been selected as the principal and Elmer admired his administrative style enormously.[7] Singleton had decided he wanted a particular kind of staff — one that bore some contrast to those being gathered in new secondary schools in the burgeoning educational system of North York where schools were to pop up, one each year, for the next decade. He was anxious to pull together people who were not just university graduates of the past few years but who had distinguished themselves in the world "out there." The physical education teacher had been a professional football player, the drama teacher had been an actor on stage at Stratford, and now Elmer, the music head, was by this time a conductor of a prominent choir, the Festival Singers, which had within a couple of years reached the heights of excellence never achieved before by any other comparable ensemble. Elmer also knew his way about the Stratford Festival, the CBC, and countless other arts venues. As well, he had established his reputation as both an orchestral and a choral director at York Memorial, a unique high school in a small borough that Elmer realized offered little opportunity for advancement compared with huge systems like Scarborough and North York, the latter municipality then the home of Northview Heights but now included in the enlarged Municipality of Toronto.[8] Singleton knew that Elmer could be enticed to be part of this Northview Heights experiment in a fast expanding jurisdiction.

However, for Elmer all these external factors were insignificant compared to the main factor — he was being invited by Lt. Col. James Singleton to join this extraordinary staff. Elmer had come to realize that in having Rutherford and Singleton as the administrators at York Memorial he had been singularly fortunate. Both men were cultured individuals who saw the advantages to students of extra music classes, trips to distant places, and the extracurricular activities of choirs and instrumentalists even though they might disrupt the regular routine of participants and the academic schedules of other teaching colleagues. They made every effort to support the Iseler musical extravaganza that was bringing such delight to students, exciting their parents, and enhancing their lives. When the opportunity arose, Elmer was more than ready to accompany Lt. Col. Singleton to Northview Heights.

There was a further reason to move on. Though not yet official, Elmer's marriage had essentially ended and his liaison with Jessie had blossomed into a deep and abiding love. The latter years at York Memorial had been difficult for both of them. As one might expect there is evidence of some harassment from colleagues and parents who were outraged by this interaction of teacher and student even though every effort of the couple was devoted to ensuring their relationship was focused on Elmer's musical activities. They both hoped that Elmer's going to a new school devoid of all the baggage of previous appearances together that distracted others from the normalcy of their relationship was the right choice. Elmer became head of music at Northview Heights Secondary School and a renewed enthusiasm for teaching was aroused.

Yet there were those even in the new setting who condemned the unconventional association of student and teacher that had developed at York Memorial Collegiate Institute. Colleagues, even members of Elmer's new choir, the Festival Singers, tittered at the uninhibited caring for each other that Elmer and Jessie demonstrated — but magically the same intensity was present forty years later. In the wisdom of time, the warm, supportive partnership of Jessie and Elmer Iseler became legendary among all those who came into contact with them. They were inseparable intellectually, artistically, and physically. It would become an accepted truth by all involved in choral music performance that without Jessie, Elmer could not have survived the incredible workload, the clashes of artistic vision, and the brutal physical handicaps that on occasion threatened to end his career.

By 1957 and Elmer's arrival at Northview Heights, Jessie and Elmer were comfortably established in the Balsillie household — and it was a happy arrangement that amazingly lasted for several years. It included sharing meals and their preparation but most of all the common concern for collective well-being. By October 1958, a son, Noel, was born and celebrated, as was the birth of their daughter, Jessie Jr., or Buffy as she would affectionately be called, when it occurred in May 1961. Both would be accepted and loved by the entire Balsillie family,

Jessie had a younger brother, David, who shared a number of Elmer's non-musical enthusiasms. He had an interest in the natural world that Elmer could understand and encourage as well as a recreational enthusiasm for building model airplanes — a hobby that became an important extension of their relationship. They were more than brothers-in-law living in the same house and sharing a common table at meals. Both found the other perfect company for a mutual enthusiasm built around a love of nature, the wonder of the night sky, and sporting activities that included a mutual obsession for a popular tabletop hockey game. David was to become a forestry graduate and eventually a deputy minister in the Ontario government's Ministry of the Environment and Natural Resources, engaged in such activities as saving the province's trees and wilderness areas as well as finding a place for the disposal of the province's waste and securing its energy future. Little wonder he was led to join Elmer's efforts to understand the natural world around him. Besides having a perfect companion, Elmer found he could even borrow money between paycheques from this extraordinary relative who along with his family remains a staunch supporter of sister Jessie and the choir that bears Elmer's name a decade after his death.

In the Balsillie household, Elmer had found a context in which he could thrive. The warmth of an extended family surrounded him, a home life that was a retreat from the enormous pressure of a bloated professional teaching career and the leadership of Canada's most prestigious chamber choir. Behind him in a few years would be the prolonged process of divorce that had challenged his mental stability. He was among people he could trust, who understood his hopes and plans and recognized and appreciated his vision. It was an uninhibited love that had no strings and contained none of the judgmental surroundings that had pressed down on him during his teenage years in the parental parsonage.

With the first years of any new institution, including a secondary school like Northview, comes a period of euphoria normally identified as the "honeymoon phenomenon." Everyone is equal in terms of seniority, positive expectations have not been dashed by conflicts or financial constraints, old confrontations have been forgotten — there is the joy of discovering new opportunities and new interactions. But with Elmer there was more than the usual delight. The Northview Heights experience would be totally unique.

Former Northview student Jean McKay concedes that Elmer was not universally popular — but he was never the ogre his enemies depicted many years later. He was rigorous and demanding. He expected every orchestra member to be in his or her chair before the rehearsal commenced. He expected his musicians to be prepared and those who had not practised their parts bore his anger. Students who could not read music and lacked security in addressing the score did not escape his censure. Elmer's dictum was that it was better to get every note wrong but to know where you were in the score. Being under the baton of Elmer you always knew you were involved in the "real thing", both as a musician and person.[9]

Ironically, it was Elmer as a human phenomenon who moved Jean McKay and her colleagues most: "It was a revelation to see a musician who was so much more than just a musician. He knew what it was to be alive. With all his interests in plants and animals, in photography and astronomy, he was a splendid role model at a time when kids were learning how to live their lives."

His relationship with male staff members became legendary. He joined them in their annual fishing, beer, and bridge foray to fellow teacher Charlie Joliffe's cottage on the Severn River and, though in financial straits, Elmer bought land and a cabin where he, Jessie, and the young family could spend time in the summer. With the state of the family finances in mind, Jessie's initial response to his announcement that he had invested in a Northern Ontario property was an incredulous, "You bought what?" Once again, it had been a sensitive Jim Singleton who had advised him that it would be a wise investment. It clearly turned out that way. With a modest cabin containing three bedrooms, a front room that included a kitchen, dining room, and living room, it was far from luxurious, but with its inevitable rural backhouse, it was sufficient.

Even the Iseler's eventual property in the Caledon Hills, Quail Hill Farm, had already come as a result of the initiative of a fellow York Memorial teacher, Walter Dunbar, who lived in the Caledon Hills and recognized Elmer's need for the quiet and beauty of the countryside. He knew of a property owned by James MacSpirit Horan, and knowing Elmer's penniless state, arranged for him a purchase that contained no upfront cost and a mortgage that could be carried with a very low monthly investment. It would become Elmer's beloved "castle" throughout the rest of his life. It was, however, a considerable drive into the Caledon area and in the late 1950s and early 1960s, Jessie, now with two young children, could not see how she could operate at such a distance, especially without the Balsillie family support system. There was also the sharing of the nursing duties in looking after Aunt Mary.

In the modest initial structure in the Caledon Hills, Elmer's parents, with his father now retired from the ministry, were able to live for some years until Theodore's death in the early 1960s. Elmer, Jessie, Noel, and Buffy picnicked on the weekends over the years that Elmer was teaching and conducting choirs "on the side," until, finally, Theodore's widow's decided to move to Galt (now Cambridge), where her other son, Leonard, lived and worked. By the mid-1960s, Quail Hill Farm had become the permanent Iseler strikingly beautiful and deeply beloved homestead.

The extent of Elmer's impact on a significant number of Northview Heights students was monumental. Forty years later, when Elmer was dying, a coterie of "Northview kids," now mature, middle-aged women of some accomplishment, brought food, provided companionship to Jessie, and cleaned the home over the months when he was totally bedridden. Northview was for Elmer a veritable paradise during the years he sought to balance the demands of his public, private, and professional life.

By the early 1960s Elmer had years of successful teaching under his belt. He knew there were some things that worked and others that did not. He was still convinced that fine music as repertoire was the basis of his success as a teacher of orchestral music, and Wagner's *Die Meistersinger Overture* and Mozart's *Jupiter Symphony* were revived as favourite pieces in his new teaching venue. Only now, in a more prosperous neighbourhood, he was favoured with some students who had previous experience at the Royal Conservatory as private students with competent instructors.

One special performance stands out. Elmer engaged Hyman Goodman, the concertmaster of the Toronto Symphony, to play the solo part of the first movement of the Beethoven Violin Concerto — a challenge for even the finest professional accompanying ensemble. It was remarkably well done, a performance that was remembered for a lifetime by the participating musicians and awe-struck parents. That evening's orchestral playing set a new level of performance for aspiring conductors of secondary school orchestras.

Yet even at these heights students at Northview saw a glimmer of the insecurity that was to beset the artist in Elmer at every stage of his own life. Being an orchestral music teacher seemed to mean being competent on every instrument in the ensemble. This was impossible. As student Jean McKay states, "He did not face personal limitations well," even when the task before him was seen to be manifestly unachievable.

Elmer insisted on providing external opportunities for his students to observe and perform at Northview Heights as he had at York Memorial. As the 1960s approached the CBC had come to realize that younger audiences needed to be nurtured. Louis Applebaum, a composer and first music director of the Stratford Shakespearian Festival, had been brought on the CBC staff as a consultant. It was his view that a youth music television program was essential, one that would feature Canadian artists and the work of Canadian composers. It was to Elmer Iseler that Applebaum turned, and with Executive Producer Bruce Attridge's help, a CBC Youth Choir was created. Elmer immediately organized auditions and, as might have been expected, ensured his Northview Heights students were on hand. However, he insisted on quality and commitment and some Northview applicants were rejected. For those who succeeded, it was a marvellous introduction to the professional life of working in the arts.

As he had done at York Memorial, Elmer gave early morning Grade 13 classes in music at Northview so that his students could pick up an extra credit towards their honours diploma. One of the elements of the curriculum was the ability to identify and describe major compositions of the masters. Elmer's strategy was not just having his students listen to these selections on recordings but also transcribing the work for the instruments they played, thereby illustrating, hands-on, the themes and variations that distinguished the work. The music was no longer part of the academic examination game but the property of the students as performers.

Ultimately, in 1960, the pressure of maintaining and enhancing the performance of the Festival Singers, assuring top-quality singing by his CBC Youth Choir, the full impact of a heavy teaching schedule over many subject areas, and the haunting spectre of a failed marriage took their toll. Elmer was exhausted and disconsolate. In the fall of that year he collapsed at school and had to be taken to hospital. The first report was that Elmer had suffered a heart attack. A group of students who had gathered to rehearse a musical production were specifically told that this was the diagnosis. However, his disintegration was obviously more mental than physical. In those days it was termed a nervous breakdown, and Elmer spent some months hospitalized in a provincial institution associated with the healing of the mind, emotions, and spirit. All these concomitant pressures had produced an eruption that simply made continuing his work as a full-time teacher and choral conductor impossible. Elmer was granted a leave of absence from his duties at Northview Heights and did not return until the fall semester in 1961.

One of the greatest contributors to Elmer's recovery was John Bird, who combined a business trip to British Columbia on behalf of his music publisher employer Gordon V. Thompson with a search for Trudie and her adopted daughter. He discovered her happily remarried and caring for her beautiful little girl, who was bright, articulate, and obviously well looked after. It enabled John to return to Ontario and assure Elmer that all was well with his estranged former spouse and adopted offspring. He accompanied this news with personal advice to Elmer that all his guilt over a broken relationship was delaying his own recovery and that he must get on with his life as quickly as possible.[10] For Jessie it was a time of deep trauma but she realized she must contain her own grief in order to give strength to the man to whom she had given herself.

Fortunately, at Northview Heights, Elmer had an advantage — an assistant in his music department, who in this case could take over his responsibilities as head of music. David Smith had taken on teaching the brass and woodwinds, leaving strings and the full symphonic orchestral leadership to Elmer. It was a positive relationship. David had joined the Northview Heights staff to work with Elmer, who had by 1957 achieved remarkable recognition not only for his work at York Memorial but as a force in the choral music world with his Festival Singers. Smith was aware of Elmer's preoccupation with "good" music repertoire. Indeed it was Elmer's "innate sense of good taste" that initially drew Smith's admiration. That, and his capacity to attract the devotion of music students, in particular, made him "a kind of Pied Piper."[11]

It was during the years at York Memorial and Northview Heights that Elmer developed what became known as his famous rehearsal techniques. In the educational system of that time he was expected to train his choir, not on school time, but as an extracurricular activity for students who might want to learn to sing. In Elmer's case, it meant one evening a week, usually in the school cafeteria. His choristers had to bring their supper, eat it while doing their homework, and then rehearse. The challenge for Elmer was to make the experience as excitingly seductive as he could in the realization that a few moments of boredom might result in the diminishing of his choir the following week. Elmer, with his sense of duty and his love of music, was not prepared to let that happen.

Each rehearsal became an exercise in theatrical dynamics. It began with a lively opening composition, preferably a familiar and well-liked piece that would arouse initial interest. Elmer ensured there was no long explanation and certainly no idle chit-chat about the agenda for the evening but rather an immediate immersion in the excitement of musical creation. Every chorister had to be engaged in the work at hand, demanding full attention and hearty voice production. Elmer expected his singers to come before him fully warmed up and ready to perform even at this level of maturity. Then it was on to the main work of the evening. Elmer moved from one demanding passage to another, never spending too long on any aspect of the composition that provided difficulties but ensuring that his singers felt confident about their subsequent interaction with that musical challenge at the next rehearsal.

Inevitably there were pages of score that were beyond his young charges. Elmer, by this time, had moved on from his New Hamburg days and had learned that he must not embarrass or humiliate individual choristers by pointing out failures in their reading of the score. Rather, he identified entire sections of the choir as malefactors and engaged the team spirit of the basses, the sopranos, the altos, or the tenors in correcting the notes before moving on to the next passage.

Elmer had known from the outset that the correct notes were the foundation of the choir's sound just as the appropriate rhythm drove the composition as a whole. The quality of the rendition depended on these simple facts. Lack of attention to either would ultimately destroy any hope of achieving excellence. However, an obsession with picking away at individual bars in the score could undermine not only the delight of singing itself but the very concept of the piece of music being rehearsed. It was the constant dilemma of every conductor. Elmer was to become known among musicians as the conductor whose introductory words "from the top" (that is, from the beginning) would be repeated constantly during the evening's rehearsal. He was determined that his choir have the sense of the total experience rather than a memory of musical fragments repeated over and over, if he was to achieve the dynamic, the blend, the tone, and the interpretive quality he craved.

With his mature chamber choirs, the Festival Singers and his Elmer Iseler Singers, he demanded that when choristers knew they had sung a wrong note or notes, they were to raise their hand. There was no doubt that Elmer's incredible ears would have heard the mistake but the hand signal would inform the conductor that the chorister knew that a mistake had been made. There was no interruption. The music went on. It would be assumed that the singer's score had been marked for future attention. The rest of the choir were relieved of the boredom of repeating bars of a score that except for that error were being correctly performed.

Thus, the drama of a rehearsal increased moment by moment as Elmer moved gracefully from one composition to another, sections from larger masses and passions contrasting with shorter selections, some works for performance at upcoming concerts, other for events some months hence, from the more familiar and to newly acquired scores — a seeming mélange of compositions, each placed strategically in the time period of the rehearsal best suited for its effective conquest by his singers. Elmer spent many hours choreographing his rehearsals, and this preparation was essential whether the venue was the cafeteria at Northview Heights, the upper room at Lawrence Park Community Church, the Hydro Hall on College Street, or the low-ceilinged basement room of Roy Thomson Hall. Where the experience transpired mattered little, but at the end Elmer knew his choristers must march out of the rehearsal on a high of delight and reignited confidence.

Many choristers speak of arriving at rehearsals exhausted from a full day's work only to find new strength and vitality and a commitment to the cause of singing full out for two hours and leaving the hall refreshed and waiting expectantly through the next week for the same event to be repeated. There had to be a transmission of energy, an artistic interaction of the most basic nature. Many singers found that performances, with all the adrenalin produced by an attentive audience, were very special, but more were impressed by the engagement of the weekly rehearsal. Here was the opportunity of being part of a collective and intimate interaction with great music and a charismatic conductor determined to see that the composer's expectations were being met. The author and his spouse sang under Elmer on more than one occasion. This writer met his brief introductory comment — "I'll have an eye contact with every one of you in the next two hours" — with disbelief, but, in fact, it happened. As it did for Elmer's Northview Heights students, these moments came to be treasured.

The music program in a secondary school, with its emphasis on extra rehearsals and trips to special events, tends to disrupt the regular schedules of other subjects, and its purveyors are often the objects of the considerable fury of history and classics, to say nothing of mathematics and science teachers on each staff. Yet Elmer was a popular figure in the eyes of most of his colleagues. One example suffices. He had met Nancy Fockler (now Thomson) in the Northview staffroom on the first day of school. She had moved from the Kitchener-Waterloo Board of Education to North York's newly opened school with some trepidation. Elmer put her at ease immediately. His opening comment was "I really like the skirt you are wearing," and then he spoke knowledgeably about the style, the colour patterns, and the nature of the fabric. His interest in her attire was genuine and not a come-on. It was a remark that sprang naturally from a photographer's interest in appearance, particularly that of an attractive young future colleague who in this case had just become engaged to be married. Later in the fall term she found that she enjoyed the sounds coming from his music room and she asked whether she could drop in when she had a spare period. "He graciously consented and I was introduced to classical music."[12] Some fifty years later, Nancy remembers Elmer as a "fine teacher, a wonderful colleague, and a musical genius."

Throughout his years of triumph as the conductor of Canada's best-known chamber choir and, by the 1960s, the country's premiere oratorio choir, Elmer was constantly asked by journalists why he had left teaching. He would consistently reply, "I was a failure as a teacher." On those occasions he tended to remember the times of trial when he was exhausted, indeed overwhelmed, by the pressures of all his responsibilities.

Just as important as his desire to return to his school duties, Elmer's healing from his 1960 breakdown came as a result of the realization that he wanted to be back with his choirs. The CBC had enticed Lloyd Bradshaw, a fine choral conductor perceived by some as Elmer's main competition during these years, to take over the Youth Choir leadership in his absence. Nevertheless, the choir members, particularly those from Northview Heights, were calling for his return.

Even more seductive was the plan of the CBC to bring Igor Stravinsky to Toronto for an eightieth birthday celebration that would include the broadcast of his choral works with Elmer's choir, the Festival Singers. CBC producers and Singers alike knew it was essential that the Festival Singers be led by its founding conductor. By the fall of 1961, Elmer was back in his classroom and on the various podiums before his choral ensembles. Rest from his onerous duties had released him from depression and physical exhaustion. As well, he experienced the delight of knowing his second child was on the way, as Jessie had been pregnant during this crisis. All these factors combined to bring Elmer back home to Jessie, his young son, and new baby daughter, back to Northview Heights, and back to the CBC studios with his Festival Singers now training itself to sing the complex choral music of Igor Stravinsky.

Former Norhview Heights students Susan Silverburg and Barbara Myers remember his return to the school with particular warmth. Both of them had arrived with Elmer in 1957 and his collapse in 1960 had been a shock. Without him Northview Heights was simply not the same place. Their memories of Elmer revolved around his commitment to young people that went far beyond the normal expectations of traditional secondary school teachers. As early as Grade 10, he had taken a group of his students to a music educators conference in Buffalo, New York, where they performed with flair and distinction. That same year Elmer had taken a carload to the Stratford Festival, where a production of Arthur Honegger's *King David* was featured on the opening night of the music program, involving, of course, his own Festival Singers. It was a success, as Elmer knew it would be, filled as the performance was with tense drama, lyrical music, and splendid solo voices and with his Festival Singers providing the ultimate assurance of excellence. Elmer wanted his students to experience the excitement and inspiration that such a work could release. He also wanted them to feel at home in such a venue and even instructed his female choristers and instrumentalists on how they should act in this setting, including an insistence that they wear white gloves.[13]

Elmer invited his Northview choristers to his Festival Singers' Monday night rehearsals, at that time several miles south of North York at Upper Canada College, and, even though opera was not a favourite musical genre for Elmer, once to Maple Leaf Gardens to see the Metropolitan Opera's productions of Gounod's *Faust*. Maple Leaf Gardens was a more appropriate venue for Toronto's ice hockey team of the same name, and Elmer took his students to hockey games as well. Years later, Jean McKay recalled that experience: "During class that day, he explained icing and the offside rule, to get us ready. So that when we were playing fugues, say those of Gabrielli, and tossing the tune around, it felt like the perfectly completed pass in a hockey game. Elmer never explained the connections in so many words. He simply showed us 'the stuff' of the game and let us draw our own conclusions. He was the consummate teacher."[14]

At weekly school gatherings in the auditorium, music students became the envy of the student body (just as athletes captured attention in the gymnasium and on the playing field). With John Bird, T.L. Roy, and Keith MacMillan contributing the music and text, Elmer put on skits based on popular songs of the day. One memorable example was a takeoff on "The Yellow Rose of Texas," in which gunshots resounded to the shock of the filled hall. Jean McKay remembers "the look of blind horror in Elmer's eyes as he fell off the podium into the arms of fellow teachers Charlie Jolliffe and Baz Mackie." Music students were not the only beneficiaries of all this energy — Elmer took his science students up to his Quail Hill Farm property in the Caledon Hills to watch tadpoles being born.

Even the summer music camp experience was enhanced by Elmer's presence. Colleague David Smith had been central in arranging for Northview students to attend a summer music camp, Manitouwabing, near Parry Sound in northern Ontario. Realizing that many of his students could not afford to attend, Elmer organized the funding of scholarships that included reduced fees for serving fellow campers in the dining hall, kitchens, and infirmary. When he heard complaints that his charges were being exploited and did not have any time to enjoy the water or sports facilities, he appeared one day as a waiter himself and checked their stories by following their schedules. As a result of his research, a more restrained timetable of work was arranged and his students were able to participate more effectively in the recreational aspects of the camp program.

A bonus for his work at Manitouwabing was a friendship with the founders of the camp, Ben and Sheila Wise, who became supporters of his career for the rest of his life.

The full assessment of Elmer's success as a teacher must come from the memories of his students. Linda Sword, who was to spend the rest of her life working in the arts, described Elmer as the ultimate "free spirit," prepared to bend the rules when it meant something important to the learning and development of the student. Linda was caught in an academic dilemma. She wanted a language credit (German) and she could not fit requisite classes into her schedule along with playing violin in Elmer's orchestra as a music student. Elmer gave her permission to take German and still perform in his orchestra. At a time when such exclusion was simply following the rules, "Elmer simply let it happen."

Linda sensed that Elmer's colleagues regarded him warmly but as "totally unmanageable" in terms of expected behaviour. Close colleagues kept a collection of neckties in the staff room cupboard for occasions when Elmer would arrive at school inappropriately dressed for some state occasion. Nonetheless, the words "fabulous" and "inspiring" came from a Linda Sword well versed in what was appropriate academic performance in a typical secondary school setting.[15]

Northview student Pat Hartman both "worshipped" and was terrified by Elmer. He was "loaded with charisma." She was a member of the CBC Youth Choir that was singing Godfrey Ridout's *The Dance* along with selections from Orff's *Carmina Catulli* on air accompanied by Mario Barnardi and the CBC Orchestra. "We knew we were so fortunate," she said, to be in his music program. He was "at the top of his game," and though she sang later under splendid conductors like Lloyd Bradshaw and Ian Sadler she remembers Elmer as "the most influential person" she met in her life. Her response was one that was common to these young people who came into his orbit and were changed forever.[16]

Elmer's reputation as a Canadian musical icon came with little formal musical preparation that would impress the most supportive of his colleagues. However, as it turned out, his work in the classroom replaced a graduate degree in music performance that might have provided Elmer with confidence in the more traditional ways of acquiring knowledge about choral technique and appropriate repertoire. The dozen years at York Memorial and Northview Heights were crucial to his success as a choral conductor. These years of experience resonated at every rehearsal and the performances that brought audiences to their feet. Like any great teacher, he was striving not for titillation but for transformation, and this showed in the commitment of his years in the teaching profession.

Chapter 5

Founding a Chorus

ELMER HAD PURSUED HIS PASSION FOR THE
classroom at York Memorial Collegiate Institute for two years when, in
1954, a momentous event changed his life. He was invited to conduct a
group of splendid singers with whom he had worked and who wanted
to create a new ensemble, a crack chorus that would be devoted to
performing the most prestigious repertoire of the ages, beginning with
the baroque period and eventually reaching the romantic era, and to do
so at the highest level of professional music-making.

There was a prospective client — the Canadian Broadcasting
Corporation, to be precise, CBC Radio. The CBC was at the height
of its desire to broadcast the sounds of great choral music to a devoted
audience that had been proven to be out there. The presence on air of
the aforementioned choral ensembles of Leslie Bell, Carl Tapscott, and
Don Wright was an indication of the CBC's commitment. Many of the
individuals who turned up for Elmer's initial gatherings of vocal forces
had sung in one or all of these choruses. Others were prominent soloists
in religious institutions in this "city of churches," as Toronto was called. It
was a time when Sunday morning attendance was burgeoning and music
budgets in these faith communities were expanding exponentially and
thereby able to respond more generously to the presence of such an army
of quality singers now being produced by the University of Toronto's
Faculty of Music and the Royal Conservatory of Music.

Even Elmer had been attracted to a church choirmaster's position.
During his first year of teaching at York Memorial, a Lutheran church in

West Toronto, aware of his success in New Hamburg, had contacted him. There was a place for him as a choir leader and it seemed to be a perfect opportunity to add to his teacher's income, but also, more importantly, to revive his enthusiasm for the music of his Lutheran past.

However, after just a few months, Elmer had quarrelled with the minister, who had a strange penchant for having his choir and congregation hum a verse at some point in the presentation of every hymn. When Elmer asked, "Why all this humming?" the reply was simplistic and unconvincing: "They just like it!" Although Elmer's faith was at low ebb at this point, and one might have expected passive accommodation, he drew the line at this abomination. The hymns had a text that expressed a vibrant faith experience that was all-important to the relevance of the worship service. As well, the beauty of the human voice was being muffled and made ineffective. Elmer refused to compromise and retired in disgust.

This experience ended any further forays into church choir leadership and thereby left Elmer open to the assumption of a dominant role in the wider musical community. As well, it convinced him that he would find his spiritual dynamic, not necessarily in church buildings, but in the structures for the great orchestral and choral expressions of the masters, specifically for *Messiah*, *The St. Matthew Passion*, and the magnificent renditions of elements of the Roman Catholic Mass. In Elmer's own words, "When I am on the podium, my faith is secure. In spite of all the havoc in the world around, I know it will turn out well."[1] He was determined that the sound of his vocal ensemble would serve the inspired concepts of the composer, not the convenience of any institution, not even a church.

Beginnings are important. They often provide an explanation for events that transpire many years later. This particular collection of choristers that eventually became known as the Festival Singers had been organized after a discussion over a restorative glass of beer in the King Cole Room of the Park Plaza Hotel at the corner of Bloor and Avenue Road in Toronto, a popular drinking venue close to the University of Toronto. It was a regular gathering place but on this occasion was being enjoyed by chorus members who had just completed a gig at the CNE Grandstand Show. Their names were Gordon Wry, Tom Brown, Elmer Iseler, and Joanne Eaton — all well known in choir circles, both sacred and secular.

It was this small group who listed the acquaintances they believed would share their desire to create a new choral ensemble devoted to a more demanding repertoire and a more sophisticated tone and presentation. It was this quartet who provided the list of invitees to a second gathering a few days later.[2]

Elmer Iseler had been working in that same CNE Grandstand Show. His friend Howard Cable was responsible for the production and had actually handed over the directorship of the chorus to Elmer. There is no record of any discussion at the King Cole Room about who the conductor of this proposed ensemble would be. Elmer had spent that night conducting and had every reason to believe that this discussion was a continuation of his evening's work and that the conductor-chorister relationship with his singing colleagues had been a part of the reason for his inclusion at that late night chat.

As well Elmer's exploits in New Hamburg and with the All-Varsity Chorus at the University of Toronto, the Toronto Mendelssohn Choir, and Willan's St. Mary Magdalene Choir were now common knowledge. Also, by that time, the reputation of his York Memorial Choir had reached beyond the school boundaries to the studios of the CBC and into the consciousness of serious music listeners. Had the gathering on Bloor Street been a random collection of individuals for whom selecting the conductor was merely appointing a first among equals? Or had the original founders approached Elmer that evening to become "The Conductor" in the full recognition of his previous experiences? Had the other three choristers initiated a movement to hand over the proposed ensemble to a particular dominant figure or had three of the four simply assumed that any one of their group could take on a minimum leadership role that would suffice to serve the interests of such an experienced and well-trained contingent of singing colleagues? A quarter of a century later, in a decade filled with less generosity of spirit than the 1950s expressed, the confusion over "beginnings" was a part of the bitterness that ended the life of Canada's most respected choral ensemble, the Festival Singers of Canada.

Tenor Donald Bartle was one of the names listed that night in that pub. He remembers vividly the next meeting, in early September 1954, of these invited choristers. The site of their meeting was in a building that had once been a private home but was now part of the Conservatory complex at the corner of University Avenue and College Street. Bartle had been approached by Tom Brown and, though intending to follow the teaching profession, still wanted to pursue, at least on a part-time basis, his first love — choral music. Etched upon his memory is the image of Elmer sitting on a coffee table, making motions with his fingertips that signified the essential motivation for the gathering — the remuneration they could expect for the expert singing of a splendid repertoire, such as the chorales of J.S. Bach, that they could sell as a series of concerts to the CBC. Two decades later, with all the recognition and honours showered upon the chorus that finally rose from these discussions, it was ironic to remember that the financial hopes and aspirations of this largely penurious collection of singers stood at the top of any list of reasons for moving ahead on this project. Significantly, at this gathering, there seemed to be no dispute over who would play the role of conductor.

Although groups of singers had already been meeting in homes at the prospect of some choral development that might transpire, proper rehearsals soon began in classrooms of Toronto high schools (Harbord Collegiate, Central Tech, Jarvis Collegiate — all central city institutions) that could be utilized at no cost because they were the regular workplaces of the aspirants for membership in the new chorus. People came and sang, and some left, never to return. There were those who lost interest in the exhausting rehearsals or who found the repertoire too elitist. Elmer, though, carried inexorably on. He was the one choosing the compositions that were to be rehearsed, deciding the choristers whose voices blended — and discouraging those whose attitudes, talents, or voice production did not suit his purpose. It was his vision of repertoire, tone, and choral flexibility that won the day. In these early days, there was no doubt about whose vision and whose perception of the choir's future was being pursued.

The 1950s was a time in Canada's and particularly Ontario's history when big artistic plans were springing up everywhere: a tent theatre for Shakespearian drama at a festival in a railway town in western Ontario, a dance company in central Toronto ostentatiously calling itself "The National Ballet of Canada" that would astonish international observers, an opera school at the University of Toronto singing in the Hart House

Theatre making possible within a few short years the Canadian Opera Company — all emerged in these magical years.

In the fall of 1954, for these aspiring Canadian singers under Elmer's leadership, a special opportunity presented itself. Louis Applebaum, a popular composer and arts administrator had just accepted the role of music director at the Shakespearian Festival established in Stratford, Ontario. Tom Patterson, a local journalist, had invited Tyrone Guthrie, the respected British theatre director, to mount the plays that would initiate a Shakespearian Festival in a declining railway town that needed an economic boost of some kind. Alec Guinness and Irene Worth, along with the cream of Canadian actors, had mounted a successful theatrical experience in 1953 on a site overlooking the town's Avon River. The music component that Louis Applebaum had organized to display Canadian talent both in presentation and composition had not fared as well artistically or financially. People just did not turn up to form the sold-out audiences that the quality of the participating Canadian musicians and composers deserved.

Louis Applebaum had cancelled the music performances for the summer of 1954 and concentrated on a new launch of the Stratford Music Festival in 1955. He wanted a good orchestra and an effective chorus to form the base of his concert programs that summer. Hearing about these singers rehearsing with Elmer Iseler in various Toronto schoolrooms, he turned up at such a rehearsal one night with his colleague Ezra Schabas (later to become principal of the Toronto's Royal Conservatory of Music) to listen to this still-to-be-named group of singers. Both men were overwhelmed by what they heard. Ironically, a collection of choristers, gathered essentially to prepare themselves as a radio choir, found itself selected for its first public appearance at a music program being presented in conjunction with the drama festival.

At Applebaum's insistence, in order that the choir could be formally hired and recompensed, Elmer was forced to organize this group as a corporate entity that could carry on its own business affairs. For Lou's approval Elmer called the ensemble "The Festival Singers" in honour of its first public appearance in the summer of 1955, to be followed in 1956 and 1958 with concerts at that same venue.[3] These concerts announced the presence of the Singers, but it was the splendid repertoire and the special sound that carried the day in defining this new addition to the several choirs already performing in Ontario. Giles Bryant, a Festival Singer, observes that to a large extent Elmer took over his former mentor Healey Willan's favourite compositions, adding his own choices of Palestrina, Byrd, Purcell, and Monteverdi, and that this glorious repertoire, along with Elmer's additonal selections of J.S. Bach, saw the Festival Singers ensemble through its early years.[4]

There were not many other formal concerts in the first years but those few were in Toronto or nearby in smaller communities around the city. Indeed as John Kraglund, the *Globe and Mail's* music critic informed his readers in the early 1960s, "Most concerts of the Festival Singers were for CBC radio and television programs. In one season alone, the Festival Singers made 31 broadcasts — 14 in the last two months of that season."[5] The development of this instrument had a slow trajectory but one that could be maintained by a group of singers who, in many cases, had their own voice students to teach and held positions in the numerous churches and synagogues across the city[6] and were often themselves still studying at the Conservatory or the Faculty of Music.

In acting as the conductor of the Festival Singers, Elmer realized he had made an important decision, one that would define his life's work. Being a choral conductor was not a role that was recognized as one of prestige in the musical life of any country in the world. Compared to the "star" image of a Toscanini, a Furtwangler, a Koussevitzky, a Beecham, an Ernest Mac-Millan, or even an Arthur Fiedler, there were few famous choral conductors in North America or abroad who were known beyond their own communities, with the exception perhaps of Robert Shaw and Roger Wagner in the United States. Even including these latter examples, there were no choral conductors visible and appropriate for emulation by Elmer Iseler in his own country. In Canada, except for Willan and leaders of radio choirs such as Leslie Bell, Carl Tapscott, and Don Wright, his choral conducting colleagues were virtually faceless. Nearly all supported themselves as church choirmasters, like Lloyd Bradshaw, or were supporting themselves as music teachers with private students or, in the case of a very fortunate few, were academics in a music faculty on a university campus.

Above: Iseler family gathering in Port Colborne on the occasion of Lucy's nursing graduation. Left to right: Elmer, Leonard, Theodore, Lydia, Lucy, and Edna.

Below: The original Festival Singers, 1954–55.

The young maestro!

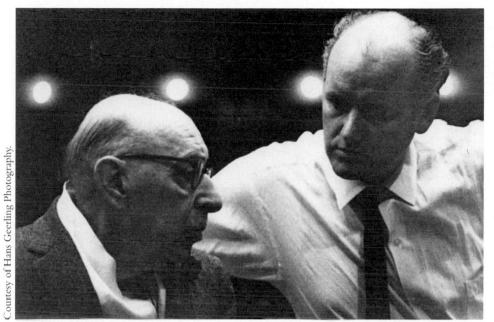

Above: Elmer Iseler with the world-renowned Igor Stravinsky. They worked together for several years in the mid-1960s to record Stravinsky's choral music with the Festival Singers, Massey Hall, Toronto.

Below: Festival Singers of Toronto, circa 1965.

Elmer with Zoltan Kodaly and his wife at a Faculty of Music, University of Toronto, celebratory concert.

Above: Noel and Jessie ("Buffy") Iseler at home in Thistletown, circa 1967.

Below: In the presence of President Lyndon Johnson the Festival Singers of Canada perform at the Lighting of the National Christmas Tree on the White House lawn in Canada's Centennial Year, 1967.

Above: Karel Ancerl, conductor of the Toronto Symphony Orchestra from 1969 to 1973, with Elmer. They enjoyed each other immensely!

Below: Nicholas Goldschmidt with Krzysztof Penderecki and Elmer Iseler. Elmer and the Toronto Mendelssohn Choir gave the Canadian premiere of the *St. Luke Passion* to great critical acclaim in 1971.

Above: Elmer and Jessie with Robert Shaw and his wife, Caroline. They enjoyed a lifelong and devoted friendship.

Below: On tour in Europe with the Toronto Mendelssohn Choir in 1972: Maud McLean, Jessie, and Elmer.

Fishing catch at family homestead in High Falls, Quebec: Noel, Jessie, and Elmer, circa 1972.

Above: Geneviève Bujold, actress/narrator for Leonard Bernstein's Kaddish Symphony, Massey Hall, Toronto, with Elmer and Jessie.

Below: Receiving the Order of Canada at Rideau Hall, Ottawa, with Governor General Jules Léger and Madame Gabrielle Léger, June 25, 1975.

Above: Toronto Mendelssohn Choir, Dr. Elmer Iseler, conductor, at the Kennedy Center in Washington, D.C. in 1976, with the Canadian Brass.

Below: Elmer and Jessie at Red Square, Moscow, November 1977. A grown man wept openly when we performed "Nobody Knows the Trouble I've Seen" and said to the person next to him, "It's about Jesus." They sold apples, caviar, and champagne with a straw during intermission at all the concerts!

The pensive and passionate conductor, Elmer Iseler.

Above: Elmer and Sir David Willcocks shared the podium at Choirs in Contact. They are seen here with Executive Director Mary Willan Mason, Peter Partridge, and Robert Cooper.

Below: Following a Toronto Children's Chorus concert, founder and conductor Jean Ashworth Bartle entertained at her residence, seen here (centre right) with Elmer, Lieutenant-Governor Pauline McGibbon, and Sir David Willcocks.

The Festival Singers perform the world premiere of *African Sanctus* by composer David Fanshawe (foreground, with Elmer) at Metropolitan United Church in 1978. The work has since been given more than three hundred performances internationally.

Above: Celebrating great friends Jim and Dorothy Singleton's fortieth wedding anniversary, 1981. Campbellville, Ontario.

Below: Elmer Iseler Singers supervising the building of the extension at Quail Hill in Caledon East, 1981.

Elmer relaxing at home in Caledon with family pet Laddie.

Above: Ontario Place Midsummer's *Messiah*, an outdoor spectacular enjoyed by thousands. Elmer Iseler conducts the Toronto Mendelssohn Choir in Handel's most favourite oratorio, circa mid–1980s.

Below: The Elmer Iseler Singers at the Seoul Cultural Olympics and Asian tour, August 15 to September 15, 1988.

Choral music creation had, down the ages, been connected with the Church. Composing and presenting such music, if considered at all, was seen as an act of divine worship rather than the revelation of a supreme talent. The magnificent mountaintops of choral music, Bach's Mass in B Minor, Beethoven's *Missa Solemnis*, and Mendelssohn's *Elijah*, were expressions of biblical texts and theological statements — too often the seriousness of the text was seen as sufficient inspiration, thereby demanding less attention to the quality of the composition and its performance.

Those identifying themselves as choral conductors were caught in a scenario of penury, never receiving an appropriate level of remuneration that reflected the genius demanded for performance or composition of great church or secular choral music. Part of the problem as well as the glory of these compositions was that they required massive orchestral accompaniment at a cost comparable to a symphonic performance. Because of these circumstances, it was inevitable that choruses capable of conquering these masterpieces were often adjuncts of the local orchestra, and when the time for performance came, it was the orchestral conductor who took over. The choral conductor was normally invited to take a bow during the applause at the conclusion of the performance, but there was little recognition of the fact that he or she had been responsible for hours of intense preparation that had created the magic of that evening.

The other reality that imposed itself on every choral director was the fact that choirs were normally made up of amateur musicians. In this case, the word "amateur," which in proper translation means "lover," had a special meaning. In many cases, the singers were excellent musicians, with all the capacities to read a score, produce sounds that had beauty, and articulate texts of profound meaning beyond that possible through the playing of any stringed or wind instrument. However, in the light of the fact that in the arts the term "amateur" normally meant "unpaid," the reality was that a choral conductor was too often unhappily dependent on the volunteer, often unintelligent, even incompetent, chorister. Few choirs required proof of even the most minimal musical capacity that would have been exposed during the process of an audition. Many choirs were and are today simply groups of volunteers who enjoy a night out singing with each other. The chorus members may have little talent and even less commitment. The role of the choral conductor too often became to cajole and bully a collection of unattractive, untrained voices to achieve at least a sound to which it was possible to listen with some degree of comfort and, hopefully, on occasion, true enjoyment.

And there was the ultimate trivializing assumption expressed in the statement "anyone can sing" that was so often repeated in order to encourage participation of those with limited interest or capacity. "We all have voices" was the gloriously inclusive invitation. These statements marginalized those who saw singing as an art form that required not only outstanding vocal chords that demanded attention and careful training but also a musical intelligence that demanded years of concentrated development.

Under all these disadvantages, why would anyone like Elmer Iseler wish to pursue this form of relentless self-flagellation? Even today many reasons leap forward. In some cases, choral conducting was the only choice of the economically strapped youthful enthusiast who had the resources neither to purchase an expensive instrument (many thousands of dollars) nor to pay for private tutelage that would make such an investment pay off. The human voice became a precious door to a valuable musical experience in youth that was transformed at some point into a desire to give leadership to the voices of others, an obsession for a genre of music presentation that offered so much to those with little material wealth.

In his own lifetime Elmer was to change the very image of the choral music performer and the choral conductor, giving the term "professional" a relevance to this form of music making.

Choral music was, and continues to be, by all accounts the most democratic, the most inclusive and participatory, the most inspiring and profound segment of the wide range of performance that can be called the "music industry." It attracts people for social and humanistic reasons that have been examined at some length. Most objective music enthusiasts would concede that the textual underpinnings of choral expressions provide a philosophical revelation that is more intense than anything that can be created by the vibration of strings or the blowing of air into brass and woodwind instruments.

There is also strong evidence that a symbiotic relationship develops among choristers, and between choristers and conductor, that is quite beyond that achieved in the instrumental ensemble. For one thing, in the typical chorus a kind of equality reigns — there are no clear distinctions and no obvious hierarchy of first chairs or supremacy of one section over another like that of solo instruments over the collectivity of the strings to be observed in most orchestral presentations.

It is significant that in the past century, scholars seeking to define the quality of life in a post-industrial-age community have seized on the presence of choral societies, along with such sporting institutions as football clubs, as essential to the development of a civil society amidst all the impersonality, noise, violence, and confusion of the modern urban centre. The presence of choirs produces an expectation of decency and order and positive public behaviour that has been observable both in the Americas and Europe.

It is even more surprising that in these troubled times of a new century, community choirs that have enormous difficulty in raising the money to pay the costs of venues, soloists, and professional instrumental accompaniment have taken on the support of great external causes. For example, part of the proceeds of ticket sales of Toronto Children's Chorus concerts go to the Stephen Lewis Foundation, seeking to bring relief to those facing the AIDS pandemic in Africa. At conductor Robert Cooper's insistence, Chorus Niagara and the Toronto Orpheus Choir have adopted the Regent Park School of Music and that same Stephen Lewis Foundation. Lee Willingham's Bell'Arte Singers are providing help to Covenant Home, Kisumu, Kenya, assisting children with disabilities in that part of the world. Thus the choristers in such groups not only sing as their contribution to a better society but do good work that goes beyond making music to including charities as the beneficiaries of their concert admission revenues. In doing so, these choirs and conductors were following the Iseler example. Elmer throughout his career recognized this extraordinary commitment to doing good that went beyond artistic vision and performance excellence. In the early years of the Festival Singers, Elmer gave the proceeds of concerts to the Israel Bond Drive, supporting the establishment of the State of Israel. On the occasion of the tenth year of Israeli independence, he received a handsome plaque that displayed the map of this new nation and a citation that the recipient had made a "Distinguished Contribution to the Cultural Interchange Between Canada and Israel."

Unfortunately, because of the perceived amateur status of choral performers, choral concerts are rarely covered for review by the major media sources — a fact that exposes the values of the media rather than the relevance or quality of the musical event. Thus little public attention is given to the plethora of fine vocal performances that are taking place in communities large and small throughout our modern society. That same word, "amateur," makes impossible the support of funding agencies such as the Canada Council for the Arts and the Ontario Arts Council, committed as they must be to the remuneration of professional artists. Though the presence of professional leadership and administration has been used as a reason for the distribution of minimal resources to choirs made up of amateur singers, in circumstances of reduced government resources choirs can be the first dropped off the funding agencies' list of priorities.

The choral conductor must deal with all these issues, which may both enhance the choral experience but also minimize its role, making it more difficult to bring focus and relevance to the work of a choral ensemble. It was one of Elmer's great contributions that he faced all these problems and sought to bring them to public attention and understanding in the interests of all his choral conducting colleagues.

At the outset, the Festival Singers were almost entirely dependent on the willingness of the CBC to commission concerts or studio presentations for broadcast. In Elmer Iseler, the Singers had adopted a leader, a virtual unknown certainly in the context of the Ontario's major cultural centre, Toronto. It took many hours of unremunerated rehearsal to place a tentative foot in the established choral world of a major city. However, during the late 1950s the choir slowly developed an audience and during these years was being regularly being heard on CBC Radio. Elmer was amazingly patient. Some of his choristers were convinced that recognition and appropriate remuneration were taking too long to achieve. When this view was expressed, Elmer resigned to stave off their complaints, but there was a unanimous move to attract him back to the helm of the choir. By the early 1960s the Singers were offering a series of concerts to enthusiastic audiences at the Trinity College chapel on the University of Toronto campus.

Iseler was not alone in the Toronto context. There were other familiar names in the choral community who had major responsibilities. Besides Willan at St. Mary Magdalene, there was David Ouchterlony at Timothy Eaton United, Charles Peaker at St. Paul's Cathedral, Eric Lewis at St. Simon's, and John Hodgins at Grace Church On-the-Hill. The names of Douglas Elliott at St. Andrew's and particularly Lloyd Bradshaw at St. George's had much greater cachet than Elmer Iseler, this young and energetic man with little experience or focused training who had so recently arrived from rural western Ontario. However, this newly minted ensemble, the Festival Singers, could not have appointed a more vision-driven leader. Iseler had acquired from all his experiences a clear perception of the kind of chorus he wanted to create, the sound it should produce, and the kind of music it should aspire to sing in the most sensitive manner and in the most appropriate style of performance.

The most important development in these years was that the choir gained an almost immediate recognition for the purity of its "white sound" and the careful tuning that was possible when Elmer found he could eliminate the vibrato prized by trained singers and secure the most seamless musical expression possible In these circumstances, a unique blend could be attained, one that was particularly appropriate for the baroque repertoire the choir was singing.[7] It was apparent that the members of the chorus had made a commitment to their individual preparation that meant that rehearsal time rarely had to be spent on finding the notes — but rather in honing the interpretation of the text. Most important, Elmer was determined that every member was to be an intelligent and thoughtful human being, rather than merely a voice. They were to be chosen for the quality of character they brought to the Singers. He insisted that this strength of personality was the most important characteristic he sought.

Then, in 1960, disaster had struck. Elmer had collapsed in a state of mental and physical exhaustion in the gymnasium of Northview Heights just two weeks before the opening concert of the series the Festival Singers had established for the 1960–61 season. It was not clear immediately how long Elmer would be indisposed. The Singers had to carry on, making use of interim conductors. The most successful replacement was Lloyd Bradshaw, a man gifted with immense musicality and a breadth of repertoire knowledge that astounded his many admirers. It was in the fall of 1960 that Bradshaw made use of Elmer's preparation to present a tribute to Healey Willan, now eighty years old. It was a successful concert, but other interim conductors did not fare as well.

The reviews of concerts were highly adulatory in the early years, but soon began to slip into pointed criticism. In December, when Toronto Symphony conductor Walter Susskind was engaged, in Elmer's absence, to lead the Festival Singers, an unidentified reporter in the *Toronto Daily Star* commented that the already famous balance had been lost. "Tonally, its soprano section has taken on a rather over-balancing fullness since I last heard it," complained John Kraglund, now the *Globe and Mail*'s music critic. He then used his review of the concert to ruminate that the audience for the choir had not reached a level that gave confidence for the future of the Festival Singers (fewer than two hundred had ventured out on a wintry night). He lamented prophetically, "It is unfortunate they have arrived at the familiar artistic impasse which makes venturing abroad seem risky because of the lack of support at home, and the latter is improbable because they have not been proclaimed abroad."[8] Here was the colonial mind revealed at its worst — a valid judgment of quality could be made only by someone else, somewhere else. It was a red flag to a convalescing Elmer, who, as it turned out, had not suffered a heart attack but rather had been felled by a mental breakdown — the result of a host of pressures that he had failed to overcome.

The emphasis on white tone had, by this time, attracted complaint for lack of "lustiness," particularly as the choir turned to the romantic choral repertoire. In a February 1962 concert that included Brahms's motets where the composer's melodic contours call "for vehemence, for strong enunciation, and in his climaxes, for emotional power. Not many of the characteristics were present in the Festival Singers performance of these motets," observed one unnamed reviewer. John Kraglund's review of the same concert was headlined "Singers fail to show significant progress," and he concluded, "Last night it had made no significant advances in any direction."[9]

It was clear that many months of Elmer's absence in 1960, 1961, and 1962 had badly damaged a choir that was on a remarkable musical trajectory to performance excellence. It was now stalled and faced with likely disintegration of its future hopes unless Elmer returned. However, throughout these months, Elmer had been distraught by a sense of failure, a perception that came to envelop him, including a loss of confidence as a musician but most of all, a dreadful guilt over the broken marriage with Trudie. Now he was filled with foreboding over the well-being of his new family, Jessie and Noel, tempered by a joy of knowing that a second child was on the way, Jessie Elizabeth, known to Iseler intimates as "Buffy."

Though Elmer's trauma seemed to be ebbing, the Festival Singers appeared to be faltering. "Did the Festival Singers have any future?" became the question of observant choral devotees. Elmer's renewed leadership seemed to be the only solution.

Elmer's immediate return to the podium was fired by CBC Radio's decision to celebrate the eightieth birthday of one of the greatest composers of the twentieth century — Igor Stravinsky. This major commitment included both the public performance and a national broadcasting of his works and the involvement of Canada's most prestigious symphonic orchestra at the CBC, but also the Festival Singers of Toronto. The CBC wanted a fine choir to sing all of Stravinsky's choral works, known to be challenging to the best of choral forces on the continent and beyond. Producers, in particular, John Peter Lee Roberts at CBC Radio knew it could happen only under the baton of Elmer Iseler. Thus, Elmer was persuaded to return to the podium, first as the Singers' coach, with others taking regular public performances, and then, once again, as the Singers' permanent conductor.

The 1960 to 1962 breakdown had made a considerable difference in Elmer's outlook on his style of conducting. The Healey Willan form of choral terrorism was not for him. In a 1962 article, Kraglund referred to the "high strung temperament and occasionally violent temper" that Iseler demonstrated at York Memorial, but it was not a reputation that Elmer coveted.[10] He returned in 1962 with a different philosophy of choral conducting. "During my illness I realized that the most important relationship — musically and otherwise — between persons is sympathy ... I realized that to establish rapport with singers, I did not have to storm and rage."[11] Giles Bryant puts it simply: "Elmer became a new man."[12]

As well, Elmer had come to realize how precious had become his relationship with Jessie and his two children, which promised him such a "wonderfully balanced life." It was during these difficult years that the divorce with Trudie had reached its final stage. In a quiet moment, Elmer had told Jessie, "I think I am allowed to love you now." There was a quiet ceremony overseen by the Reverend Theodore Iseler and they were legally married! By that time they had gone through so much together that the ceremony was virtually superfluous. They never celebrated their wedding anniversary. "Every day was an anniversary" is Jessie's comment on the absence of this date in the Iseler family calendar.

There had also during his illness been time to review his vision of making music. Elmer had not originally addressed contemporary music, particularly that of living Canadian composers. Already, the CBC had pushed him in the direction of modern works. The production of a program in the 1950s had demanded a performance of American composer Aaron Copland's *In the Beginning* and the Festival Singers were given only a few days to prepare the work. But he had found the experience most satisfying and he became attracted to the presence of contemporary Canadian composers. Now he had to convince them that they should write music for choirs and voices rather than just orchestras and instruments.

It was clear that in these few years Elmer had become almost an instant icon in the choral music world. Alex Jozefacki, who sang with him in both his chamber choirs and shared his reincarnation in the 1960s as the leader of Canada's most celebrated large ensemble, the Toronto Mendelssohn Choir, speaks reverently of Elmer's discovery of his strength during these years — an ability to captivate, to command attention every moment he was on the podium. He took on a "regal bearing" that exuded a confidence that infected his choristers and brought new energy and purity of sound to their performance.[13] Elmer began to take pride in being able to say of his Singers, "This choir can sing anything."[14] And he was right.

Chapter 6

Total Collapse to the White House Lawn

THE EXTRAORDINARY CBC RADIO COMMITMENT to choral music in the early 1960s, and particularly to the music of internationally respected composer Igor Stravinsky, brought Elmer back to the Festival Singers, first as the ensemble's vocal coach and ultimately as, once again, its permanent conductor. The Singers' self-image changed and, even more, the public perception of the ensemble was transformed. The Festival Singers, begun initially as a participant in a modest music program alongside theatre presentations at the Stratford Shakespearian Festival and as another CBC Radio broadcasting choral ensemble, took on a new aura.

Stravinsky arrived in Toronto accompanied by Robert Craft, his ever-present professional associate who tended to his octogenarian physical needs as well as acting as a rehearsal coach for whatever ensemble the master might be conducting. Most important of all, Craft was gathering the information and inspiring the performances and recordings that would assure Stravinsky's legacy for centuries to come.

The simultaneous presence of three conductors produced some hilarious moments. On one occasion, before major decisions about tempo for a particular composition had been agreed upon, Stravinsky occupied the podium, but both Craft and Elmer were to be found standing slightly behind the master providing a more vigorous beat — with the choir completely baffled by the question of which conductor they were to follow.[1]

It became clear that the splendid CBC Symphony Orchestra was very much prepared to address his challenging scores but the surprise for Stravinsky was the artistic brilliance of the Festival Singers. One TV special was to include his popular *Symphony of Psalms* and the creator was ecstatic over the sound of the Singers, announcing at the end of the rehearsal that he "could not find another choir in North America who could take the *Psalms* at the pace [he] wanted."

The decision to take advantage of Stravinsky's presence in Toronto by scheduling a public concert at Massey Hall resulted in a North American premiere of his latest choral work, *A Sermon, a Narrative and a Prayer*. Also on the program was his *The Dove Descending Breaks the Air*, which Robert Craft would conduct. A rapt Canadian audience enjoyed the unique experience of hearing these excellent works, conducted by the famous composer and his trusted associate, being splendidly performed by its own choral ensemble, the Festival Singers.

The Festival Singers, after so many months of wondering whether there would ever be a permanent conductor — or even a continuing choir — were excited. The remuneration produced by the CBC initiative was also welcome. Being referred to as "the best choir on the continent" by perhaps the world's most prestigious composer had restored the morale of the entire group. On April 10, 1962, a Festival Singers concert, though still not conducted by Elmer, was declared "outstanding." John Beckwith's review in the *Toronto Daily Star* was headed "Festival singers in best concert": "Either inspired by guest conductor Roland Pack or nice things that Stravinsky had been saying, there was an unmistakable new animating quality in the Singers' work ... in sum, it is no exaggeration to say this was a rare evening of distinguished choral singing."[2] The Singers knew it was more than Pack's conducting and Stravinsky's praise that was inspiring the ensemble to new heights — it was the return to weekly rehearsals and the intense choral preparation now in the hands of an at least partially reinvigorated Elmer Iseler.

The April 29 concert performance in Massey Hall was hailed by one critic as "a massive victory" by an ensemble "securely trained by Elmer Iseler." By the last concert of the Festival Singers' 1961–62 series at Trinity College in May 1962, Elmer was back on the podium. John Beckwith reported that the "former director of the group returned as a guest conductor for the occasion and drew from the choir a top caliber performance of predominantly modern repertoire pieces."[3]

On *CJBC Views the Shows*, a Toronto radio station's weekly program on the arts, R. Murray Schafer, a recognized Canadian composer not noted for his flattering reviews of arts performances, commented that the Festival Singers had "executed Stravinsky's *The Dove Descending Breaks the Air* the way no other choir in North America could do it." Stravinsky himself congratulated them at the conclusion of his composition, stating that "there was no choir in the world that could perform this work as well." Needless to say, such accolades assured the performance of the Stravinsky repertoire in Festival Singers' programs for years to come, but they also encouraged Elmer to look beyond this music creator to other contemporary composers — and particularly Canadian composers. In 1963 alone, Elmer premiered two major works, *The Tokaido* by Harry Freedman and *Jonah* by John Beckwith. Both continued as respected compositions included in the repertoire of Canadian choirs.

As it turned out, the years 1962, 1963, and 1964 were focused on the Stravinsky project with all the fallout that was initially beyond the Singers' imagination. The composer returned to the United States and cancelled a recording contract in California, returning to Canada again and again, indeed, four times in a fourteen-month period in 1962 and 1963, in order to place his entire choral repertoire sung by the Festival Singers on the Columbia record label.

Elmer's reputation and that of the Festival Singers was now established beyond question. Indeed, Elmer speaks of both he and his Singers "treading on air" after one of Stravinsky's visits that included "the crowning glory of five hectic days of rehearsal and recording sessions." However, health problems continued to beset Elmer. He was able to conduct a sold-out 10 Centuries Concert in early December 1962, but the taping of a ninety-minute CBC Radio concert to be broadcast on Christmas Day of that year was instead conducted by Sir Ernest MacMillan. In spite of Elmer's continued mental and emotional illness, reviewer George Kidd's analysis of the 1962 musical life of Toronto would include how impressed he was with "the strides made by the Festival Singers under the guidance of Elmer Iseler."[4] Within a year the National Film Board had made a documentary on the Festival Singers that would be shown from coast to coast.

Early in 1963, music critic John Kraglund, on the occasion of a concert in a sold-out Festival Singers subscription series, chose to take an historical look at the choral scene in twentieth-century Toronto. Headlined "Choir of 33 upholds city's claim to fame," his review contained a reassuring analysis of the Singers' new position in the country's musical life:

> Choral music has enjoyed a long and frequently distinguished career in Toronto since the end of the nineteenth century. But I would wonder if it has ever flourished with greater enthusiasm — or in one of two instances, more brilliantly — than it does at the present time ... At the apex of today's revival of quality choral singing is the ensemble known as the Festival Singers of Toronto whose guiding genius is founder-conductor Elmer Iseler.

The major work of that March 12 concert had been Ralph Vaughan Williams's Mass in G Minor. Critic John Kraglund had been more than a little impressed:

> It happened to be my first opportunity this season to hear the Singers and to marvel again that these 33 performers — most of them soloists and frequently members of other choirs — can achieve a uniform quality, spirit and style which seems to elude most other vocal ensembles ... Rarely have the meanings of the separate parts of a sung mass been so vividly communicated as in the performance of the R.V.W. Mass.[5]

In the summer of 1963, Udo Kasemets, writing in *Maclean's* magazine, while adding to the general acclaim of virtually every reviewer of the Festival Singers, revealed the very issue that was ultimately to bring the illustrious chorus down. "In 1963, he is Canada's leading choral director and his choir is often referred to as 'The Iseler Chorus' ... the Festival

Singers have from the beginning so mirrored Iseler's own personality."[6]

The year 1964 was a watershed for Elmer and his Festival Singers. He became the conductor of the Toronto Mendelssohn Choir. He called it a turning point in his life. A later chapter will explore the drama around the surprising developments that concluded with his acquisition of Canada's most distinguished oratorio chorus — but both Elmer and his Singers had now embarked on a new course.

For a host of reasons, the Toronto Mendelssohn Choir was in a tattered condition. Indeed, the ensemble was nearly out of business. Elmer had been chosen because of the miracle that had produced the Festival Singers. Now he was faced with performing a second such wonder — one in many ways more difficult than the first.

His additional challenge was fortuitous in one sense — it solved the continuing problem of Elmer's financial well-being and the lack of security he had faced through the first decade of his working life. It was simply impossible for him to teach full-time and direct a major choral organization — that was the lesson of the 1960 collapse. It was Lt. Col. James Singleton, his Northview Heights principal, who understood this dilemma most clearly. However, the Festival Singers' remuneration was minimal at best as an income base to support Jessie and their two young children. Singleton saw in the plight of the Toronto Mendelssohn Choir a window of opportunity. If Elmer could be recompensed by both choirs for his work, a resignation from his teaching position would be possible. It would either be his salvation or "Elmer will be out on the street," Singleton figured. Defying Singleton's negative possibility, Elmer Iseler accepted the invitation in 1964 to be the Mendelssohn Choir's artistic director and became Canada's first full-time professional choral conductor.

For the Singers there was a particular advantage as well. Raising the quality of the Toronto Mendelssohn Choir by the addition of the thirty-plus Singers with their sight-reading abilities, their quality voices, and their interpretive skills was a solution to another problem. It could be a path to a more lucrative future as a Festival Singer. But there were serious problems. The combination of volunteer choir and a paid core of singers on that scale had never been tried before. The TMC was an old, staid operation that had been proudly made up of volunteer members from the outset and still was after the many decades it had performed since the mid-1890s. Would TMC members resent the fact that Festival Singers choristers would be paid to perform exactly the same function in a chorus when as TMC members they had to contribute a fee in order to sing and received not even the remuneration to subsidize their travel and parking expenses? Would this change undermine the morale and energy of the regular singers? As it turned out, the experiment was successful, indeed, was financially advantageous for the TMC, as the presence of professional singers made it possible for government granting bodies to make a contribution to its well-being that its formerly entirely amateur status made impossible.

What of the Festival Singers? Would the ensemble lose its identity when seen as a part of the massive Mendelssohn Choir organization? Would working with amateur singers diminish the reputation and self-image of the Festival Singers? Would the very different repertoire for chamber choir assure the Festival Singers that important distinctiveness on which their future success would be based? With Elmer's appearance as the conductor of both, these problems seemed to vanish, particularly in the extreme pressure of work facing both ensembles.

Elmer ensured that the 1964–65 Festival Singers concert schedule was filled with exciting events. It commenced, significantly, on August 16 where it had all begun — at the Stratford Festival with a full program of Bach: Motet no. 6, *Lobet Den Herrn, Alle Heiden*, Cantata no. 2, *Ich Hatte Viel Bervümmern*, and the Magnificat in D Major. Not an easy or "popular" program. However, the capacity audience rewarded Elmer and his Singers with a standing ovation obviously agreeing with critic W.J. Pitcher that "all had performed with distinction … and achieved both sonority and lucidity" under Elmer, who demonstrated "the drive and assurance of a natural conductor."[7] The *Toronto Star*'s critic, Ralph Thomas, later that year was to comment that Elmer looked healthy and relaxed, portraying none of the "tension and exhaustion which in the past showed itself in a terribly short and volcanic temper."[8]

Though delayed by the events surrounding Elmer's acquisition of a second major choral organization, the preoccupation for Elmer on his return had been to make his Singers into the first truly professional choir in Canada, and, in a sense, in North America. A comparable ensemble on the continent was the Robert Shaw Chorale, but it was essentially a pick-up choir for radio broadcast and recording purposes with no regular performing responsibilities. The economics of these changes were bound up in the fact that the TMC rehearsal and concerts could now be charged to that organization's budget, as Festival Singer professional appearances and thus the full "professionalization" was now easier to achieve. Elmer wanted choristers to be respected and honoured in the same way as orchestral players who were devoting time, talent, and energy to the performance of challenging works. He believed that the amateurism that pervaded choral work came from the conclusion that its performance required less skill and commitment. Elmer wanted to change that perception. Professionalism was the most direct way of revealing the intellectual and physical demands of singing — as well as placing a challenge before composers that would result in music of the highest calibre appearing on the music stand.

However, there had to be a more broad-ranging role for such an ensemble than simply CBC broadcasts and a regular subscription series in Toronto and a few run-out concerts in nearby urban centres. Elmer wanted the Singers to accept a wider responsibility to spread the appreciation for choral music — and to raise the quality of its performance in communities in Ontario and ultimately in every region of the nation. This meant touring to those regions across the entire country, not only performing but also the exhausting activity of providing workshops for choristers and conductors from church and community choirs from coast to coast.

As well, Elmer wanted Canada to be recognized as a country with a splendid choral tradition. Touring his Singers to the United Kingdom and European communities, indeed any part of the world where western choral music was played and sung, was an essential strategy in achieving that goal.

Finally, it meant taking on the cause of encouraging Canadian composition of choral music — the creation of a repertoire that would be available to all choirs, one that would express something of what it was to be Canadian. Almost as an acceptance of this role, in 1964, in a celebration of the warm and inspiring association with Stravinsky, the Festival Singers appeared at New York Philharmonic Hall to participate in a performance

of the great composer's music conducted by both Stravinsky and Robert
Craft. Included in the same trip was a recording session with the New York
Philharmonic. By this year, Igor Stravinsky had accepted the role of a patron
of the Festival Singers along with a host of other distinguished figures.[9]

From a personal point of view Elmer had added another priority.
He wanted to remain in contact with young people. With his secondary
school teaching career over, he could now consider instructing at the
university level. It would not command as much of his time but would
provide the satisfaction of working with young musicians eager to pursue
choral music as a profession. He succeeded Dr. Charles Peaker as a special
lecturer in choral technique at the Faculty of Music at the University of
Toronto. Probably no faculty member had been hired with fewer paper
qualifications and with greater promise.

Dr. Fred Graham was one of Elmer's students during those two
academic years, 1966–67 and 1967–68, and was enormously impressed
with the manner in which he carried out his responsibilities.[10] Elmer
had specific objectives and all else, such as the provision of formal
lectures, was ignored. Paramount in his mind was the determination that
his university class in a course leading to a Bachelor of Music degree
should be connected to the real world of professional arts performance
and that appropriate standards of musical expression should be established
as part of the academic program. He had watched students of previous
classes sink into the mire of mediocre activity beyond the mainstream of
music creation, accepting the inadequate standards of music making in
churches and schools and in private instruction. His students would not
be allowed to emulate these inadequacies. In order to establish some sense
of expectation, he insisted that all students attend his Festival Singers'
rehearsals now held in the Upper Canada College auditorium.

As well, Elmer was anxious that all students acquire a personal repertoire
of choral compositions that were familiar to them. He requested that each
member of his class purchase twenty-five pieces from a broad list representing a panorama of some ten centuries of choral music composition. His
graduates would know a representative collection of the masterpieces of the
ages. His only lecturing was concentrated upon a profound analysis of how
each composer had revealed the text of each individual composition.

Elmer realized he was teaching young men and women who would be waving a baton before countless choirs, but he had little interest in teaching the technique of choral conducting. "He emphasized the heart more than the head," Graham succinctly observed. Elmer wanted to stress the importance of the intellectual and experiential that every student brought to the podium. He saw the desire to conduct coming from the intelligence, the energy, and the dynamic of individuals living their lives fully and consciously. Only then could they benefit from their time with him.

In the realization that many of these students would be working with children, he brought in a teacher whose school choirs were the pride of the Toronto region, Jean Ashworth Bartle, and simply let her demonstrate her genius with young choristers. He knew her skills, if observed and understood, would lead to the improvement of singing in hundreds of classrooms around the province.

Elmer remained only two academic years and then retired. Some have suggested that, once again, he had overextended himself. Both his choirs, but especially the TMC, needed his attention. The more perceptive believe that resistance to his more unorthodox methods and untraditional views on the purpose of post-secondary education led to a rapid deterioration in his enthusiasm for the university classroom. There may even have been interference in the syllabus he pursued and his personality brooked no such intrusion or meddling. When questioned specifically, Elmer simply replied that university teaching was too much like the secondary school experience he had left but a few months before. His retreat was a blow to the preparation of a phalanx of fine music teachers that Ontario and Canada desperately needed.

Elmer realized that the Stravinsky pronouncements on the quality of the Festival Singers would have a very short shelf life and that unless the ensemble increased both the quality and number of its performances and broadcast appearances, all this advantage would soon be lost. He was determined to see that his Singers received a regular stipend for their services — thus becoming Canada's first professional choir. Ralph Thomas, a Toronto music commentator, recognized the prejudices that Elmer faced. He observed, "One big reason that choral music has never gained its proper place in Toronto's music calendars is that, generally, it has been done badly … Audiences have come to expect something way short of perfection at a choral concert. They associate it with slipshod technique as they have usually had to put up with a wall of bad sound and wrong notes between them and the meaning of the music." Thomas expressed his confidence in Elmer as "Canada's Mr. Choral Music."

During the 1960s it could be said that Elmer, in pursuit of reversing these prejudices, went from triumph to triumph. The struggle involved the entire choral world. In the ten years since the Festival Singers had been formed other choral ensembles with ambitions to reach similar heights had been established — the Montreal Bach Choir and Renaissance Singers as well as choral groups in Vancouver and Winnipeg. Well before the end of the century, there would be a few professional Canadian choirs and others on the road to some level of professional status. It was Elmer's dogged determination that cleared the way, establishing a reputation for excellence in choral presentation by justly and appropriately paying singers to give time and study and as well as their appealing voices to this cause.

Shortly after the Stravinsky years, at a concert of the Festival Singers offered by the Women's Musical Club of Toronto, their singing could be declared as "stunning … the best Bach performance I have heard in ages" by no less than the well-respected composer and commentator John Beckwith.

William Littler, now the *Toronto Daily Star*'s regular music critic, became particularly interested in the struggle for professional status for choristers, as he saw the possibility of improving the entire choral music community through grants and private donations. If members of ensembles like the Festival Singers were supported like public school teachers by being put on a salary they would be able to carry on regular educational work. Such an ensemble in a school for a few days could make an enormous difference. Littler advanced his cause by pointing out that the Festival Singers "have arguably achieved professionalism" artistically and now it was only a matter of "making the transition happen."[11] At the same time he was realistic about the fact that Elmer had created a unique musical entity: "Iseler's choir is something more … It's a reflection of one man's approach to the art of making music chorally, a living witness to his integrity and skill."[12] Though wishing for more colour and forcefulness, critic Ken Winters in the *Toronto Telegram* could say of the Festival Singers, "When one finds fault it is not according to standards set by other choirs — but according to the standards set by themselves ... but more lust please."

These years were also an opportunity to look back over past influences. Elmer never lost sight of his roots. The 1964–65 concert season included a trip to Waterloo College, where his decision to pursue musical studies had been made, and in the presence of most of his relatives he led his Festival Singers in a concert in Galt, where his father, Theodore, had come to live and work after ending the pastoral care of his flock in his Port Colborne Lutheran Church. Now semi-retired and living with Lydia on Elmer's property in the Caledon Hills, Theodore was thrilled to have his son leading his choir in this beloved western Ontario community. Again Elmer appeared in Galt with his choir in 1966 to "thunderous applause and a five minute ovation following the final number." Elmer's genius was in full view: "The 40 voice choir seems to be attuned to every gesture — perhaps every thought of the conductor."[13] The proceeds of ticket sales for the concert went to the Rehabilitation Foundation for the Disabled in that region.

The mid-1960s was an exciting time to be in a Canada preparing itself to celebrate its centennial with the greatest explosion of music and dance performances the country was ever to witness. Though the celebration year became focused on Montreal and Expo '67, the Government of Canada had placed Niki Goldschmidt, who would become the nation's most prestigious arts entrepreneur, in a position to exercise his promotional skills in every corner of the land some months before. Orchestras, string quartets, vocal soloists, and dance companies moved from urban centres to villages and hamlets across Canada entertaining and inspiring audiences of enthusiastic Canadians. By 1966, citizens had been made aware that Canada had become a country whose creativity must be recognized and that singing, playing instruments, and dancing was how that should happen in 1967, what Pierre Berton was to call "the last great year" in the country's history. That year even occasioned a Festival Singers' choral celebration of the life of Healey Willan (who would die at eighty-seven within the next year) that was so enthusiastically received that *Telegram* reviewer Ken Winters was unable to get into the crowded sanctuary of the host church.

The Centennial preparations and celebrations gave Elmer a valuable opportunity to increase the number of Festival Singers' concerts and thereby the quality of his chorus through almost continuous rehearsing. Also, the Centennial was a godsend in terms of increasing the Festival Singers' commitment to touring. In a spasm of generosity, the choir was given $5,000 by the Canada Council in order that concerts could be presented in Hanover, New Hampshire; Rochester, New York; and Boston, Massachusetts, as Canada's centennial gift to a friendly neighbour. The Centennial was also a raison d'étre for Elmer to expand his commissioning program to enlarge his repertoire of Canadian choral music. Unlike the many first performances of contemporary works that were scattered across orchestras in larger cities, Elmer tended to conduct these new pieces a second, third, and fourth time, and in the cases of his favourites, on countless occasions.[14]

At Expo '67, the Festival Singers were, of course, the featured professional core of the Toronto Mendelssohn Choir and were at the centre of that ensemble's contribution as the nation's first and most prestigious large community choir. The Singers also performed concerts at the Canadian Pavilion as a distinct chorus between July 4 and 7, demonstrating their special status in the celebrant country. By this time, the Festival Singers were known across Canada. Touring might not have been extensive in the early years but by 1967 the chorus had contributed more than 250 broadcast performances to the CBC — an incredible record in the annals of Canadian choral presentation. Observing one of these Expo pavilion performances, Eric McLean of the *Montreal Star* effused that their program "was an impressive one, worthy of any choir I have heard in the last 15 years."[15]

The post-Expo period was somewhat dismal for many arts organizations, but for the Festival Singers it could not have been better. It began at Queen's University, where Elmer scheduled Kodaly's *Jesus and the Traders*, which was described by Ted Bond as "extremely dramatic and full of sharp contrasts of rhythm, dynamic and tempo that enabled the 30 singers and the brilliant Mr. Iseler to show us all what they were capable of right at the start and the effect was stunning." The program also included Canadian composer John Beckwith's *Sharon Fragments*, about which Bond commented on the "perfect blend of voices, superb ensemble dynamic and precision of attack ... a wide range with perfect control."[16]

A Saskatchewan tour ended what must have been the most frantic month of the Singer's history. Before heading west, though, the Singers fulfilled a mid-October commission at Notre-Dame-de-Grâce in Hull, Quebec, before another such event at the National Gallery nearby in Ottawa where Poulenc's Mass in G was sung, described as a "strongly rhythmic work and under Mr. Iseler's conducting was strong and forceful, so that the work had great impact." Then it was off to the Saskatchewan Festival of the Arts in Saskatoon with stops in a number of other provincial cities, including North Battleford, Swift Current, Weyburn, Moose Factory, and finally, Regina — all by bus.

Choir directors and members unanimously agree on the positive impact of touring on both the morale and the quality of performance. Choirs leap forward in their development by years through the preparatory rehearsals and the intense "concertizing" that occurs while on the road. But even more, hours of enforced intimacy for groups of choristers, whether on planes, trains, or buses, increases the sense of being a team that is achieved by no other comparable experience. In spite of the administrative time and the costs that have to be covered, choir leaders like Jean Ashworth Bartle push the value of touring at no small cost to boards of financially beleaguered ensembles because no other activity can replace this method of giving a motivational charge to her choristers (in her case, the Toronto Children's Chorus) over the days and weeks of singing and travelling together in an unfamiliar part of Canada or in a strange land.

As soon as Elmer felt the Festival Singers were ready, it was off to other provinces and countries. The Saskatchewan tour was something of a revelation. Elmer had taken his Singers to smaller communities close to Toronto, but this was on a scale that produced very different results. He discovered that these lesser venues produced audiences who were ecstatic — treating every singer as a god come down from on high to sing just for them. There were tears of joy and sadness, unrelenting applause, and automatic standing ovations.

Elmer's vision from the beginning had included a sense of mission to take his choir to every hamlet in the country. The touring experience never failed to fuel his nationalism. The more of Canada he experienced, the more unwilling he was to leave it. Certainly there were other elements to this missionary spirit — the delight of being able to take Jessie and the children and drive with them for hours at a time, a practice for a large man like Elmer that unfortunately played havoc with his overall health and, in particular, the well-being of his legs. This kind of touring also put him in close contact with the kind of people he loved. Not for Elmer was the experience of small-talking the sophisticated devotees of Paris or Vienna. He could not ignore the need to make such pilgrimages in order to satisfy those in Canada whose passion for the Singers seemed related to the wild enthusiasm aroused in those cultural centres. Elmer arranged tours to those places because he was expected to, and he ensured the best performances because people at home would be impressed, but it was in the smaller communities that he really loved to be.

Elmer enjoyed enormously the opportunities that touring provided to conduct in church sanctuaries and concert halls that had great acoustics. But even those that were wanting were a challenge to a man who had raised the capacity of his ears to position his singers to the best advantage of every performance no matter what the available space did to his singers' sound. On one occasion when his choir had tramped back and forth, up and down, in yet another cathedral, chorister Jean Ashworth Bartle questioned the wisdom of this obsession with acoustical perfection. Elmer replied, "Every concert is like presenting a great masterpiece of Monet or Turner — the presentation makes all the difference." Elmer was prepared to exhaust his choristers in the search for the right place to sing in every venue he encountered. All these factors came into play on the Saskatchewan tour resulting in references to "this magnificent choral aggregation" in the review of all their concerts in a province that had no overabundance of cultural experiences and where audiences were thrilled with the Festival Singers' quality of performance.[17]

There was another strategy in his desire, particularly in Centennial Year, to move his ensemble across the country and beyond on tour. He could present the considerable repertoire of Canadian music his singers had conquered. It was in September of that year that the publication the *Canadian Composer* identified the Festival Singers as "one of the most consistent champions of Canadian music." Most of this music had been commissioned through the good offices of the CBC and had become included in the regular repertoire of the Singers' concert presentations. It was little wonder that Elmer soon received the prestigious Canadian Music Council Medal for outstanding service to music in Canada.

Shifting to contemporary music, particularly the work of Canadian composers, had been an enormous challenge for Elmer, the Singers, and their audiences. It was often more difficult, thus requiring more hours of rehearsal. There were fewer moments of ecstatic euphoria that produced the standing ovations following old choral favourites as listeners sought to comprehend and appreciate unfamiliar sounds of Schafer, Beckwith, Glick, Henderson, and Holman. Elmer had faced criticism from all sides, and in the September 1967 issue of the *Canadian Composer* he fought back: "I have a particular liking for Canadian music and the new avenues of expression. I wouldn't blame anyone for becoming ear-weary at a totally contemporary concert but I've found you can program a complete concert of Canadian music. Now because of the backlog, you can also affect a nice balance of contemporary and traditional works."

Realizing that some of his audience were not enthralled with his choice of contemporary repertoire, he issued his challenge: "I prefer unbounded enthusiasm or down-to-earth distaste rather than indifference to what we are performing."

However, Elmer placed some of the blame for the negative response on the shoulders of Canadian composers: "Some new music asks the human voice to do things that just don't suit it ... I haven't seen the burning desire or diligent choral composing necessary to produce great choral works and not enough composers are conversant in the element."

Elmer expressed his disappointment in the shortage of non-commissioned choral works and that composers should produce new works without immediate expectation of performance. "The monetary rewards will come," Elmer predicted.

Centennial Year touring culminated with the pièce de résistance, a Washington, D.C., invitation to participate in the Christmas Pageant of Peace at the White House on December 15, where President Lyndon Johnson and a crowd of ten thousand would gather on the lawn to light the traditional national Christmas tree. There would be a television audience of many millions and all the accoutrements of the Festival Singers presentation would be in the hands of a people who excelled in celebrating religious and secular holidays. Even the United States Marine Band would be present. Elmer provided the expected Christmas fare but included a composition of Healey Willan — even an American presidential Christmas program would not escape at least one Canadian composer's creativity. Repetition of the choral fare took place when the Singers gave a short half-hour presentations in the U.S. Senate Building and at the Canadian Embassy.

Elmer drove to Washington with his entire family and time was provided for some relaxation. Daughter Buffy, now an attractive teenager, was invited to a White House party and had the thrill of dancing with the son of an American senator. For Elmer, it was the end of the most exhausting extended choral season of his life. He and Jessie, Noel, and Buffy returned to Canada with some sense of relief and with some hope of a complete rest. There had been twenty-five concerts in the last six months of 1967 — and by the spring of 1968 that number would rise to sixty. The Festival Singers had performed for 26,000 (excluding those at the White House Pageant), and the budget for the choir had tripled, as had grants from arts councils and from earned income. Yet there was still $30,000 to be found through donations. It was a perfect example of the phenomenon that remains to be true in the arts — sudden phenomenal success can destroy any organization. In the case of the Festival Singers the money was found.

There was another cost. Elmer was to pay the price of all this activity. In early 1968, he was hospitalized with a severe attack of phlebitis in his legs. It was serious enough that it kept him off the podium — a March concert to include the Bach Mass in B Minor had to be delayed until June.

At the most serious point, Jessie was informed that gangrene had been discovered and that it would be necessary to amputate one of Elmer's legs. She was shocked beyond description but gathered her strength to protest such a severe intervention. "Just one more night," she pleaded. That night the drugs took hold, the tide turned, and Elmer's leg improved marginally — enough to ward off an operation that would have affected his future dramatically. For the rest of his life, Elmer had to endure the discomfort of legs that were never to be restored to their previous health and sometimes conducted in pain that could have threatened the quality of his performance.

After all this activity, in 1968 the penny finally dropped. The Festival Singers became Canada's first fully professional choir. A minimal stipend would be provided every month. It would not be generous and the coming years would be devoted to raising the amount the Festival Singers could pay its members. Elmer could report that the stipend could probably keep a single person alive — but as the head of a family the chorister would have to find other income. Unfortunately, the heavy concert, broadcast, and recording schedule would make that task very difficult.

Rejoicing was stifled by the many ramifications this triumph promised. There would be even greater expectations for every concert to be a stellar experience. For the choristers, there would be greater demands of their time for rehearsal. Elmer could express the expectation that their paid employment put special pressure on them to eschew other career opportunities and concentrate on their roles as professional Festival Singers. Many members of the choir who had full-time day jobs, such as, for example, teachers Don Bartle and Frank Taylor, found they could not attend afternoon rehearsals and had to resign. Also there developed in some members a sense of now being members of a workforce that, even in the arts, should signal certain limitations on the power of a conductor over the affairs of Festival Singers' choristers.

There was another factor that had nothing to do with the Festival Singers' struggle for professional status. The world had changed. The 1960s had ushered in new perceptions of the roles of leaders in every area of life — the church, the university, the business community, and the arts. The belief that in joining an orchestra, a choir, a theatre, or an opera company an individual had given up all right to artistic opinions or any rights over the pattern of his or her own careers had eroded. The idea of the orchestral or choral conductor as autocrat was being challenged on every side.

The financial implications of more properly remunerated choristers would put more pressure on the fundraising role of the official board of the Festival Singers. The need for members who could raise money, much more of it, became paramount. A stronger, more efficient board became a top priority. But giving more responsibility to any board of any institution runs the risk of blurring the role of professional and volunteer. In the arts, the artistic staff is expected to direct the creative activity. But the raising of money can be the most critical activity, which, if unsuccessful, can decide the very continued existence of the choir, orchestra, or theatre company. Artistic and financial decisions as well as power relationships tend to interact to the consternation of all involved. For example, the repertoire of concerts is an artistic decision, but it may affect the size of the audience and box office receipts. Artistic decisions thus have financial ramifications that involve the voluntary board members quite directly.

It was soon apparent that the achievement of professional status, which had been so much desired by Elmer, created a new dynamic that now had to be accommodated as the Festival Singers faced the 1970s and even more challenging circumstances for the survival of a now more expensive choral ensemble.

There was a charming naïveté about Elmer Iseler. It was part of his artistic nature — a vulnerability that gave his conducting even greater appeal. On occasion, he exhibited a total unselfishness and infinite kindness that was unrestrained and childlike. This innocence helps explain his inability to recognize and appreciate the individual ambitions of Festival Singer members who had visions of their own.[18] It was beyond his imagination that members of a choir engaged in singing the great music of faith and love could turn on each other so engaged and threaten the very life of the collectivity. That was the lesson that Elmer had yet to learn as he entered the 1970s.

Chapter 7

The Festival Ends

THE FESTIVAL SINGERS FACED THE 1970s WITH enormous confidence. There was no doubt that the ensemble was now the nation's pre-eminent chamber choir. True, there were few competitors, but the Singers had achieved this national presence through a commitment to radio broadcasting and extensive touring across the land. The Centennial Year had placed the Singers at the centre of the Montreal Expo choral celebrations, and the chorus had participated in the expanded touring program that the Government of Canada had funded and encouraged. The achievement of professional status and the international recognition of the Stravinsky years culminating at the White House at the end of the 1960s were perceived as evidence of inexorable artistic progression towards the heights of universal acceptance of the Singers' unique place in Canada's choral universe.

For Elmer, in spite of his own health problems that continued into the 1970s and 1980s, it was a period to cherish. All his dreams were coming to reality. The 1967 Saskatchewan tour had been but a prelude to comparably successful trips to Alberta and British Columbia — the latter a province he would return to often and with extraordinary affection.

Successful recognition in the recording sphere had been achieved when Elmer had shared a Grammy (an internationally recognized best serious music award) with Igor Stravinsky in the early 1960s for the *Symphony of Psalms* disc. Elmer had a dichotomous attitude toward recordings, whether vinyl, tapes, or CDs. He realized how important they were in extending the reach of the Festival Singers beyond the Toronto home base. He was aware that the promotion of his vision of improved and enriched choral performance was pushed forward by every disc that was produced. However, he was also deeply concerned that recordings not be seen either as definitive performances of any composition or any substitute for live concerts. Elmer had watched Stravinsky adopt very different tempi for his compositions during a series of recording sessions. He had no illusion that a particular work could be captured for all time on any recording. Nevertheless, he was pleased with his collaboration with the great composer at the peak of his creative power and the Grammy Award provided a record of this significant event.

However, there were Canadians who believed that the choral tradition had come from the United Kingdom and Europe and that until the Festival Singers were accorded acceptance there local accolades could be just a display of the ignorance and lack of sophisticated taste of the colonial unwashed. Elmer set out to prove that he had created Canada's choir of the century — one that could stand up to the critiques of audiences anywhere on earth.

During the 1960s Elmer had kept the faith of the early years. He had maintained the most rigorous standards of repertoire selection and per-formance. As a Canadian musician and artist he was in a small minority of those whose careers were growing in the post–Centennial Year slump that followed in the final years of the 1960s and early 1970s. Tragically, all the excitement of expanded presentation and increased funding of the national birthday celebration had turned out to be a political aberration. Restraints on funding from provincial granting ministries and the Canada Council had devastating effects on fragile theatre companies, orchestras, and dance companies. Choirs were not as intensely affected simply be-cause they had always received but minimal funding for project grants or support for particular functions as a result of their status as non–professional recipients — but they shared the general impact of shattered expectations. The arts community had expected the activities of the pre-1967 period and the enormous success of the Centennial Year would bring an under-standing of the advantages of appropriate support for the arts — but it was not so. Arts organizations were forced to endure the unpleasant process of cutting back — the country's birthday party was over!

However, in spite of being the only professional choir at risk over the reversal of national priorities, there was no pause in the fortunes of the Festival Singers. The 1969–70 concert season turned out to be one of the busiest in its history. An area of increased development became that of choral workshops. As far back as the summer of 1963, Elmer had taken all thirty-six voices to Stratford to share in the program of making chamber music with the members of the Festival Orchestra. On July 8, after working with local choristers for two weeks every evening for three hours, a concert had been presented that included all these vocal and orchestral forces. It was enthusiastically received by the audience and the Stratford area choristers were euphoric.

Elmer came to realize that workshopping could have dramatic effects on the quality of performance of both isolated singers and prospective conductors who through the process could find themselves connected to a whole new perception of what was possible. On that Stratford occasion the participants had sung a Stravinsky cantata and Vivaldi's Gloria in D Major. Choristers who had previously performed only the most pedestrian repertoire discovered their own musicality and a memorable performance had emerged. Elmer was delighted. He had already engaged the Festival Singers in giving workshops in elementary and secondary schools but now recognized that the choral workshop with adults could be a positive experience for both the invited choristers and his own Singers, who soon saw another role they could collectively play in the development and improvement of choral music in Canada. Even more advantageous was the fact that workshops could be combined with regular concert appearances, enlarging the audience and the gate receipts, particularly in more remote corners of the country.

As chorister Alex Jozefacki observed, Elmer discovered he could take one hundred untrained singers and, within an hour, turn them into a chorus. Previously, working with amateurs over a short period had seemed a less-than-exciting prospect for Elmer, whose focus had been on the professional experience, but strangely it became a treasured role for him. Observers commented that at no other time was Elmer more relaxed and congenial, more patient and accommodating. Increasingly, he realized that he especially enjoyed working with these enthusiastic amateur choristers and their appreciative prospective choral conductors without the pressure that presenting yet another outstanding performance placed on his shoulders. Indeed, he believed he could, through these workshops, pass on the torch to younger conductors.

It was a perfect moment to increase a commitment to workshopping. A close associate of Elmer's, Keith Bissell, had become the coordinator of music for the Scarborough Board of Education (the eastern borough of the City of Toronto), but more important, he was also a musician and composer and an advisor to the Ontario Ministry of Education. By the end of the 1960s there was general despair over the state of music education in the province's school system. This focus had come originally from a conference that the Province of Ontario Council for the Arts (POCA) had organized in 1966 on the topic "Music in Ontario." All the main figures involved in the province's music presentation and education were at a Lake Couchiching resort, including both Elmer Iseler and Keith Bissell. The depressing state of music presentation was perceived to be the result of the lack of both quantity and quality of music composed for schools and performed in the Ontario educational system. The main culprit for what was described as the inadequacy of musical expression was seen to be the pathetic state of musical preparation in the average school classroom. There lay the responsibility for the inadequacy of music education across the entire province.

A study on choral music was commissioned from Keith Bissell and a colleague, Ezra Schabas, a fine musician and effective teacher who would become the Conservatory of Music's principal in later years. Schabas's blunt and unadorned expression of the truth as he perceived it was already widely respected and was the major source of inspiration for the content of the report. His description of the problem was based on a widely distributed questionnaire to choral conductors, choristers, and academics associated with the choral art in the province. Responses came in that recorded the "declining interest, low budgets and dusty repertoire" that discouraged music education in the schools and undermined the efforts of choral conductors everywhere.

Respondees to the questionnaire who considered the plight of contemporary music "hinted at the irrelevance of texts," suggesting that choral music was now "out of touch with reality." Indeed, conductors felt "helpless before the secular world of folk and pop, the trashy and debasing rock and roll, Tin Pan Alley and the Hit Parade." There was general agreement that the schools were to blame. "Children don't learn one note from another, are burdened with unmusical and poorly trained teachers in the elementary school and develop attitudes to singing which persist like smoke clouds from Vesuvius for the rest of their lives ... Standards in the elementary school are low to non-existent," the study concluded.

It was obvious that choral music needed an injection of quality in the schools of the province. However, there was little hope that the existing phalanx of music teachers could bring any inspiration to the task of improving choral music in the schools. The study was ruthless in its assessment of the conducting skills available. Elmer must have cringed along with his conducting colleagues at the study's perception of the results of inadequate conductor training: the evident lack of taste or knowledge of repertoire, the lack of attention to baton technique or voice production. As for the school system's contribution to musical development of the community, the consensus was that classroom music teachers "don't even earn the low salary they usually get."[1]

Elmer must have been pleased that the study conceded that "Ontario has one of the best professional choirs in the world"— an obvious reference to his Festival Singers. When Keith Bissell proposed a series of workshops in his own Scarborough schools, Elmer was anxious to proceed. Although the Schabas-Bissell Report had focused on the elementary schools, Bissell believed that Elmer, with his previous experience in secondary schools, would be more effective at that level and remarked to John Kraglund that his schools were "a wasteland in choral terms and in Scarborough the only way to go was up." When half of the cost of the program was donated by the Atkinson Foundation, the program was "on" in 1969.

With the co-operation of the aforementioned Keith Bissell, the Festival Singers were hired for a year to give six workshops for both teachers and student choristers. The Singers would be dispersed among both, for the consideration of choral selections and the emphasis on the reading of scores, proper voice control, and the sheer joy of singing well together would enliven the choral work in both the classroom and the school auditorium. Elmer understood only too well what the teachers faced. The program represented a turnaround, and the Scarborough Board of Education ultimately developed one of the finest choral music programs in the province. The program was expanded in North York, an adjoining board in the Toronto area, by the efforts of Laughton Bird and Elaine Mason, who encouraged their students to observe Elmer's open rehearsals in their school cafetoriums and classrooms.

Alas, the initiative was only a single beachhead at one level in one school board jurisdiction. Choral music as a whole continued a downward course partly as a result of an extraordinary shift to instrumental music that came as a result of enormous resources unleashed in the 1960s by the federal government in the name of vocational training. A music room filled with strings, brass, and woodwinds became the norm in virtually every secondary school. The choral art was too often ignored or allowed to erode. Much later there were interventions in the school programs by conductors like Doreen Rao (Faculty of Music, University of Toronto), and recognizing the need of a full choir commitment, Jean Ashworth Bartle annually took her Toronto Children's Chorus singers with her into elementary level institutions. But it would require more than a handful of committed conductor-educators to achieve province-wide improvements and there was no official willingness to make that happen.

As it was realized that artists could make an enormous impact on impressionable school children and youth, it was essential that these artists have some understanding of the learning process, including the attention span of young people at particular points in their development. Elmer was an expert and required little advice on these points at issue. Also needed was a command of the scheduling process if music, visual arts, theatre, or dance were to be fitted into the pattern of timetabling students. Elmer needed no instruction about how schools worked — he had been there and could bring this expertise to the attention of his colleagues.

Elmer understood that it was necessary to provide directions to conductors that would carry these individuals beyond the single day's intervention. An annual conductors' workshop had begun in the mid-1960s at the time of Elmer's assumption of the role of conductor at the Toronto

Mendelssohn Choir and it had run through the 1970s as another aspect of being employed by the Festival Singers. Conductors and would-be conductors from Ontario and other provinces would be invited to apply and, once again, the main attraction was a close association for some days with Elmer and his Singers — attending rehearsals and, if possible, a formal Festival Singers concert. Normally, successful applicants could also become involved with the total spectrum of Elmer's musical life by attending Mendelssohn Choir rehearsals and possibly a performance and, even more helpful for some, after it was formed, rehearsals and performances of Robert Cooper's Mendelssohn Youth Choir. For the teacher-conductor, the latter experience was a revelation. The age group that was the most difficult to attract and hold to choral music were teenagers, and to witness these young singers rehearsing under Cooper's dynamic baton the works of Mozart and Haydn, Beethoven and Berlioz, Derek Holman and Robert Evans, was to observe a clear message of hope.

Workshops increased but performance remained the central role of the Festival Singers. The first concert of the 1969–70 season was a celebration at Yorkminster-Park Baptist Church of Elmer's favourites — the Poulenc Mass in G and Ives's *Symphony of Psalms* followed by Beckwith's *Three Blessings* and *Sharon Fragments* as the centrepieces of the program. With Holst's *Tomorrow Will Be My Dancing Day* as the final selection audiences were sent off happily humming a familiar tune. The December concert of that season was at St. Anne's Anglican Church. This venue was fast becoming a favourite for Iseler for both presenting concerts and producing recordings. The sanctuary had not only decorative art produced by the Group of Seven but also fine acoustics. Elmer never allowed the trivialization of the sound that he wanted and the text it celebrated, insisting on a visual integrity that would surround his singers appropriately. Thus churches became a favoured venue for the presentation of the best of his religious repertoire. On one occasion critic Kenneth Winters made the point rather poetically in relation to a performance of a splendid work presented in such a context and acoustic: "The *Comus Magnificat* was the choral peak of the evening — wondrously elaborate, vigorously posited, meltingly sung, its long reveled lines lifting your spirit out of this time and place. This is the kind of music conductor Elmer Iseler and the Festival Singers do matchlessly, handling its internal antiphonies with secure mind-widening freedom and a genuine elevation."[2]

It was to Hindemith, Britten, and Baker that Elmer turned in his February 1970 concert and once again Winters was ecstatic: "Now each of these works in turn was remarkably sung, and one could sit and appreciate, on one level, Mr. Iseler's control of his superb assembly of blended voices. They are a phenomenon, without any doubt, a major choral achievement."[3]

When the CBC provided a festival in Toronto that summer of 1970, Elmer's Singers were very much at the centre. Significantly, Canadian composers dominated the Singers' concerts, with compositions by Oscar Morawetz, Norm Symonds, John Beckwith, Srul Irving Glick, Robert Aitken, Bruce Mather, Alexander Brott, Healey Willan, Talivaldis Kenins, John Weinzweig, R. Murray Schafer, and Harry Freedman all included. The repertoire and the quality of the singing throughout the season presaged an important announcement — in the following 1970–71 season the Festival Singers would be travelling, for the first time, to the United Kingdom and Europe. There had been invitations to several festivals and concert series just months before and particularly to the annual illustrious Prom Concerts in London's Albert Hall. Opportunities to participate in the Adelaide Festival in Australia with an extension allowing the ensemble to sing in Manila, Bangkok, Hong Kong, and Singapore had arisen, but, as with all previous opportunities to go abroad, Elmer had turned them down. The unanswered question around where the funding was to come from was a constant challenge he faced whenever the opportunity to tour arose. He had no confidence that the Festival Singers board was prepared to back the cost of sending a professional choir abroad.

As well was the question of whether the Festival Singers were really ready. Elmer had definite ideas on this point. With his intense nationalism very much showing, he wanted people in other countries to see Canada at its best in every aspect of its choral being. As a hockey fan, he felt personally humiliated when a Canadian team failed to display itself well at the Olympic Games or in other international competitions. As it transpired, in spite of his hesitations about touring abroad, one of Elmer's greatest contributions to his country's cultural reputation came from the performance of his Singers in foreign lands.

If there was one criticism of the Festival Singers, it was the "coldness" of tone that was an aspect of Elmer's desire to achieve that pure, white, perfectly tuned sound, devoid of any tremolo, that so enhanced the quality of the Singers' performance. However, this purity of tone was not appropriate for every choral occasion. Kenneth Winters had called for "more lust," and in November 1970, Elmer confessed to critic Peter Goddard that "in the last year or so there have been some changes in the choir ... I've tried to get them to sing with more ... uh ... warmth. And it's starting to come."[4] It was one aspect of "being really ready."

Finally, the commitment was made — a month-long tour of Europe was to begin in early May in Ljubljana, Yugoslavia, and end a month later in Paris. The Singers would perform on thirteen occasions and participate in a BBC recording session. It meant that on the average they would be singing in concert every two days and between these appearances would be travelling from Yugoslavia to Austria, to Germany, the United Kingdom, and finally France. Rehearsing in all the contrasting venues would be a challenging experience for his Singers in Europe and would, Elmer knew, be both exhilarating and exhausting.

There was one problem. With all the subsidies there was still too little money and the Singers had to accept a modest reduction in recompense per appearance. Resentment among a small number of Singers was recorded in a letter dated October 24, 1972, some months after the Singers' returned from Europe. It was signed by chorister Malcolm Russell and was about the "unprofessional way in which the choir was paid for the European tour, and an enquiry into how a similar situation might be avoided." This missive was the first display of discontent, and although securing adequate resources was a board responsibility, the discontent was to grow until, in 1978, there was a breakdown in the relationship of Elmer with some of the Singers and board members, a breakdown that was to end his role as the ensemble's conductor.

However, in May 1971 the Singers' morale was at its height. The first stop in Europe was in Yugoslavia in order that the Festival Singers could be a highlight at the Sixth Zagreb Biennial. Although the Singers were a familiar name to every choral enthusiast in Canada, they were virtually unknown across the ocean — but soon it was clear that a performing wonder had landed on the continent. Never had a Canadian performing group received such reviews! It began with a warm critical response in Zagreb by Djordje Saula, who was quoted as writing in fractured English that "everything was here, before all, a brilliant colour of a rarely suggestive and noble art of chorus singing which was perfectly worthy to be performed at the Biennial."

The choristers were looking forward most of all to the full week in Austria and the concerts in Graz, Vienna, Salzberg, and then in Mainz, Germany. It was also Elmer's first experience in Vienna, the magical city whose inhabitants had played such a role in his life. He was to return with his Singers to an even greater triumph a decade and a half later but it was in Austria that the critical reviews for the 1971 tour were overwhelmingly positive. At the first concert in Graz, the headline clamoured "Choral Music of Highest Perfection." The program had begun with Stravinsky (what better place to start!) and a local critic commented, "His *Pater Noster* floated in on a transcendental sphere, seemingly outside of expression. One must witness the performance of this choir — how the 44 singers according to need, sound as a single voice or as a vault of sound encompassing all possible dimensions."[5]

When the Festival Singers reached Vienna they sang in the Minoritenkirche "with exemplary precision and immaculately trained voices capable of all modulations." However, it was in Mainz that the presence of a magnificent choral ensemble was fully recognized:

> There is naturally no trace of any rigid interpretation, everything is accomplished, even in the finest shade of expression, everything is expressed with an unheard novelty of sound ... it is absolutely perfect as far as design and colour of contemporary works are concerned ... the greatest success with the public belonged however to Murray Schafer and his Epitaph for Moonlight which was presented with a resounding clearness and delicate artistic interpretation.[6]

It was in the United Kingdom that the most astounding reviews were written. The issue of *Time* magazine of June 14, 1971, carried a *Financial Times* review by Ronald Chickton:

> Rumour had murmured of their excellence, but nothing had prepared me for one for the electrifying effect of their London appearance here last night … virtuoso technique, brilliant attack, discipline which does not stultify but encourages a degree of "giving" we too rarely meet in our crack choirs, marvelous control, a kind of gusto I can only describe, quite inadequately as breeziness.[7]

The *Daily Telegraph*'s reviewer went even further: "This chorus easily belongs to the best international teams in existence. The unanimity of attack was astonishing, the intonation flawless and the tonal balance well-nigh perfect."[8]

The critics had decided that the Festival Singers "have been ranked with the finest choral groups in the world by discerning audiences and critics."

The *Eastern Daily Press* covered a concert at the Norwich Cathedral under the headline "Virtuosity of singers from Canada":

> It is rarely, one must admit, that European ears are turned towards Canada in the expectation either of original compositions or outstanding performances. How deaf we can be … Festival Singers under Elmer Iseler gave a concert of such virtuosity that we are unlikely to hear excelled, let alone surpassed … We do not hear musicians from Canada but the skill with which they tackled an elaborate programme of intricate, unaccompanied choral works could be matched by few other choirs … the overall effect from these 38 musicians is of tonal perfection, the ultimate in ensemble singing. Under their founder-conductor Elmer Iseler, I am sure they will be as celebrated in Europe as in their own country.[9]

At Llandoff Cathedral in Wales, Elmer's capacity to select repertoire and effectively place singers was demonstrated:

> We were not expecting the Festival Singers to "cunningly" choose a repertoire that exploited the virtues of the Cathedral. Yes, this was the effect and one was constantly lost in admiration of the way in which Elmer Iseler tapered dimendi so that they seemed to disappear into the Cathedral corners ... and gave it a sense of belonging in this environment. Their versatility was impressive and so was the professionalism of their presentation.[10]

The choir completed the tour with a final concert in Paris and flew back to Canada to participate in a memorial CBC concert honouring Igor Stravinsky just a few days after landing in Toronto. The *Globe and Mail* headline for the review of that appearance was a rather overly bombastic "Festival singers wildly cheered at homecoming concert" and Kenneth Winters remarked that the concert was a return home at which the Singers "sang with marvelous poise and simplicity of line." In a Sir Ernest MacMillan composition "they held vigor and balance, singing with impeccable modesty, wonderful clarity and great style. How fortunate we are to have them back home safe." The only critical comment came from John Kraglund, who commented on the fact that Robert Craft, a guest conductor for a portion of that concert, could not balance the sound in the MacMillan Hall as astutely as Elmer was able to do. Elmer now set about building on all this unanimous foreign appreciation of his Singers in a now impressed Canada where it would mean something in practical terms.

The 1971 European tour was the veritable Himalayan range for his Festival Singers. In an interview with *Toronto Telegram*'s Sid Adelman, Elmer included in his national triumph those who had been his supporters through the early years: "The reason the Festival Singers were so successful in Europe was because we've been supported by the Ontario Arts Council, the Canada Council and the CBC."[11] This generosity of spirit towards supportive public institutions was to be repeated many times over in the future. (It was not a 1971 aberration. As early as 1964, Elmer had dedicated a Festival Singers concert to Metropolitan Toronto, acknowledging the generosity of the municipality, conceding that "without assistance of this type the Festival Singers could not continue.")

It was characteristic that Elmer followed his European tour, just two years later, with one that concentrated on Ontario's north. He even slipped over the border to a largely ignored region of the United States and gave a concert in Marquette, Michigan. Touring the largely empty miles of the province's forests was a demanding experience. Uncomfortable buses, unappealing performance venues, and challenging accommodation all threatened minor disasters — but Elmer loved the small towns and their appreciative though unsophisticated audiences. The 1973 northern Ontario tour revealed that Elmer was not prepared to sing down to the people who lived in these isolated communities. The concert repertoire, night after night, included in the first half several religious works of little known Hans Leo Hassler (1564–1612) before moving into both the twentieth-century favourites of Healey Willan — *Rise Up My Love* and *Gloria Deo* — and the compositions of English composer John Paynter, with whom Elmer had established a close working relationship. Leading up to the intermission came a work by Igor Stravinsky. The program then moved entirely to twentieth-century composers: Thomas Baker, John Cook, and then the very popular R. Murray Schafer's *Epitaph for Moonlight* and the *Folk Songs of the Four Seasons* by Ralph Vaughan Williams. A considerable listening challenge to even the most knowledgeable choral enthusiast!

The schedule during the 1970s took on a regular pattern. Along with CBC broadcasts, short or longer tours in communities near Toronto, and concerts sponsored by presenters in and around Toronto were school workshops and workshops that were directed at adult choristers or groups of choirs and their conductors. These years extended the contribution that Elmer and his Singers made to the quality of choral music in Ontario and provinces beyond. The Ontario Arts Council was pleased to support these activities in both schools and church basements in a host of communities. For Elmer, it was a positive experience. His years in teaching had prepared him magnificently. He knew exactly how to organize a day or a series of days in a way that attracted the attention and ensured the enthusiasm of both teacher–conductors and choral students, whether adolescent or mature.

There were years in the 1970s when a Festival Singers concert series, with all the costs of renting a suitable venue, hiring an orchestra and soloists, and providing adequate promotion and advertising, was occasionally abandoned. There just was not enough money to support the most minimal compensation to professional choir members. It was sometimes simply more profitable, as long as there were sufficient engagements, to be a "choir for hire" by presenters who had the resources to look after all the organizational details. As long as the Singers were available on Monday night for the regular Mendelssohn Choir rehearsals, an absence for short tours was easily arranged. Longer stints and especially international tours demanded more organizational flexibility — but, with Jessie's help, Elmer could arrange his choral forces to provide both artistic satisfaction and performance excellence. As long as he could maintain his standards, the Festival Singers could continue to be a beacon to his colleague conductors and their choristers. However, it meant there was no pause in the pressure on the Festival Singers. These unrelenting high expectations ultimately had their deleterious effect.

Ironically, before the final explosion in 1978, the Festival Singers arguably experienced its greatest triumph — another three-week tour of Europe accompanied by Lois Marshall and the Canadian Brass. To veterans of the 1977 tour, it seemed at first like a replay of the 1971 experience. However, the inclusion of the Soviet Union and Baltic countries was a new aspect of this tour. The Cold War gave a special patina to every artistic intervention — whether it was Glenn Gould in the USSR or the Red Army Choir in Toronto. The visit by the Festival Singers gave another extension to the relationship of West and East. Here was a country whose choral history was unsurpassed. The Russian audiences overflowed every venue and were emotionally unrestrained. The Soviet news service, Tass, in covering the Leningrad concert, described it as a "brilliant performance of sheer magic."

Elmer had been warned that he should avoid "religious music." He ignored the warning. It was the right decision. He described his wife's experience: "Jessie went out to join the standees in the halls. She saw tears running down people's faces during the singing of the Bach motet."

Tenor Christopher Grounds told William Littler, the tour chronicler from the *Toronto Star*, that "the audience would not let us leave the stage and when we did they ran up and kissed us on the cheek." When the Festival Singers visited the three Baltic countries, Latvia, Lithuania, and Estonia, the crowds were ecstatic. The Estonian Male Chorus made Elmer an honorary member.

The Canadian Brass accompanied the choir and played popular selections before and during the concert. However, it was soloist, soprano Lois Marshall, well known to vocal devotees, whose presence caused standing ovations before she had sung a note.

The tour had begun in England and Paris with the Singers taking part in an External Affairs program, "Musicanada," that included concerts in Paris, at King's College, Cambridge, and at St John's Church in Smith Square in Central London. Of the last offering, David Murray, writing for the *Financial Times* of London, commented, "Their concert made an incredible impression. Few choirs anywhere match their standards. The sound they make is full but transparent, superbly balanced, wonderfully clean-edged; their phrasing has the flexibility and precision that might be expected from a small group of soloists. The proportion of tone to mere breath is uncommonly high."[12]

The Bonn Concert, the single offering in Germany, was special as it was sponsored by the Canadian Association of Publishers, Authors and Composers, one of Canada's primary performing rights organizations. With a concert title "Rendezous with Canada," Canadian contemporary music was appropriate and received programming emphasis. Barbara Kaempfert-Weitbrecht, critic for the Bonn newspaper *General-Anzeiger*, wrote of the Festival Singers that the chorus had "demonstrated a sumptuous clarity of tone and a sovereign security and precision in the execution of polyphonic passages and rhythmic complexities. The Singers were especially impressive in the truly difficult blending of conflicting intervals, in the opposing rhythmic figures and demanding phrasing of most contemporary works."[13]

It was an important revelation of Canadian repertoire in a country that knew little of the creativity of Canadian composers.

The Festival Singers returned home in a state of collective euphoria. This trip made all their hard work worthwhile. It is hard to believe that while this tour that had dazzled Europeans was going on, Elmer's role as conductor was seriously in question, and that before the 1970s were over he would be asked for his resignation as artistic director of the Festival Singers by the board chair, Barbara Heintzman, and some of her board colleagues who had even been present in Europe and had viewed the choir's triumphs.

Later in the decade, an Ottawa performance of Handel's *Messiah* by the Festival Singers with the NAC Orchestra took place. Robert Richard, the *Citizen's* music critic, sought to bathe the Singers with the kind of accolades that his European colleagues had accorded in 1971 and 1977: "Iseler gave depth and plasticity to the work, a three-dimensionality to its emotive content. His approach was by turns dramatic, smooth, mystical and even sometimes if rarely tending to the earth, but with a definite propensity to the beautifully finished, the finely rounded shading and phrase. Not a striking *Messiah,* rather a deeply stirring *Messiah*."[14]

How ironic that within days of this triumph in the nation's capital Elmer was formally asked to submit his resignation.

For Elmer, these months of late 1977 and early 1978 were very diffi-cult. On the one hand, there was the feeling of having captured for Canada a recognition abroad that would have been unthinkable just a decade be-fore, but this was offset by trouble at home. He had known for some time that things were going wrong, but could not put his finger on the precise problem. He was faced with a mélange of issues in some cases demanding conflicting solutions. John Fenton had been a valued member of his Festi-val Singers board for many years and had watched the membership change towards the inclusion of more representation from the corporate sector with some dismay. There was an inevitable clash of values. On one occa-sion in the mid-1970s, as they were walking down the street after a tense board meeting, Elmer had asked him, "If I established a new choir, would you come with me?" and John's response had been, "You bet I would."[15] It convinced Fenton that Elmer was already aware of the undercurrents that threatened the continued excellence of the chorus and the presence of a board that did not seem to understand its role as a fundraising body.

In order to maintain the pre-eminence as the nation's choral broadcaster Elmer felt he must search out new Canadian composers and commission them to do their best work. The lack of a first-rate chamber choir concentrating on serious music had disillusioned many able composers and that, along with the task of competing in creative production with the one giant — Healey Willan — had discouraged others. Elmer had taken on the challenge of turning that situation around, and it was the Festival Singers and the extraordinary team of producers at the CBC who unleashed a veritable torrent of Canadian composition that surprised the nation and astonished choral music devotees in other countries. It was as both an initiator and an example that Elmer shone. It was during the 1970s that other Canadians conductors in other cities, such as Jon Washburn in Vancouver and Wayne Riddell in Montreal, had taken up the challenge and commissioned composers, and in these decades a national reputation for choral work was built that caught the attention of the world.

Touring, workshopping, broadcasting, and recording, along with performing, assured a varied and rewarding lifestyle for Festival Singers' members. However, along with increased expectations came an increasing sense of inadequate remuneration, now recognized not just for touring, as in 1971, but as an ongoing problem. Those with working spouses or partners with regular jobs, thereby making Festival Singer remuneration simply extra family income, could survive. Choristers who had spent years and a great deal of money preparing for a singing career had reason for bouts of discontent at the increasing expectation in terms of preparing repertoire and setting aside blocks of time for touring and broadcasting gigs that made it impossible to acquire extra income. Pioneering is exciting and exhilarating — but there is a practical limit that reality enforces. By the early to mid-1970s that limit had been reached. It is recorded that Elmer constantly attempted to make his board realize the inadequacy of the remuneration for his choristers — but to no effect, there simply was not enough money and no acceptance of a fundraising role that would need to accompany a professional choir.

Elmer demanded very high quality voices and some of the graduates of conservatory or faculty who could reach his expectations also had hopes for a solo career. But Elmer was adamant — a Festival Singers rehearsal was even more important than any single artist's Carnegie Hall debut. He made the point that "You are my singers!" again and again. He realized that choral excellence demanded a full commitment from a consistent membership. Indeed, in 1972, there had been some uneasiness around the rumour, recorded in Malcolm Russell's letter to Elmer, that the choristers "would shortly be asked to sign contracts limiting [their] professional time entirely to you."[16] The rumour had no basis but it was made plain that there could be no effective stand-ins at Festival Singer rehearsals or performances. Thus, there was considerable turnover, sometimes amicably processed but sometimes with a break in relationship that caused considerable bitterness. Some choristers found that their own visions of an artistic future were too much in conflict with Elmer's expectations for choral supremacy and moved on.[17]

Indeed, as professionals, various members of the Festival Singers developed an alternative vision — one that ensured a continuing salary as a Festival Singer but allowed space for personal ambition. It was believed, at least by a few, that by organizing themselves more expeditiously they could achieve a miracle of flexible timetabling. When a choir social committee was formed it was perceived by some to be a body that could encourage recreational events for singers, spouses, and partners, but others saw it as a complaints committee — and the road to confrontation with Elmer was soon clearly defined. A management assessment report by Barry Cole had been commissioned by the Festival Singers board, but the recommendations would, in Elmer's view, have cost an estimated $100,000 extra per year. Elmer understood that, but the document, with no hope of increased Canada Council funding, was of no help in avoiding the impending conflict.

The 1970s, as government commitments were reduced, placed great emphasis on private sector fundraising for all arts organization. There was an enormous expansion in the numbers of both musical organizations and musicians (as there was in every arts discipline) that could not be covered by government grants. Every orchestra and choir needed a board that could raise money. The amateur background of choirs had placed this aspect of survival at a very low level compared to other performing arts institutions like orchestras and dance and theatre companies, but as the 1970s progressed, the Festival Singers board became increasingly made up of corporate representatives.

The main Festival Singers figure in this transformation was board chair Barbara Heintzman, a very intelligent and handsome woman, who was unfortunately to become a victim of cancer a very short time after the unpleasantness of the Festival Singers' disintegration. She cared about the financial security of the Singers and invited and acquired individuals with business values and styles of operation to become members of the board. She, too, had a vision. It was a Festival Singers organization that could attract large audiences, many of whom could become donors. Her focus was on a more popular repertoire — perhaps to include evenings presenting Broadway hit songs. She noted at one point that even the Toronto Symphony had played an evening of Lerner and Loewe, the creators of the popular musical *My Fair Lady*. The future demanded increased financial resources and the present repertoire would not reach to larger numbers of choir enthusiasts, but with perhaps some "repertoire bridging" that might be possible.

Elmer, though believing in the efficacy of quality music of all kinds, fought against this erosion. He perceived the alternative as a trivialization of the choir's repertoire. Nor was he anxious to consider more gigs that had little artistic purpose but expended enormous energy and time that could be otherwise used to advantage. In particular he was unmoved by complaints that he was commissioning and conducting too much inaccessible music by Canadian composers. It is fair to say that more public financial support would have made the conflict less intense, but there were different views about repertoire, scheduling, and choir administration that were not being resolved.

Back in the 1960s Elmer had eschewed the outbursts of temper as a strategy to get his way (or to follow his vision, depending on the sightline one adopted). However, changes in mood and temperament still occurred to arouse anger. In spite of the changing times and the democratization of relationships at all levels of administration in business and educational institutions, there was no undermining of Elmer's belief in his direction as conductor and his methods of achieving his purposes. What Elmer called strength and determination, his critics called autocracy and even dictatorial behaviour. The struggle had gone on for years without any perceptible erosion in the quality of the Singers' work. But by the late 1970s, the standoff was complete: It was Elmer's view that democracy, in the sense of collective decision-making, was compromised when the singer joined a choir. Leadership was his responsibility. However, there were Singers who believed that certain accommodations in scheduling and organizational style would not destroy the quality of the choir's presentation. It was simply the intensification of the age-old tension to be found in all choirs now raised to a new level by the introduction of professional status and expectation.

There were unfortunate incidents, and one in particular became the opening salvo that ended in a disaster. A twenty-minute Christmas presentation in 1977 to a Canadian Club luncheon at the Royal York Hotel in central Toronto became the *cause célèbre*. Not surprisingly, in December, even the weather had intervened to create considerable havoc — a wicked snowstorm that made it difficult for the choir to reach the Royal York Hotel from its north Toronto rehearsal hall at Lawrence Park Community Church. Elmer was upset by the failure of members to arrive at rehearsal on time — only ten of thirty-six had been successful in weathering the storm. Elmer was beset with considerable questions about whether those present could sing the seasonal repertoire effectively, as there was no sectional balance, and cancelled the appearance just a few hours before the scheduled noon-hour appearance. For Elmer, it was an artistic decision.

Understandably, board members who had arranged the presentation were outraged. They had secured a small honorarium for the appearance and saw it as a coup in connecting the Singers with prestigious members of the business community. Not only that: these board members, including the chair, had been invited to be present and had to explain the choir's absence to disappointed Canadian Club members. Elmer saw it as a matter of artistic policy that a reduced complement would threaten the quality of any attempted performance; board members and some choir members saw it as obstinacy and disobedience. The fact that the Canadian Brass, all of whose members were already ensconced downtown, was contacted and the ensemble was able to arrive at the luncheon to replace the Singers convinced certain board members that Elmer was guilty of insubordination and that it was he who should be replaced.

The Canadian Club fiasco took place on December 12. By December 15, the executive committee of the board had passed a motion "that a recommendation to the board of directors that Dr. Elmer Iseler's engagement as conductor and musical director be terminated at the expiry of his present contract on August 31, 1978."[18]

The entire board met on January 3, 1978, but refused to accept the recommendation. It then passed a motion that Dr. Iseler "should be reprimanded and advised that, in the board's view, a repetition of action of such a nature or other action evidencing his disregard for the authority of the Board could be considered just cause for his dismissal."[19] It was obvious that it would be only a matter of time before an irreparable explosion would take place. Unfortunately, the explosion came just as the choir was approaching Elmer's twenty-fifth season as the Festival Singers' conductor. The Canadian Club luncheon was seemingly a minor incident but it represented a host of issues that needed to be resolved. The struggle between a small group within the choir, a larger group in the board led by Chair Barbara Heintzman, and Elmer as artistic director was intensified and by May 1978 resulted in a decision on the part of the board that shocked and outraged the musical community: Elmer was asked to submit his resignation.

There was chaos and dissension in the Singers' ranks — some remained with the Festival Singers in the hope that these confrontations would end and Elmer might be back. Others cheered and encouraged the board to hold tough. At the board level, members John Bird and John Peter Lee Roberts resigned. Elmer retired to his Caledon farm, alone with his family and separated from Toronto by some miles of country road but by light years of understanding. He was crushed. For six long weeks he simply sat in his rocking chair on a small porch at Quail Hill Farm unable to cope with what had happened. He had been fired!

It was a family tragedy as well. Jessie and Elmer had decided it was time to extend their small home and the steam shovel was ready to move onto the property. With no Festival Singers income the entire project had to be cancelled. Jessie took on the role of a go-between, protecting Elmer from the press and from a host of individuals, many of whom wanted to give him support, others who wanted to give advice. Some welcome counsel came from singer Elizabeth Elliott and composer, CBC producer, and friend John Reeves, both of whom told him to form a new choir and call it the Elmer Iseler Singers — the name they believed should have been adopted from the outset in 1954.

It quickly became a public battle. The board refused to provide any rationale for their action — a position its members justified as an effort to allow Elmer an opportunity to leave with dignity. However, the Festival Singers were receiving considerable resources from the public purse. It was not a matter that could be decided in private with no explanation to the shareholders created by grants from the Ontario Arts Council and Canada Council — that is, the taxpaying citizens of the nation.

Music critic William Littler wrote the defining explanation under a headline "Why did Elmer Iseler get the old heave-ho?" The facts of the conflict between artistic director and volunteer board were outlined and the basic issue of who should determine direction was exposed. Littler concluded, with what turned out to be unfounded optimism, "Sure, the Festival Singers can go on without Elmer Iseler. But is that what we really want?"[20]

In the press, letters to the editor recorded a range of responses. Composer Harry Somers, outlining the role that Elmer played in supporting Canadian music, spoke for many of his colleagues: "It is impossible for me to believe that a board made up of intelligent, hard-working people would willfully, thoughtlessly or for insubstantial reasons, take it upon themselves to overrule one of the finest musicians Canada has ever produced."[21]

Former Festival Singers joined the fray, including a founding member, Tom Brown, who addressed the question of a more popular repertoire:

> I was a member of the choir from its founding in 1954 until 1967, and I can attest that none of the people who contributed their talents or money in those days was ever under the misapprehension that we were trying to

> be Canada's answer to Fred Waring's Pennsylvanians, or
> a co-ed version of the Leslie Bell Singers ... please let
> us avoid creating a sing-along-with-Elmer (or whoever)
> ensemble in an ill-founded attempt to rake in more
> dollars at the box-office.[22]

Not all the letters were on Elmer's side, but Canadian conductor Boris Brott certainly was, claiming the board had removed "the greatest choral conductor this country possesses — perhaps the greatest choral conductor in the world."[23] Radio features producer John Reeves at the CBC commented in a letter to the *Globe and Mail* that the decision to dismiss Elmer was "ill-judged, mischievous and incomprehensible," and posited the possibility of another Iseler-led choir continued with a threat that unnerved many of Elmer's enemies.

> I think it would be my duty, as a spender of public funds,
> to engage for CBC programs whichever choir was the
> better. And very probably a new choir conducted by
> Elmer Iseler would be better than the Festival Singers
> without him. I have thought it to be my further duty
> to make this known to the Canada Council and to the
> Ontario Arts Council. Since both of these bodies support
> the Festival Singers with public funds, it is their duty to
> consider whether their support should be continued to
> the Festival Singers or should be transferred to whatever
> choir Elmer Iseler may next found. I do not envy them
> their dilemma.[24]

Reeves was driven to request legal action when members of the Festival Singers board attempted to threaten their choristers with charges of disloyalty if they were to appear on CBC with any newly created Elmer Iseler Singers. (Indeed, an injunction was sought to prevent Festival Singers from performing at the first public performance of the Elmer Iseler Singers at St. James Cathedral a few months later and Elmer had to carry on without a full complement.)

It was a turning point in Elmer's life but, even more, also that of his entire family. Elmer was, in Festival Singers' chair Barbara Heintzman's words, "hurt and confused" and in seclusion. Jessie was devastated but yet a tower of strength. Both Noel and Buffy were in shock — how could the board members and choristers they believed to be friends and associates countenance the "firing" of their father? He was a father whom they had observed spending his lifetime at great personal sacrifice promoting a vision of choral excellence based on professional commitment that would bring honour to his nation.

There was no common ground. Legally the board had the law on its side. Or did it? As a corporate entity publicly responsible for the financial health and institutional well-being it could make this choice. Elmer was an employee — the board technically had the right not to renew his employment. However, in Elmer's view and that of his followers, the Festival Singers, a national institution, was his choir. Their accomplishments had been his life work. He had been a founder, the only regular conductor in the history of the chorus. He had taken responsibility for the complement of singers who had been chosen, it had been his sound that had prevailed for more than twenty-four years as the hallmark of the ensemble, his choice of repertoire that had dazzled real and broadcast audiences, his contacts and reputation at the CBC and the granting councils that had brought in revenue, his determination that had led to professional status. The idea that he had been fired for insubordination paralyzed him for weeks, even affecting his health. Yet even in this valley of despair, he could advise an unhappy soprano Judith Young to remain with the Festival Singers, realizing to maintain her voice and sense of well-being she had to sing and had a right to be remunerated.[25]

In June 1978, Elmer gathered his strength and ventured beyond Quail Hill Farm to work with choristers gathered at Laurentian University for the annual session of "Choirs in Contact," a program of the Ontario Choral Federation that brought hundreds of choir members in countless choirs from all over Ontario to engage in discussion and prepare a major choral work under the baton of a distinguished, internationally recognized conductor. This particular year Elmer had agreed to carry out this task, choosing Vaughan Williams's *Dona Nobis Pacem* as the major selection in his repertoire, surely an appropriate prayer in the circumstances. Not only did he appear, he was perceived to be at his very best. Choristers from across the province expressed their dismay over the events of past weeks and encouraged him to create a new chamber ensemble.

The letters that arrived at Quail Hill Farm from across the country, in particular from choristers and former Festival Singer managers, that rejected the charge he was "difficult" and "uncooperative." Elmer was supported by a flood of letters not only from former choir members but also from choral giants from overseas such as David Willcocks in the United Kingdom and Canadian colleagues like Lloyd Bradshaw, all offering him their sympathy and their willingness to intervene in any way they could.

The integrity of Elmer's position was borne out by the outcome. Advised by members of the Singers, the board had sought out Giles Bryant, a former Festival Singer but a respected organist and choir leader in his own right. Fortunately he had returned to England to a new marriage and new choral responsibilities and thus had played no part in the events that had recently transpired. Yet he knew the repertoire and the qualities of the Singers' performances that must be maintained. He was engaged on a temporary basis by the board, conducted the rehearsals and the initial and Christmas performances, and acted as artistic director as well for concert appearances of a string of quite prestigious Canadian conductors (Jon Washburn, Derek Holman, Peter McCoppin, Brian Law, John Barnum), all of whom were commissioned for individual concerts that filled the proposed 1978–79 season. The Festival Singers board's decision to move to a series of conductors, in spite of the obvious prestige that Bryant brought to the choir, ensured that the quality of the Singers was at risk.

Unfortunately, performance presenters of engagements already planned wanted Elmer Iseler and were not prepared to accept the Festival Singers without him. There was a dramatic fall in the number of single tickets sold at the door for concerts. There was a postponement of a Canada Council grant for touring in Western Canada and a considerable reduction in the revenues for radio broadcasts.[26] The reviews of early concerts in the Festival Singers series were not good, nor were the tapes submitted to the granting councils in applications for the continuance of support. As it transpired, the Festival Singers ensemble was soon facing bankruptcy and could not complete the subscription series they had announced.

Internally, the chorus was rent by tensions between those who, like Judith Young, were angry by what they saw as a successful conspiracy to remove Elmer and those who felt that their courage and determination was devoted to the best interests of the Festival Singers. They felt simply that the leadership was no longer adequate — that is, not directed towards creating a more synergetic approach to conductor-chorister relationships, finding solutions to economic problems, and alleviating the severe pressures of the demanding and in some cases enormously difficult repertoire.

In spite of the new appointees to the board from the corporate world, there was only a modest strengthening of the private fundraising function. Survival was still dependent on the number of choral opportunities presented by the CBC as well as generous grants from the Ontario Arts Council and the Canada Council. The ability to provide a regular monthly stipend to the members of the chorus was dependent on these revenues and they were obviously drying up. A few recalcitrant choristers blamed it on Elmer's connivance with the bureaucrats at the summit of these institutions. Elmer's absence had resulted in a dramatic reduction in the number of broadcast appearances on CBC. Obviously, stated his enemies, Elmer's conspiratorial friends at the Corporation were unprofessionally punishing the Festival Singers board for its behaviour towards their long-time friend and colleague. John Peter Lee Roberts, a CBC executive and Festival Singers board member who along with John Bird had felt impelled to resign in protest over the board's treatment of Elmer, was seen as a villain, as was Robert Sunter, once at the OAC and now at the CBC, who claimed, when confronted in an exchange of letters with Malcolm Russell,[27] that recent broadcast tapes indicated a demonstrable erosion in quality.

The issue of quality of performance was at the centre of the response of granting councils to criticism that there had been unfair treatment of the Festival Singers. These councils were also confronted by the possibility of two competing chamber choirs in Toronto and wanted no part of being responsible for that situation. Russell, who had been for a period of time the manager of the Singers, sent letters appealing for fairness and equity in the wake of the impending financial breakdown of Canada's major choral ensemble. But to no avail.

The degree of hurt and humiliation for Elmer was massive and unendurable. It eventually resulted in an irrational and destructive response that sought legal recourse. Ultimately it did little damage to all involved, but it did indicate the angst that he had suffered. In 1979 Ron Hambleton wrote a column in the *Toronto Star* that sought to explain the situation to a baffled public and quoted angry choristers who sought to "set the record straight." In their fury over the impending demise of the Festival Singers, they cast doubts on Elmer's capacity as a musician, focusing particularly on what they perceived as his insensitive and cruel treatment of the Singers, including charges that indeed questioned his integrity.

On the advice of legal counsel, Elmer struck back in the only way he knew — he sued Hambleton, the *Toronto Star*, and choristers Russell and his colleague Michael Dufault for $10 million each, as well as the CBC, which had broadcast commentary by Dufault that Elmer found especially reprehensible and defamatory. Stephen Clarke, a singer and a lawyer who represented Russell and Dufault, claims that Elmer had no illusions that a sum of money like that could be extracted from penurious artists — but was aimed at securing the attention of a newspaper, a journalist, and a broadcaster and those they had quoted who might wish to carry on a vendetta into the future. It certainly had that effect.[28] The action sputtered on for a few years into the 1980s but never reached a courtroom, as it was finally withdrawn by Elmer.

As one would expect, the action was seen by those who had reason to resent Elmer's leadership as an indication of his determination to intimidate and vilify. Those who loved and respected him saw this as a strategy to prevent any further personal vindictiveness and to protect the choral community from further disruption. His enemies, of course, perceived his actions as the behaviour of a desperate, almost a deranged man seeking to protect his reputation. It was seen by those at some distance as a mindless though heartfelt strategy to offset the attacks of a group of "turncoats" who had caused enormous heartache both for Jessie and his children and within the entire Canadian choral community.

Even with all this uproar, the Festival Singers board made no public statement regarding the causes of Elmer's dismissal, even though reminded that the ensemble had received considerable public funds from taxpayers through granting councils at all levels of government.

The inevitable disintegration and bankruptcy of the Festival Singers brought the institutional conflict to an end. By the summer of 1978, Elmer was contacting those who were his supporters in the Festival Singers, promising them a place in his new ensemble, the Elmer Iseler Singers. As long as public money was involved and granting councils insisted on the presence of a board of directors to represent the public interest, the danger of conflict was ever-present. But having the choir called the Elmer Iseler Singers gave its founder and conductor more leverage and expressed the fact that it would indeed be "his choir."

The Festival Singers tried to raise the tens of thousands of dollars needed to avoid bankruptcy — with little success. In a last effort to save the choir the new Festival Singers board chair, Charles Tisdall, sent Elmer a letter dated May 15, 1979, asking him to return as artistic director. In the light of all that had taken place, a very restrained reply indicated that Elmer would not accept such an invitation:

> In looking at the total picture which now obtains for the Festival Singers organization as outlined by you to James Singleton and myself, I must put aside what might be immediately attractive to me. The Singers were of infinite concern to me for twenty years of my life … I have, unhappily, come to the conclusion that I could not in all conscience ask men and women to begin or to continue in a situation which had arrived for one reason or another at a position of considerable deficit … I therefore sincerely regret that I am unable to accept the … offer to return as Artistic Director.[29]

The newly minted Elmer Iseler Singers retained the music library that had been acquired over the years, largely because the Festival Singers had, at the time of dismissal, owed Elmer some $30,000. In the case of bankruptcy the first call on any organization is to pay the wages owed to its employees. By putting the Festival Singers' music library as the basis for compensation for wages owed to him, thereby making it his personal property, Elmer was able to arrange for this most valuable asset to be saved from possible sale and dispersal. Many of the Festival Singers found their way into the new ensemble, and within a few months singers from that source made up half the membership of the Elmer Iseler Singers.

One of the problems that the Festival Singers had failed to solve was a lack of consistent excellence in the management of the ensemble. There were often as many as two or three managers in a single year — many of them intelligent and efficient but beset by internal conflicts that seemed irresolvable. That position was now to be filled by Jessie Iseler, who remains the Singers' manager now into the new century. Her enormous capacity for sensitive leadership and organizational genius has been recognized and celebrated. In 1997, the Elmer Iseler Singers received the Lieutenant Governor's Award, a sizeable sum of money, for the choir's success in raising money in the private sector. It was truly Jessie's award, as manager of the choir, for her efforts to ensure its financial health.

The other issue was the scale of the sound produced by the Elmer Iseler Singers. There was no doubt that the quality of sound and stretch of repertoire were increased by the size of the Festival Singers (some thirty to forty and, on occasion, more]. William Littler put it succinctly: the Elmer Iseler Singers would be "leaner" and "tougher" for a leaner and tougher age. It would continue to be a professional choir of some twenty singers who could be afforded without increases in grants, donations, and earned income. Particularly, the cost of touring and workshopping would be drastically restrained.

Elmer, in his quiet moments after the shock and amidst the elation of a new beginning, making use of his superb ear and his understanding of the basics of acoustic excellence, was able to accommodate and adjust his singers in such a way that the presence of that great sound and an even greater flexibility was assured. Also, he recognized that, in some ways, he had created his own anguish for the future. He had inspired other professional choirs, notably by this point the Tudor Singers of Montreal and the Vancouver Chamber Choir, who would now share grants, broadcast opportunities, and recording sessions. But he was ready both to collaborate and to compete.

Elmer had endured an intense trauma. As a student and assistant to Sir Ernest MacMillan he had survived the humiliation of rejection by the Mendelssohn Choir, but then he had been but a youth. By 1978 he was accepted from coast to coast as Canada's prime choral conductor, and he had been fêted in the United States, the United Kingdom, and Europe. He was determined that he would not allow himself to be placed in this situation again. Unfortunately, history is a poor instructor, and though a situation never repeats itself exactly, the pressure of inadequate resources and conflicts of traditional administration expectations versus artistic vision do, in the arts, encourage the replaying of tragic events and their unavoidable consequences. Elmer, as an artist, still remained vulnerable to the assaults on the part of those who could not accept the implications of his vision to achieve and sustain choral excellence.

Chapter 8

An Alternative Theme

THE UNEXPECTED FORCED RESIGNATION FROM
the role of conductor of the Festival Singers was a traumatic experience for
Elmer. There were moments during the late spring of 1978 when he came
to the conclusion that perhaps one choir was enough. He would remain
in the roles of artistic director and conductor of the Toronto Mendelssohn
Choir (TMC) that he had acquired in 1964. He would still have control
over who would be members of the TMC's professional core. Whether
they were also members of the Festival Singers (now under another
conductor) or another collection of singers under his own direction, the
opportunities to direct the affairs of the TMC would continue to be in his
hands. In fact, during these incredible months of conflict, Elmer and the
TMC board, with Suzanne Bradshaw taking the lead, were planning the
splendid tour that would take the TMC back to Europe in August 1980.

Yet Elmer soon realized that without a chamber choir not only was
his income severely diminished but his quality of working life would also
be eroded. He needed such a chorus that he could rehearse within a more
intimate context, one that could perform a wider range of repertoire that
could not be addressed by large vocal forces. As well, he could lose contact
with his professional choristers and would be restricted to working with
a TMC that was largely amateur. He did not wish to restrain himself to
the preparation and performance of familiar oratorio favourites that were
inevitably the main repertoire for such large choruses and would certainly
continue to fill the hall with an audience but would not sufficiently
challenge him or his singing colleagues.

As well there would be things he could no longer do. He realized that the TMC had been expensive to tour in the 1960s and 1970s, but now, in the more rigorous 1980s it might become almost impossible. Being restricted to a large oratorio choir and thus restrained in its touring would also diminish his access to the people he most wanted to reach — people who lived in smaller distant centres in Ontario and in other provinces across Canada. A huge choir rarely had an opportunity to sing in those places because, first, there was rarely an appropriate venue — size was once again an unavoidable factor. Second, though he had taken the TMC to the United States on a several occasions and to Europe and the United Kingdom on a major tour and was now planning a second such experience for the TMC, the cost of travel and accommodation was now becoming virtually prohibitive. An alternative was that of touring with a part of the TMC, perhaps less than one hundred singers. This, he believed, would have negative effects on the performance of the entire TMC. He could not risk that possibility. It was a dilemma that could only be solved by the presence of a separate professional chamber choir completely dedicated to his artistic vision of what could be achieved with such vocal forces.

As well, there was the reality of the broadcast studio — either radio or television. The CBC, virtually the only source of funds and the will to broadcast serious music, had neither the facilities nor the technical capacity to give regular broadcast opportunities to such massive vocal forces as those represented by the TMC. Broadcast performance for this chorus would continue to be a CBC taping of regular concerts either with or without the Toronto Symphony Orchestra.

Elmer had brought new life from the old days of the TMC's very narrow repertoire (*Messiah* and *St. Matthew Passion*) to a new age of limitless choral possibilities. How ironic if restrained public support now provided less promise of new and experimental repertoire commissioned especially for chamber choir. Certainly Holman's *Jezebel* and Srul Irving Glick's *The Hour Has Come* were to be TMC triumphs during these years. But the availability of composers prepared to write large on every occasion of a commission from the TMC would be limiting.

By the summer of 1978, Elmer had made his decision. He would form a smaller ensemble called the Elmer Iseler Singers (EIS). It was no surprise that he would turn to those singers with whom he had worked, in some cases for a quarter of a century. Some were now otherwise engaged, but given a few months to complete contracts or finish other choral projects — they would be thrilled to join Elmer's new ensemble. There were also, of course, the Festival Singers members, now engaged in a survival effort to produce a 1978–79 series of concerts and making themselves available to presenters across the continent. However, even by the winter and fall of 1979, rumours of the Festival Singers' financial troubles were rampant. It appeared that an Elmer Iseler Singers ensemble would soon be the sole source of Elmer's famous choral sound in the absence of any competition.

Just as important for any new chorus was the administrative challenge of finding resources and managing the choir. It was a matter of starting all over again. An entire new board had to be found and new links with both the granting councils and private sector donors had to be forged. As important to any success was the reconnection with the CBC and its desire to broadcast quality choral music. That had been the basis of the resources that had allowed the Festival Singers to begin its work in the 1950s. Once again, in the late 1970s, it would play a central role in giving an immediate reason for the presence of a new ensemble with initially nothing to exhibit but the name of its highly distinguished conductor and his enormous reputation.

There was no lifting of the eyebrows when Elmer turned once again to his old mentor, friend, and colleague, Lt. Col. James Singleton. This time the enthusiasm of the entire family was engaged and Jim's son Paul was invited to participate in the search for new board members who would provide leadership for the EIS — and also for new sources of revenue from the private sector.

By the late fall of 1979, after countless gatherings of one or two potential members at Quail Hill Farm and undistinguished venues in Toronto and beyond, a board of directors had been named and the first formal meeting held. In the chair, providing Elmer with infinite support, was Jim Singleton, and in the group being recruited, as one would expect, were John Bird[1] and John Peter Lee Roberts. There were other familiar names, all friends and admirers of the Iseler vision, for example, John

Fenton, whose financial expertise was essential. Soon, George Pennie, a former Festival Singer board member and once Elmer's brother-in-law, would be recruited and would eventually take over the reins as chair of the EIS board after Jim Singleton's passing. The selection of board members would be given greater attention than ever before, and after George Pennie stepped down the choir would turn to James T. Chestnutt, who, along with his choral vision, has, in turn, given devoted service to the Singers with the recruitment of new and effective board members, a major aspect of his contribution over so many years.

The minutes of the first board meeting reveal that much business had already been carried out. Incorporation was essential in order that a formal appointment of directors could take place, and, just as important, an application had to be made to Revenue Canada for an official number designating charitable status and allowing income tax receipts to be given for the donations that were now crucial, whether from individuals, corporations, or foundations. As one might expect, Richard Shibley had looked after those details.

As essential was a strategy for establishing a relationship with the Ontario Arts Council, the Canada Council, and the Toronto Arts Council, all of whom had been kept aware of the steps toward creating a new choir that had already been taken. Directors and officers of these bodies had been shocked at the loss of Canada's most prestigious chamber ensemble and were anxious to provide at least some bridge funding for individual concerts in Ontario until the choir could apply for normal annual funding for its entire program.

There was a need to establish a contractual relationship with the Toronto Mendelssohn Choir in order that the Elmer Iseler Singers could replace the soon-to-be-defunct Festival Singers as the professional core of the TMC, an essential element of the budgetary and artistic situation for both choral enterprises. The TMC board came through with magnificent support for which Elmer was eternally grateful. This step assured the TSO that the singing quality the orchestra demanded for its choral repertoire would be present in future concerts of any such works that Elmer might plan to present in upcoming seasons.

Needless to say, fundraising was the major preoccupation of the new board. Enormous lists of previously approached corporations were assembled and Jim Singleton led the effort to reach out to these and new business representatives. However, the most important action of that initial meeting was the formal hiring of Jessie Iseler as the manager of the Elmer Iseler Singers. She had been the informal glue for all the multitude of activities that had filled the previous year, but now it was time to pay remuneration for the enormous amount of work she was already doing. She had become the driving force behind every aspect of Elmer's regeneration as the conductor of a new ensemble, as well as the essential source of his mental and physical stability.

An Elmer Iseler Singers brochure that could be given the widest possible distribution to concert presenters had already been prepared through Jessie's foresight, as had opportunities for immediate touring in the realization that a formal concert series in Toronto could not be immediately mounted. That would create a base for income and, simultaneously would be a signal that the Singers were ready to travel, sing, and provide workshops across the continent. Although the possibility of a tour of the United States had risen, the Department of External Affairs had no money to contribute. Though initially thought to be a disaster, this circumstance turned out to be a stroke of good luck, as Elmer was able to present his new ensemble as aspiring to serve and to be seen to be serving Canadians as its first priority. The first EIS tour was in the Canadian West in March 1980. Elmer declared to his new board that, even withstanding past wonderful touring experiences with the Festival Singers, this one had turned out to be "the finest ever."[2]

However, finding money remained the major preoccupation of the board and administration of the Elmer Iseler Singers. It drove the board to sell a portable organ once used by the Festival Singers to a north Toronto synagogue, Temple Emanu-El, with the agreement that it could be rented out to the new choir when needed for only $100. At one point there was serious discussion of a proposal brought by Richard Shibley that the Singers be hired out as a regular choir for the services at Blessed Sacrament Church in Toronto. The idea was ultimately abandoned both by the church and the EIS board, but the discussion revealed the desperate need for sponsorship. The plan represented as well a desire to bring hope and beauty through sensitive and meaningful repertoire to a large downtown parish on a regular basis. Fortunately, the former need was partially overcome — the Singers were soon hired by an array of Ontario presenters. The members of the ensemble were engaged as part of the TMC for a special Healey Willan celebratory concert in 1980 and for the regular TMC series concerts for the 1980–81 season.

Perhaps the most creative solution to the Elmer Iseler Singers' financial woes came from the CBC and producer John Reeves. He presented for CBC radio broadcast a series, not of concerts, but of public EIS rehearsals from Timothy Eaton Memorial Church. It gave Elmer the opportunity to explain on air, in some detail, the steps taken to produce the choral sound that was now so famous, and to do so in an informal setting that humanized the process and made it very effective for radio listening. It also provided proof that a new chamber ensemble was being prepared, one that would have the qualities, if not the volume, of the previous larger Festival Singers ensemble. Indeed, it was these CBC appearances that resulted in a heartwarming letter that Elmer received from a listener, Helen Law of Leamington, Ontario:

> You are living proof of the healing, renewing power of music As if by a miracle, you have risen from the hurtful, bruising experience of the recent past to produce that exquisite sound that I am hearing on the CBC–FM (Mostly Music). You have achieved that remarkable and unmistakable Iseler sound once more — and, if possible, even more beautiful. I am moved to tears! You have that sound in your head and have assembled the gorgeous voices and modified them to produce that incredibly beautiful sound, and flexibility and musicality.[3]

It was not until March 13, 1980, that the Elmer Iseler Singers made its concert debut in St. James Cathedral in downtown Toronto. It was a great occasion heralded by John Kraglund's review that no choir could have been accorded "a more enthusiastic reception and deserved it more," making the point that the emphasis in the singing was "on tonal quality rather than emotional expression"[4]

They were now ready for any challenge of presentation that could be conceived, even one that involved other choral ensembles. Within the first year, Elmer had taken his Singers to Montreal for a joint concert with the Tudor Singers and, in the early 1980s, he established a relationship with the Netherlands Chamber Choir that resulted not only in a visit to each other's home base but the production of a recording, *Serenade in Harmony*, in which both choirs participated. In 1984, the recording won a Juno nomination (the highest accolade the Canadian recording industry offers) in the classical category. Working cooperatively with such a choir satisfied Elmer and his choristers' need to occasionally hear the larger sound that could only be produced by the presence of more voices. It also allowed the Elmer Iseler Singers to address repertoire demanding two full choirs interacting with each other.

Elmer had to work hard to achieve the fullness of sound that could fill cathedrals across Europe, and his Singers found that it was much more demanding being in this smaller ensemble. When there were multiple lines within sections, singers found they were alone, virtually soloists, singing with colleagues who were also feeling rather lonely in their parts. In some cases, there was previous repertoire that simply had to be abandoned.

But the fewer numbers had an enormous advantage as it turned out. There was a new excitement being part of a smaller ensemble — the sound could be even more elegant. As well, a new relationship developed between Elmer and the individual singers. Ed Weins, a former Festival Singer and now ready to join Elmer's new chorus, puts it simply: "We became more than members of his choir — we became close friends, indeed a real family."[5] On tours, both Jessie and Elmer rode the bus with the Singers and shared the same accommodation as the choristers.

There were obvious financial advantages. Not only were the costs of presenting workshops now reasonable for smaller communities, the numbers of singers did not dominate the choral forces they were seeking to support. The scene became more intimate and sensitive. The same could be said for the conductor workshops: the inexperienced conductor was faced with a less imposing array of singers. The atmosphere became extraordinarily warm and compassionate. Ed Weins speaks of workshop participants who, after a strenuous workout, stated unequivocally, "I want to sing like that for the rest of my life."

Lydia Adams accompanied the Elmer Iseler Singers for many years and witnessed the transformation that took place in countless workshops across the country:

> Elmer had the ability to take singers outside the confines they had built for themselves and the will to do what they thought was the impossible. He focused so totally on the music — he drew them in with him and they had no choice but to go with him on the journey! He had that strong personal aura — an aura of greatness. I think that sometimes when Elmer entered the room that it had the same effect as if the singers were seeing the Monarch. Now those singers knew they could achieve something great. After the session, their lives had been changed — they had taken part in something far greater than themselves and they now had confidence to do something more with their talent and ability. He did this many, many times in his life.[6]

An invitation to mount one of the Elmer Iseler Singers' first performance-workshop tours resulted in a sixteen-day tour of Nova Scotia in 1980. Travelling east nicely balanced the tour of the western provinces a few months before. This part of Canada had already come to mean much to Elmer. In 1979, he had been invited to be a guest master at Nova Scotia's Institute of Choral Conducting. Dr. Fred Graham, a graduate of Elmer's class at the University of Toronto back in the mid-1960s, was organist at the Halifax Cathedral and, with other choral musicians, including his wife, Melva, had become aware of the appalling state of choral music across the Maritimes. In that year, Elmer had taken only Jessie with him, but in 1980 he brought his entire complement of Elmer Iseler Singers with him. The workshop at the Institute of Choral Conducting radically changed the quality of choral performance across the provinces of Nova Scotia and New Brunswick for the rest of the century and into the new millennium. It was another example of a communing with people he knew and trusted and had come to respect.

One of these participants turned up at an EIS concert in Ontario several years later. He sought to meet Elmer after a strenuous concert but was confronted by an attendant who was protecting the exhausted conductor from the informal interventions that face performers on such occasions. He presented the attendant with his name and a few seconds later heard Elmer's booming voice: "Send him in, he's from Nova Scotia." To Maritime choristers and conductors both Elmer became an icon and his influence cannot be overestimated. The pattern for workshopping had been revived by the Elmer Iseler Singers and for the next decades communities across Canada shared in this form of continuing choral education with enormous implications for the cultural life of the nation.

These Maritime events continued to the end of his life. In the 1980s and 1990s it was Newfoundland that received the attention of Elmer and his singers. Douglas Dunsmore is the conductor of the Memorial University Festival Choir and Chamber Choir, the Newfoundland Symphony Philharmonic Choir, and the Choir of Gower Street United Church. He writes:

> Elmer Iseler's visits to Newfoundland and my specific choral program in 1985, 1992, and 1997 are worthy of special mention. In these instances, the host choirs were not "sung to" but rather "worked with." Elmer's workshops were magical. He and his professional singers invariably raised the bar of excellence for every participating singer in our choirs. Concerts of very ambitious proportion enjoyed splendid results. Perhaps most important, from both a pedagogical and community building point of view, the host conductor always shared podium time, and the spotlight, with Elmer.[7]

Dunsmore's colleague in Newfoundland, Susan Knight, the conductor of the Newfoundland Symphony Youth Choir (now known as "Shalloway") and a student of Elmer's at a Maritimes conductors' workshop and at the

University of Toronto, shared in this chorus of adulation: "Elmer is one of the reasons I am doing what I am today. He was extraordinarily inspiring as a teacher, mentor, musician and human being. He and his wife Jessie took me under their wing, and continued to be a source of inspiration and encouragement to me throughout my life."[8]

A few years later, at the other end of the country and considerably farther north there was the workshop experience of Bill Gilday, conductor of the Yellowknife Youth Choir, the Gumboots. He writes of Elmer's tour of Canada in 1996 and his stop at Yellowknife:

> Elmer brought us all together in our local theatre where we worked on Oscar Peterson's "Hymn to Freedom" and Allistair MacGillvary's "Song for the Mira." Elmer was so kind to my girls and told them what a lovely sound they produced, much to their delight. When Elmer rehearsed his own choir, the rest of us sat in the auditorium and watched while he put them through their paces. That was the first time many of the girls had seen and heard a professional choir, an experience that made a strong impression on them. They were dazzled by the power and beauty of those voices and were struck by the tremendous breath control that they displayed.[9]

Don James had been inspired at a concert by Elmer Iseler and his Festival Singers while he was still attending a junior college in Saskatchewan: "I still remember the incredible, interesting sound he got from that group. That choral sound could be so powerful and so expressive was a revelation to me. I decided to take music courses full-time, and entered a bachelor of music program at Seattle Pacific University."[10]

It was in 1984 that James initiated an extraordinary event in, of all places, the modest community of Powell River on the north coast of British Columbia, some distance from any major urban centre. He had attended the International Society for Music Education in London, Ontario, in the mid-1970s and had created his own Powell River Boys' Choir. By the early 1980s, he came to the conclusion that he could organize a world-class festival in this small Canadian community that could draw children's and youth choirs from all around the world for what could be termed a major international choral experience.

In 1982, the International Choral Kathaumixw Festival was born, and after two years spent raising funds, the first choirs were invited. Part of the festival's attraction was the unpronounceable name, Kathaumixw, a native word meaning a gathering together of different people. The first festival in 1984 involved the entire Powell River community and was an unqualified success. It became an event that took place every two years and it was one to which Elmer came back again and again. It included both competitions and individual choir concert presentations for some thirty ensembles. The crowning event was the gala closing concert, for which the entire complement of young singers rehearsed for the entire week. Elmer was invited as the conductor of this event three times in the late 1980s and early 1990s and never tired of the opportunity to participate. Even on his deathbed, Elmer asked Jessie for maps of Powell River and the adjacent region to sharpen his memory of glorious times in that part of Canada.

James describes the final gala concert in words reeking of understatement: "The chance for all choirs to sing together is a unique component of the Festival. It never fails to be a highly moving and exhilarating experience for the singers." Kathaumixw became another example of Elmer's willingness to appear in every corner of the country supporting the cause of bringing choral music to young people.

It had been back in May 1980 that the Ontario Arts Council had received the first submission for funding from the Elmer Iseler Singers prepared by Jessie as the ensemble's newly appointed manager. Rarely had such a document exuded the enthusiasm this one did. It was particularly miraculous having been developed in the shadow of all the trauma of Elmer's conflict with the Festival Singers that had preceded its arrival at the OAC's office. In the initial paragraphs Jessie could exclaim, "It has been a heart-warming and encouraging year both artistically and financially. In other words we're going to make it!" There followed an extraordinary account of the successful events of the past year.[11] More important, the application for funding assured the Council that the Elmer

Iseler Singers could overcome the trials of the 1980s and 1990s — the choir had survived that difficult first year.

In the fall of 1981, the Elmer Iseler Singers went on a tour in the United States, and at the October 29 meeting of the board, Elmer was able to report that "it was very successful in every way and the Singers maintained their health and enthusiasm."[12] It was followed by several other such tours later in the 1980s and 1990s. Indeed, there were parts of the United States that received almost as much of the Elmer Iseler Singers' presence as did some regions of Canada.

There were other times of euphoric success that allowed Elmer to feel his decision to create a successor to the Festival Singers was the right one. For Elmer personally, the very mountaintop of his life came in 1987, when he was invited to be the lecturer and presenter on "North American Contemporary Choral Music" at the first World Congress on Choral Music, to be held in Vienna, Austria. Under the auspices of the International Federation of Choral Music, it was a most prestigious world gathering. Elmer insisted on bringing his Elmer Iseler Singers. Once again, it was an Elmer who had little interest in just talking about music. He wished to illustrate every point he wanted his audience to remember. The invitation recognized the status that he had achieved worldwide and the fact that he had been chosen to play this role rather than a host of other prestigious conductors from the United States and Canada. The opportunity was understandably a matter of great pride. Elmer took a suitcase full of Canadian compositions and was able to state on arrival back in Canada that he had made use of every selection. In spite of the theme of all his sessions, that is, "North American Contemporary Choral Music," there has probably never been so much Canadian music performed abroad in the space of a few days as during the 1987 Vienna World Congress on Choral Music.

The Vienna concerts had been heard by officials who were planning an international choral festival to accompany the Seoul Olympics in 1988. As a result, the Elmer Iseler Singers were invited to be one of the few non-Asian choral ensembles assembled at the Seoul Art Centre, with only the Olaf Choir from the United States, the Ars Nova from Brazil, and the Kammerchor Stuttgart from Germany included in concerts and gala occasions along with several choirs from Japan and Korea. Elmer, in his individual EIS concert, insisted on presenting works of Holman, MacGillivray, Schafer, Healey, Gould, and Somers along with familiar selections of Handel and Bach.

Patti Walker, a close friend of Elmer's daughter, Buffy, accompanied the Iseler family on the Far East tour and expressed in an unpublished handwritten account the excitement of the welcome with flowers and banners after the fifteen-hour air trip from Canada. There were sensational moments of performance. In Walker's words,

> The Elmer Iseler Singers represented Canada and her culture as no other choir could have done. The quality of the performances and the variety in the program provided the Korean audiences with a wonderful opportunity to listen to and love the music. And they did! The Iseler recordings that were brought were sold out in ten minutes and the choir members were exhausted by repeated encores ... the massed choir performance of Beethoven's 9th Symphony was a moving experience.[13]

Walker was also impressed, as were members of her Iseler Singers hosts, with the parties after the gala, and especially with the dancing: "We polka-ed in long gowns and tuxedos, Japanese women did a fan dance and the Brazilians led us in a congo line." They shopped, toured the Olympic facilities, and enjoyed the excitement of an event that would soon catch the attention of the world.

The Singers had arranged for a concert in Hong Kong, and after some hours of exploration it was back to work. The Singers were declared by critics to be "in excellent form" and had received a "response that was overwhelming." Then it was off to Singapore, where Elmer had been asked to adjudicate at a competition of Singaporean choirs. "Among the group was a delightful Children's Choir whose members skipped on the stage and stole the show with the gestures, smiles and voices," Walker reported. After a wildly successful performance it was on to Taiwan, where they were met by a representative of the Chiang Kai Shek Cultural

Centre who sang traditional folk songs on the bus to the city. For a few moments it became a duet with chorister Robert Missen, who had studied Mandarin Chinese.

Even though exhausted, the Singers "rallied and performed an outstanding concert": "It was an emotional evening as it brought together all those who had contributed to the different aspects of the tour … Lydia Adams, the dedicated and exceptionally talented accompanist, the management team of Jessie Iseler and Patti Sun … and Elmer Iseler who has created a unique sound in Canadian and world choral circles and who consistently requires and receives from each performer his or her best work." For tour chronicler Patti Walker "it was over," even the shopping, but for the Singers it had been but another peak of performing in strange lands on an unfamiliar continent.

The Elmer Iseler Singers had been invited to appear at Expo '86 in Vancouver, where the choir was to premiere in six concerts an unusual item of repertoire — an *Electronic Messiah*, which horrified some conservative choral enthusiasts but delighted many who saw this as another example of Elmer's courage. A supreme moment of the decade was, however, the choir's appearance at the 1988 Winter Olympics in Calgary, Alberta. It had taken a long time to secure some attention for the arts at these gatherings of the world's greatest athletes. In recent years Olympic host cities have used the Games as an opportunity to expose the quality of their performing artists along with visiting artists to the world that was now watching. Calgary was determined to outdo previous Winter Games hosts and the Elmer Iseler Singers were to be featured along with other professional choristers who were to be found in Wayne Riddell's Tudor Singers, Jon Washburn's Vancouver Chamber Choir, and Michel Gervais's Pro Coro Canada in a choral concert spectacular and were also participating in the gala opening with the Calgary Philharmonic under conductor Mario Bernardi.

In 1985 Elmer had commissioned Srul Irving Glick to write an extended choral composition for his Toronto Mendelssohn Choir and the result had been *The Hour Has Come*, a melodic appeal for peace and brotherhood based on a text by Carole H. Leckner, and the final movement was the crowning moment in both the Calgary Olympic gala opening and the choral spectacular. For the gala, the Elmer Iseler Singers were part of a massed choir that included all the professional choirs along with the Calgary Choral Society and other singers from local church choirs. It was a moving climax to a program that was a launching pad for the greatest fortnight in Calgary's history, when its citizens astounded athletes and visitors with both the amazing organizational skill and the collegial warmth of the Canadian West's citizens.

In the choral spectacular, the four Canadian choirs moved through an extraordinary spectrum of repertoire that included Ralph Vaughan Williams's Mass in G Minor, R. Murray Schafer's Psalm, Frank Martin's Mass for Double Chorus, Arnold Schoenberg's *Friede auf Erden (Peace on Earth)*, Jonathon Harvey's *Come Holy Ghost*, and Michael Tippet's arrangements of *Five Negro Spirituals*. It was an opportunity for Elmer to view what he had achieved — none of the other professional choirs had existed in the 1950s when Elmer had formed the Festival Singers. Needless to say, it was a highlight of the "cultural olympics" and enhanced a Calgary event that had already set a new standard for Winter Olympic presentations for the rest of the century. The experience also created a sense of camaraderie with Elmer Iseler Singers and other professional choristers, reminding them that they were no longer isolated and unique but part of a growing community of Canadian singers who were devoting their lives to the art of singing together.

Although Elmer was but one of four conductors on this occasion, he was honoured by being given the task of bringing the spectacular to a conclusion. University of Calgary associate professor of music Kenneth DeLong described the final moments of the celebratory concert:

> The final member of the quartet was Mr. Choral Canada himself, the old sorcerer, Elmer Iseler, who presided over the grand finale in a grand manner. The concert concluded with the final movement of Srul Irving Glick's recent choral symphony, *The Hour Has Come*. Composed in a musical style at once popular and compelling, it brought the concert to an end with the audience leaping to its feet in appreciation of this most sumptuous of choral feasts.[14]

The third and last responsibility for Elmer and his Singers was a performance of the Verdi Requiem, which involved all four professional chamber choirs, but also the Calgary Choral Society. It was a reminder that those who were now finally professional and paid to sing had a historic connection with those who were called amateurs but who simply sang because for them it was so important to enhance the quality of their lives.

In 1989, Niki Goldschmidt's International Choral Festival was taking place in Toronto and the Elmer Iseler Singers were very much involved. Critic Peter Mose commented on a performance that took place at St. Patrick's Roman Catholic Church in a special report for the *Toronto Star* headlined "Iseler sets the standard for all choral groups":

> Palestrina's well-known unaccompanied *Pope Marcellus Mass* led off. Iseler leading his 27 professional voices (the EIS slightly augmented) with his customary, musical motions. Here we are in the midst of a blazing international choral festival and our home-grown Iseler Singers chamber choir virtually defines the standard by which to measure other groups.
>
> That says an enormous amount about its namesake: Iseler is indeed someone whose arms and upper torso breathe music. Ever shaping and sculpting while urging a flow onward. Plus the insider's choral word is that his eyes communicate with searing intensity.[15]

Yet in the fall of that same year, Elmer could give his attention as completely to a tour of sparsely populated Northern Ontario towns with little expectation of any accolades from important individuals in the music community. The trip included Timmins, Kirkland Lake, Wawa, Marathon, Geraldton, Thunder Bay, and Kenora. Some days were spent entirely on the bus, travelling, for example, from Thunder Bay to Kenora. Only in Thunder Bay was the choir able to spend more than a single day. The adjective "exhausting" took on new meaning.

Significantly, the repertoire for the concerts in northern Ontario was drawn from the same quality of compositions that were selected for

Toronto audiences, as well for those in American and European cities —
Handel, J.S. Bach, a collection of spirituals, and the amusing *So You Want
to Write a Fugue* of Glenn Gould. The evening ended with the music of
Derek Holman, Allister MacGillivray, R. Murray Schafer, Derek Healey,
and Harry Somers. The audiences were enthusiastic to a fault, knowing
that they had not been sung down to.

Even on concert days, Elmer and Jessie found ways to involve the
wider community. In Timmins the warm-up rehearsal was combined
with a workshop for the Timmins Youth Singers. Rosanne Simunovic,
the director of the ensemble, was quoted as saying, "I have had the
chance to hear them [the Elmer Iseler Singers] in Toronto and they are
truly exceptional. Their standard is so high, which is something you
always aim for." She had captured perfectly the outcome that Elmer
was striving for, particularly in his interactions with young people. In
Thunder Bay it was with the Lakehead University Vocal Ensemble with
whom Elmer spent most of a day and Rita Umbrico, writing in the
Thunder Bay Chronicle Journal, focused on one aspect of the choral art
that is often forgotten: "Though numbering only four each, the Iseler
altos and tenors were an inspiration to the local forces. Seldom have the
inside parts been so well defined."

The early 1990s presented Elmer with what turned out to be the
ultimate experience in reaching out to young people. He was now in
his mid-sixties, and the organizers of the National Youth Choir (NYC),
the Association of Canadian Choral Conductors, in all this attention to
youth, must have asked themselves about the wisdom of bringing an
older man, even an Elmer Iseler, to appear as the NYC's conductor in
1992. The days of rehearsal for a concluding concert tour would bring
Elmer and Jessie into close contact with the choristers. These young
people would be worked relentlessly to achieve Elmer's standards. Would
they accept this kind of discipline? Would they ever reach the standards
that Elmer expected?

Elmer had picked the repertoire carefully. It was not just for
performances that would take place after all the rehearsals had concluded.
Here was an opportunity to provide an experience in the history of choral
music for these young people from across the land who needed to know

something of the basic selections that were essential to the choral art. As well, they would be made aware of the excellent Canadian composers living among them. Elmer wanted these young people to know that their country now had a reputation for being a "singing nation" and to know why that reputation had emerged.

A work was commissioned from Derek Holman, a composer whom Elmer had commissioned on several occasions, and he presented the choir with *The Present Time*, an appealing composition with a text that stirred their minds as well as their musicality. Elmer wanted to ensure that these choristers were aware of glorious music from the Renaissance, so works by Byrd and Mundy were included, and, of course, every one of these young people must experience the delight of Mozart's *Sancta Maria*. Also, there had to be recognition of a swath of contemporary composers from other countries. Arthur Honegger's great oratorio *King David* provided *Three Psalms*, and Norman Dello Joio's *Psalm of David* brilliantly represented American composition. The three choruses from Aaron Copland's opera *The Tender Land* included particularly attractive fare — *Stomp Your Feet*, *The Promise of Living*, and *Simple Gifts*. Elmer wanted these young people to experience the music of Canada's best-known living composer internationally, R. Murray Schafer, and his *Epitaph for Moonlight*, written originally as "a study piece for a youth choir," was a perfect choice.

When public performances finally did take place, audiences were staggered by what they heard. Harry Currie in the *Kitchener-Waterloo Record*, under a heading "National Youth Choir May Be the Best Kept Secret in Ontario," wrote a review of a rehearsal at Wilfrid Laurier University. By that time these thirty-six young singers had been in rehearsal for sixteen days and were about to give six performances in Ontario cities including Kitchener-Waterloo, St. Catharines, London, and Toronto. Their debut concert was to be at Podium '92, the biennial conference of the Association of Canadian Choral Conductors. It was obvious that Elmer had done his job well. Currie was enormously impressed:

> Listening to the rehearsal, I was struck by the pitch sense
> and intonation of the choir … it was bang-on in every
> moment, and seemingly without effort. Their dynamic

control was amazing from triple piano to double forte
with no forcing, no tempo change and no pitch shifts.
The steadiness and blend of tonal quality was remarkable,
each chord able to resonate with its own harmonics and
not coloured by vibrato modulations which destroy so
many community groups.[16]

Something unexplainable but quite extraordinary had happened at
that National Youth Choir program that went beyond the rehearsals and
performances and has to do with revelation and transformation. Was it
the daily interaction between Elmer and Jessie and these highly motivated
and clever young people at mealtime, the parties around the campfires
in the evening, the one-on-one sessions that Elmer and Jessie had with
individual choristers? Was it that the circumstances gave an opportunity
for Elmer and Jessie to provide an example of personal relationship that
cut through all the adolescent reticence that normally hampers intimacy?
It is impossible to say. However, before the choir's intense sixteen days of
rehearsal ended, the choir members decided they wanted to show that
they had not only experienced new understandings about choral music —
but had, as well, learned something about living a good life.

The choristers bought a copy of the incomparable Lorraine Monk's
Canada With Love, a magnificent coffee-table volume expressing in glorious
photographs the unexcelled beauty of her Canada. Each chorister chose
a page, often containing pictures of the corner of the land from which
they had come (one found her grandmother's house behind the depicted
grain elevator), and wrote something of what they believed had happened.
Hugh Russell exclaimed, "You have made this one of the richest musical
experiences of my life I'll treasure forever." There were several others who
simply wanted Jessie and Elmer to know they had learned something
about a loving relationship. Krista Joy wrote directly to Jessie, "You and
your husband have such a splendid love," but to them both Adrienne Lewis
wanted to express her appreciation for their "warmth" and "patience" as
"the most stunning couple I have met." Kristen Brough commented that
"you are 2 of the coolest people I have ever met," conceding that she
had also "learned so much." From a group of young people preparing

for university, for a first job, for a first serious relationship, the comments of Maureen McDonald — "thanks for letting us get to know *you* rather than the famous Iselers" — expressed a general theme, but her final entry had special poignancy: "Thank you for your happiness. You both have given me confidence in love." Maudlin, adolescent excess? Scarcely. These young people had experienced a defining moment in their young lives and had found a way to express themselves with appropriate intensity.

There was a more formal recognition of this unique occasion a few years later. The National Youth Choir was singing in May 1998, just a month after Elmer's death, and in its concert program was included the response to Elmer's passing written by Margaret Champion MacLean, a member of that National Youth Choir of 1992 but now vice-president of the Nova Scotia Choral Federation: "Elmer and Jessie were compassionate, caring and fun-loving with all the National Youth Choir members, and they enriched all of our lives as choristers."[17]

Two years later, in 1994, the Ontario Choral Federation invited Elmer to conduct the Ontario Youth Choir and there another love-in took place, dramatic but not as intense as the 1992 experience with the National Youth Choir. It was also the period of time when Elmer finally came to realize that he had not been a failure as a teacher — that he had touched the lives of many young people at both York Memorial and Northview Heights. It was a revelation that made a difference in the quality of his last years and particularly his last days.

Chapter 9

Confronting Everest

THE CONTRAST BETWEEN A CHAMBER CHOIR of some thirty voices and the massive forces of an oratorio chorus with up to two hundred voices has been described as that between a rowboat and a battleship: both are dependent on water, but there all comparison ends. Elmer, back in 1954, had been a part of the founding of the Festival Singers and, continuing the analogy, had transformed the rowboat into a sleek, easily manoeuvrable canoe, strong and flexible, devoted to a largely forgotten repertoire. Now, in 1964, he was presented with the challenge of leading a large, unwieldy, some would say unmanageable vessel, a chorus devoted to a familiar repertoire that had captured the interest of Victorian music lovers.

Unlike the Festival Singers, which had been founded by a quartet of singers including Elmer Iseler in the mid-1950s, and the Elmer Iseler Singers, which had been formed by Elmer single-handedly in the late 1970s, the Toronto Mendelssohn Choir in the 1960s had been in place for nearly seventy years when Elmer was invited to become its leader. In Canadian terms, this was an ancient and formidable institution. Elmer had been just thirty-seven years old when, unexpectedly in 1964, just ten years after he had played his part in starting the career of the Festival Singers and fourteen years before he had created the Elmer Iseler Singers, he was invited to become the artistic director and conductor of Canada's oldest existing arts organization and most prestigious large choral ensemble. He was still teaching at Northview Heights and was already overwhelmed by the effort to juggle his school responsibilities as well as his choral conducting. Both he and Jessie were aware this situation could not continue. He had already collapsed once in 1960 and Jessie was determined that it should not happen again.

Elmer knew exactly what he was facing. It was a chorus with a long history of accomplishments that had fallen on hard times. He had, of course, known the Toronto Mendelssohn Choir when, scarcely out of his teens, he had sung in its ranks in the late 1940s and early 1950s and had been declared its rehearsal assistant by Sir Ernest MacMillan for the 1951–52 concert season. It had not gone well and he had been "fired," largely for his "over-exuberance," at the end of that initial year.

As the conductor of the Festival Singers for most of a decade, he followed the fortunes of the TMC closely. He saw that the choir had become a victim of its mythology and longevity. Although able to trace its beginnings back to the end of the nineteenth century and its development and survival to the talent and musicality of Augustus Vogt, the TMC had experienced great moments of triumph but had now seemingly lost its way.[1]

Under Sir Ernest MacMillan, conductor from 1942 to 1957, the choir had scaled the heights of *Messiah* annually and had developed a reputation as Canada's major choral ensemble devoted to J.S. Bach's *St. Matthew Passion*. Even before Sir Ernest, the TMC had been available to the Toronto Symphony for its frequent performances of Beethoven's Symphony no. 9 (a supreme achievement of combined forces of instrument and human voice) but to these performances had been added the more popular choral works of Elgar, Berlioz, Walton, Vaughan Williams, and the ensemble's namesake, Felix Mendelssohn.

Sir Ernest's main preoccupation was, of course, his leadership of the Toronto Symphony Orchestra, and he also had administrative duties as dean and principal of the University of Toronto's Faculty of Music and the Royal Conservatory and a sense of responsibility for the support of virtually every national music organization in the country. The TMC, by the 1950s, had become increasingly peripheral in terms of his focus and energy. Finally, by mid-decade, Sir Ernest had decided to resign as its conductor.

In 1957, MacMillan was succeeded by Frederick Silvester, who had been assisting Sir Ernest as a chorus master since 1946, but Silvester remained as conductor for only three years before retiring and being replaced by John Sidgwick, who remained only four years before he too took his retirement from the TMC's leadership role. Sidgwick's resignation had surfaced a basic fault in the structure of the TMC's relationship with the Toronto Symphony. Because the TMC had preceded the establishment of the TSO, this choir, unlike many such North American choruses that had been established simply to serve the interests of an already existing symphony orchestra in the city, had a reality of its own. Indeed, in the early decades of the choir's history there were periods when the TSO had not been in operation and the TMC collaborated with the Pittsburgh, Philadelphia, Detroit, and Cincinnati Symphony Orchestras as well as the New York Philharmonic, often appearing in the home city of each of these distinguished ensembles.

However, as the twentieth century proceeded and the Toronto Symphony Orchestra had strengthened and developed as the city's pre-eminent orchestral musical presence, the TMC had become the TSO's regular chorus as well. This relationship was solidified after 1942, when both the TSO and the TMC were conducted by Sir Ernest MacMillan. By this time, though, the TMC had established its own independence and sovereignty. It had its own board of directors and administrative officers and retained the right to present its own series of concerts and accept invitations to perform in association with other orchestras, either in Toronto or elsewhere, completely unconnected in any way with the performing schedule of the TSO.

All the issues around the relationship of the TSO and TMC came to a head after Sir Ernest's resignation. Silvester was prepared to accept only a short tenure as the choir's leader. He had been offered the role of chorus master, with Walter Susskind, MacMillan's successor at the TSO, taking on the position of conductor. John Sidgwick, Silvester's successor, was not prepared to accept this subservient role and he left to lead his own Orpheus Choir. Thus, the TMC found itself without a regular conductor even though Susskind was at the helm when the choir sang with the TSO. The impact of all this confusion and friction, along with the succession of three conductors in a single decade, had undermined the quality of a proud and resilient Toronto Mendelssohn Choir. Elmer was very much aware of all the chaos surrounding the decline of the choir. By the early 1960s, it was plainly losing its audience and the respect of the choral community.

In 1962, observing there were only a thousand people that less than half-filled Massey Hall for the last TMC performance of the concert season, Canadian composer Udo Kasemets, in his review for the *Toronto Daily Star*, asked a pointed question:

> Why then is the public slowly withdrawing its support from the events of this organization? Maybe the public has become disillusioned with the performing standards at the TMC concerts. Judging by last night's experience this would seem a logical conclusion. For with the Mozart, Walter Susskind gave his worst performance during his tenure of the conductorship of the TMC. All choral members were forced, overly loud and heavy. No attention was made to give musical shape, to individual phrases nor to the contrapuntal web of the parts.[2]

In that same year, George Kidd, another Toronto music critic, commented that it appeared that the public only wanted *Messiah* from the TMC and were unprepared to attend other concerts in sufficient numbers to make the choir's performances worthwhile.

Also in 1962, John Beckwith, by century's end one of Canada's most prolific composers and musical thinkers, under a headline "Mendelssohn Choir Needs Reform," questioned the very nature of the TMC's choral response to a twentieth-century repertoire, declaring that recent efforts to justify the big-choir texture were somewhat pointless: "That texture is indeed in need of justification. In terms of today's musical tastes it is an anachronism. Today's characteristic musical sounds are linear, selective, precisely pointed — whereas a 250 voice mixed choir like the TMC is none of these."

Beckwith opined the TMC's lack of commitment to contemporary works but pointed out how inappropriate the ensemble would be if it did attempt to address such a repertoire. In his view the presentation of the baroque repertoire posed even greater problems: "The TMC does not do much contemporary … but it is even less suitable to present day taste and knowledge in Bach or Handel performance as was proved by Wednesday's distressing and unstylistic rendition of the former's B Minor Mass at Massey Hall."

However it was more than simply an unacceptable performance:"The choir itself is, to judge by last Wednesday, a more uneven and undisciplined mob than in several season's past."[3]

Indeed, by 1964 it was the view of leading members of the TMC board that the choir, even with its prestigious history, would soon go under, perhaps to be succeeded by the TSO aligning itself with another Toronto based chorus (such as the newly created Orpheus Choir) or by a pickup collection of singers to be identified specifically and uniquely as the Toronto Symphony Chorus. Neither option was appropriate in the minds of those who remembered the glory days of previous decades of an organization that had survived for seventy-five years, through two major world wars and a devastating depression. The chair of the board, James Westaway, a most respected businessman and arts supporter, accompanied by Paul Mills and Elmer's close friend Keith MacMillan, turned up at Northview Heights, asked to see Elmer, and, standing in the hall outside Elmer's classroom, put forward a proposition. Westaway, MacMillan, and Mills (the latter had ironically been the person who had informed Elmer of his "firing" as the TMC associate conductor many years before) were determined to save the choir, and having watched the impressive record of Elmer's work with the Festival Singers asked Elmer if he would take over the role of conductor of the Toronto Mendelssohn Choir. Westaway was quite blunt: it would be a mammoth task. The choir was sinking into oblivion at heartbreaking speed. But there would be unimaginable rewards if Toronto's most prestigious chorus could be revived.

Elmer had decided views on the state of the TMC. He had declared to Jessie "if I am ever offered the role of conductor of the TMC, stop me from having anything to do with that operation." He had already suffered one humiliation by this organization almost a decade and a half before and he had also heard the choir at its worst in recent performances.

To revive and to enrich this chorus would not only take a monumental effort, it would be an unpopular undertaking both with choir members who would not survive his initial audition and would have to be asked to leave and with those who remained and would have to be relentlessly rehearsed until the choir's musical prestige was restored. Elmer was already overwhelmed with work as a full-time teacher and with the increasing load of Festival Singer appearances and broadcast dates. He saw no possibility of adding to his responsibilities the transformation of the Toronto Mendelssohn Choir.

What was he to do? One man saw an opportunity in this TMC invitation — his Northview Heights principal and close friend, Lt. Col. James Singleton. He advised Elmer well. The opportunity was very straightforward. Conducting the TMC along with his leadership role with the Festival Singers could allow him to achieve the position of dominance in the choral life of the nation. Surely, with appropriate remuneration for his duties with the TMC, the situation could be manipulated to secure sufficient resources to give up his teaching position and become a full-time conductor of the two major choruses of their kind in the land. It was the only way it could be accomplished. Just a couple of years before he had seen Elmer collapse in his school gymnasium, at least in part from the pressure of overwork and massive responsibility. Singleton also realized how tenuous Elmer's financial situation was, and would be, unless he could replace his teacher's salary with sufficient remuneration to support his maturing family from both these roles. These two sources of revenue, along with other opportunities, perhaps a part-time role with the University of Toronto and other consulting and adjudicating gigs, would surely make it all possible. This was the course of action Singleton advised, along with the caution that if it failed to work out, Elmer would be desperate and penniless, no longer receiving a regular teacher's salary and with no hope of a stable financial future.

In 1964 Elmer accepted the role of conductor of the Toronto Mendelssohn Choir, along with a growing realization that if he could perform a miracle he might take a major leap toward the achievement of his vision of a Canada that was recognized internationally for its choral achievements. Not only did he leave the teaching profession and add the

TMC to his list of activities, he was also able to contemplate moving his family to the Quail Hill Farm property in the Caledon Hills. After so many years of Elmer's ownership and its more recent occupation by his father, Theodore, and mother, Lydia, Elmer was now determined to build his life on that land with Jessie and his children and any other members of the extended Balsillie family, such as Jessie's mother, Elizabeth, who might wish to move with them. It was forty-five minutes from the centre of Toronto, now with well-paved and lighted roads, all making its isolation less threatening. With both children ensconced in schools nearby Jessie could then accompany Elmer to rehearsals and performances of both choirs. As a special enticement, Elmer could see his stars through telescopes that were not overwhelmed by Toronto's constant illumination. He could grow his crops on the rich soil of the Caledon Hills, could feed and watch birds and engage in all the other activities with which he filled his life. Most of all, it would be truly an Iseler family homestead for Jessie and his children.

Elmer knew the TMC restoration would be an enormous challenge. Perhaps the greatest contribution to a solution leading to the creation of a great choir was the fact that the TMC's first conductor, Dr. Vogt, had, with some considerable difficulty, been able to establish a tradition that every choir member would face an annual audition. Voices that had lost their vitality and minds that had perceptibly declined could be weeded out. With this he had addressed the major problem that faced large community oratorio choirs. Their validity was based on the production of exciting massive choral sound but they had also been faced with the conflict of two competing forces — the pursuit of excellence and the ideal of inclusiveness. However, after the Second World War, it was found that large, undisciplined choirs could not address the increasing complexity of choral composition, especially if they were dependent on singers who could not read a score effectively and did not have the vocal quality and impressive volume to contribute to the stunning sound that composers were wanting to create and audiences were expecting to hear.

Yet, the warm ideal of the inclusiveness of the community choir was the pride of such choruses, particularly in the homeland of such institutions, the United Kingdom. Industries, both mines and manufacturing operations, had subsidized the costs of these choirs with some sense that they were raising the morale and increasing the feelings of well-being of the participating employees and their families. The Canadian experience had more to do with the creation of similar ensembles that served people who had left the United Kingdom and were now feeling geographically isolated. The issue was politically explosive and divisive. A.S. Vogt dealt with it by initiating a process that each year disbanded the entire choir in the spring and then recreated it in the fall for the next concert season. All were invited to reapply and, most importantly, to audition, and those who were deemed capable were invited to join the choir for another year. Thus it could be said that all were being treated equally, even extending to those who were applying for membership for the first time and were thus only hopeful applicants rather than returnees.

Needless to say, this potentially unpopular tradition had been allowed to lapse to some extent as time went by and the choir was seen to be sailing on without dramatic erosion of its quality. It was particularly difficult for Sir Ernest to find the time to audition some two hundred singers. Elmer determined that this tradition would now be ruthlessly applied to ensure that a number of choristers with weakening voices and insufficient skills in reading scores could be dropped from the choir's membership list.[4]

Elmer knew that size was not the only contrast that would face him in terms of replicating his success with the Festival Singers. The TMC's membership had very different motivations and expectations to bring to their participation. It was a traditional volunteer community choir. Whereas his Festival Singers were almost all trained, and, indeed, many were soloists in church choirs, and though not yet fully professional with expectations of regular pay, they did by this time receive remuneration for concert appearances and broadcast dates. Mendelssohn Choir singers would be largely recreational in their attitudes and were expected not only to contribute an annual sum to support the choir but also to pay all their expenses of travel, parking, and in some cases child care from their own pockets. Elmer would now be leading a very different ensemble and his success would be tied to his understanding of the members' reasons for singing in the choir and responding to their hopes and fears.

At the turn of the century, Lee Willingham, the conductor of the Bell'Arte Singers of Toronto and now a professor in the Faculty of Music at Wilfrid Laurier University, wrote a doctoral thesis, "A Community of Voices," on the expectations as well the effects of being a member of his choir. He gathered his results around four themes, "Community," "Self-identity," "Means of Restoration and Healing," and "Means of Developing Discernment and Connoisseurship." Through questionnaires, one-on-one interrogations, and small group discussions, Willingham gathered an enormous amount of information about why his Bell'Arte Singers gave up every Saturday morning to rehearse and many evenings to perform when they were living busy and fulfilling lives as heads of families and carrying the heavy responsibilities of demanding employment. Willingham's thesis provided a "story of people who come together regularly to sing: a community of Singers who partake in a meaningful art making experience." It was just such "a community of singers" that Elmer had now agreed to lead.[5]

In Willingham's study, under the heading "Community," certain phrases surfaced: "the sharing of a common bond," which was, of course, "the common love of music"; "a sense of teamwork, of interdependency, of pulling together"; "a safe place to be," with "people who care, take responsibility for each other's well-being" and together "strive for excellence." At the same time, it was recognized that "people bring their anxieties, personal issues, strained relationships, loneliness, shyness ... and their own sense of inadequacy ... and artistic frustration."[6]

Elmer, in his first experience as a very young chorister and TMC rehearsal assistant, had little understanding of these matters, but he had learned much about "community" from his experiences in the classroom, in his work with choirs including the Festival Singers, and in observing the behaviour of teaching colleagues and mentors. Most of all, he had come to know the value of "community" from Jessie, whose family had been his support system through his darkest days. It was a very different Elmer Iseler who now stood before the grand forces of the TMC in 1964, one who now knew something of the psychology of choral performance.

The second collection of the expectations of choir members seeking a "Means of Self Identity" was built around such phrases as "self-esteem, reinforced by singing well," "buying into a standard of excellence," "development of skills," "pride," acting with honesty and truth," "connection to beauty," "belonging to something larger than ourselves," "sense of self-worth," and attitudes that express lives of abundance that are "joyful" and "hoping."[7]

Elmer had entered choral conducting at his father's church in Port Colborne, at the Lutheran church in New Hamburg, in the chorus at the University of Toronto, and with his school choirs with an extraordinary sense of confidence, but the crowning opportunity to understand this need had come from the incredible success of his Festival Singers. Ten years of increasing quality had convinced Elmer that raising the standards of the TMC was his first task, one that would benefit every choir member and lead them to accept his rigorous rehearsals and his demanding quality of performance. Indeed, much to the surprise of those who saw him in these narrow circumstances seeking excellence, he stressed his determination to have people who already had "full-filled" lives in his choirs and his desire to enhance their lives even more intensely. Elmer insisted on recruiting people of warmth, receptiveness, and a sense of humour — none of which attributes could guarantee quality of voice or accuracy of technique. Yet these were elements of character that he stressed at every audition, even in making judgments about those who were to fill the ranks of the chamber choir he eventually sought to make fully professional at the earliest opportunity. He was convinced that membership in the TMC could have the same objective and at his best rehearsals stressed the role of choral singing and its possible role in the living of a full life.

Not many would see choral music as a "Means of Restoration and Healing," but Bell'Arte Singers surfaced such phrases as "brings mental order" and "being receptive to the transcendental" and "a loss of ego." There was the belief that singing in a chorus "opens the human spirit for aesthetic experiences and non-temporal and non-material realities." In short, singing "enlivens the spirit … inspires the soul, replaces boredom with animation" and provides a "sense of peace and well-being," the Willingham study concluded.[8]

Elmer could most certainly find empathy with those seeking to find in their singing a healing of their minds, bodies, and souls. In 1960 he had literally broken down, physically and mentally, but with Jessie's support had returned to his choirs and their music and saw that commitment to greater synergy was the most restorative factor in his new experience of health and well-being. He had emerged from his personal depression of 1960 to 1962 with a very different attitude toward his singing colleagues and a desire to grow in empathy and sympathy with them while achieving the highest choral quality.

Finally, Willingham's singers' identification of "Developing Discernment and Connoisseurship" as a major reason for their participation in choral music was a position Elmer could have readily appreciated. A rehearsal was surely a learning experience, emphasizing the acquisition of "skills in singing" and "vocal technique," the "formation of vowels and consonants," and the opportunity to "express the profound poetic texts"[9]

Though he stressed that performance was the raison d'être for the struggle to achieve choral perfection, Elmer used all the pedagogical techniques he had learned as a classroom teacher for over a decade.

Willingham's questionnaires had revealed no connection between the choristers' concern with ongoing social issues and their performing in a choir, yet he found that there was a general realization that singing had some influence on "the 'cultivation' and 'nourishment' of a mythos that celebrated the notion of a world of justice containing hundreds of musical compositions, plays, poems and paintings."[10]

Elmer spoke and wrote little about these predilections as he faced the immediate challenge of leading the country's most prestigious oratorio choir, but the years of maturity and broad reading since his last interaction with the TMC had created a socially conscious individual who had now connected his music making with the intellectual and spiritual expectations of a troubled society. Clearly, TMC choristers were facing a much more mature and sensitive Elmer Iseler than his colleagues had known some decade and a half earlier and would be better for it.

There was also the matter of the TMC's repertoire. As John Beckwith had observed, the choir had never sought to be a major voice in the presentation of new choral works. Elmer decided he would have to face that issue during the first honeymoon years of his tenure as conductor. Otherwise, the choir would never spill out of the ruts of old favourite oratorios, passions, and masses that they had sung many times before.

Nor had the TMC, since the beginning of the Second World War, been active as a touring choir, either in the United States or Europe. (There had been an attempt to organize a major European tour before the First World War but, surprisingly, as of 1964, no recent effort had been made to revive such an initiative.) Ironically, it was Elmer Iseler, no great lover of travel, particularly by air, who was to take the choir to prestigious performance venues both in the United States and in countries on the continent across the Atlantic.

His years with the Festival Singers had convinced him that mandatory attendance at regular weekly rehearsals as well as a schedule of more performances by the TMC, both in Toronto and outside, could have a real effect on the quality of the choir's sound. Like the annual audition, it would not be a popular step. It would demand energy and time of the choir members and some would not want to make that commitment. It was the only course. Elmer could recreate the success of the Festival Singers — but only at great personal risk — but he had to take a chance that the results would be seen to have made these changes necessary.

Elmer knew it would take a few years, but he was determined to secure a dramatic increase in the quality of the choir's performance. These reforms would outrage those addicted to the established image of voluntarism and the relaxed mode of operation of the TMC. Yet these attributes accommodated and celebrated the amateurism that in turn legitimized the lower standards of presentation. It came to him that the incorporation of the thirty-six voices of the Festival Singers would assist him in making that substantial improvement. This step would, in part, be a solution to another challenge — that of making the Festival Singers into a fully professional choir. More paid nights of choral activity were essential. If those paid evenings were spent with the TMC, both in rehearsal and performance, and were remunerated through the TMC budget, his thirty-six professional Singers would be earning money some fifty nights a year, thereby moving a long step towards raising the revenue to create a monthly stipend.

Even more important, Elmer thought, if he could add the skill and quality of voice of the Festival Singers to TMC ranks, the sound would be significantly better. In 1968, with the assistance of a supportive board filled with directors who shared his vision (the names Westaway, Lawson, Mills, Bradshaw, and MacMillan surface constantly), he made this inclusion permanent and the Festival Singers were now members of the Toronto Mendelssohn Choir. It was a coup of significant proportions, raising the quality of the TMC's sound and enabling them to address and sing a more complex repertoire.

And the coupling of the TMC and the Festival Singers solved yet another issue. The government granting agencies (Canada Council and the Ontario Arts Council) could not support choirs, as normally they were, by definition, amateur. Except for professional leadership, administrative support, and special project grants, choirs were ineligible for operating funding. With a core of paid choristers, these councils could provide grants for the costs of major improvement in choral performance created by this core of professional singers. The fear that such support would have to be extended to every choir in the country was successfully countered by the argument that only the Festival Singers were truly professional and thereby eligible. Elmer had found a way around the professional-amateur distinction that obscured the spectre of money being passed on from government granting councils to every choral organization in the country — at least insofar as this argument could be used against such support of his own Singers. He could improve the sound and technical performance of his TMC, while simultaneously finding resources for his professional Singers and a support mechanism for the TMC. As well, he had found a way to reduce the time for preparation of new works, as the professional core could give leadership to every section of the choir.

Immediately upon his appointment, and within a few months, Elmer was faced with performance challenges. TSO conductor Walter Susskind had scheduled, for the last concert in his final season in Toronto, the Canadian premiere of what was arguably the greatest choral composition of the twentieth century — Benjamin Britten's *War Requiem*. In spite of the TMC's chaotic situation, and aware of all the loud accolades the work had received in other countries, Susskind was determined that the performance of this monumental work had to go ahead even if newly appointed TMC Elmer Iseler had only a few weeks to prepare the choir for conquering what was then perceived (and still is) to be a very difficult score.

As well, the annual *Messiah* had been scheduled in December 1964, with Ernesto Barbini conducting (but with the new TMC conductor preparing the choristers as would be expected). It was a Christmas tradition in Toronto that Elmer could not dare to threaten. It was essential not only that the *Messiah* performances be presented but also that there be some major improvement in the presentation.

Elmer soon realized there was on the prospective TMC's conductor's desk an invitation for the choir to participate in the celebration of the 150th Anniversary of the Boston Handel and Haydn Society in 1965. All these had to be faced with some immediacy. As it turned out, though appointed in mid-1964, Elmer himself did not lead his new choir in public performance in Toronto until the winter of 1965.

The first hurdle, and by far the most challenging at first glance, was to ensure that the *War Requiem* received an outstanding performance. Every major choir of this size around the world was struggling to give premiere performances of this work in its own country. To overcome the shortfall in talent he had inherited and could not sort out immediately, Elmer doubled the number of rehearsals each week. That certainly captured the attention of every member, and a number whose commitment was lacking fled the choir, saving many hours of auditions that would have exhausted him in the coming year. Even regular members who had conquered their auditions were mildly disgruntled at the increased time and effort Elmer demanded. However, the extra rehearsals began to pay off. As the score became more familiar it became increasingly "singable." The performance of the *War Requiem* under Susskind's baton was an unquestionable success.

Reminding his readers of the TMC's former limitations, the *Globe and Mail*'s John Kraglund commented of the *War Requiem*'s performance:

> Yet last night's interpretation held few disappointments
> and set a new standard for the Mendelssohn Choir. But
> then this is a new Mendelssohn Choir reduced to 140
> voices and prepared by its new conductor, Elmer Iseler.

It is a choir that is precise in its attack ... that is capable
of producing flawless, almost inaudible pianissimos ...
that is remarkably securely pitched, and enunciates Latin
with surprising clarity ... The Mendelssohn Choir sang
with the interpretive sensitivity and conviction that
comes only from a full understanding of the work.[11]

Iseler had met the first test and passed with flying colours. On the
basis of that preparation Kraglund, looking back over the musical events
of 1964, could express some satisfaction over Elmer's success in providing
the "improved standards of the Mendelssohn Choir" but reminded his
readers that Toronto "still had to look forward to its first performance
under his direction. So far we have witnessed only the rewards of his
preparation for others."[12]

John Beckwith, whose criticism of the TMC in previous years had been
particularly savage, was thoroughly delighted with the new Mendelssohn
Choir: "We have not had so thought provoking an observation of
November 11th in many years as provided by Benjamin Britten's *War
Requiem* ... its presentation was in almost every respect first class."[13]

Barbini's *Messiah* performance also went better than in previous years,
with a fuller sound and a more precisely articulated text Under a review
headed "Skilled *Messiah*," John Beckwith gave the TMC hesitant praise
by referring to the presentation as "a skilled and effective repair job on
the organization's former good *Messiahs* rather than a totally reconsidered
revival" but conceded that it had been "finely prepared."

The first Toronto concert of the TMC under Elmer's leadership, in
April 1965, was characterized as a festival of choral music and included
the participation of other choirs, two of which (the St. George's United
Church and North York Youth Choirs) were prepared by Lloyd Bradshaw.
Iseler had selected his program carefully, ensuring that the works were a
balance of baroque and modern works. Gabrieli, Monteverdi, Holst, and
Debussy were all included in the eclectic program.

George Kidd pointed out that though there was no great single work
included in the program, the concert had been a success:

It was a rewarding evening and probably the best the Mendelssohn Choir has given us in a number of years. Under the guidance of its new and energetic conductor, Elmer Iseler, it threw away the lethargy of the past and made everything sound right … Watching him conduct one is impressed by the quiet, almost dignified attitude he takes introducing the printed score and making it fully convincing.[14]

John Beckwith wrote admiringly of Elmer's "flair for the musically spectacular" that had made this first public concert under his baton quite an occasion. Elmer had made use of the balconies at Massey Hall and in doing so had "achieved an astonishing freshness of projected sound with antiphonal brass ensembles, one high above the stage, the other in a balcony position, supporting the massed choirs." The Monteverdi had gone particularly well: "And everyone seemed infected by the theatrical rhythmic pulsations of Monteverdi, to which Iseler himself obviously responds with spirit and drive of a special and highly communicative sort."[15]

However, it was the TMC appearance at the Boston Handel and Haydn 150th Anniversary International Choral Festival that truly signalled a different direction. A series of concerts had been arranged featuring such stellar ensembles as Sir Malcolm Sargent's Huddersfield Choral Society from the United Kingdom, New Zealand's Christchurch Harmonic Society, and the Helsinki University Chorus, as well as the host choir, the Handel and Haydn Society Chorus of Boston.

Each choir was expected to give a full concert that would display its own best qualities. The Huddersfield Choral Society performed Handel's *Israel in Egypt* and the Christchurch Harmonic Society presented the Verdi Requiem. Elmer chose to provide a varied program that he had rehearsed for the TMC's 1965–66 subscription series concert presented in October in Toronto. It had included Vaughan Williams's *Serenade to Music* — a work normally sung by a small collection of fine soloists. Elmer had ensured his Canadian content with Godfrey Ridout's *The Dance*, a work that Elmer knew from his secondary school choir days, along with Sir Ernest MacMillan's *Blanche comme la neige* and the work performed by the

Festival Singers that had changed Elmer's career, Stravinsky's *Symphony of Psalms*. Finally, Poulenc's Gloria, a composition that would demonstrate the capacity of the TMC to cope with a recent twentieth-century work of a demanding nature, closed the program. The program repertoire had not excited the Toronto audience that much (though it had challenged the perception of the dull and "tubby" TMC), but Elmer had rehearsed the TMC in that repertoire and had decided it was too late to change.

Comparisons may be odious, but in a situation that provided a concert performance from choirs from all over the world, they were inevitable. To even the general observers of the international choral scene, the conclusions reached by the Boston music critics were astonishing. In their eyes, the TMC was simply the best in the roster of choirs that had been gathered. It was the review of Michael Steinberg in the *Boston Globe* that provided the finest critique the Mendelssohn Choir had ever received, under the headline "TMC best yet"·

> It took just two measures of the Vaughan Williams "Serenade to Music" to establish that the Toronto Mendelssohn Choir is by light years the best of the choruses that have appeared in Boston during the Handel and Haydn Society's International Festival ... There is something fresh, stimulating, vital, about the Iseler-Mendelssohn combination and the result, vocally and musically, is remarkable.
>
> The Mendelssohn Choir's work is pure and transparent ... pitch is impeccable, even in the rather difficult a cappella portions of the Stravinsky "Psalms" ... The direction is superb ... chord and polyphonic textures are always in perfect balance ... the fortissimos are brilliant. ...
>
> Elmer Iseler is a man obviously capable of achieving the best that can be achieved with a big, non–professional chorus.[16]

Elmer and his choristers were ecstatic. The TMC might seem a dull and worn ensemble to some Toronto music lovers — but now, accolades from critics covering an international gathering of great choirs had brought a convincing authenticity to those who had predicted positive results from the TMC revitalization that Elmer had produced. Choral music enthusiasts with long memories had created in their minds a golden age of the early years of the TMC when regular appearances with great American orchestras in major American cities had been initiated and been deemed successful. They had been silenced. As were the pens of the colonially minded who refused to believe that a splendid choir with an international reputation could be singing in Toronto, Ontario. It thrilled Elmer to realize he had triumphed over the small minds who could not believe that high quality was possible in the backwoods of a former British colony in North America called Canada.

Back home in Toronto, the choir was greeted ecstatically and it was obvious that only Elmer's preparation could have brought such adulatory comments. John Kraglund made the uncomfortable point that the TMC had been given a "lukewarm reception in Toronto for the same program" and, quoting Elmer, had been forced to "leave Toronto for recognition."

That summer Elmer was back to Stratford, this time with the entire TMC. He presented a rarely heard work in Canada, Handel's *Solomon*. Performing in the Festival Theatre he had the Stratford Festival Orchestra to accompany members of both his Mendelssohn Choir and his Festival Singers. It did not thrill critic George Kidd, who could only describe it as a "satisfactory but only occasionally exciting reading."

On the other hand, Jackson House, writing for the Stratford paper under the headline "King Solomon is splendid," felt "Elmer Iseler's singers caught the spirit of the piece and delivered every phrase with expert rhythmic drive and warm tonal beauty."

Messiah in 1965 would be the point of success or failure of Elmer's transformation year in the minds of many Torontonians. Barbini had been the object of all the criticism for any failures in 1964. Elmer had accepted the accolades for the better trained and prepared choir but the performance had not been his responsibility. Both critics and audience members had come to resent the slow, ponderous readings of past Christmas seasons. Elmer decided he would make use of the recent rendering of the work by British scholar and composer Watkins Shaw. The Watkins Shaw edition had been produced after a rigorous effort to discover Handel's original concept of the work. The nineteenth century had encouraged choirs to enlarge and distort the work by the use of forces that magnified the output of singers and orchestral accompaniment quite beyond anything conceived by the composer. As a result the tempo had slowed, the nimble movement had disappeared, and the effective articulation of the text had become blurred. The result had become a boring and interminably long evening. Elmer determined that he would change that performance to one that was lively and dynamic and moving. The results could be disastrous. There were those who had become used to this traditional "Victorian" presentation and would be upset by the loss of expectations for a solemn rite that justified their annual trip to this spiritual trough at the Christmas season. Elmer, once again, decided to take the risk — and it worked.

Messiah continued to be sung by the TMC at Christmas in Toronto for many decades to come. It became also an annual journey for Toronto critics Kenneth Winters, John Kraglund, and William Littler, who provided a yearly introduction and assessment of the Iseler *Messiah*, making the city's *Messiah* habitués perhaps the most appreciative, knowledgeable, and sophisticated in the world. Their interplay of *Messiah* critical comment became a favourite topic over Toronto Christmas dinners for years.

As 1965 closed, Elmer's future looked favourable indeed. In spite of the dozens of singers who could no longer find themselves in the TMC's ranks and the many more who did not wish to be driven so relentlessly towards choral excellence, the choir had prospered artistically. The malcontents were to be joined by those who resented both his delving into the archives for rarely sung choral gems and, even more, his commissioning of contemporary repertoire and bringing the results to the attention of both choir and audience. But for the present, Elmer had triumphed. He could not have been more secure and more confident of his capacity to lead the TMC in directions never before pursued before audiences here in Canada and, in later years, internationally.

Chapter 10

Celebrating a Nation's Birthday

AFTER THE TRIUMPH OF BOSTON AND THE success of the first concerts in Toronto, Elmer's Toronto Mendelssohn Choir choristers must have felt they had truly arrived at the some kind of choral nirvana. However, having leaped these initial hurdles had not convinced Elmer that his choir was ready for the future he had in mind. He had, for example, persuaded himself that the choir was not ready for the challenges of touring to the world's great centres of choral music. The 1964–65 concert season with its *War Requiem*, its *Solomon*, its revitalized *Messiah* had certainly taken the choir some distance along the path towards the excellence he believed was achievable, but there was a long way to go.

By the mid-1960s, it was apparent to most Canadians that the centennial of the country's creation as a nation was an opportunity for celebration, not just in 1967 but through the year or two before as well. The British North America Act had been passed in the legislature of another country, the United Kingdom, and had been achieved through no exciting war of independence. Yet the significance of that year 1867 had to be portrayed with some dramatic purpose. The date meant nothing to any part of Canada west of the Lake of the Woods, where in the mid nineteenth century only small colonial outposts existed on Lake Winnipeg and the Pacific Coast. The province of Manitoba was some years away from birth and the provinces of Saskatchewan and Alberta did not exist until decades later. Indeed, even on the East Coast, Prince Edward Island had rejected any part in the new union until 1871 and Newfoundland's involvement in the Canadian nation came only in the mid twentieth century. Amidst all these complications, it would take all the talents and creativity of Canada's artists to make anything of the 1967 festivities.

For Elmer it was an opportunity to display his choirs, particularly the large and vocally powerful Toronto Mendelssohn Choir. The glories of 1965 had been but a quick glance at what was possible. Elmer, with his blatant nationalism on his sleeve, was determined to have the TMC ready for whatever the Centennial Year might bring. There was no doubt that the choir would be invited to Expo '67, the Montreal main stage for Canada's celebrations. But that was only a fraction of the excitement that could be mounted by a country desperate to express its hopes for the future.

Canada had won its independence through shrewd and thoughtful diplomatic action. Two warring peoples had been untied, becoming equally legitimate English- and French-speaking citizens, and had discovered the accommodations to make it happen. In doing so they had been able to make an enormous contribution to the manner in which nationhood could eventually be secured by other colonies of a disintegrating British Empire. Further, this comparatively newly minted nation state had played its part in ensuring the freedom of European and Asian countries in the two ghastly world wars of the succeeding century. As well, in that twentieth century Canada had welcomed more immigrants from other countries to its shores in proportion to its population numbers than any other country on the planet. These were no mean achievements and they deserved celebration.

In Elmer's view, it would be a year in which artists could exponentially raise Canada's awareness of its own strength and artistry. Music, dance, and theatre were historically the mechanisms for remembering the past and its achievements and Canada in 1967 would be no exception. Even more, after a post–Second World War loss of directions in which Canada had seemingly been selling off the control of its economy largely to the aggressive and expansive United States, there was an opportunity for this Centennial to be a source of inspiration for the development of a more positive collective future. With Niki Goldschmidt, the nation's prime arts entrepreneur, as a leading figure providing know-how, 1967 would be an explosion of composing and performing contemporary music and of writing emotionally moving text from coast to coast.

In such a huge land mass, cultures had developed almost in isolation. English Canadians knew so little about the splendid singers and dancers in "la belle province," and French-speaking citizens were unaware that there had been an explosion of artistic activity taking place in English-speaking Canada since the late 1940s and 1950s.[1] These celebrations would begin in the mid-1960s in preparation for the Centennial Year, and musicians, dancers, and actors could thus move across the vastness of the land, bringing both knowledge and the appreciation of the different cultures that now made up a united Canada. Elmer knew well that singing was, by far, the most traditional way of expressing the fact that a different and effective political entity had emerged in the northern reaches of the American land mass a hundred years before. From that realization could come a strong international presence, one that the nation's prime minister of the day, Lester B. Pearson, had already utilized to bring at least an uneasy peace to the Middle East and had received a Nobel Prize for his efforts.

In terms of readiness, the Centennial Year could not have come at a more propitious time for Elmer and the TMC. Elmer did not allow his choristers to rest on the laurels of their Boston experience. When the TSO's new conductor, Seiji Ozawa, included the TMC in his April 1966 performance of Beethoven's Choral Symphony, Kenneth Winters could describe the Mendelssohn Choir as "stunningly good … I don't think I have encountered either the TMC or the Festival Singers in higher spirits or better form."[2]

The TMC had been invited to participate in the gala on July 1 at the Salle Wilfrid-Pelletier in Montreal sponsored by Robert Winters, minister of Trade and Commerce, and Jean Marchand, minister of Manpower and Immigration. The presence of Expo '67 in that city had assured that Montreal would be the central focus of the 1967 celebrations. The gala program exhibited the essential bilingual reality of the celebrating nation. Elmer placed on the program Godfrey Ridout's *The Dance*, a familiar Iseler choice, along with Healey Willan's *Apostrophe to the Heavenly Host* and John Beckwith's *Flower Variations and Wheels*, a new commission with meaning and relevance to such an event. These selections were balanced with exactly the same number of compositions from the pens of French-speaking artists: Pierre Mercure's *Cantata pour une joie*, Calixa Lavallée's *La Rose Nuptiale*, and Roger Matton's Concerto for Two Pianos.

The political balancing had overshadowed the excitement of presentation and any hope of playing and singing a repertoire that could emotionally move an audience. The concert was a perfect mirror of the nation's basic frustrations as well as, ironically, a recognition of its overarching success in joining the futures of the two founding peoples. Even the accompaniment to his singers had to be provided by the Montreal Symphony, an orchestra Elmer knew only by reputation. However, the limitations of the program did not restrain the *Montreal Star*'s music critic, Jacob Siskind, from joining Boston and Toronto colleagues in praising the TMC that had performed "with a sensitivity and professionalism that suggest that the choir can already be ranked among the great choral societies of the world. Under Elmer Iseler's direction it has developed into an instrument of marvelous flexibility."

When in November 1967, the TMC gave its own Centennial concert at Massey Hall in Toronto, it was an amalgam of Elmer's favourite composers, Britten and Haydn, with the centrepiece provided by John Beckwith's musical offering *A Place of Meeting*, including a text written by Canadian author Dennis Lee. It was described as a "gritty poem" that revealed the problems as well as the strengths of the century-old union, particularly about two artists' solemn pessimism over the impossibility of living human lives "in their awful Americanized native land."[3] Not for Lee, not for Beckwith, and certainly not for Elmer was the usual focus of celebration on nothing but the positive achievements of the past century to be expressed in celebratory fashion without also a warning regarding the next decades and their possible threats to Canadian sovereignty.

However, for Elmer, Canada's birthday deserved the performance of what, with all its inconsistencies, is described as the mountaintop of choral expression — Bach's Mass in B Minor. William Littler, in his review of the initial August performance in Stratford, emphasized the fact that the work was "beyond any ensemble ... Bach made this so difficult that we may never hear an ideal B Minor Mass. Perhaps we shouldn't expect to."[4]

However, he conceded that Elmer had come as close to conquering the masterpiece as anyone who had attempted it.

In January 1968, James Westaway, as chair of the TMC board, was still providing stellar leadership. Appropriately it was Westaway who presented Elmer with the Canada Centennial Medal that had been awarded to him "for his contribution to the Centennial celebrations." It was accepted with pride and appreciation. It was during these years that the silver Medal of Paris was awarded to Elmer, an expression of that city's recognition of a man who was making a splendid cultural statement in his performance of fine choral music. It was an appropriate recognition for a conductor careful to commission French-speaking as well as English-speaking Canadian composers.

In his appraisal of the annual *Messiah* at the end of the Centennial Year, Kenneth Winters had provided his readers with a nostalgic review, informing his *Telegram* readers that the Mendelssohn Choir had been "unbelievably transformed" and that the performance had included singing that was at times "quite dazzling" and at others "quite moving" and was an "enormous advance over previous years."

However, there was a price. Elmer was a big man, and his constant standing to conduct many hours at a time, as well as his insistence on driving many miles to reach faraway destinations, had placed inordinate pressure on his legs. As a result he was hospitalized for two and a half months in the winter of 1968, and it was the thrombosis in his legs that had struck him down. It meant that he could not conduct the scheduled performance in that year of the *St. Matthew Passion*. Metropolitan United Church's organist and choirmaster Melville Cook had to take over that responsibility. To his TMC choristers Elmer penned a note that he was "overwhelmed by the affection which you have shown me in your cards and letters. That I had a positively sentimental feeling for you must have been obvious long before this time; I had no idea that the affection was so reciprocal. What a help you have been in my darker moments." In that note to his choir, he expressed his love of the *St. Matthew Passion* in quite emotional terms: "The work is dear to me because it contains the very essence of what is most important in man-God relations and man-man relations — forgiveness and the dissolution of guilt through love. For years I have wanted to bring that message to an audience through the music of Bach and the word of scripture and poetry."[5]

In a perceptive aside in his letter, Elmer wrote that the orchestra had "forgot to resist a choral conductor." This was Elmer's reference to the undercurrent of demeaning comment about his orchestral conducting that he had never fully buried. Year after year, decade after decade, he had been constantly criticized for his technique on podiums in front of symphonic ensembles of able instrumentalists. "We cannot find the beat" was the continuing complaint of orchestra members.

Yet Elmer had taught instrumental music at least at the secondary level for a dozen years and knew the obsession of such ensembles for exact timing. He knew the instruments of the orchestra and their sounds and technical capacities; he had been fascinated by orchestral music long before he had chosen to follow the choral path. Yet, watching Elmer's style of circular, inclusive movements one could understand what the complaint was all about. But, as needed, Elmer could quickly correct that seemingly indecisive baton beat when orchestras specifically requested a clearer time sense. (Howard Cable had once advised a group of instrumentalists that they use his baton's passing of his second shirt button as the beat.)

Elmer was intent on the sculpting of choral sound through expressive hand gestures, often abandoning the baton, drawing attention to the text and its need to be clearly phrased, and, especially for non-professional choristers, providing leadership that encouraged the shaping of an appropriate phrasing to the composition. With sufficient rehearsal his singers understood Elmer's choreographic movement. However, there was rarely time for such rehearsal with a symphony orchestra. Elmer seemed to have made a conscious decision to choose the style with which his choir could achieve the most inclusive and individual interpretation of the music and that would be the most comfortable and expressive for his choristers. He relied on the capacity of professional instrumentalists to look after themselves. Thankfully, there were orchestral players, for example, members of the Canadian Brass, who did recognize his strategy and appreciated the challenge of being a part of his style of music making. They realized that Elmer allowed the music to breathe.

Ron Hambleton's review of the 1968 *Messiah* was particularly flattering. Under a headline that proclaimed "Messiah something of a miracle" Hambleton wrote, "I think he has succeeded in taking Messiah away from the Established Church and giving it back to Handel."[6] James Kent, a CBC Radio music producer who often recorded Elmer, in a letter to John Lawson, the president of the Mendelssohn Choir, expressed the view after he had "compared with work of several outstanding choirs ... the TMC presentation of Messiah is the best in the world."[7] Elmer had evidently passed the test of comparison with the finest choruses in the world.

There were other ways of celebrating the country's birthday and paying homage to a man whose past contributions deserved the appreciation of a nation. Even if this recognition was a year late, it was, in Elmer's view, essential. The man in question was Sir Ernest MacMillan, who, though now retired, had been the towering figure over so many years between the world wars, throughout the Second World War, and during the extraordinary expansion of cultural opportunities in the 1950s and 1960s. Elmer believed that only through music could there be an appropriate recognition. He became the organizer of a concert both of Sir Ernest's own music and of that which this great Canadian musician had most loved. It was certainly a memorable occasion to celebrate a man who had dominated the musical life of the country for several decades, as well as having been Elmer's own mentor at his most vulnerable time.

However, Elmer's most unpleasant task during these early years of his association with the TMC was to dissuade TSO conductors who arrived on the scene (knowing something of the choir's most recent triumphs) of the belief that the ensemble could perform at a moment's notice any composition that included choral involvement. Seiji Ozawa was a dashing figure and had taken on some of the extravagances of his mentor, Leonard Bernstein, and immediately upon arrival in 1965 expressed rampant enthusiasm for the choral repertoire. Elmer cautioned him not to expect too much from the TMC initially. It almost resulted in Ozawa seizing the opportunity to create another TSO chorus under his complete control. But Elmer was adamant.

Yet he could not be too negative. There were in fact other choruses available to Ozawa in Toronto. Karel Ancerl, on his arrival in 1969, also had to be restrained. He, like Susskind, wanted the TSO to perform the Britten *War Requiem* during the first year of his tenure as conductor. However, in this case, it was a work that the TMC now knew well. After the performance Ancerl wrote to Elmer, "I just want to thank you again very much for preparing the Mendelssohn Choir in such a wonderful way for the Britten 'Requiem' performances. All credit to you for contributing so much to the success of the evening."[8]

Elmer's desire to accommodate TSO conductors had to be balanced with his determination to stay on course in the development of a full sound, a stunning intonation in regard to text, and a sensitive capacity to react to the dynamics of every musical phrase. If accomplished, the TMC would be eminently presentable in the large choir category of performance anywhere in the world. It was not an easy task.

The addition of the Festival Singers as the professional core of the TMC certainly had its effect. There was a marked improvement in all the areas of Elmer's concern. The sections were better prepared as regular TMC members sought to keep abreast of their professional colleagues and rehearsals were more productive. Elmer's obsession with tonal quality was indeed paying off, and unlike many large choirs whose specialty seemed to be focused on overwhelming volume, the TMC was developing a most moving rendering of pianissimo passages. Elmer's determination that text must be respected, yea, worshipped, was ensuring that the great poetry set to music could be heard, understood, and appreciated, though there were critics who complained the text was often sacrificed to achieve the most pleasing musical phrasing. As well, the TMC was developing a reputation for singing, whether a cappella or with accompaniment, completely in tune. In the light of the more complex, sometimes atonal scores that were being addressed, it was no small accomplishment.

The 1969–70 concert season marked the seventy-fifth anniversary of the TMC's presence in Ontario's capital city. Though Elmer had been only a small part of that history, he saw it as an opportunity to arouse the pride and raise the morale of a chorus whose latter years before his arrival had given it little reason to celebrate. Elmer felt he could accommodate in January a first-time TMC presentation of Handel's *Israel in Egypt*, in February present the *St. Matthew Passion*, and in May successfully prepare for Dvorak's Requiem. In that year, he also prepared his TMC to conquer a score he came to describe as "complicated as a road map to Florida," Penderecki's *St. Luke Passion* for its Canadian premiere in 1971.

Handel's oratorio *Israel in Egypt* had been ignored for decades even though it was a masterpiece that emphasized choral dramatic expression even more intensely than the infinitely more popular *Messiah*. William Littler indicated that "it was worth a 75-year wait," and Kenneth Winters declared the Mendelssohn Choir "superb" in its interpretation of the work.

Perhaps through lack of rehearsal time, the *St. Matthew Passion* performance of that year received a widely divergent response. John Kraglund was uncharacteristically critical: "In too many of the choruses, the choir was ragged in its attacks and rough in tone, often seeming uncertain what Iseler was after."[9]

Kenneth Winters, however, was positively ecstatic, informing his readers that even though he had come to Toronto only in 1966, he had heard the chorus on the radio on several occasions. He wrote with evident passion: "It was the finest and most meaningful performance of the work I have ever heard ... I have not been more moved or more chastened in years."[10]

Elmer took the occasion to write to his choir about that performance:

> I was moved beyond measure by your complete knowl-
> edge of the score, your physical stamina [three hours] and
> your incredible ability to overcome the break in conti-
> nuity which we all suffered. [The lights went out for
> several minutes during the performance.] None of these,
> however, was as moving as your commitment to the Bib-
> lical text and to Bach's matchless setting! As well as the
> audience, I, too, was a listener. I am most grateful.[11]

That same season, the TMC's Dvorak Requiem was astonishingly the Canadian premiere of the work. Maestro Ancerl once again depended on Elmer's capacity to rehearse the choir in an unfamiliar composition.

He was not disappointed. Kraglund, who had been most impressed by the technical improvements under Iseler's direction was overtaken by "the added bonus of real emotional involvement to make this seem the highlight of their [TMC] season."[12]

Krzysztof Penderecki's *St. Luke Passion* was a composition that had received enormous attention in Europe and had already gained the reputation of demanding the highest expectations of vocal capability. The work took months of rehearsal and without the core of the Festival Singers to provide leadership might have been a disaster. Fortunately, the performance of the *Passion* was a huge success. William Littler was enormously impressed both with the work and with the April performance of the TMC: "What matters most is what was right about the performance, and Iseler ... gave us so much that was right that we owe him more than applause. Last night's achievement was one of the most remarkable of his already distinguished career."[13]

Elmer had every reason to believe that the Penderecki association with the TMC might rank in stature with Stravinsky's adulation of the Festival Singers, bringing international recognition of a similar nature. It was not to be. Even a repeat performance of the *St. Luke Passion* a year later — an unheard of concentration of attention on a single contemporary work — along with the North American continent's premiere of Penderecki's *Magnificat* some years after, failed to capture the audience reactions and certainly did not draw the interest of recording companies as Stravinsky's compositions had done. Nonetheless, the composition's successful presentation of the difficult score indicated that it was now plain that the TMC, under Elmer Iseler, was ready for any choral challenge.

Elmer's arrival at the helm had put the attention of the Toronto audiences upon the unique contribution of the choral conductor. It became evident that one could not overestimate the significance of leadership in achieving excellence in choral presentation. Particularly with untrained voices, it came to be realized that only constant, relentless attention to detail could accomplish anything worth hearing. Every observer of the Iseler performance during these years mentions one attribute, Elmer's extraordinary hearing — the capacity of his ears to catch even the off-key entrance of a single chorister amidst a sea of open mouths arrayed before him.

There was also the matter of continuing attention to taste. Elmer at Christmas 1971 handed over the conducting of the annual *Messiah* to the popular American conductor Roger Wagner. No matter how many times he conducted this Handel masterpiece, Elmer would never admit to a moment of boredom with any performance. He stated again and again that every rendering of the masterpiece brought new opportunities for astonishment. However, he felt this season of the Christian calendar was being monopolized by one composition when there were so many other great works that should be equally familiar to discriminating audiences. Elmer decided, on this occasion, to break the mould.

In early December, the TMC presented an unusual and varied program, including Honegger's *Christmas Oratorio*, Schoenberg's *Friede Auf Erden (Peace on Earth)*, and Roger Matton's *Te Deum*. However, these substantial and quite accessible twentieth-century works simply did not stir the emotions. It was also apparent that no alternative repertoire to *Messiah*, no matter how exciting, could draw the "sold out" sign night after night at Massey Hall. It may seem crass in the euphoria of Christmas to place such emphasis on the number of people in the audience, but the fact is that *Messiah* plays the same role that *Nutcracker* and Beethoven's Choral Symphony performs for ballet companies and symphony orchestras. These works draw a solid box-office response that strengthens the budget of the presenting ensemble and allows the exploration of less popular compositions to be attempted on other occasions. Ultimately, it is this balancing of the wildly popular and the less accessible but important works that allows arts institutions to survive in a world not given to an excess of artistic exploration. However, in 1972 and each year after, Elmer was back on the podium for the multiple offerings of *Messiah* as usual. It was a tradition he could not break.

As well, the decision to invite Roger Wagner as his replacement to conduct the 1971 *Messiah* performances was unfortunate. With all his reputation, Wagner was unable to reach the standards that had been achieved in the previous years. It was clear that the serious Toronto music community wanted *Messiah* as Christmas fare and they wanted it at its best, or if not at its best, then in a format that allowed the full participation of audience members. Elmer returned to the podium in 1972 not only to provide the normal choral presentation, but in that year and for a couple of subsequent years he initiated a singalong *Messiah*, much to the horror of some purists who thought this audience participation was an abomination, indeed, a reprehensible manipulation of the greatest choral work of the ages.

Mendelssohn Choir readiness for any challenge was, by the century's seventh decade, established. Even by the late 1960s Elmer had begun the long journey of planning what would be an incredibly expensive tour to Europe for a choir several times the size of any comparable choral ensemble that had previously visited. It meant convincing government ministries and granting agencies that the appearance of such a choir in major centres in several countries in Europe would enhance the perception of Canada's culture and lead to an understanding that this sophisticated country's economic development deserved investment or at least the establishment of branch plants of major corporations. Also, the presence of excellence in music would convince individuals and families in Europe that Canada had more than just mountains and lakes to visit, but also an array of music, theatre, and dance that deserved attention, thereby enhancing the tourist industry.

It is staggering to realize that the TMC had waited some sixty years through the tenures of several conductors before finally making a foray to the epicentres of choral music in the United Kingdom and European countries across the English Channel. It took all of Elmer's persuasive powers to convince board members, granting agencies, and corporate sponsors that such a tour with so many singers was even possible. It was one thing to take a chamber choir of thirty members, a substantial size for that category of performance, but to transport, feed, and accommodate 160 members was a gargantuan undertaking that would stretch the capacity of both the choir manager, Patti Tompkins, and the choir librarian, the indefatigable Roger Hobbs. The enthusiasm of the choristers was massive, but the practical obstacles were enormous. However, Elmer was convincing, support was forthcoming from both public and private sectors, and it was decided that in the summer of 1972 the Toronto Mendelssohn Choir would go on an extensive European tour.

Having decided that this was the next rational step in the TMC's history, Elmer was relentless in his determination that such a tour should be worth the effort. He was adamant that the choir sing in England, followed by France and Switzerland, and then (after a return stopoff in France) conclude its tour in England. There would be moments for sightseeing, but Elmer ensured that the singers realized that their main focus must be upon performance. Rehearsals must take place before every single concert. He wanted to assure himself that in every venue he could place his singers in the most appropriate setting with full recognition of the varied acoustical properties of each performing space. In some cases, he drove the TMC slightly berserk with his assembling in one configuration, only to rearrange and reconfigure again and again. He was determined that the sound of the Mendelssohn Choir would be remembered for years after the TMC had departed back across the Atlantic. He was also very aware of the risks. It would take only one bad performance and a few negative reviews for this tour to backfire and destroy the careful buildup that had gone on now for nearly a decade since his appointment as the TMC's conductor.

There were those who claimed that Elmer was adding to his own career by such overwhelming preparation. Yet Elmer was not "preaching for a call"; he had no interest in using either the Festival Singers or the Toronto Mendelssohn Choir as a stepping stone to another more lucrative and perhaps more prestigious post either in Europe or the United States. He had already turned down several invitations from abroad. He simply wanted the TMC as Canada's premier large choral presenter to be seen as the equal to any other choir in the world.

The tour began at the Harrogate Festival in Yorkshire. The first performance was in Ripon Cathedral, a magnificent, inspiring structure to initiate the enterprise. It was a perfect venue for the voices of the TMC; indeed, in rehearsal the choir had never sounded better. Although the choir did not receive the wildly glorious reviews that were to greet its appearance on the second tour in 1980, it was clear that the audiences were enthusiastic. Elmer placed on the program several Canadian compositions, including Derek Holman's *Make We Joy*, Healey Willan's *O Quanta Qualia*, and R. Murray Schafer's *Epitaph for Moonlight*, providing an extraordinary range of Canadian music writing. These, along with the compositions of Rachmaninoff, Vaughan Williams, Stravinsky, and Copland made up a wide repertoire of music both familiar and, in some cases, the first hearing for audience members.

John Paynter, a British composer, had been invited to hear the TMC sing his *The Rose* and declared to Elmer that it was the best performance he had ever heard of his motet. The critic for the *Harrogate Evening Post* referred to the evening as a "thrilling experience." Ernest Bradbury in the *Yorkshire Post* told his readers that "the large choir is now without doubt a virtuoso ensemble, hand-picked one would think, and capable of the most varied shades in choral sound, springing from an attention to detail that is most praiseworthy. Added too is a sense of professionalism in programme presentation that British choirs might well copy."[14]

In Paris, at the Church of St. Germain des Près, Elmer was warned that ovations were not a matter of course. In fact, such emotional outbursts were actively discouraged by the church authorities, who considered them an inappropriate response in such a sacred setting. The audience defied tradition and their clerics by giving the TMC a standing ovation. As Elmer put it to a press conference on the choir's return to Toronto, "The reception was beyond belief. The audience almost mobbed us."

However, it was the London critics that Elmer most feared. There were those who resented these colonials seeking to emulate or even outdo those at the very centre of the old empire whose choral tradition they had borrowed. "How dare they?" was a question on the lips of British choral devotees. Thus, the Albert Hall presentation at the famous Prom Concerts was a particular challenge. The critic of the *Financial Times* was obviously impressed: "This is a superb choir of 200-odd voices [which] produced a beautiful sound of great firmness, with plenty of easy power in hand for the climaxes, serene and pure in the chording ... it is plainly a choir of world class."[15]

The TMC tour ended, for Elmer, at the Maltings, the Aldeborough Festival, a distinguished gathering of the finest musicians originally established by composer Benjamin Britten and his partner, tenor Peter Pears. There could not have been, for Elmer, a more intense emotional experience than to have been invited to perform there. For decades he had championed the works of contemporary composers. Britten was the central figure in mid–twentieth-century British music and that country's hopes for the creation of serious music when the composing community seemed to have lost touch with the people around the world. Britten and his colleagues had kept connected. Elmer never gave up his belief that there was a Canadian Benjamin Britten out there, if only he or she would concentrate on choral music making, not waiting for a commission but experimenting with compositional techniques in the confidence that with commitment rewards would eventually come.

The 1972 tour was another turning point for the TMC. Even Torontonians realized that they had in their midst a great choir about whom they could speak with pride. Choristers struggled to be seen as competent and committed when facing their auditions with both courage and foreboding. Prospective singers applied for membership and, realizing the upper limit of numbers had been reached, took auditions but waited year after year hoping that their time would come.

Throughout the 1970s, the TMC was borne aloft by the memories of England and Europe, though appearances at Montreal's Olympics in 1976 and an invitation to sing at the Kennedy Center in 1976 and 1978 added fuel to the pride of place as members of one of a handful of choirs that had captured international space occupied by only a small contingent of ensembles around the world.

Chapter 11

Maintaining Momentum

ALFRED BRENDEL, THE GREAT CONCERT PIANIST, once commented, in a discussion of a performing artist's career, that there is a clarity and focus around both the launch of a career and its conclusion. The area of difficulty resides in interpreting and assessing that long stretch called the "middle years" when the initial excitement must be sustained over an interminable period of time. How does one keep one's edge?

It was a particular challenge for the conductor of an oratorio chorus like the Toronto Mendelssohn Choir. There is not a wide range of works for such an ensemble that can attract a large audience on numerous occasions throughout a single season. The very volume of sound such a chorus produces demands a large, often expensive hall and a multitude of listeners to give the evening a context of success. As well, the wide range of ability and commitment in such a choir forces conductors to choose repertoire wisely, recognizing that for some compositions an extended rehearsal period may be necessary. How does one's conducting and musical leadership serve the less able without boring the most experienced and most capable?

Also, in a large choir, there is the inevitable turnover that may result, not from any disaffection on the part of the chorister, but from the fact that a spouse has been transferred to another city and the singer must resign and move in order to keep the family together. Then there is the reality that new replacements must be gradually introduced to what for them is a new repertoire. Inevitably the conductor is met with an impatience emanating from the established members who know and have sung the composition many times. All this demands a balancing and accommodation that makes a long conductor's tenure with an oratorio choir an exercise in creative imagination.

Yet, there are many excellent conductors who have long tenures on the podium in Ontario and beyond. The host of the exceptional CBC Radio 2 program *Choral Concert* heard across Canada every Sunday morning, Howard Dyck, has been the conductor of the Kitchener-Waterloo Chorus for some thirty-five years and has now taken on the leadership of the Bach Elgar Choir in Hamilton as well. The producer of *Choral Concert*, Robert Cooper, was conductor of the Mendelssohn Youth Choir for over two decades, is still with Chorus Niagara after a decade and a half, and has been with the chorus of the Opera in Concert program for some thirty years. He has recently added the Orpheus Choir of Toronto to his list of responsibilities. Jon Washburn in Vancouver has served his choirs for some thirty-five years, and Gerry Fagan, in London, Ontario, has conducted his Singers and Fanshawe Choir for almost the same period of time. Noel Edison can now measure in decades his work with the Elora Singers, as can Lydia Adams with the Amadeus Choir. On her retirement, Jean Ashworth Bartle could measure a quarter of a century conducting the Toronto Children's Chorus that she founded.

Elmer had soon surpassed all expectations of what he could accomplish with the TMC. There had been a string of successful TMC appearances, under both his baton and those of the TSO conductors, Walter Susskind, Seiji Ozawa, Karel Ancerl, and Andrew Davis, all of whom had come and gone during his regime. He and the TMC had received accolades on the rare occasions he had been able to take his choristers beyond the Canadian borders, in particular, Boston in 1965 and the United Kingdom and Europe in 1972. He was constantly faced with the challenge of finding new horizons to enliven the singing careers of this group of choristers whose expectations had been raised and were making great sacrifices of time in order to be available for both concert and weekly rehearsal.

Elmer had no illusions about the fact that conductors have to earn their right to leadership on every occasion they appear before such an organization. Like soloists, conductors are only as good as their last performance or even their last rehearsal. Choristers must be engaged and inspired week after week and care little about any track record no matter how impressive. Elmer, in a decade, had achieved an incomparable reputation in the field of large-scale choral presentation. There was a long way to go before he could consider retirement perhaps a quarter of a century down the road.

In that short time Elmer had successfully placed his imprimatur on the TMC — it was most certainly recognized as an Iseler ensemble by the 1970s. It had a special sound and flexibility of performance unusual for such a large choir and its reputation had grown gradually but inescapably. It could now be compared to the dominant role the Festival Singers had achieved as a chamber choir in the musical life of the country, a role still unexcelled by any competitor after Elmer's two decades at the helm by the end of the 1960s.

However, there was an important difference between these two choral enterprises that Elmer never quite understood. He might truthfully state that since he had been a founder and the founding conductor, the Festival Singers was *his* choir. However, the Toronto Mendelssohn Choir had been around for nearly seventy years before he had assumed the leading role. After the retirement of the indefatigable and incomparable Sir Ernest MacMillan and a succession of conductors and choral assistants, there was a clear sense among some singers and on the part of some on the board of the TMC that the choir could survive the loss of any conductor. The TMC was now an institution, an ongoing tradition within the musical life of Toronto and beyond. At Elmer's arrival the organization had experienced three choral conductors within a decade, and by the mid-1970s its members had sung under four TSO conductors and several guest conductors for special occasions. Even in spite of its dishevelled state in 1964, there was some confidence in the capacity of the choir to continue no matter the changing face of leadership either on the TMC or TSO podium.

It was now assured that the TMC's *Messiah* would receive multiple presentations each year. From the original single performance, *Messiah* now reached five sold-out evenings at Massey Hall (and eventually Roy Thomson Hall) each Christmas season. Indeed, its presentation would creep into the summer with a performance before a huge crowd at Ontario

Place, the recent provincially created recreation area in the Toronto bay directly in front of the Canadian National Exhibition grounds. There could not have been more effective audience development event for encouraging a full hall at performances of the choir's regular subscription series concerts.

It could be predicted that the Bach *St. Matthew Passion* would have a significant place in the regular repertoire of the choir with a performance at least every few years. However, Elmer realized that only a dynamic repertoire that explored areas never approached in previous decades could keep the TMC spirit alive. There were compositions that had received little attention, ironically, those of Felix Mendelssohn being on the forefront. Other great Bach works had received few performances and deserved more. But even the familiar did not always attract an audience — a performance of the Brahms *German Requiem* presented at a Toronto symphony festival of the composer's work in the O'Keefe Centre drew only a half-filled auditorium. Yet when, in 1974, the TMC sang Vaughan Williams's *Dona Nobis Pacem* for the first time, John Kraglund wrote of the "high excitement" and the "remarkable verbal clarity" and concluded that it was the kind of performance to make one wish Iseler would direct his efforts more often to the less familiar repertoire. Even so there was hope but not an iota of assurance that the finest composition sung perfectly would inevitably bring a crowd to a choir's succeeding performance.

As well there were works by other twentieth-century British composers, particularly Elgar and Walton, whose works had produced a sensation internationally and might well prove to be popular. However, Toronto was changing rapidly by the 1970s. There were people coming from every land on earth and the city was becoming the most multicultural of any in the world. Just singing the works of the mother country's composers would not do. In North America, there was composer Aaron Copland, whose *In the Beginning* was a particular Iseler favourite, and Leonard Bernstein, whose very accessible works *Chichester Psalms* and *Kaddish Symphony* were sung several times by the TMC in the 1970s, but there were others much less known who deserved a hearing, like Norman Dello Joio, whose works would receive more than one performance from Elmer in this decade.

The Stravinsky experience had opened windows for Elmer that he never allowed to be closed. There was some irony in the fact that Elmer had begun his choral efforts in the direction of reviving the great music of the baroque period but had received his greatest acclaim from conducting his singers in twentieth-century repertoire. The highly attractive *Symphony of Psalms* was sung several times in these years and was joined in concert with Honegger's *King David* and Sir Michael Tippet's *Vision of St. Augustine*, the latter in a North American premiere. Even more important, in these years there came a flock of Canadian contemporary compositions.

The arrival of Andrew Davis in 1975 as the TSO's conductor had an enormous impact on Elmer. He had been forced to subdue Susskind's and Ozawa's desire to perform choral works that the choir was not ready to perform, and though Ancerl was certainly a choral enthusiast, he had died after only a few short years at the TSO helm and before he could engage the TMC more than a few times. With Davis, Elmer had a real champion. Andrew Davis was young, had not led an orchestra of his own before, had been trained by David Willcocks in choral music at King's College, Cambridge, and had made his mark conducting the Janacek *Glagolitic Mass* in England and Europe. He actually chose that composition as his introduction to the TSO and its audience. He was energetic and demanding of singers and could appreciate the work that Elmer had put into the Toronto Mendelssohn Choir's transformation.

With Andrew Davis, Elmer was introduced to the symphonies of Gustav Mahler. Davis had announced on his arrival that through his tenure with the TSO he would perform all of Mahler's symphonies. There was considerable reliance on choral involvement in his Symphony no. 2, the *Resurrection Symphony*, and the Symphony no. 8, the *Symphony of a Thousand*, as well as a place for TMC women's voices in his Symphony no. 3. It was clear that Davis would be calling on Elmer quite often.

The other composer for whom Davis had a particular enthusiasm was Edward Elgar. Though Elgar was perceived as a favourite orchestral composer, his *Dream of Gerontius* had become a revered oratorio in the United Kingdom. Davis was determined to give it prominence in Canada as well, and to bring Elgar's other choral works, like *The Kingdom*, to Toronto and to New York's Carnegie Hall listeners. Elmer realized he had an ally in Andrew Davis, and their relationship thrived throughout the dozen years Davis remained as conductor of the TSO.

Elmer revealed that his sense of the dramatic had not eroded by giving Leonard Bernstein's *Kaddish Symphony* its Canadian premiere in the mid-1970s with the actress Geneviève Bujold as the speaker. John Kraglund, while questioning its description as a symphony (a "three-part monologue" suited his perception better), appreciated the TMC as being "in its customary excellent form." It was a work Elmer would repeat a few years later with Canadian actress Martha Henry in the role of commentator. On the initial occasion of the Bernstein work, the TMC had presented Stravinsky's *Symphony of Psalms* "sung with insight and musicianship few other choirs could match," and included in this very full program was the first Canadian performance of Godfrey Ridout's *Pange Lingua*, a work that was soon picked up by other Canadian choirs.[1]

The TMC's tour of Europe in 1972 had made Elmer deeply aware of the cost of touring a couple of hundred singers. A few months after that tour he created a chorus of one hundred voices that could be both toured and presented in the many Toronto venues that were much smaller and more visually attractive than Massey Hall. The choir's new configuration made its debut in a CBC concert of sacred music in St. James Cathedral in central Toronto. Elmer was comfortable with this experiment because it allowed him to introduce works that were less appropriate for either a mass choir or a chamber ensemble. Under a heading, "Enjoyable new choir," a review by Harvey Chusid explained that this chorus would "combine the dynamic range of the former [TMC] with some of the intelligence and intensity of the latter [Festival Singers] to produce immensely enjoyable singing." After hearing the chorus sing Vaughan Williams's Mass in G Minor and a commissioned work by French-Canadian composer André Prévost, *Missa de Profundis*, along with selections of Charles Stanford and Harry Somers, Chusid was impressed by the fact "the choir seized every opportunity for sensitive expression."[2]

The idea of establishing a smaller one hundred-member choir remained on Elmer's choral agenda throughout these years. However, the solution had serious disadvantages. Prospective hosts wanted the full-bodied sound of the entire Toronto Mendelssohn Choir. There were occasions when the case could be made for a smaller number. For example, two of the regular concert programs in the 1974–75 season were shifted from Massey Hall to Yorkminster Park Baptist Church, a structure with splendid acoustics that handled the hundred-voice choir perfectly. Yet a year later, when the National Arts Centre invited Elmer to bring his TMC to Ottawa to a performance with the governor general in attendance, it was clear that the full chorus was expected.[3] The hosts were right — it turned out to be a spectacular occasion with the full 180 voices filling the national capital's magnificent concert hall. The triumph did nothing to resolve the issue of travelling with just one hundred TMC choristers as a way of reducing costs as well as extending the choir's repertoire.

Elmer was to return to Ottawa at the invitation of Governor General Jules Léger a mere two and a half years later for a very different reason. It was the occasion of his appointment as an Officer of the Order of Canada, the nation's highest honour for those who have made a difference to the life of the country and its people. It had been just twenty-two years since his founding of the Festival Singers and just over a decade since his assuming the directorship of the Mendelssohn Choir. He was in good company at Rideau Hall on the occasion of its presentation. The Hon. Paul Martin, Sr., a most respected statesman, was appointed a companion of the Order; W.A.C. Bennett, a former provincial premier; and outstanding publisher Jack McClelland joined Elmer as officers. Elmer never failed to wear the insignia on his lapel at every concert performance.

Elmer had predicted that it would take many years to bring the Mendelssohn Choir up to his standard of choral excellence. Over a decade had now passed and it was obvious that the TMC had reached Elmer's vision of its possibilities. In a review, William Littler ruminated in this vein under a headline "Mendelssohn Choir improves with age." His *Toronto Star* piece began, "There is nothing in Canadian choral music quite like the sound of the Mendelssohn Choir, 180 voices strong, pouring down the nave of a large church."[4]

The year 1976 was a time of celebration in the United States of America. It was the nation's bicentennial and celebrations were in order in Washington, D.C. The Toronto Mendelssohn Choir was invited to give a concert in Washington's Kennedy Center. Elmer was ecstatic, knowing that the TMC would enjoy the tour and the recognition it would bring. However, he believed that the best musical gift that Canada could present was a collection of the more creative works of its own composers now a part of the TMC repertoire. Elmer included in the program Harry Somers's Gloria, Willan's *Apostrophe to the Heavenly Host*, and the Canadian contemporary selection that was the most often sung by his Festival Singers, R. Murray Schafer's *Epitaph for Moonlight*. In spite of the nature of the occasion, these compositions received a particularly enthusiastic ovation.

Elmer himself was especially anxious to present great works that had mysteriously been ignored or forgotten. In some cases, he discovered that sometimes these works did not carry an entire evening, nor were they able to keep an audience fully engaged. He developed a format that brought excitement and public acclaim. A 1977 performance of Liszt's *Missa Choralis* was given a new relevance by inserting between the movements short but appropriate compositions of Britten, Brahms, Schoenberg, Verdi, and John Paynter. It aroused an excitement that the work presented in a traditional presentation could not have achieved. Though this arrangement aroused the ire of some church music aficionados, Elmer replied that in a normal presentation in a church setting, the work would have been interrupted by prayers and various readings from scripture. The more traditional were not convinced, but the most amazing event took place on one occasion after such a concert had concluded. The most enthusiastic audience response to an encore was not for the repetition of the Brahms or Verdi — it was for a second hearing of the selection by John Paynter. One observer, Fred Graham, a student of Elmer's and a respected organist and choral director, concluded that contemporary music had made some strides in acceptance with Toronto audiences.[5]

Another composition that Elmer believed deserved performance was David Fanshawe's *African Sanctus*. He was determined to give the work its Canadian premiere. This unusual but exciting work sought to link the Christian message to the colour and exotic sounds of the African continent. It required special tapes of African equatorial forest rainstorms and chanting voices along with a full symphony orchestra augmented with extra percussion. Elmer brought Fanshawe to Toronto on the TMC's Canadian premiere but critics failed to find the music original or particularly attractive. The technology of directly inserting the African contribution by playing tapes rather than integrating the authentic music with his own western European style of composition was, for some, a distracting methodology. Elmer repeated the work again in 1979 but the technology failed and the performance was distorted by the absence of the essential taped interventions. Despite this lack of enthusiasm, this composition has had three thousand performances around the world since Elmer's advocacy in Canada.

In 1978, the TMC returned to the Washington, D.C.'s Kennedy Center, this time with the Canadian Brass. On this occasion Elmer provided a program largely made up of works by Canadian composers André Prévost, Derek Healey, and Harry Somers. It was an enthusiastic audience that brought Elmer back for encores, and once again the Canadian Brass excelled as the accompanists. Members of this brass ensemble developed a special relationship with Elmer and his choirs during the 1970s. Indeed, the Canadian Brass came to credit the success of the ensemble to the exposure they received participating in Festival Singer and TMC appearances, both in Ontario and on the Continent in these years when the group was just starting a unique career that combined splendid arrangements of the classical repertoire with a capacity for high comedy. Elmer particularly liked using them as accompanists, first, because they were flexible, and their playing could meld with singing to produce a superb sound. The balance of voice and instrument was perfect. As well, they enjoyed playing selections as a solo ensemble that gave variety to a choral concert without diverting audience attention from the central theme.

On the other side, the members of the Canadian Brass were Elmer's greatest supporters. Trombonist Gene Watts, one of the founders of the ensemble with tuba player Charles Daellenbach, puts it quite directly: "Working with Elmer was the highlight of our musical career — he taught us so much, how to reach out to an audience, how to develop effective programs." It was Watts's view that Elmer intuitively organized the repertoire of his programs to create the most dramatic effect. Some instrumentalists found his beat lacking "definition," but the Brass revelled in the shaping of sound under Elmer's hands moving and moulding sensitively every individual phrase. Indeed, Elmer was hired by the

Canadian Brass to conduct a recording session of vocal music composed by Gabrieli but arranged for brass instruments. The Brass was joined by members of the New York Philharmonic and the Philadelphia Orchestra. "Elmer was superb," Watts concluded. "He captured the attention of the major troublemaker in the ensemble from New York and bonded with him immediately. It all came off splendidly."[6]

As for Elmer, he revered the Canadian Brass's excitement for performing that was displayed by their willingness to entertain TMC audiences before concerts, during intermissions, and long after the choristers had left the stage. Their delight in making music led Elmer to make use of their services and to encourage other musical organizations to hire them on every possible occasion. Elmer became the ensemble's foremost informal promotion agent!

In these years Elmer himself had to face the question of "where do I go from here?" By the end of the 1970s, he had conducted the TMC for a decade and a half. In the last two years of that decade he had faced the most devastating experience of his career — he had been removed as conductor by the Festival Singers board, ignominiously "fired" as the conductor of the choir he had founded and had developed to extraordinary heights. Could an even longer tenure with the TMC result in a similar debacle?

Although he had faced extended absence for illness on two occasions — the early and late 1960s — his health, except for some bother with his legs, was excellent in the 1970s. He was only in his fifties, but orchestral conductors, perhaps because of the enforced exercise that is central to the function of the job, have tended towards extraordinary longevity. Indeed, the final octogenarian years of such a career were often perceived as the best of their lives. There was no reason why he could not emulate his orchestral counterparts (an Arturo Toscanini) and extend his performing life for another two or three decades. Surely the same mental and spiritual motivations of addressing the great masterpieces of the ages, bringing new insights to their interpretation, would lead a choral conductor to enjoy a comparatively long and productive life.

Elmer had been subjected to a flood of invitations from prestigious organizations such as the Handel and Haydn Society in Boston and from a number of faculties of music in American universities who saw in Elmer an opportunity to occupy a distinguished niche in the preparation of choral conductors. However, Elmer never seriously considered these invitations — and for good reason. He had the finest two choirs of their kind in Canada, perhaps in North America, and comparable to any in the world. He knew from experience how much effort would be required to bring any new choir up to his standards of performance: "I would have to start all over again." He knew this struggle would then replace all the excitement of discovering little-known gems of the past or commissioning new compositions from contemporary composers and experiencing the thrill of giving them stellar premieres.

Most convincing of all his reasons for remaining as the conductor of the TMC and the Festival Singers was that he did not want to leave Canada. He had attended the Faculty of Music at the University of Toronto along with a host of musicians, composers, and arrangers who had made the choice in the late 1940s and 1950s to remain in Canada. Thankfully there had been a large number who caught the collective virus of Canadianism, and their presence in the 1950s, 1960s, and 1970s had resulted in an explosion of musical achievement in their homeland. Elmer had no desire to leave all that.

His vision was to be a contributor to the choral culture of his own native land, one he cherished. If he went to the United States, there might be an increase in remuneration but there would be no sense that he could accomplish comparable results in the lives of that huge population. Yes, there was also the "big frog in a little pond" syndrome that undoubtedly influenced his choice. Especially by the mid-1970s, with his Order of Canada on his lapel, he was receiving acclaim and recognition in his homeland that as a choral conductor he would have had difficulty achieving in the more heavily populated country to the south. But perhaps even more important, he had no confidence that he could live as closely tied to the values he cherished as his remaining in Canada allowed. The thought of abandoning the Caledon countryside and adopting the competitive style of the American dream had no capacity to seduce Elmer from the country whose citizenship he treasured.

Elmer, in his career flight, had experienced an almost instantaneous success followed by a stunning trajectory by the mid-1960s that meant that before he was thirty years old he had established his pre-eminence as a conductor of Canada's finest chamber and eventually its first professional choir. Before he reached the age of forty, he had been appointed conductor of Canada's most prestigious large oratorio choir. Where else could he replicate that experience? Where could he now go to achieve the personal level of satisfaction in exploring not only the finest repertoire from the ages but also the twentieth century's contribution to that genre of music presentation? Even more, he would have to give up that relationship, abrasive as it might be on occasion, with all those Canadian composers who had emerged from John Weinzweig's classes at the University of Toronto and who had been joined by colleagues from abroad to settle in a country they believed had excellent prospects of success.

There were those critics who would claim that Iseler feared the competition of working close to others in a more musically established context like New York City or Paris. There he would not have been the acclaimed prestigious pioneer but would have had to accept the genius of other colleagues and accommodate himself to their visions of a choral paradise. That theory falters with the realization that Elmer was not alone on some mountaintop in Canada but was in contact with dozens of other conductors; from abroad, in the 1950s and 1960s, there were Helmuth Rilling, Sir David Willcocks, Robert Shaw, and Dale Warland, and in Toronto there were Lloyd Bradshaw, Melville Cooke, Roland Pack, and Giles Bryant.

In Canada, by the late 1970s and 1980s, Fagan, Washburn, Riddell, Dyck, Adams, Barnum, Fallis, Willingham, and Cooper were all making choral music of considerable quality and were simultaneously pushing against the inadequacies of the choral music community. In the West, there was Bruce Pullan and his Vancouver Bach Choir and Diane Loomer with her Electra Women's Choir. Certainly by the 1980s, several splendid choral ensembles were reaching professional status. Jon Washburn was making enormous strides in Vancouver moving toward the creation of his own ensemble. Wayne Riddell had established his Tudor Singers in Montreal. Both were determined that their choirs should also become recognized for their choral excellence. Michael Gervais, inspired by Elmer and Jessie, was creating another professional choir, Pro Coro Canada, in Edmonton, Alberta.

In Elmer's own home base of Toronto, his example was having the effect of producing a plethora of fine choirs both in the city and in southern Ontario. They had come to include a Tafelmusik Chamber Choir led by Ivars Taurins that, in association with the Tafelmusik Baroque Orchestra, was splendidly addressing a baroque repertoire and competing with Elmer for a *Messiah* audience each Christmas. Decades later Brainerd Blyden-Taylor established a professional chamber choir dedicated to Afrocentric music of all styles, including classical, spiritual, and gospel music. North of Toronto, Albert Greer was singing and conducting, thereby making a major contribution to the collective choral arts expression in the Barrie-Orillia region. This is only a bare sampling of the rich phalanx of colleagues who were to be found on other podiums leading both amateur and professional ensembles. Elmer welcomed each one, indeed expressing the view that there should be a professional choir in every province. He did so knowing they would dilute the support of both the CBC and the granting arts councils as well as the audiences upon which his own choral organizations depended.

Of particular interest was the work of Barbara Clark in the nation's capital, who became a legend in her own time, reaching young people with outstanding leadership and in co-operation with a colleague, Brian Law, improving the choral response of the entire Ottawa Valley. By the end of Elmer's life, in the Kingston area, Mark Sirett was carving out a unique career as both a conductor and composer. To the West of Toronto, Noel Edison had established his Elora Singers, and even before that ensemble was in place, Gerald Fagan had established a reputation for extraordinary performance by his choirs in the London, Ontario, region. Wayne Strongman had founded his Tapestry Singers but had moved west to Hamilton to lead the Bach Elgar Choir to new levels of achievement. Gerald Neufeld, too, had blessed Elmer's university haunts in the Waterloo area with his impeccable treatment of the great classics, and Deral Johnson was making an intense and ongoing commitment to the development of young choristers. Even farther west, Richard Householder had made great strides in both teaching and conducting choral music. This sampling ignores the excellent work of Jean Ashworth Bartle, Linda Beaupré, Eileen Baldwin, and their colleagues with children's choirs that were excelling far beyond what was expected in previous decades.

There was no reality to the image of a solitary choral genius at work through all these years from the 1950s to the 1990s, either in Toronto, in Ontario, or across the nation. One could fill a page with the names of choral conductors being trained and inspired by a perambulating and indefatigable Elmer Iseler, then taking over existing choirs and founding new choirs, thus making Canada into the "singing nation" that Niki Goldschmidt constantly celebrated.

These same critics would claim that Elmer's lack of formal training, his personal unwillingness to engage in established patterns of formal education, his reported reluctance to accept a sabbatical that might result in his taking new directions, and his perceived disinterest in travelling abroad to interact with other conductors in other countries from whom he might learn were indications of a fear that such engagements would only reveal weaknesses he could not face. These unsubstantiated negative observations reveal a lack of appreciation that Elmer was almost continuously in a learning mode that he fashioned from his own experience. He had a splendid library and spent extraordinary numbers of hours in his study at his own Quail Hill Farm. He consciously considered all the options before him and decided that concentrated attention to his specific learning needs was the only path that appealed to him and, for practical and financial reasons, the only one open to him. For those captured by society's loyalty to paper qualifications from famous learning institutions, and convinced that all wisdom must come from abroad, Elmer was an enigma.

It could be argued that Elmer might have struck out on other new paths. An example of one option that was never considered was the one taken by the respected choral conductor Robert Shaw, whose work with the Atlanta Symphony and its Chorus was unexcelled in the United States of the late twentieth century. He was very much a contemporary of Elmer's who had, like him, achieved enormous prominence in the United States in the 1950s and 1960s, but who in mid and later life had found his place as a conductor of an orchestra with a chorus that could be shaped into a splendid ensemble. With his orchestra and choir in a wealthy community, he was able to present an outstanding array of great choral performances and could, as well, see that these treasures were preserved in numerous recordings.

However, the Robert Shaw phenomenon occurred in a country with the many symphony orchestras available to invite his leadership. Certainly in Canada there were only a handful of professional orchestras of sufficient quality to play the role of the Atlanta Symphony Orchestra. As well there was the colonial mindset that refused to concede that Canadians could possibly aspire to such heights of musical activity. With the exception of Sir Ernest MacMillan, Victor Feldbrill, Mario Bernardi, Boris Brott, Alex Pauk, and Simon Streatfeild, there have been few who have conducted major orchestras in Canada. Orchestras, even those at the community level, with only a professional core at their disposal, seemed to prefer to be kept safely in the hands of European conductors with European experience on which to draw.

For Elmer, seeking out this possibility held no attraction. He had eschewed orchestral conducting even though he had taught orchestral music for a dozen years at the secondary level until he had abandoned that genre of music in order to bring his entire attention to the choral repertoire. His vision of what he could achieve was based on that decision of how he might best use his time and energy. His career from that point was focused on voice and text and the special relationship of chorister and conductor, one so very different from the cooler, more distant, sophisticated interaction with instrumentalists, one that pervades the internationally accepted models of orchestral conducting and leadership.[7]

John Reeves, a Canadian composer and distinguished CBC producer, as well as a close friend of Elmer's, suggests that it was a tragedy that Elmer did not have the opportunity to launch a series of recordings of the great choral works of the past — perhaps interspersed with the works of Canadian composers. The choirs were in place, but the resources were absent, especially in Canada, which had no viable commercial recording industry.[8]

There was another option — one that had been followed by another of Elmer's closest colleagues, Sir David Willcocks in the United Kingdom. He had established his reputation as a pre-eminent choral conductor but kept a strong hold on an active and creative academic career. This might have been Elmer's choice. He had been invited to teach in the Faculty of Music at the University of Toronto in the mid-1960s. He was an experienced instructor but the timing of this intervention was off. It had only been a couple of years since his full-time employment as a secondary school teacher. He needed more opportunity to forget the exhaustion and frustration of York Memorial and Northview Heights. He took on this responsibility when the pressure of raising the sights of the Toronto Mendelssohn Choir was too much in his thoughts. A few years later he might have been able to concentrate on the complexities of balancing all the roles with choirs and his work at the university. Unfortunately he could not seize the opportunity to establish a proper relationship with the university community that would have grounded his academic colleagues' confidence in his unorthodox philosophy and methodology of teaching music to younger people.

It was Doreen Rao, in the last months of his life, who secured an adjunct professorship for Elmer at the University of Toronto, and he was delighted with this work in the few opportunities his failing health allowed him to be with students. But it was too late — he died in the year following Rao's initiative.[9]

Elmer himself spoke of a dream. With minimal construction, Quail Hill Farm could become a college for the training of choral conductors. He made no specific plans, but a graduate school for only a handful of conductors at a time might just have been an answer to the lack of such training in Canada at that time. There would have been no overseeing process, no formal degree-granting power, just the genius and commitment of Elmer Iseler. With Jessie at his side to look after the practical details, Elmer could have invited other colleagues to assist in carrying out his ambitions.

Thus Elmer remained in Canada and provided leadership for almost another two decades. During those years, to be known here and abroad as the "golden years" of choral performance, Toronto audiences continued to be thrilled by great concerts of magnificent choral works. It is hard to believe that during a few months in 1978 he was confronted each week at rehearsal by a TMC that included some of the Festival Singers who continued to sing for him even though the latter organization had rejected his leadership. These Singers continued to make up the professional core that Elmer so depended upon. It lasted for only a short period. By the 1978–79 concert season, members of his planned Elmer Iseler Singers (sometimes the same individuals) were replacing choristers from the soon-to-be defunct Festival Singers.

By the 1980s, Elmer was preparing perhaps the most exciting experience that his Toronto Mendelssohn Choir would have — a second trip to Europe and the British Isles. It was to be another triumph that would bring honour to the country he so passionately loved.

Chapter 12

Clearing the Bar — Keeping the Faith

ELMER REALIZED THE EXTENT TO WHICH THE 1972 tour had established the Toronto Mendelssohn Choir's international reputation both at home in Canada and abroad. Another trip by 1980 was an opportunity to prove that the 1972 adulation had not been misplaced — the TMC at the very top of its form was a choral ensemble second to none of its kind in the world. Those who were working so hard to find the resources could not have known that this tour would be the last such event for the Toronto Mendelssohn Choir, not only in the twentieth century, but to this point in the twenty-first century as well.

Thus, in August of 1980, it was back to Europe for the Mendelssohn Choir, accompanied by the Canadian Brass. The tour began, as before, at the United Kingdom's Harrogate Music Festival, but, on arriving on the Continent, moved to Belgium, particularly the Flanders Festival in Bruges, and on to the Huy and the Stavelot Festivals. As in 1972, a return to the United Kingdom was scheduled later in the tour, in this case to the vaunted Edinburgh Festival, where the TMC would sing for the first time, initially in St. Mary's Cathedral and two days later in Usher Hall, accompanied by the London Philharmonia Orchestra. Then it would be on to the BBC Prom Concerts in Albert Hall — the tour's artistic culmination at what had become the very centre of musical attention every summer in the British Isles.

Although Ripon Cathedral in Yorkshire was the host venue for the tour launch as it had been in 1972, this time Elmer had complete confidence in his command of the cathedral's acoustics. The critic of the *Harrogate*

Herald generously commented, after reminding his readers that the TMC had been there eight years before, "it is evidently an exceedingly well-trained and disciplined body of singers, and Elmer Iseler the conductor conveys his instructions by firm gesture without a baton. The result is a magnificent clear ringing tone, thrilling at climaxes, yet flexible enough to provide varied degrees of expression."[1]

At the Flanders Festival, the choir was faced by an audience prepared to greet them warmly. It was the final event of the festival's program and the presentation was called the "Canada Memorial Concert" in commemoration of the Canadians who had lost their lives liberating Belgium from the Nazi forces in 1944. The TMC rose to the occasion. A local critic observed, "The ensemble leaves a powerful and imposing impression. The choir of 160 persons is quite something ... the flexibility of the choir, the extraordinary homogeneity, its well measured vocal balance captivate the audience. Moreover the choir gives evidence of great erudition."[2]

At the next stop in Huy, Belgium, the TMC performance was equally satisfying. The review in the Huy press exclaimed, "It would be too little to say that this exceptional group of Canadians [160 choristers and musicians and the members of the Canadian Brass] drew enthusiastic response from the two hundred music lovers present. These choristers and musicians, who demonstrated a dazzling vocal technique and rare musical sensitivity, received a genuine ovation at the close of the concert."[3]

At the Stavelot Festival a day later, Elmer and the TMC were confronted by a series of disasters. The abbey in which the choir was expected to sing turned out to be an uninhabitable ruin. When the choir completed its trek to the small Église Primaire nearby, it was discovered that the only organ accompaniment would have to be produced by a tiny portable instrument of highly questionable quality.

There was some uncertainty around whether an audience would appear — the presence of the choir had been heralded by an outdoor speaker on top of a car that had wended its way through the town all day — but this rather unsophisticated promotion did in fact create a crowd for that evening's performance. The TMC received a standing ovation and the antics of the Canadian Brass at the end of the concert "created a sensation." An invitation to return to the Stavelot Festival as soon as possible was immediately transmitted to a delighted Elmer Iseler.[4]

The Edinburgh Festival was perhaps the most prestigious such event in Europe and that was the next stop. The *Edmonton Journal's* drama critic, Keith Ashwell, began his review of the concert with a question: "Curtain Call in a Cathedral?" "That's what the applause amounted to at the end of the 34th Edinburgh Festival. It was so sustained the audience, that filled every chair that could be found in St Mary's Cathedral, got its reward — an encore. It was a triumphant evening."[5]

However, there was no doubt about which presentations would be the climax of the tour. It was the two performances at the BBC Proms in the Albert Hall in London. Not only would there be several thousand in the audience, but the radio broadcast of the event would reach possibly 37 million listeners across the United Kingdom and over the BBC World Service. Elmer, who had begun his career as a singer and conductor with CBC Radio was aware of the importance of this invitation. The choir sang Walton's *Belshazzar's Feast* with the BBC Orchestra and Chorus under Mark Elder and, two nights later, the Bruchner *Te Deum* with the Philharmonia Orchestra under Andrew Davis, that year still officially the conductor of the Toronto Symphony Orchestra.

William Littler reported the review of Robert Henderson of the *Daily Telegraph*, who wrote of the TMC, "Its firm, decisive, clearly textured sound was admirably suited to Bruchner's weighty, totally unsentimental choral writing. Sensitive to the music's spiritual incandescence as well as to its breadth and grandeur, it made a majestic climax to a program devoted to works composed during the 35 years between 1880 and 1915."[6]

Perhaps the best response had come from the mouth of a hardened trumpet player in the back row of the Philharmonia Orchestra who called to his colleague, "How can this Canadian city afford to have a professional choir of some hundred and fifty singers to send to the U.K.?" It was clear that these musicians who had accompanied a host of choirs from their own country and nearby European centres had actually concluded from its quality that they had been listening to a fully professional chorus. What higher accolade could there have been?

There was no doubt that the tour had been an outstanding success. How sad that a quarter of a century later, with the increase in the costs of travel and accommodation, the TMC has not been able to return to the touring glories of the 1970s and 1980s. As William Littler, after three weeks of assorted delights and discomforts in the company of the TMC, put it, "They were a choral army, disciplined <u>on</u> stage, full of individuality <u>off</u>. They did their job well."

The loss of international touring was tragic, particularly since invitations continued to come to the TMC from festivals taking place in every part of the western world. Unfortunately even U.S. cities some distance from the international border became out of the question as destinations to which large numbers of singers could be transported. For choristers who had revelled in the excitement of great cathedrals and glorious concert halls and who had been treated as gods from the resplendence of the New World after singing in the finest arts venues of Europe's past, it was disappointing. The decade that included the 1972 and 1980 tours later became the golden age now, in the 1980s and 1990s, beyond all reaching. The impact of this restraint on morale did not affect the quality of performance by the choir in Toronto and its environs in the 1990s. There is no evidence that the choir remained in a state of debilitation for all these years awaiting the return of those past triumphs, but there were moments of nostalgia shared by older choir members with new recruits who listened in obvious awe to those who had experienced those magnificent weeks abroad.

Elmer took the Mendelssohn Choir almost annually to Niki Goldschmidt's Guelph Spring Festival, realizing that it was not only the first of the music festivals that had come to grace the province of Ontario but, at that time, also undoubtedly the finest. Elmer particularly loved to conduct his singers' voices in the impressive Church of Our Lady that towers over the city. Another of Niki Goldschmidt's festivals in Sault Ste. Marie also attracted the TMC, even though it was at some distance from its base of operations. It was particularly significant that even before foreign travel became prohibitively costly Elmer had given equal, indeed pre-eminent attention to local provincial festivals rather than confining his TMC's appearances to those in other lands at great distance. As the

TMC entered the 1980s, this commitment to Canadian culture, through festivals in provinces both west and east and more restrained tours that included workshops with local choristers and their conductors, stood the choir well now that such foreign invitations were now virtually impossible to accept.

The choir's 1985–86 concert season included the ninetieth anniversary of the TMC itself as well as the centennial of the birth of Healey Willan, Canada's most prestigious church music composer. A "Willan Week" was proclaimed in Toronto and his *Coronation Suite* was part of a TMC concert. But Elmer was determined that Willan's fame would not be allowed to overshadow the presence of a dedicated and talented group of composers who had now become the master's successors. In that same concert, the works of Harry Somers, Derek Holman, and Norm Symonds were also given performances. By this time, performing contemporary Canadian composers had become an Elmer Iseler challenge and passion. Just a week before the Willan celebration he had his singers perform the work of one of his favourite composers, John Reeves, in particular, his Four Motets. He realized it was a feat of balancing the unfamiliar with the historical and traditional, but he was determined to lean towards a greater recognition of the contemporary and the experimental that he believed necessary if Canadian culture was to be served.

The decades of the 1980s and 1990s were characterized by a worldwide emphasis on choral music that without question placed Toronto on any map of cities with a commitment to that genre of performance. The guiding force for the two Toronto international choral festivals that took place during a single decade was Niki Goldschmidt, who on both occasions gathered a prize committee of choral music enthusiasts and successful businessmen and convinced federal and provincial ministers of culture, the Canada Council, the Ontario Arts Council, and the Toronto Arts Council, along with a bevy of corporate donors, that nothing could make city, province, and country more culturally respected than the presence of great choirs gathered to sing the most sublime choral music ever written. However, without the presence of a TMC that could now perform anywhere in the world and be greeted enthusiastically, the presentation of such festivals in Toronto would have been ludicrous.

On each occasion, the TMC performed several times and addressed an exciting and demanding repertoire. Choir people around the world now knew of Elmer's reputation for both his chamber and his oratorio choirs and were willing to make the effort and pay the cost of travelling to this northern land to be on an illustrious program with great Canadian choirs as well as those from other countries.

By the 1980s Elmer had achieved many of his early goals. He had produced two choirs with a sound he knew could compare with choirs of equal size around the world. But the world was changing and it was not in a kindly fashion for those who saw their future in the arts. Amidst the letdown after the Centennial Year, it had been thought that time would prove the need for society to invest in the dynamic forces that would alone bring prosperity and development in a world economy that now elevated creativity and imagination as opposed to cheap energy and a trained mass of workers. However, Canadians and their political representatives could not connect the arts, too often termed "entertainment," with the creativity that resulted in the brilliant management and the emergence of invention that could transform a tired economy.

When a recession occurred as it did in the early 1980s, and government revenues decreased, it was seen prudent to severely limit the public resources going out to both education of the young and the artistic initiatives that were perceived to be an inconvenient drain on public resources. The government restraint was severe, and those things perceived as peripheral in the wake of the economic turndown, or not connected to arts industries that raised the gross national product, or not centred on an expansion in the private sector, were seen to be trivial. Needless to say, by the 1990s, amateur choirs were dropped from the Canada Council's list of granting priorities. Elmer travelled to Ottawa again and again to meet Canada Council officers, to argue for at least a restoration of the limited support previously provided to choirs across the nation. As late as 1994, when the TMC was celebrating its hundredth birthday, Elmer found himself back in Ottawa seeking to secure the $45,000 grant to his TMC that had been cut off the previous year.

In spite of these frustrations, Elmer's energy and creative vision was focused on opportunities for the Toronto Mendelssohn Choir to sing great music, now almost exclusively in Toronto and nearby, but never losing hope that the winds of change would blow in the proper direction and international touring could be resumed. Ultimately, as a result of this persistence by Elmer and his colleagues, there was indeed some reinstatement of funding for choral music — but only after an enormous output of time and energy.[7]

In the meantime it was a matter of carrying on with style — no matter the continuous pressure of financial need. One of Elmer's strategies during these years was to include the Toronto Mendelssohn Youth Choir in its programming. His interest in young singers never waned and Robert Cooper had produced a splendid ensemble quite capable not only of singing a challenging series of concerts in their own right but also of distinguishing themselves performing in joint concerts with the members of the TMC.

There was also the attraction of presenting great solo voices. International star Kathleen Battle was one of Elmer's significant finds and received flattery beyond compare when she performed Handel's *Solomon* with the TMC. The glorious sounds of Maureen Forrester were heard often but these were also years when Catherine Robbin came into her own as one of the finest soloists that the country had produced. Elmer ensured that the soloists he hired were of the highest quality his budget could afford. There was the rare occasion when Elmer's soloist had to be replaced after a first *Messiah* performance proved the inadequacy of a soloist's voice production or preparation. It proved Elmer was human — he could make a mistake.

Elmer saw the advantage of providing a variety of solo voices, but there were certainly favourites such as Lois Marshall who sang year after year with the TMC. He also ensured that a great emerging Canadian talent, like a Michael Schade or a Russell Braun, was given the opportunity of singing with a splendid TMC and before a large audience. Elmer's Canadian nationalism did not lead him to restrict his choice of soloist to Canadian voices, as this would in itself have diminished the value of such a presentation both for homegrown singer and local audience. Thus, Elmer became responsible for the presence of an extraordinary array of outstanding solo voices before Toronto audiences.

He was well aware that the soloist can also be a factor in creating that moment of magic in presenting a great work. Very often, at the end of a concert, the response of the TMC singers to an outstanding solo performance was more spirited and enthusiastic than that of the audience. On many evenings, choir and the soloist inspired each other to heights unattained by either on previous occasions.

Elmer never lost sight of the extent to which his reputation for dazzling performances came from the mouths and minds of his choristers. A long-time performer in the Elmer Iseler Singers, David King, quotes Elmer's admission upon receiving a compliment from Queen Elizabeth on one of her trips to her North American subjects. He pointed out to Her Majesty that under sensitive leadership a choir can take on energy and quality of its own in performance going beyond anything a conductor can predict.

Of course much of the scheduling for the Mendelssohn Choir had to be built around the various celebrations that seemed to dominate these years. There was, for example, the opening of a new concert venue, to be called Roy Thomson Hall (RTH). In its earliest days at the end of the nineteenth century, the TMC had participated in the opening of a Massey Hall that would then serve Toronto well for over a century. However, Massey Hall was a venue built for less demanding audiences and performers. Many of the seats were uncomfortable and the decor was drab and always appeared dusty and unattractive. It was unbearably hot in summer, had virtually no foyer in which people could gather, and had a lack of amenities for artists that was an embarrassment to all those who were aware of the limitations. Several steps had been taken to improve the building's acoustics. At one point the hanging of long drapes over the orchestra led one observer to comment that the auditorium stage looked like a tall ship in full sail. Elmer, who had suffered all these years in Massey Hall and looked forward to a new venue, was enthusiastically positive on the RTH arrival. From a position of performance comfort and as an administrative home, it was a considerable improvement over the old building on Shuter Street that had served the Toronto Symphony and the Mendelssohn Choir for so many years. Tragically, for many musicians, orchestral ones in particular, and for many patrons, the RTH acoustics left much to be desired.

The new hall designed by Canadian architect Arthur Erickson, with its round glass outer shell, was certainly visually exciting. The oblong auditorium style had been abandoned, which seemingly led to serious sound transmission problems that had to be rectified with special accoutrements. There was an enormous amount of space to fill in the domed hall, more than in almost any other hall on the continent. The sound had to be pushed out into the audience by huge plastic reflectors hanging over the stage from the ceiling. These additions could be raised or lowered to adjust the amount of sound reaching the listener. As well, there were tubes shaped like cigarettes protruding from the very summit of the ceiling elevation and these too could also be raised and lowered. It was plain that the conductor of the performing ensemble now had the additional responsibility for tuning the hall. Fortunately it was not a problem for Elmer, who had special talents in that regard, but other conductors found the challenge frustrating and debilitating. Surprisingly, the new hall brought astonishingly increased attendance to the TMC in the first years of its operation.

However, along with the distance of the chorus from accompanying orchestra, there was the problem that the large reflectors could not be adjusted once the audience was in place. Every composition in a varied program needed different patterns of acoustical adjustment, but that was not possible. It was Elmer who understood the acoustics of Roy Thomson Hall and, though initially supportive of its design, soon realized the limitations of what was now the TMC's performance base. Large-scale choral presentations were particularly at risk. The reflectors, when raised high, would prevent the full chorus from overwhelming the audience but would leave the soloist unsupported and indeed responsible for filling the hall's massive dome, a task that frustrated even a Ben Heppner at his Wagnerian best. Iseler became a favourite figure among the technicians as the one conductor who could adjust the various protuberances to affect the sound, though even he could not regulate the auditorium for the varying needs of a full evening's choral program.[8]

Sound problems at RTH were a burden that neither the TSO nor the TMC needed to carry at a time of overall lessening support for the arts and a staggering increase in the number of entertainment options offered by competing commercial arts presenters in the city. Substantial advertising budgets were convincing large audiences to pay sizeable sums of money for single seats at popular musicals. Yet, even with increased promotion, audiences for "serious" music were not increasing. Searching out new audiences for choral music especially among young people eventually became a challenge of savage proportions when the role of the arts was being cut back within the schooling system. Elmer himself had a most eclectic taste in music, appreciating good performance in almost any genre (even including country and western). But he could find no path from his attraction to more popular contemporary music and the expectations of the older audience awaiting the performance of a familiar oratorio.

Elmer saw that he was faced with a seemingly impossible situation. The TMC in full voice needed a large hall, though Elmer himself was quite prepared to move performances to a smaller venue — a position seen as a retreat by some TMC board members. Thus, he now had the RTH, with all its limitations to cope with, at a higher cost to rent but with more seats to fill. All this at a time when finding an audience was a substantial challenge. Was the TMC an anomaly in the last decades of the twentieth century? Elmer was determined to prove that this was not the case. He successfully held back the seemingly inevitable erosion through his emphasis on pure tonal quality and precise articulation and his willingness, despite the criticism, to champion new works. One concert included the melodic, some would say derivative and superficial, Andrew Lloyd Webber Requiem to attract those who had been captivated by his popular musicals, *Cats* and *Phantom of the Opera*. Yet this tentative exploration did not restrain him from returning to Carl Orff's *Carmina Burana* and the Berlioz Requiem as well as the works of his beloved J.S. Bach as prime examples of music that could inspire his singers and motivate his audiences.[9]

Perhaps most important in the long run were Elmer's efforts to support contemporary Canadian composers by ensuring their compositions had a hearing, not just once, but where possible repeatedly, and even more importantly, a place on the recordings that he was producing. Perhaps the most obvious case was Elmer's enthusiasm for Srul Irving Glick's TMC commission, *The Hour Has Come*, and particularly the last movement of the work that has now become a part of the repertoire of choirs around the world. The works of his accompanist for many years, Ruth Watson Henderson, were given a frequent hearing.[10] Her *Missa Brevis* was one of Elmer's most prized selections and the TMC and his own Elmer Iseler Singers performed it often. Needless to say, it was easier for Elmer to find new repertoire for his chamber ensemble. This fact led to the unfair accusation that he was losing interest in the TMC and centring his creative activity on the Elmer Iseler Singers.

The mid 1980s seemed awash with celebratory events. There was the TMC adieu to the old, but soon to be refurbished, Massey Hall. The Berlioz Requiem with all its bravado seemed an appropriate way to leave on a high note. But 1984 was the ninetieth birthday of the TMC as Canada's longest-surviving arts institution (celebrated with a splendid performance of *Elijah*). The year 1984 was also the twentieth anniversary of Elmer's appointment as conductor of the TMC. The City of Toronto proclaimed November 3 "Elmer Iseler Day." The promotional document emphasized that the TMC was "one of the finest ensembles of its kind in the world" and continued with no hesitation to claim that it was due to Elmer's "distinguished achievements that this choral organization continues to set unprecedented standards of performance, unsurpassed for its magnificence of sound, remarkable clarity and expressive power." Just a few weeks before Elmer had been named the first life member by the Association of Canadian Choral Conductors. Yet even amidst these accolades, he could not escape the critiques that sought to erode his reputation.[11] Of all these honours, in his mind none superceded his aforementioned appointment in 1975 as an Officer of the Order of Canada. Only a Nobel Prize could have placed a more valued garland on the brow of this consummate patriot.

These years in the century's last decades continued to provide anniversaries and celebrations that engaged Elmer and the TMC. The year 1985 brought Bach 300, the recognition of possibly history's greatest choral composer, and Elmer had to include his Mass in B Minor in the TMC concert season. Once again, Maureen Forrester outdid herself in the contralto role. In that same year came the premiere of the John Reeves *Veni, Creator Spiritus: Music for Pentecost*, a moving composition that demanded the addition of voices from the Toronto Mendelssohn Youth Choir and the Toronto Children's Chorus. It was enthusiastically received, as was Derek Holman's *Night Music*, a composition commissioned in that same concert season and one that pleased Elmer enormously. It was recorded by his Elmer Iseler Singers in the early 1990s.

The following year, 1986, was the one hundredth anniversary of the Royal Conservatory that filled the seats in the newly opened Roy Thomson Hall. Elmer was there with his TMC, obviously the ensemble without whose presence no event could be celebrated musically. That same year Walter Homburger, the managing director of the Toronto Symphony for a quarter-century, announced his retirement. The TMC and an array of world-renowned artists gathered at Roy Thomson Hall for a concert of unsurpassed prestige that was a crowning moment for both the TSO and the TMC.

By the late 1980s, the number and intensity of celebrations began to erode. However, in 1989, the musical community decided that it was time, once again, to celebrate Elmer Iseler — in particular, his twenty-fifth anniversary as conductor of the TMC. The occasion was a choral tribute presented by the TSO, who had commissioned Derek Holman to write *Tapestry*, a work with a text based on five medieval poems. It was truly Holman at his best as the successor to Healey Willan as a composer of religious, or perhaps, rather, intensely philosophic music for voice.

The TMC declared the 1989–90 season a gala marking Elmer's anniversary and determined that a number of popular choral works would be performed under either Elmer's baton or that of other conductors. A list of major compositions by Bach, Beethoven, Prokofiev, Mahler, Orff, and Janacek emerged. When, in 1994, the TMC's one hundredth anniversary came about, there was the realization that Elmer had been the conductor for almost one-third, and certainly the most active and acclaimed fraction, of the choir's existence as a musical organization. At a time when change was being worshipped Elmer had outlasted, in years of service, every other conductor on the TMC historic roster.

The twentieth century saw the inclusion of film as an art form with enormous potential and Elmer recognized that reality. He hoped that involving the choral art in film might be a means of reaching out to young people. In the 1980s and 1990s he grasped the opportunity with both hands. Norman Jewison, Canada's most distinguished film director, was producing a major offering, *Agnes of God*, that depicted the problems faced by a woman who had given her life to her Lord. The soundtrack needed a choral intervention, and Elmer and his Elmer Iseler Singers were able to provide precisely the sound he wanted. After the studio session, Elmer could inform his singers that Jewison had been delighted with the professionalism displayed during the recording and the quality of the sound that had been thus achieved.

A few years later, the TMC was once again invited into this world of film. John Williams, American composer and conductor, had written a moving score for the movie *Schindler's List*, the story of a heroic European who had saved large numbers of Jewish people from extermination in Hitler's concentration camps. It included choral music that Williams became convinced could be sung beautifully by the choir he had heard about in Boston many years before. Now he would discover just how splendidly they could learn his music and respond to his inspiration. The recording session went exceedingly well and the resulting performance of the TMC was a stirring moment in the lives of the participants.

All these pressures were being imposed on an art form that was historically aligned with amateur performers in many cases devotedly singing to the Glory of God. As a result, it was a longer stretch for choirs, even the TMC, to find their place in the busy world of corporate fundraising that other art forms of music, drama, and dance performance had recognized as essential for survival. There had always been an element of private donation that had allowed the TMC to continue, but now, with lower government commitment, all the art forms, including choral music, had to become intensively involved. Indeed, fundraising rose to the top of the list of management priorities by the end of the 1980s. In spite of these efforts, the events of 1997 and 1998 can be seen as a seeming replay of the Festival Singers' time of troubles.

There were heroes in the struggle for survival, both artistic and managerial. George Brough was, throughout most of Elmer's time, the TMC accompanist. With a reputation for keyboard accuracy that was legendary, he became the recipient of Elmer's admiration and respect. On a scrap of paper that Jessie found after his death, Elmer had outlined his thoughts about the man on whom he had depended: "a narrow fellow at the keyboard … over many years, a million notes; the slender fingers, now so gentle, now so unfathomably strong and quick … George, a gentle man, a gentleman, a magnet for affection."[12]

Another towering figure on whom Elmer depended was Patti Tompkins. She had come to Canada from the United States, had joined the TMC as a singer, and in 1967 had taken on the role of manager. She provided the stability and reliability that Elmer needed. There were none of the surprises with which Elmer had been confronted in Festival Singer days when he had coped with two or three managers in a single concert season. He knew from experience how much it meant to have all the administrative details of developing a regular concert series, monitoring the relationship with the TSO, to say nothing of the chaos of North American and particularly European tours that included seeing that 160 singers were in their places at every rehearsal and performance in a host of different venues in many cities in several countries. However, in 1989, Patti Tompkins resigned and there was no figure of that stature who could take her place.

There had been one potential managerial successor, one whom Elmer liked and respected: Michael Ridout, the son of composer Godfrey Ridout, who with his feet firmly placed in the new technological era had arrived at the TMC office and had brought a rich experience from other arts forms to which choral music might have connected. Michael Ridout could have provided Elmer that same sense of security that the Tompkins's style had encouraged. However, soon after joining the TMC organization, he began to have concerns over the tensions in the TMC board and decided he should leave his TMC post with some hope of returning when the situation cleared. Unfortunately, before this transition could occur, Ridout was struck down with cancer. It was a sad loss for Elmer and Jessie, not only on a personal level, but on an institutional one as well. The result was a blow to Elmer's need to be sure that the day-to-day affairs of a complex organization were in hand, and that someone was on top of all the relationships with concert presenters and the TSO — that indeed everything was being done to attend to the matters on which high morale and deep commitment were built. It was this assurance, seemingly basic to inspired singing, that was at risk during these years.

In the midst of Elmer's tensions with some of the TMC board members, the quality of the administration and, even more, the presence of dependable and loyal volunteers were crucial. However, the bylaws of the TMC placed great emphasis on the role of choristers in the governance of the organization. To be specific, the TMC board was required to have a substantial presence of choir members and there had to be a majority of choristers on the executive committee of the board. Today, with the pressure on arts boards to be fundraising mechanisms, no choir could thrive with such a constitution. Boards simply need the corporate strength to engage the private sector and to ensure that these board members have confidence in the working of the organization and effectiveness of its governance. Influential membership from outside chorister ranks on the TMC board was essential. John Lawson, an active member of the TMC for many years, a prominent force in the legal profession as well as a participant in many arts initiatives, explains that at the time of the founding of the choir in the nineteenth century, male members were drawn from that very sector of business and the professions that now needed to be attracted to board membership.

The idea of chorister control of the governing structure complied with the democratic tradition that had grown around the choral community and its board and seemed appropriate when male choir members had virtually synonymous backgrounds and vocational callings. At that time and well into the twentieth century a sociological shift in the sources of voices for the choir had taken place. No longer did professionals from medicine and law along with businessmen dominate the bass and tenor sections. Rather teachers, social workers, librarians, civil servants — all concentrated in the public rather than the private sector — had become the mainstay of the male sections of the TMC. Though their commitment to the musicality of the chorus could not be questioned, their capacity to find generous sources of funding in the private sector to cover the rising costs of administration and presentation was less effective than it might have been if it had been possible to maintain previous patterns of choral involvement. Sadly as well, the TMC was slow to involve female choristers and supporters in the practical affairs of administration and fundraising.[13]

These trends had developed long before Elmer's arrival at the helm, but he was to bear the brunt of this situation. The TMC was seemingly always in financial difficulty. But Elmer was not even invited to board or board executive meetings. It was in the 1980s that the author of this volume, though never a TMC chorister, accepted membership on the TMC board. Experience on the boards of other choirs led him to believe that the artistic director of any arts organization should be involved in the deliberation of any such body. It was also apparent that the presence of a majority of TMC choir members on its board inevitably led to questions of artistic policy that only Elmer's contribution could adequately settle. This uninformed author raised the question in all ignorance, "Why is Elmer not here?" The query was met with an embarrassing silence. At the end of the meeting he was taken aside and informed that Elmer was never invited to be present. The reason: Elmer was considered "difficult" with a tendency to dominate the meeting. Even in the 1980s there was already reason for concern for the future well-being of the TMC governing structure.[14]

In 1996, the Toronto Mendelssohn Choir and Elmer were honoured by the presentation of the Roy Thomson Hall Award for their contribution to the Toronto's rich musical heritage. Nancy Westaway, chair of the awards committee, had sought to make this a prestigious municipal honour and TSO conductor-in-residence Victor Feldbrill and choral conductor Jean Ashworth Bartle had already received the annual award. On previous occasions of honours bestowed on him by governments, universities, or arts agencies, Elmer had stated to his singers, "This is as much yours as mine." This time the award itself included a recognition and reference to his Toronto Mendelssohn Choir. Elmer was delighted.

There was a sad irony in the timing of the presentation of this award. It was a scant year away from the time of the disastrous events that ended his work with the TMC. In the spring of 1997, in his own words, he was "removed" from his post of conductor by the Toronto Mendelssohn Choir Board of Directors. A year later he was dead.

Chapter 13

Living the Abundant Life

ELMER AND JESSIE KNEW EXACTLY HOW THEY wished to live their lives and prepare their children to face their journey in a troubled world. For both of them, the arts in general and music in particular had to be accompanied by a lifestyle that expressed what they most profoundly believed. Elmer and Jessie's vision of day-to-day living included a quiet restraint in their daily activities that allowed time to appreciate visual beauty, in both their natural surrounding as well as those whose source was the result of human creativity. As soon as it was possible, they wanted their family living in the country amidst forest, field, and rolling hills even if their work was totally centred on the performing arts, perhaps the most urbanized form of making a living there can be, based as it is on the gathering of crowds of people and providing them with comfortable accommodation to watch and listen.

Even when financially constrained in his early days of teaching, Elmer had bought land that could serve both his and Jessie's future together. At that time, the Caledon Hills property had been an investment in a future lifestyle that was still several years away. The area was a largely rough landscape with forested hills the main feature but with agricultural land to be found on patches of soil now ploughed and expanses of empty grazing lands nearby. This countryside, with its gentle valleys and flowing streams, ensured magnificent vistas from every window in the modest structure that Jessie and Elmer had initially built from logs imported from the West Coast of Canada. Most important, what became Quail Hill Farm was sufficiently distant from the developing megacity of Toronto to make them both feel they had entered another world when they turned north to their home on Gore Road from Highway 7, a major transit route across the southern expanse of the province of Ontario. The only noise to break the silence of the countryside was that of airplanes rising from the nearby airfield. The Pearson International Airport, as it was to be named, served Elmer's delight in observing aircraft at a distance and led him to discount the sonic interventions of the flight patterns that included the air space over Quail Hill Farm and imposed the roars of engines on the quiet of his bucolic setting. Robert Cooper, often a guest along with his singing wife, Megan, met a very different Elmer Iseler than the man encountered in the concert hall. Here, cooking a meal on his outdoor barbecue oven, he could be warm, relaxed, and engaging, far both in mind and body from the places where he felt he had to assume a persona of infallibility and dominance.[1]

Jessie had realized in the late 1950s and early 1960s, while living in the Balsillie family home, that it was impossible for her and Elmer to bring up two young children in that rural context where schools would be distant and the availability of stores, libraries, and professional services would be minimal, particularly for a family with but one car that would be sitting in a school parking lot all day. She realized as well that, until her own father sadly passed away, she had a responsibility to assist her mother in looking after him, and then, as well, to care for a fragile aunt. She recognized that calling upon Elmer to transport himself daily to Northview Heights, his children to a spectrum of activities, and herself to a host of local destinations made necessary for shopping, banking, and domestic arrangements would not serve his mental well-being. Even when regular employment at Northview Heights ended in the mid-1960s, he still had to drive himself to Festival Singers and Mendelssohn Choir rehearsals, studio sessions, and concerts in the city. Even though she sought to accompany him whenever possible, these activities inevitably led to complicated arrangements for looking after the children. Elmer, Jessie, Noel, and Buffy remained in the Balsillie's Thistletown household for several years, visited the Caledon property on the weekends for picnics and exploration, enjoying the company of on-site parents and grandparents, and waiting patiently for the time when it would be their Quail Hill Farm homestead.

Fortunately, the presence of this property worked well for Elmer's parents. The Reverend Theodore Iseler was retiring from his Galt Lutheran Church pastoral charge after many years that had seen a considerable increase in the numbers who made up its congregation. Elmer and Jessie's house was a perfect solution to the age-old problem of finding appropriate residential accommodation for men and women who had served their faith community by living in church parsonages throughout their careers, thus finding themselves homeless when they stepped down from their final charge. In the early 1960s, Theodore and Lydia moved to Quail Hill Farm on Elmer and Jessie's invitation. The arrangement worked well for a few years until Theodore's death, but the loneliness and isolation made it difficult for Lydia to stay there, and she moved back to Galt, where she could be near her friends and her son Leonard, who still taught industrial arts in the nearby senior public school.

Jessie understood better than anyone that these arrangements were not just about living space. Elmer needed the support of an extended Balsillie family. Together they determined to replicate in the Caledon countryside the family commune of their Thistletown experience. Jessie and Elmer's first years together had been in a household that included, along with her parents and brother, David, her mother's sister, Aunt Mary, in a healing environment that had provided support to Elmer in the struggles he was waging in the secondary school classroom as well as on the forefront of choral performance.

Finally, in 1968, the Iseler family moved from Thistletown and occupied the Quail Hill Farm home and prepared to enjoy the delights of the Caledon Hills countryside. By now local schools had been established, and Noel and Buffy attended Palgrave Public School and then went on to Mayfield Secondary School, both under the Peel Board of Education. The latter institution eventually came to specialize in the arts! Although transportation to these schools was by means of big yellow buses, the distance was not too long and the trip not too exhausting for the Iseler offspring.

By this time Jessie's father had died, and her mother moved to Quail Hill Farm with the Iseler family and became a beloved matriarch in their new community, appearing at local events and becoming a familiar sight on the streets and in the stores of small nearby communities. Jessie and Elmer now had a home of their own and could become citizens in a close-knit neighbourhood made up of people desperate to maintain the rural nature of their surroundings as long as possible in the face of an expanding Metropolitan Toronto.

Elmer and Jessie made it apparent to all the local citizens that the Iseler family was there to stay. There was not the slightest indication that Quail Hill Farm was a temporary stopover on the way to a prestigious Rosedale address, the luxury of Forest Hill, or the Post Road of North Toronto. Elmer had chosen a career path that promised, even to the most successful, a level of penury that would deny him the lifestyle of the rich and powerful. But he and Jessie had made a very clear decision about the things that were important in their lives, and family and community were at the top of the list. They became recognized figures in the shops, tea rooms, and service stations and at community gatherings. When the opportunity offered itself, Elmer and Jessie brought the Singers to nearby venues and gave concerts that left their neighbours speechless. They had lived since the mid-1950s in the Balsillie household and, for them, moving to their house and eventually extending it to serve both their two children and other possible family occupants was an adventure they had long anticipated. Circumstances had led to Elmer's sudden assumption of the TMC leadership in 1964, the abandonment of his teaching career that same year, and a move to the Caledon Hills a few short years after — and all had come together in an exciting and seemingly inevitable fashion.

Their new home became their treasure, panelled throughout in natural cedar and including a large living room with a fireplace to bring warmth on cold, snowy nights. Picturesquely situated in the centre of the room was a rocking chair framed by a shelf of Elmer's current reading. The entire floor plan celebrated easily accessible space; one could move from kitchen to dining room and back to the living room with ease. Architecturally, it expressed both openness and inclusiveness, as there were always windows that brought the beauty of the country into every corner of each room, providing every chair and sofa with a sightline that swept some part of the Caledon Hills yet also included nearby neighbouring homes. For the ensuing decades, Elmer and Jessie bought Canadian-designed and

-manufactured furniture along with antiques that exposed their love of Canada and its people to every visitor. Each area exuded the intimacy and affection that expressed the family values dominating their lives. This homestead drew friends and acquaintances to realize that when they visited they were occupying a special place of warmth and welcome.

A verandah surrounded the house and bird feeders seemed to be everywhere. Elmer and Jessie could view a remarkable collection of birds and animals that were frequent visitors. Deer and foxes came fearlessly to be fed in winter. In short, the glory of the Caledon Hills was brought to their doorstep every day of their lives. Though the touring of the Iseler choirs took on new meaning in the 1970s and early 1980s, Jessie, Elmer, Noel, and Buffy returned to their Quail Hill Farm with anticipation and gratitude after every triumph abroad.

Jessie and Elmer slept in a white eyelet canopied bed in a room whose windows gave a breathtaking view of the lawns and the flowering bushes and trees — but it was placed in the farthest corner of the building that assured privacy and precious quiet. Elmer had his own study and music scores lined the room. Jessie, particularly after she took over the administration of the Elmer Iseler Singers late in the 1970s, also had her work space. They had built a structure that perfectly served their social and vocational needs as well as their aesthetic predilections. Quail Hill Farm became increasingly a haven from the unpleasant pressures of coping with institutional and public expectations and a launching pad for yet another experiment in programming musical performances that would attract and inspire both singers and their audiences.

The interconnection of garden and home was the product of a grand strategy. Elmer had an extraordinary capacity to concentrate on the scores of works he was preparing himself to conduct. As Elmer put it, he did not depend on the presence of a keyboard (there were none at Quail Hill Farm) and spent no time constructing piano versions of choral works. Rather, he said, "I hear it in my head." And his analytical powers were legendary. While reviewing the unpublished conductor's score of Penderecki's *St. Luke Passion* that had been delivered to him after a performance of the work in Europe, he found and corrected ninety-four errors. More than one music critic mentioned that a major factor in

Elmer's success had been the careful preparation that had preceded every concert or broadcast performance. The quality of Elmer's environment had much to do with his capacity to concentrate and focus on the works he was preparing for performance.

Elmer found that he could work for only short periods of time, perhaps an hour, before the notes just swam before his eyes. However, if he alternated his study of scores with his other activities he could be more productive. Gardening in beds just outside his window was a perfect alternative pursuit, particularly in the style he had adopted. He had read Mel Bartholomew's *Square Foot Gardening*. Elmer discovered that he could spend an hour at the study of a score, then take a single four-foot square and work until it was seeded or weeded, raked or hoed, composted or harvested — and return to his study and his scores. In 1983, he had 127 such squares. His property looked like an archaeological site. He discovered that from each square he could harvest 120 pounds of potatoes or 256 pounds of carrots. Needless to say the Iseler household spent little of their food budget on any vegetables that could be grown in a Canadian climate. Friends were constantly flooded with the results of a crop that had matured in amounts beyond the consumption of the family. Elmer found he could grow corn in his squares — a crop that had defeated the expert Mr. Bartholomew but only posed a challenge to a man who had infinite confidence in his green thumb. This organization of his garden made the process of alternating study and manual labour both pleasurable and profitable.

Gardening was not his only enthusiasm. On evenings when he was not conducting a rehearsal or concert, he scanned the skies through one of three telescopes mounted on Quail Hill Farm's verandah. He was overwhelmed by the panoply of stars he could view in the true darkness of his rural abode. It was not only viewing that captured his interest. He read widely in the field of astronomy and viewed the skies with purpose, identifying particular constellations and exploring others as they were discovered. He developed a highly personal understanding of the vastness of the glorious exhibitions of stars and planets he examined each evening he could wrench from his busy schedule.

As important, his love of the universe was an extension of his interest in broadening and deepening his faith experience. He had begun his life in the cocoon of a simple Lutheran belief in a living and personal God. His early experiences in choral music had strengthened that faith. However, he found that only the most glorious musical expressions of the tenets of the Christian faith could hold his theological attention. Music, particularly Bach chorales, was his inspiration in addressing the meanings of the sacred texts of the Jewish and Christian scriptures.

During his university years Elmer had sought answers to the profound questions of human existence and the implications of these explorations on his own ethical behaviour and that of humankind. He had found answers wanting. He discovered, as years passed, that a serious study of astronomy, with his constant viewing supported by wide reading and contemplation, gave him another window on the universe, its immensity and its mystery. He could find lasting significance in his artistic efforts in the context of the universe's incredible order and beauty that he observed through his telescope. Astronomy was not some offhand hobby or transitory interest. It had been a passionate object of his attention from his teenage days. He regarded the study of the stars as an intense journey towards greater understanding of what he had originally perceived as a simple Garden of Eden creation story, with the purpose of achieving a greater understanding of the life force that had included music in the great plan. This visual statement gave a context to the very traditional archaic statements of faith, the creeds and interpretations of history that were to be found in the texts of the Masses, the Glorias, and the Passions he presented to his choirs and, through them, to his listeners.

Elmer never wrote or spoke publicly of the theological transitions he experienced over the decades except in the very informal responses to probing interviews. He never took the issue of faith and the stars further than an expression of faith in a benevolent Being that was revealed by his observation of the heavens and his exploration of the creativity of the human mind and spirit to be found in the scores that were on his music stand and those of the singers he was conducting. These were his moments of intimacy with the Eternal, moments he hoped he would share with his choristers and his audience.[3]

Elmer never engaged in casual hobbies to fill his time. As Jessie puts it, "Elmer worked hard and he played hard."[4] His play was the inspiration for his work. Just as astronomy strengthened his intensity for conquering the intricacies of human creativity devoted to the wonder and beauty of the universe (and thereby the quality of the divine mind and hand behind it all), his commitment to the visual arts had a comparable role.

Elmer had been attracted to the technology of photography at an early age. It was a path to a sensuality he himself appreciated but saw repressed in the strict and narrow limits of his home setting in Port Colborne. Photography became his means of learning about the excitement of form and texture. It was a legitimate though arguably questionable corridor to the mysteries of his own sexuality. Posing attractive female colleagues and fellow learners and taking their pictures could be a step towards greater intimacy and closeness that, at that time, he could find in no other way. After the mid-1950s, it was the beauty of Jessie, his partner, that fulfilled his need to explore the human form and examples of his work covered the walls at Quail Hill Farm. Individuals who visited the Iselers were mildly shocked at the number of professionally posed pictures of Jessie, Buffy, and other attractive females from the choral community that graced the walls of his home. There was nothing pornographic or even titillating but there was certainly an indication that the sensual as well as the intellectual was a welcome attribute within the handsome structure that was the Iseler homestead. Ultimately he reached extraordinary heights of expertise in the art of photography, recognized by professionals as having achieved the quality of a *Vogue* master.

Just as the heavens exposed a magnificent universe, the beauty of nature captured Elmer's interest in the more obvious delights that the eye beheld in the countryside he came to love. From the early 1950s to the late 1960s he had lived in a dull and undramatic neighbourhood. He had compensated by throwing whatever pennies he could find into opportunities for a long-term communion with the natural world. Quail Hill Farm had been but one example. The Severn River cottage lot could not be called a real estate investment either. These were plans for visual experiences that would serve his soul. Just as the discovery of the human form engaged Elmer's attention, the countryside around Quail Hill Farm and the Severn River in the Ontario northland became the expression of this impact on his and Jessie's body, mind, and spirit.

It was not only in producing images of objects that he served his visual needs, although even in his last years he planned to connect his music making and his photography to create shorts films that would demonstrate his horizontal sensitivity to the interaction of various art forms. On a visit, journalist William Penfield found that Elmer had just brought home a beautifully woven hornet's nest from Tennessee, a ball of tumbleweed from Saskatchewan, and a decorated candle from Austria.[5] These were items that were a feast for the eye and a remembrance of an experience of choral delight that had transpired in each of these areas. Elmer was not the relentless tourist when he was travelling with his choirs through Europe, the United States, or Canada. He did not always join his singers as they sought out museums, art galleries, or cathedrals. Usually his mind was concentrated on the music that he knew must be served. However, he did bring back small but simple natural objects of beauty and remembrance that he could place on the shelves or pin to the walls of his beloved home.

Quail Hill Farm was a perfect site on which the Iseler children could grow and develop. Noel and Buffy were sources of great pride for Elmer and Jessie. Although by the 1980s they were soon to be adolescents, they took the move to their new home most comfortably. Pictures taken in childhood and youth, carefully processed, enlarged, and framed, show two very handsome young people. They were popular with teachers and their colleagues. Whenever possible Elmer and Jessie took them on tours with his choirs and were delighted to have them present.

Noel became a sensitive and thoughtful young man. He found he was much more comfortable in the quiet of the Caledon Hills than the urban workplaces of nearby Toronto. He had come to love Elmer's dedication to the land of Quail Hill Farm. Indeed, Elmer's devotion to nature became the legacy that Noel seized, caring for the farm with all the intensity of his famous father.

Eventually, it seemed more appropriate for Noel to have his independence and a separate home on the Iseler property. A bungalow was placed not far from the main Quail Hill Farm structure for Noel. After Elmer's death, Noel became a source of strength to Jessie, looking after the farm property, cutting and piling wood for the winter's consumption, and working construction jobs. Both children always knew they had the love and support of their caring parents.

Buffy, a very intelligent young woman with her mother's organizational and multi-tasking skills and her intense love of children, felt no pressure to follow in her father's footsteps as a musician. However, she had been imbued with his love of learning and his desire to help others learn. She became a teacher and an educator.

Both Buffy and Noel had a positive experience in the nearby Mayfield Secondary School. Their presence was appreciated by one teacher, a Mr. Rose, who added a note on the border of a page of an essay that Buffy had submitted in her American history course: "Jessie, my 'historical' comments are on the back page. I have to get out of my 'sarcastic character' but I did want to tell you that it has been a real pleasure knowing you at Mayfield. You always brought a realm of sanity to a world of chaos. My congratulations to your parents for producing two super children."[7]

It was Buffy's experience at Mayfield that led her to choose teaching as a vocation. After graduation from the University of Toronto, she attended Brock University's Faculty of Education, secured her teaching certificate, and, like Elmer, took employment, in her case, as an elementary school teacher. She soon took on tasks that required more advanced skills, particularly in the area of special education, where she could use her personal attributes with particular impact. She was the pride of her parents as she excelled in her profession and became a strong and articulate woman.

Elmer, in notes for a speech that was never made, included a lengthy excerpt from a letter that had been handed to him by Buffy as he and Jessie left for another tour, now unaccompanied by their children. It was opened as the airplane left the tarmac of Pearson International Airport and its contents moved her parents deeply. It revealed that Buffy had come to realize what her parents' commitment to making music was all about. She was obviously remembering other recent trips with her parents as they now left for the Soviet Union:

> Dear Mom and Dad,
> When the two of you fly high across the sea, I'll long
> for you to be home, sitting by the fire, watching t.v.,

listening to music — the simple things in life that make it so important.

But I know the merits of what you are embarking on. It is an honour for the name of Canada but even more is the fact that it is an opportunity for growth. Every mind on the tour is going to expand to a limit it has not reached before. Your gift to the strangers who will become your friends is your glorious music. Their gift to you is their culture and the challenge and experience of dealing with it that enriches your mind, body and soul.

So ... we stood in Red Square, looked at Lenin's tomb ... wondered about the Secret police ... stood in ancient cathedrals with their 12th century icons ... brushed our teeth in Crest and Russian champagne ... performed for audiences that stood for three days for 3 hours of music ... and demanded 35 minutes of encores.[8]

Buffy married John Bride, a fine musician, and bore a child, Vanessa, whom Elmer worshipped. Never was Elmer happier than when she was in his arms and he was showing her the birds and animals that were welcomed at the Quail Hill Farm property. Vanessa remembers with evident delight Elmer's efforts to teach her how to fish by using a pail, a length of string, and a simple, bare metal hook. He was repeating the lesson he had received from Theodore Iseler many decades before.

By the time the Iselers had taken up residence at Quail Hill Farm, Jessie's role was changing. The children were now older, soon to be in their late teens, and completing their schooling. She had, through all these years, been Elmer's constant companion, his manager, and his buffer against criticism and hurtful observation. She was also there to share his success and the accolades of those who responded to his music. She was able to predict the moments of disappointment that would overcome Elmer on occasion and take appropriate action to soften the impact of these moments of depression. She made sure that every disruptive or distracting detail at a rehearsal was taken care of — the absence of a glass of ginger ale on the podium, the lack of a marked score on his music stand. In 1978, when the Festival Singers uproar took place, she had the strength to defend Elmer from the press and their sometimes inappropriate interest. When times were darkest, she saved him from making comments publicly that might have destroyed his career. Elmer realized that one of his problems with his Festival Singers had been the lack of continuity and consistency in the day-to-day management of the choir. When a new choir was formed in 1978 and called the Elmer Iseler Singers, Robert Sunter, one of the CBC and OAC music supporters, told her directly, "You must take over the management of any new choir that emerges from this mess." She was formally hired as the manager at the very first meeting of the Elmer Iseler Singers Board of Directors.

Throughout all these dark days, she realized that her main role was that of Elmer's wife and ensured that their love, caring, and intimacy, no matter whatever transpired, would be the most important aspect of their lives. This complete faith in Jessie's support was the main link to Elmer's well-being throughout these years when disaster struck and shook his confidence in what he perceived to be his life work.

This was the time of women's liberation theory and practice and there were those who found Jessie's personal sublimation of her own career opportunities quite disconcerting. She was obviously very intelligent and articulate as well as charming. Elmer never resisted the chance to comment on her physical beauty, thereby giving the impression that he saw her as a trophy companion. It was a ruse to convince people of his humanity. But it was not so. She was wise not to make any effort to comment on the intricacies of choral performance even though her taste in music and literature was as consciously developed as her understanding of fashion and personal appearance. She never for a moment allowed her constant presence at rehearsal or performance to be perceived as any lack of confidence in Elmer's love and loyalty whenever they were apart.

Jessie's strength of purpose came from a clear understanding and sharing of Elmer's vision and a belief that in forwarding that vision by active participation and involvement, she would eventually find her place. She did not find it necessary to construct any area of musical expertise, time-consuming hobby, or esoteric form of voluntarism to achieve her own role.

By the 1980s, not only had she become the manager of the Elmer Iseler Singers, she had taken on the most unpleasant aspects of Elmer's role. She understood how important it was to have a constant membership at every rehearsal and performance if Elmer's demands for excellence were to be met. Singers now found that they had to deal with Jessie if they had reasons to be absent from either. She became the chorus "police," who often had to say no. Keeping Elmer pleased was not just a way of assuring a tolerable home life. It was simply the way that Elmer's vision could be achieved at every concert, every recording session, and every broadcasting opportunity. No one else could carry out this role. Jessie's legitimacy as the person responsible for ensuring that Elmer's expectations were met was never questioned.[9]

In that same decade the events around the destruction of the Festival Singers had affected Elmer's attitude to the world about him. There were those whom he trusted implicitly. That did not change. However, Elmer was now even more cautious in forging relationships with people he did not know well. This was painful, as he believed that creating music had a transforming power that could be the solution to the human tragedy that could be observed all around him — whether the environmental crisis or the continuing horror of war and violence. He read widely and kept abreast of the circumstances that made the arts so peripheral to the affairs of humankind. He had infinite faith in the human spirit but little confidence in the institutions that human beings created to carry out their ideals.

Elmer had lived through an incredible half-century of Canadian history. He had been schooled while the Second World War raged, had attended university with men and women who had served their country, and had witnessed the value of an investment in the education of these men and women once the hostilities had ended. He had experienced the excitement of Centennial Year and had seen what transformations were possible when cultural opportunities were exploited and a nation celebrated.

But he had seen another Canada. He had watched the country selling off the control over its economy and becoming increasingly a colony of the American empire. He was thrilled with the initiative of Lester B. Pearson, who showed Canadians what role they could play in the international corridors of power and had received a Nobel Prize for his peacemaking achievements. Indeed, on one trip to Ottawa, Elmer took the trouble to seek out Pearson's grave and pay his respects on a quiet hillside in the Papineau Hills across the Ottawa River just north of the nation's capital.

John Diefenbaker also had a vision, one that chose to develop the Canadian North and maintain the traditions of the past. However, neither he as prime minister nor his vision did much to stem the Quiet Revolution in the province of Quebec that threatened the very life of the country. With family roots in la belle province, Elmer's Canada certainly included Quebec. An enthusiasm for an independent Canada, the Trudeau style and relentless determination to keep Canada united, sovereign, and strong, fuelled Elmer's patriotism.

There was little that was partisan in Elmer's mind. His political passions were focused on the capacity of governments at all levels to see that national objectives could be reached only through the support of a dynamic arts community. The Mulroney years, with globalization on the rampage, represented the seeming inevitable takeover by corporate interests and a loss of confidence on the world's political stage. Perhaps more than anything, these would be years of retreat from the highest point of Canadian confidence when, in 1967, Canadian singers, dancers, and instrumentalists sped east and west across Canada for a year of celebration. Elmer believed that taking his choirs to small-town Canada was in fact his way of producing a stronger nation. He also believed that commissioning French-speaking composers to write for his choirs was another contribution he could make to national unity.

Even on a personal basis, Elmer was prepared to reach out to French-speaking individuals who might be separatist but who might be brought over with gestures of respect. For example, a favourite colleague of Elmer's was François Bernier, the founder of the Domaine Forget's Summer Festival in the beautiful Charlevoie area of Quebec. For a number of summers, Elmer assisted Bernier by organizing the choral program for his French-speaking choristers. It convinced Elmer that the two solitudes could be bridged when a dedicated separatist and a devoted nationalist could co-operate to produce magnificent music and simultaneously come to love and respect each other.

Before a concert Elmer would not allow distractions that might dilute the intensity of his command of the music. He would not watch news reports on television or read columns on contemporary events. Yet every performance was a statement about what Canada's culture could be in terms of excellence and relevance and how Canadians might perform on the world's political stage expressing the sensitivity, compassion, balance, and openness that he believed were attributes of his fellow citizens.

No man was more a community advocate than Elmer Iseler. Indeed, his major complaint about globalization was that it took resources, influence, and jobs from the community and placed them in the hands of corporate giants living somewhere else. Jessie and Elmer were determined to know their neighbours well, including the local hardware dealer, George Berney, and the feed merchants, the Davis family, and to support their local causes whenever possible.

In the early 1990s, the author of this volume was drawn into the environmental policies of Ontario's NDP government as they were expressed by the minister of the environment, the Honourable Ruth Grier. These included the closing of all waste incinerators that were burning garbage, thereby polluting the air that citizens breathed, as well as forcing the Greater Toronto Region (GTR) containing some 8 million people to look after its own garbage output rather than imposing its accumulation on people elsewhere in the province. There were three large landfill sites in the GTR and they were nearly full. The strategy was clear — to find three alternative large sites in the GTR that would store the waste for about twenty years until there would be even more effective recycling techniques and treatment of waste, making landfill sites unnecessary. These sites were to be placed where they would have the least impact on the region's people, would not gobble up more prime agricultural land, would not threaten endangered animals or plants, and, most important of all, could be engineered to have the least effect on the area's water table. These and other lesser criteria would be used to determine where these new landfill sites were to be placed.

The author was appointed chair of the Interim Waste Authority, an Ontario government agency whose job it was to monitor a staff of splendid young environmentalist civil servants who, after extensive testing, would recommend the three landfill sites. People throughout the vast area extending miles north of Toronto and east and west of the city were terrified that one of these sites would be established in their backyard, with all images of the past before them — the traffic congestion, the smell of unsightly rotting garbage, the masses of gulls and vermin that would surely be attracted. Assurances that modern landfills can be engineered, indeed beautified, to eliminate these problems were unconvincing.

Elmer Iseler, a resident of lands near the edge of Toronto, shared the concerns of his neighbours and was determined to express his displeasure at the threat of any landfill placement near his community. He arranged two meetings with the chair and in clear, cogent argument, indicated the folly of considering the Caledon Hills as a resting place for the waste created by the several million people in this massive GTR. Elmer's argument was flawless and persuasive. The chair's frustration was that though he agreed with Elmer's position on this part of the Greater Toronto Region, he could give no absolute assurance that his community would be bypassed. Elmer listened to the arguments that disposal of waste had enormous global environmental implications. He fully understood and appreciated the unpleasant reality that a society based on massive consumption created serious problems that were destined to require drastic action. Jessie was present and without eroding Elmer's presentation ensured that interaction between the author and Elmer was calm and civilized. At the end of the conversation, Elmer was warm and friendly and the chair came away with a CD of the particularly inspiring music his Singers had just sung and had recorded.

In the end, Elmer's neighbourhood area was not chosen to host one of the landfill sites, and, ultimately, a provincial election replaced Bob Rae's NDP government with a Conservative government led by Mike Harris, who as the new premier took no responsibility for trying to solve Toronto's waste disposal problem and passed the issue back to the several municipalities making up the GTR. Much of the waste was transported to large Michigan landfill sites. However, Elmer could feel that he had intervened on behalf of his community on an issue he felt deeply about.

There was one aspect of the political reality of his country about which he had no question — that governments had a responsibility for adequate funding of the arts. Early on when he had made the decision to pursue a career in music and had taken on the leadership of the New Hamburg Youth Choir, the debate over the direction of Canada's cultural future was taking place. The establishment of the Massey-Lévesque Commission in the early 1950s had been a turning point in the country's history. Among the recommendations was one that proposed a Canada Council for the Arts, based on the successful Arts Council of Great Britain, whose responsibility would be to provide support to the development of the arts, including the performing arts. The report of the commission came forward as Elmer was establishing the Festival Singers as a force in the choral community. He realized that, though CBC Radio would be his initial source of support for broadcasting concerts, a national body of those responsible for encouraging artistic development would want to provide resources at least for certain components of the Festival Singers' costs such as touring and commissioning Canadian music. Surely, his vision of the quality repertoire and performance would be shared by such a Canada Council.

Elmer had no doubts about the legitimacy of such public support for the arts. Politics, in Elmer's view, had been best expressed by Lester Pearson as "how we do things together for the common good." There were still hesitations about artists and arts institutions accepting government "handouts," and many Canadians preferred the American system, which placed more emphasis on corporate and foundation largesse. Elmer, coming from rural roots, knew that Canada did not have either corporations or foundations with the resources that a giant industrial nation like the United States could provide, nor did the country have a history of private philanthropy like its southern neighbour. Canada might not wish to follow the European model of total dependence on governments at all levels, but complete reliance on private money was also not an option. Soon Elmer's experience with the public sector came through Canada Council officers who had encouraged him in his work. Indeed, the first grant that came for the Festival Singers was for $37,000 and arrived from the office of the Canada Council's Peter Dwyer.

From the outset, CBC producers secured resources to commission Canadian composers and hired Elmer's Singers whenever possible. He had never experienced any pressure to popularize his repertoire or accept certain soloists who were the favourites of those hiring him and his Singers. In contrast to some arts administrators who revelled in their capacity to attract money from the private sector and seemed embarrassed to accept money from the public trough, Elmer at every opportunity praised the generosity of the country's taxpayers and their largesse through a hierarchy of national and provincial and municipal granting councils.

There was a risk that Elmer never fully realized. Governments and their policies shift and the availability of public resources shrink. Elmer regarded these shifts as aberrations rather than the inevitable swings in popular responses that make up reality in a democratic system. He didn't recognize that especially in the fragile context of choral music these unexpected redirections of public resources could be particularly savage.

On the other hand, he had experienced deterioration in his hold on artistic policy when the need for more private funds to support his professional Festival Singers had brought a conflict of values and practices within his own board and some choir members. It was an area in which he could find no compromise. There was a lack of comfort in the politics of securing increased private resources that Elmer was never able to resolve. He was caught up in the spiritual mandate of choral presentation — singing was a creative, God-given human ability that was transformational and developmental. Great choral music's role was to inspire both singers and audiences with thoughts and motivations of eternal significance. He would brook no erosion of that great mission even if more profits from the box office might come from singing a more popular repertoire. His solution to the needs of choral ensembles was to hound, harass, and ultimately convince people, their governments, and their granting agencies that in a dangerous world a strong arts presence is crucial to the well-being, even the survival, of humankind. His political philosophy was direct and straightforward. The arts were an essential burden and joy in the lives of every citizen and deserved their continuing support through the actions of their governments at every level.

Quail Hill Farm was not Elmer's only place of comfort and healing. Even before he had moved from Thistletown, he had acquired a small cottage on Copp Bay on the Severn River, accessible only by water from a dock very close to the famous marine railway on the Trent–Severn Waterway at the Big Chute. Waterfront properties on Copp Bay had been held by the Fitzpatrick family and Charlie Jolliffe, his colleague at Northview Heights, who had built a cabin on its shores. As properties were subdivided, the Singleton family had also purchased land. Soon Charlie's place became a venue for an annual fishing, bridge, and beer weekend that male staff members at Northview Heights anticipated each fall. Elmer was thrilled by neither beer nor bridge, but he saw Copp Bay was a picturesque place to wander with his camera in his hand, fish to his great delight, and simultaneously enjoy camaraderie with people he respected.

It was his mentor, Jim Singleton, who advised him that he should buy some frontage as soon as possible. Once again, Elmer was overwhelmed by the thought of making such an investment. There was a piece of property that had a small cabin with a modest living room overlooking the bay and three bedrooms — just the right size for his family. There was no running water, every drop had to be carried by pail from the water's edge, but the structure was large enough for Jessie and the children plus any of the Balsillie family who wanted a few days in the quiet of Ontario's north. As a result, Jessie's brother, David, spent part of many summers there and on his return south from a stint with the Ontario government in Sudbury built a handsome cottage for his own family on the shore of Copp Bay in sight of the Iseler cottage.[10]

Indeed, the Severn River cabin was the Iseler's first real home. It was occupied in summer while Elmer and Jessie were still living with their Balsillie in-laws in Thistletown and it was truly their own in every way. It was where Elmer could escape his "Conductor" role, wearing his traditional white shirt, trousers, socks, hat, and running shoes. Here he could be the ultimate fisherman — and he took every opportunity to outdistance his neighbours with his success. He became a living legend in the area. "River Elmer" could catch fish when everyone else was simply feeding them. Paul Singleton, the personable son of Elmer's Northview principal, today a prominent psychiatrist, describes Elmer as the perfect example of the "low-tech fisherman." Eschewing sophisticated casting rods, reels and lines, and highly touted lures, he simply put a worm on a hook at the end of a line, carefully selected his spot on the bay (later to be named "Elmer's Bass Hole"), and waited for the fish to appear. He knew exactly where the rock shelf dropped steeply just a few yards from shore, he knew which weeds attracted the kind of fish he coveted, he dropped the line down just twelve feet, and magically, he soon had his catch for the day. It was simple still fishing at its best.[11]

Elmer did not have a yacht or even a typical rowboat. Financial limitations forced him to build his own barge — a simple plywood vessel with no specifications that made much sense. He determined the depth of the barge by having Noel stand in the plywood shell and measuring the point where his son could see over the edge but was not likely to fall in the water. He painted this floating utility craft a bright red and it soon became a major attraction on the bay. But in it Elmer caught fish!

In this relaxed atmosphere he became a favourite companion of the many children who were fleeing the city for the paradise of a lakefront cottage. When holidays brought fireworks, it was Elmer who ensured there were lots of sparklers — indeed, for this host of children attending the Copp Bay neighbourhood fireworks display hosted by Paul Singleton, he was not a choral conductor but the "sparkler man."

Barbara Singleton, Paul's wife, saw Iseler as a man who loved to be with women but also cherished children. Their own young son, Jamie, found Elmer to be one of his favourite companions before he had reached five years of age. Elmer would take him out on the dock with the invitation, "Let's conduct." With only the music of water and motor boats available, he would show Jamie how to move his arms and hands and thereby conduct imaginary music, played by some invisible orchestra or sung by some angelic choir. Jamie was intrigued by this strange man who appeared on his dock and taught him something he had never seen or experienced. Soon he began practising alone, making use of music he heard on radio or record. Later he was to write a note of appreciation and after Elmer's death drew a picture that expressed his admiration. Significantly, his sketch included a very prominent Canadian flag. With the unflagging capacity of children to discover the essence of adult loyalties and values, he caught Elmer's enthusiasm perfectly.

Barbara discovered Elmer's interest in black and white photography most attractive. For her he was a thinking person's photographer who did not need colour to pique the viewer's interest. She felt his interest in magazines and articles about fashion empowered her to read them more carefully and more enjoyably.[12] Barbara felt he dignified and intellectualized the most pedestrian articles about clothing and the human form, thereby encouraging her own aesthetic predilections and giving them meaning.

Elmer developed a love for this collection of people who partied together and fished together — but also guarded their privacy tenaciously. There were those who held very different opinions on nearly every topic. They often agreed to disagree. These were the kind of people Elmer could trust.[13]

Copp Bay on the Severn became much more than a typical summer cottage experience. It could be called Elmer and Jessie's response to the values of the wilderness and its importance to the Canadian character. The cabin remains small and compact. There are no indoor washroom facilities — the familiar outhouse reigns. The Severn River represented the beauty of an ever-changing, breathtaking landscape, along with a sense of intimate community that is the pride of those who share its glory. It was the one place where the pressure of choral music presentation could be escaped. It was close enough to Toronto that Elmer could come up only for a single day. Neighbours laughed to see him in his dress shirt pulling in the fish he loved to catch, clean, and share with his family in the warmth of an evening meal.

Performing artists are not known for the stability of their personal lives. The work they do is their joy and obsession. Jessie and Elmer shared the intimacy of working and playing together, often in the company of a host of people they loved. It was the engine of their determination to change the face of Canada's culture. Their marriage appeared so strong that they were often consulted by friends and colleagues who were considering the state of matrimony in their own lives. Their advice was freely given, if not always followed. Their perceptions of likely success of such unions were always accurate and honestly provided. In cases where they saw only disaster they inevitably watched these marriages disintegrate. However, most unions were successfully achieved and the "Iseler's Marriage Advice Service" continued to the very end of Elmer's life. It was yet another intervention in the cause of the abundant life that Elmer cherished along with his partner, Jessie.

The family life, the intimacy of Elmer and Jessie's union, dwelt in harmony with their commitment to the cultural values that celebrate human love, compassion, inclusion, environmental responsibility, and sharing — in contrast to the behaviours that emerge from conflict, disinterest in others' pain, exclusion of all those who are different, the destruction of the natural world, and enormous greed that has characterized the tragedy of human history. Their life was of a piece, a single tapestry. It was their personal song of hope!

Chapter 14

The Last Days

IT WAS JESSIE WHO FIRST REALIZED THAT something was wrong. The first revelation came on another of the many trips they took to the American south looking for distance from the wearing consistency of weekly rehearsals of the Elmer Iseler Singers and the Toronto Mendelssohn Choir. They sought sunshine and warmth and an escape from the dark, cold Canadian winter for brief periods of refreshment. For Elmer and Jessie, this annual pilgrimage was a physical and spiritual lift, a contrast of lifestyle, a trip to friends they had come to know in Florida and on the Palm Beach shores over the years, and to beloved colleagues, like the Bartle, Dodington, Broderick, Gold, and Mantei families, determined to share that same experience of relief from the darkness, the drab, the ice, and the snow.

Elmer had developed routes from the Caledon Hills to Florida and the New Jersey shores that no one else he knew had ever discovered. He normally needed no maps; he just drove continuously, coming upon various highways and byways and magically finding his way to his particular destination. However, in the spring of 1997, he was having difficulty in connecting with the lesser roads that in the past had delivered him, almost traffic-free, to Florida and his friends. When they finally arrived, Elmer could hardly wait to wander the seashores and the Sailfish Marina with his camera in hand, remembering past years when he did so while the kids and Jessie were alternatively sprawled on the sandy beaches and racing into the surf.

However, the early months of 1997 had been particularly exhausting. Jessie was dead tired. Rather than providing the healing of anticipation, the trip and all its preparations had contributed to a brutal strain of flu, and instead of the enjoying warmth of the sun-kissed beach, Jessie was laid up in bed. When Buffy called to ensure they had arrived safely, she found Elmer unable to articulate the situation with any precision and she became deeply concerned about her mother's health. She called other Iseler friends she knew were in the area, telling them "Pop seems out of it," and they were able to get her mother to a nearby Florida hospital.

Jessie recovered but not without some misgivings about Elmer's condition. When it was time to return home to Canada, she found Elmer listless and unfocused. Whereas normally he would arise early to pack the car so they could be off and on the highway by seven o'clock, she awoke to find Elmer still in bed. When she remarked that it was time to leave, his response was a desultory "What's the rush?" Though still recovering from the flu, she found herself pushing Elmer to action, knowing that they had a twelve-hour drive, one that had to be interrupted several times so that Elmer could walk the stiffness and pain out of his legs, an absolute necessity if the phlebitis was to be kept in check.

As soon as they were back at Quail Hill Farm, Jessie took Elmer to his physician, Dr. John McIlraith at the Etobicoke General Hospital, for a checkup. She knew he could not be delivered to just any doctor. Elmer had reactions to many forms of medication and only Dr. McIlraith knew how to "talk him out of his discomfort" and, with advice to "take a week of complete rest," see him eventually find his way back to his normal energetic pace. This time, the doctor was concerned. Something was not right.

Then there were a series of external indications that things were not normal. Elmer and Jessie drove south from the Caledon Hills to Toronto on Highway 427 several times a week, but for the first time, Elmer missed the turnoff to the 401. He quickly recovered and found his way to familiar roads, but his confusion struck Jessie as extremely odd.

At home, trying to be helpful, Elmer would put on eggs to boil and then forget the task he had initiated. Soon the steam was rising from the stove and the pot was dry. Even more distressing, Elmer, the early riser who found he could complete several jobs before Jessie rose, continued to sleep in. When he was finally conscious, he seemed unable to remember the tasks he had set for himself and, once again, it was Jessie who had to rescue him from his obvious consternation.

At the Elmer Iseler Singers' rehearsal that started at four o'clock, Elmer would ordinarily be on the podium several minutes before its commencement providing an example and a presence that would en-sure the Singers would be in their places before the appointed hour. Now, Jessie found she had to rouse him from his chair at 4:05 p.m. and remind him that the hour had come to begin. Obviously, his incredible sense of timing was fractured. Singers began to realize that Elmer was not quite on; he found it hard to search back to bars in the score that needed attention. On occasion, they found his tempo for a composi-tion rather bizarre. In an EIS performance in early 1997, an Avro Part composition that normally took twenty-six minutes took forty minutes under Iseler's tempo. That same evening, in a collection of songs being presented in different order than found in the printed score, Elmer was baffled by his own inability to find his place with his usual alacrity.[1] As a result of these factors, this memorable concert did not end until eleven-thirty at night and was termed a "musical purgatory" by Toronto critic Tamara Bernstein. However, that was a rare exception. Concert appearances gave little indication that Elmer's mind was somehow being strangely affected by any health problem.[2] Indeed, his flair for showman-ship in public performance never left him.

Jessie decided she must take Elmer back to his doctor and secure a referral to a specialist. The return to Dr. McIlraith, a highly respected physician, founder and former chief of staff at the Etobicoke General Hospital, assured an immediate appointment for x-rays. Elmer, Jessie, and Buffy viewed the results. The worst prognosis was delivered. There was a sizeable tumour that could be seen clearly on the x-ray of Elmer's head. Dr. McIlraith moved quickly to secure the services of a first-class brain surgeon and an operating room at the Mississauga General Hospital. Within a week, in March 1997, Elmer was scheduled for surgery.

The week of waiting was simply a time of torture for both Jessie and Elmer. There were long periods of painful silence. It did not help that Elmer's younger brother, Leonard, had died of cancer but two years before, a loss that both Jessie and Elmer felt deeply. Both were obviously devastated by a sense of impending disaster. They could do no more than share their mutual fears. Jessie, while Elmer slept, found she had to do something with her hands that would give her some feeling of accomplishment. She washed, by hand, every curtain in a house that was graced with seemingly countless windows. It was almost as though she thought she might be able to expunge the reality of death in the washtubs of Quail Hill Farm.

When Elmer came out of the operating room he was unconscious and ashen. His head was bandaged but blood was seeping out and there were tubes everywhere connecting him to several pieces of technology. Jessie could not believe her eyes. However, in the waiting room there were those who cared deeply for her and her ailing spouse. As well as her family, the bevy of students from Elmer's classrooms some forty years before, "the Northview kids," were there in force after slipping past the security staff. They held their balloons as symbols of their celebration of Elmer's life, now under an enormous threat. Simultaneously, Robert Cooper, Elmer's colleague from both the TMC Youth Choir and the CBC, arrived along with pianist Lydia Adams to discover that he was emerging from the operating room. Most poignant of all, Ben and Sheila Wise, old friends from Manitouwabing music camp days, found their way to Jessie and to Elmer on the pretense that they were close relatives.

Especially appropriate was Cooper's presence. He was the conductor who had been engaged in Elmer's absence to take over the TMC rehearsals and performance of the great Bach Mass in B Minor in the early months of 1997. It all went extremely well — Cooper knew what Elmer would have wanted, and though he brought his own individual interpretation and technique to the fore, Elmer had complete confidence in his replacement. There may have been an unexpected crowd at the hospital but they were all people Elmer wanted to be near.

There was one more regular TMC concert scheduled for June 1997 and Elmer was determined to be on the podium. There were also EIS concerts scheduled for that spring as well as a summer visit to the Newfoundland Festival 500 arranged, and although conductors like Gerry Fagan, David Fallis, and Lydia Adams could take over individual events, Elmer was determined to remount the podium as soon as possible.

Also in June 1997 there was a particularly important concert that Lawrence Cherney's Soundstreams had commissioned Elmer to conduct. His imaginative arts promotion agency had established a Northern Encounters Festival of concerts around a theme of exploring music and its performance in countries that were Canada's neighbours in the highest latitudes, reaching in some cases into the Arctic regions of the planet. This particular concert in Toronto's St. Paul's Anglican Church, often referred to as "the Cathedral," featured two of the finest professional chamber choirs in Europe — the Danish Radio Choir and the Swedish Radio Choir — along with the Elmer Iseler Singers. The principal work was Gorecki's *Miserere*, a very difficult work that Elmer was to conduct with minimal time to prepare the three ensembles. In order to rehearse the three choirs as effectively as possible, Elmer had arranged all the singers in a circle around him and at least one observer questioned how these professional performers would react to treatment normally reserved for younger, less experienced choristers. Was this an aberration on the part of a very ill man just recovering from a serious operation? Would he arouse the ire of these professionals by treating them in this manner? To that query from Robert Cooper, Cherney replied, "They loved him!"

Indeed, Cherney's memory of the occasion could not be more complimentary: "I recall very vividly my impression that it was one of the best concerts that Elmer ever conducted. He was at the very top of his form ... At that time, both the Danish and Swedish Radio Choirs were thought to be among the best in the world, so Elmer and the EIS were in good company. The results were truly extraordinary."[3]

The TMC's 1996–97 choral series was to end with a concert that Elmer would conduct that people would recall for the rest of their lives. He had long wanted to have his Mendelssohn Choir perform a concert of Canadian music that would expose the true meaning of his love for Canada. The most articulate exponent of the Canadianism that Elmer espoused was bestselling author Pierre Berton, who had written numerous books about his country, led demonstrations on Parliament Hill against any weakening of its independence, put his entire public reputation on the line on behalf of many causes that sought to ensure the survival of a separate and sovereign nation.

One of Elmer's favourite experiences was having his Singers performing at James Campbell's Festival of the Sound in Northern Ontario. After experiencing a Howard Cable concert with the Hannaford Brass featuring Canadian music at that festival, Elmer had determined on a similar concert as a climax to his Toronto Mendelssohn Choir's 1996–97 series. He had met author Pierre Berton at a garden party and broached the subject of a presentation of Canadian music along with readings from Berton text that would enhance the very themes that Berton himself had exposed in his many books. Pierre was not very interested. Not to be diverted or discouraged, Elmer did his normal research, reading nearly every volume that the writer had published, marking out passages in musical scores that contained common themes that had been utilized in one or another composition of one or another Canadian composer. The strategy worked. Berton saw the clever association that Elmer had created between his own text and the proposed music program, relented, and joined Elmer in his last TMC concert in Roy Thomson Hall on Friday, June 8, 1997. It was not a normal array of favourite selections to celebrate a retiring conductorship — it was Elmer's call to every Canadian to remember what Canada stood for and a challenge to defend that country's integrity in every way that was possible.

People in Roy Thomson Hall realized they were likely seeing Elmer for the last time. The angry scar on his forehead from his surgery reminded them of his true fragility. When he came on stage, the crowd erupted with applause. Here was an open expression of support empowering a dying man who was prepared to give every ounce of energy his body could muster to the music and his audience. People simply would not stop clapping. The response was also a statement of outrage against those associated with the TMC who had made the previous months a form of hell beyond description. It was significant that the Toronto Mendelssohn Youth Choir was also on stage prepared to carry out his every strategy to ensure a concert that every singer and audience member would remember.

The concert ended too soon. The audience would have stayed all night. But the conclusion gave them another opportunity to clap, and clap, and clap — and Elmer had fulfilled every expectation. There could have been no more appropriate event to mark his departure as conductor of the Toronto Mendelssohn Choir after thirty-three years of devoted service. And Jessie and Elmer went home to Caledon still hoping for the miracle of a recovery.

It turned out that this concert was not to be his final public appearance. Later in the year, he was to conduct a concert of three choirs at St. Basil's Church on the University of Toronto's campus that provided a sensational experience of song, and Elmer had decided after these memorable concerts that, though no longer a part of the TMC world, he wished to conduct the music at the Toronto City Hall Cenotaph on Remembrance Day, November 11, 1997. He had performed this task, along with City Hall Christmas Celebrations, for many decades and he was determined to carry out that final act of commemoration. There, in the rain, in his long coat, with a regimental band and his Singers, was an ailing Elmer Iseler conducting the hymns of the occasion that spoke of sacrifice and commitment. Some of his extended family joined him — his brother-in-law, David, with his wife, Darlow, and, inevitably, close by his side — Jessie.

The operation in March 1997, Elmer hoped, had removed the cancerous tumour from his brain and he planned a return to his active way of life as soon as possible. During the months that followed, Robert Cooper always phoned the Iselers early in the morning knowing that invariably, in all his discomfort, Elmer would be out on his verandah walking in order to strengthen his body in readiness for his return to the podium. That spring and summer of 1997 saw Elmer achieve amazing feats of human courage and determination. He and the Elmer Iseler Singers had agreed to spend the late spring in Newfoundland. The Festival 500 was the celebration of that Island's discovery and colonial past and then its provincial beginnings, with conductors Bramwell Tovey, Gerry Fagan, Doreen Rao, and Halyna Kvitka Kondracki also taking part. The festival had been founded by two of Elmer's former students and Singers, Susan Knight and Douglas Dunsmore, and he was determined to be there with his own chorus. The scheduled workshop with the local choral community was to be an extraordinary experience. The choristers and the young conductors were aware that they might be the last recipients of Elmer's wisdom and they reacted with an amazing intensity of response. His accompanying EIS performance produced wildly enthusiastic accolades.

He returned to Quail Hill Farm and to Buffy's determination that he was going to experience, likely for the last time, the delights of travelling to his relatives in Quebec, to the familiar haunts of Ocean City New Jersey, to those places and to those people who meant so much to him. Though aware that he was weak and unable to be his exciting self, Elmer realized that these precious moments with his family could not be missed. Buffy understood the enormous responsibilities that Jessie was now carrying as manager of the Elmer Iseler Singers, as well as being a twenty-four-hour-a-day nurse for a deathly sick husband. She took on the responsibility for the travel arrangements. Buffy knew that neither the Iseler nor the Balsillie cars could provide the smooth drive she knew Elmer's condition demanded. She went to a local car rental agency, explained her problem, and was provided a luxury Cadillac at a highly reduced rental rate. The next few weeks were magical as Elmer visited his relatives and the beloved places of his lifetime in Quebec and then on to the southern United States, seeing people who could respond to his affection without restraint.

On his return to Canada, a visit to Princess Margaret Hospital confirmed that, indeed, the first operation had failed to catch all the cancer. Ensuing radiation and medication did relieve the terrible headaches that he was enduring, but it was all short-term. It was clear by the winter of 1998 that there could be no recovery. At one point, Elmer asked his doctor, "How long do I have?" The reply was, "With radiation, six months." As Jessie puts it, "I nearly went through the floor." But even that prognosis turned out to be too optimistic. Elmer went to bed on November 11, 1997, and stayed there until, on April 3, 1998, he quietly died.

These were the months when Jessie's presence every day and night brought comfort to a man damaged both by illness and cruel circumstances. The attending doctor offered his advice: "Take your dream trip!" Elmer replied, "I have done that every day of my life." In an offhand remark he had expressed his philosophy of living the good life.

There were moments of unexplainable energy and determination. The Christmas season of 1997 would include the typical Iseler-Balsillie festivities, with a meal of Chinese food on the eve and a full turkey dinner on the day. A week before, he had asked Jessie for his car keys. With enormous discomfort he rose from his bed, heading for Jim Bland's Caledon East Feed Mill to buy seeds for his wild birds — and then on to Orangeville to buy bird feeders for every member of the family. He went as well to the local hardware store, where owner and old friend George Berney found and sold to him a huge toboggan for his three-year-old granddaughter, Vanessa. It might overwhelm her initially, but she would be able to make use of it for years to come and that was the very point. Along with the toboggan he bought Vanessa seeds, soil, and garden boxes in which future years she could emulate his love of nature. His only expressed regret over his impending demise had been, "I don't want Vanessa to forget me." There was no chance of that happening — Vanessa remembers with a clarity undiminished by the several years of his absence her love for her grandfather. Juzzelle, her younger sister, is envious that she had not been born soon enough to experience Elmer's love, but is nevertheless enormously proud that she is his granddaughter. All the gifts that Elmer had bought were more than seasonal presents: they were symbols of what he cared about.

It was during these months that Vern and Elfrieda Heinrichs became central figures in the Iselers' lives, committing themselves to seeing that, before he died, Elmer would receive the ultimate recognition for his contribution from his own University of Toronto and that within this institution there would be assurance that his legacy would never be forgotten. Vern had spent an enormous amount of his time on negotiations he believed would result in an appropriate ending to Elmer's leadership of the TMC. It fell to Elfrieda to secure letters of support and to make contacts with university officials to see that the recognition would not be posthumous but celebrated during his last months of life. She took on this task with the relentless energy of a woman who knew what was right and was determined to see that right triumphed. In doing so she had the assistance of Doreen Rao, the director of the Choral Program at the Faculty of Music at the University of Toronto.

As a result of these efforts, Elmer would receive an honorary doctorate from his alma mater before his death in April. Although Rao's nomination had gone forward informally in the winter of 1997, and formally in June of that year, she insisted that it be moved on a short timeline that surprised every observer of an institution where time is normally measured in glacial terms. Amazingly, with the assistance of Dean of the Faculty of Music David Beach, who was most supportive, and University of Toronto President Rob Prichard's Office, a special convocation was planned for early 1998.

Even before, there were wonderful moments of pure joy. On a beautiful afternoon at the Heinrichs home at 88 Elm Avenue, in the presence of President Prichard, Elmer was the recipient of a University of Toronto jacket, and on that occasion it was announced that national choral scholarships had been established in Elmer's name and that his Singers would be "the professional choir in residence" at the Faculty of Music at a cost of $375,000, exactly the income that the EIS had lost when they had been replaced as the professional core of the TMC. Elmer and Jessie were both thrilled. As well, it was soon to be known that the Heinrichs, with Elfrieda the unstoppable force of nature, had decided to establish an Elmer Iseler Chair in Conducting. For Elmer to be aware of the legacy he would be leaving in some ways removed some of the gloom that had pervaded the Iseler home in the previous year.

As well, Elfrieda had managed to have Elmer's name and image on countless banners hanging from a sea of streetlight poles along major thoroughfares in the city — all a part of the university's fundraising campaign strategy to show what a contribution the university's distinguished graduates were making to the life of the City of Toronto. Elmer's recognition would not be just a rather private matter known only to the university community but made plain to virtually every citizen of the Greater Toronto Region.

In February 1998, in all the glory demanded by a full formal convocation, the chancellor and appropriate university officials appeared in full regalia at Quail Hill Farm and made their way into Elmer and Jessie's bedroom, where, overlooking their beloved garden, surrounded by close friends and family, they conferred on Elmer an honorary University of Toronto LL.D. Former Ontario lieutenant governor and now University Chancellor Hal Jackman remarked that it was the shortest but the most moving convocation he had ever convened. "I have never experienced such a touching moment in the conferring of a degree," he said. Though Elmer had already received honorary degrees from other universities — Dalhousie, Brock, York, and Wilfrid Laurier had so honoured him — receiving this recognition from his alma mater meant more than he could express. Indeed, as he sat up in his spotless white shirt carefully ironed by Jessie's hand he could only comment, "I feel rather underdressed for this occasion."

For the public there was an event that gained even more attention than the deserved recognition by the University of Toronto. *Choral Concert*, on CBC Radio, has long been at the very heart of the Canadian choral community, broadcasting every Sunday morning both worthy performances of international choirs on recordings and tapes of recent live performances by Canadian choirs from coast to coast, but providing as well a weekly announcement of the choral concerts being presented by choirs across the nation. In February 1998, an entire program was given over to a seventieth birthday celebration for Elmer Iseler. His life was recounted and observations of his contributions were presented through interviews with Sir Andrew Davis, Sir David Willcocks, Robert Shaw, Niki Goldschmidt, John Bird, William Littler, Harry Somers, John Beckwith, Ruth Watson Henderson, Maud McLean (a veteran TMC chorister and former Festival Singer manager), Howard Cable, Donald Bartle, Walter Homburger, and Kenneth Winters — literally the network of colleagues and critics who had been a part of the fabric of his life. Elmer's past recorded interviews on CBC were featured. It was apparent that Howard Dyck, Robert Cooper, and the *Choral Concert* team had outdone themselves in their desire to present the remarkable career of an extraordinary figure and to do so before he was gone. Letters and emails flooded the mailbox and computer at Quail Hill Farm. Jessie ensured that every one was read to Elmer and he was understandably thrilled to know that others had come to know that he had indeed carried out his vision — that he had made a difference. It was particularly appropriate that Cooper was able to take a recording of the program out to Quail Hill Farm for Elmer and Jessie to hear before it could be scheduled on air.

Not to be outflanked by radio, the television series *Adrienne Clarkson Presents* also provided a feature that spring, "Voyage to the Heart of His

Country," which made use of the June 1997 concert with Pierre Berton that had exposed Elmer as the ultimate patriot. Clarkson's warmth and appreciation for his work was evident: "A champion of modern Canadian composers and a tireless promoter of great choral music, Elmer Iseler is himself truly a Canadian treasure." The main focus of the program had been Elmer's conducting of the TMC and its Youth Choir, and the CBC cameras had to be carefully placed to hide as much as possible the results of the surgeon's knife on his forehead that would remind his audience of his ongoing battle with cancer.

Elmer never re-entered hospital, though his doctor, John McIlraith, made regular personal rather than professional visits, travelling all the way from Thistletown to Caledon to check that everything was being done to ensure his patient's freedom from pain. Often, they just sat as long-time friends quietly enjoying the peace of Elmer's surroundings.

Jessie's and Buffy's nursing skills kept Elmer comfortable and calm at Quail Hill Farm throughout his final months. His friends gathered round. John and Dolores Bird came regularly, and the Heinrichs, Viponds, Wheelwrights, and Shibleys were there often. Doreen Rao brought conductor Dale Warland from the United States, and, of course, the Balsillie-Iseler family waited upon Elmer and provided support to Jessie through these difficult weeks. Indeed, sister-in-law Darlow Balsillie took a leave of absence from her nursing work to assist, while Lucy Reid, a neighbouring nurse from nearby Palgrave, gave considerable professional and heartfelt attention to Elmer and the entire family. The "Northview kids" came every weekend, concerned that the "care crew" must nourish themselves, bringing prepared meals together with their love and good wishes. Sometimes they cleaned the house for Jessie so that she could concentrate on Elmer's well-being.

His choral conducting colleagues, Lydia Adams, Ruth Watson Henderson, and Robert Cooper, came often, as did the TSO's Andrew Davis, but they were but three of many. John Lawson, Suzanne Bradshaw, and Charlie Cutts, all representing the governance and staff of Roy Thomson and Massey Halls, arrived one day with a beautifully framed picture of the sculptured bust of Elmer that would grace the RTH lobby. The end came too soon, hurried on by the horror of the unfortunate events surrounding his severance from the leadership of the Toronto Mendelssohn Choir.

The series of events that led to the tragedy of 1997–98 already had a long history. Elmer's impending seventieth birthday had seemed to capture TMC board members' attention during the entire early and mid-1990s. As early as 1991, and initially unbeknown to either incumbent, the board had prepared a succession plan for the conductors of the TMC and the Toronto Mendelssohn Youth Choir but it was assumed, in Elmer's and Cooper's cases, that it would be a matter of negotiation. Elmer wanted only to take the choir into the new millennium and retire gracefully at the end of that first twenty-first-century season. But the TMC Board of Directors would not let that be!

The mind of the TMC board was obsessed with financial stability. The impetus for change seemed to have focused on some strange belief that a new conductor would automatically bring new audiences. It was a time of a desperate need for managerial leadership in the arts in general, and at the TMC it was a difficult transition period when infinitely more human resources were needed. Patti Tompkins had been long retired and no comparable figure had emerged to bring both efficiency and confidence. In particular, the fundraising function had become increasingly competitive. For choirs who had never been seen to be in need of massive support, it was a hard sell to a corporate community in which choral music was still perceived as an activity that involved the participation of amateurs who themselves actually paid a stipend for the opportunity of singing together!

There was also the psychological impact of the coming of the millennium — a kind of collective madness that seemed to indicate that the move from the 1900s would be accompanied by changes heralding a new world in a new century. In Toronto, it also seemed to be supported by the late twentieth century arrival of a new Roy Thomson Hall, even with its inadequate means of support for its day-to-day operating expenses. Many strange actions led institutions to behave in ways that in periods of normal development from year to year, or even from decade to decade, would have seemed mindless. People at the TMC spoke excitedly about "new directions." Today, when it appears that all the baggage of world conflict of the previous millennium has been carried into the 2000s and one looks back to the past century of Cold War as a proverbial golden age, this mindset now seems quite irrational. Indeed, the rhetoric of future hope and expectation of the 1990s sounds absolutely bizarre. But the fact that Elmer would be leading the TMC in his early seventies by the time the millennium arrived seemed incongruous to those who followed the patterns of street wisdom that a senior citizen should not be carrying Canada's most prestigious, historic choral community into the new millennium. Howard Cable, whose interaction with music performance is equalled by no other Canadian, expressed his view that the politics of choral music, with its strange alliance of amateur and professional, its lack of status, and its inadequate financial support, was the most volatile to be found in any corner of the music industry. The TMC actions proved he was right.

There were very significant immediate problems that were set out by the TMC's board chair, Irene Bailey.[4] Now ensconced in a larger and more expensive hall — both for performance and administrative offices — there were disadvantages that had financial implications. The choir was not drawing the 60 to 70 percent houses of the past. Rather, she claimed, 50 percent was becoming the norm and the choir was unsustainable at that level of concert attendance. As well, she contended there were indications of erosion in the quality of the choir, using as her evidence that the CBC had rejected tapings of a couple of recent concerts. It was true that tapes of performances of both the Iseler Singers and the TMC had been rejected for broadcast and deemed below the usual standards but there seemed to be other explanations for this phenomenon, in particular, Elmer's condition, but they were unconvincing to the TMC board and administrative officials bent upon "new directions." The full impact of that reduction in the quality of the choir could, Irene Bailey realized, lead the TSO to turn to another chorus when choral works were being performed.

Irene Bailey and the board believed that any loss of TMC revenue would savage the budget of a choir already in financial difficulty. As for the decline in box-office receipts, there was no effective analysis carried out to determine what was, in fact, discouraging potential subscribers and single ticket purchasers. It was most certainly a time when the entertainment dollar in Southern Ontario was being sought by an exponentially increased array of presenters. Could it have been the declining quality of promotion that was not exciting a new generation of choral enthusiasts? Had the decline in choral activity in the schools finally undermined any recognition of great choral work as a form of expression that merited attention by the young people who were graduating from the educational system? Or was it simply that a poor marketing strategy was failing to attract audience members? Or had demographic changes in Toronto reduced the capacity of a large traditional oratorio choir to find new audiences?

The massive oratorio choir had been a carryover from another century and another culture — in particular, the United Kingdom. Had the days of such vocal forces finally come to an end or, perhaps more likely, had a sound that was most appropriate for great celebration in giant stadiums and shopping malls ceased to attract mass audiences in more normal performance venues? The city of Toronto had become the most multicultural urban centre on the planet and later in the century most of the immigrants had come from Caribbean and East Asian countries rather than the United Kingdom and Europe. They now made up a significant percentage of the city's population, and although these citizens had rich choral traditions of their own, the music for large oratorio choruses had simply not yet reached their radar screen.

There was also the matter of repertoire. Essentially, composition on this scale had come from the liturgy of the Christian tradition. It was a time of galloping materialism fuelled by all the expectation of globalization of trade and financial transactions. The numbers of churchgoers was decreasing except in the more evangelical or charismatic wing of the Protestant community, for whom the large choir and oratorio repertoire had less familiarity. Indeed, the text of the great repertoire Elmer was committed to repeat — the Passions, the Masses, the Stabat Maters, the Glorias, and even the beloved *Messiah* — were mostly from other centuries and were written for people whose understanding of the universe was simpler, less complicated by scientific research, and could be reached by a faith statement of musical expression that reflected that perception of the universe. The music may have been divine, but the theological content came from less sophisticated levels of comprehension of divine purpose and behavioural expectation that seemed irrelevant to the theological debates that now challenged that faith. Perhaps there is no great truth more simply stated than can be found in a Bach chorale — but in the frantic toils of modern life, it was difficult to make that known and appreciated.

For at least some TMC board members, it was simply a matter of finding a bright new conductor to whom these so far untouched people would flock. There was a corporate mindset that saw the conductor as simply another employee and, in Elmer's case, one who refused to retire in a "normal" corporate fashion. It was a simplistic picture of the future but one that was easily accepted by several determined TMC board members and some baffled choristers. There was no common ground.

For Elmer it was a replay of the Festival Singers breakup. The TMC was also "his choir," even though he never had more than a one-year contract renewed year after year and had carried on without any kind of written assurance that provided any security once the board decided his talents were no longer wanted. He had no plans for immediate retirement. Elmer had been the mainstay as conductor for a good percentage of the choir's existence — some thirty-three years (a first in terms of longevity on the podium of a major choir anywhere in Canada) — and this commitment, in his view, deserved a longer and more sensitive transition, but at some time in the future. The corporate world had moved to early and immediate retirements that solved transition problems, and for some of the TMC board members there was nothing that spoke to a different style of administrative behaviour in the arts.

When Elmer had been formally approached about retirement plans, he refused to discuss the matter with any seriousness. In spite of the Festival Singers fiasco, he believed that the time would come when he would want to leave. He had openly expressed his interest in other projects — such as establishing a conductor's school on his Quail Hill Farm property. But nothing had come from the TMC succession plan documents that had been around for several years. Even the 1996–97 contract between Elmer and the TMC had never been signed by him, but in the history of annual contracts this seemed an insignificant aberration.

The decision of the board to conclude some agreement with Elmer was taken in the first months of 1997. The timing was crucial and disastrous. Irene Bailey claims that no one knew that Elmer was suffering from a brain tumour when the serious effort to change the TMC's relationship with him was initiated. There was no argument that the board had a legal right to replace its leader at will and with appropriate financial compensatory arrangements. However, they were now dealing with a man in a seriously weakened condition. The whole process should have ground to a halt as soon as Elmer's condition was known, as it most certainly became apparent after surgery in March 1997. That did not happen. In fact, Elmer's state of health became an argument to sort out the end of his tenure so that the choir could move on! To be fair, the TMC board was anxious about the continuing existence of the institution. As well, there were board members who admired Elmer and realized all that he had done. But after the entire drama had been played out, the terrible uproar was focused on the manner in which Canada's greatest oratorio choir had treated its conductor, now dying with brain cancer. A large number in the choral world were outraged and horrified. Conductors across the land openly wondered, if this kind of treatment could be meted out to their "dean" and mentor, how secure could they feel about their relationship with their own choirs and their boards. There were breaches of friendship and respect that have not as yet healed after a decade has gone by.

The board presented a proposal that Elmer's 1997–98 contract as conductor be abandoned, and he would have, instead, the honorary title of "Conductor Emeritus." He would be invited to mentor his successor (a Canada Council suggestion that had questionable merit and, under the circumstances, no likelihood of success). Elmer would be celebrated at a seventieth-birthday dinner before the first fall 1997 TMC series concert and he would conduct a millennium concert in 2000. In the intervening years, it was clear that Elmer would have no decision-making opportunities in regard to repertoire (except for the odd concert he himself might be asked to conduct) and would no longer have any part in determining the TMC's choral directions.

For Elmer, it was a humiliating offer. To a man fighting for his life against the cancer that had invaded his body, it was a devastating blow. Perhaps the most terrible suggestion was that he should produce a letter from a doctor stating that he was in no danger if he conducted rehearsals and performances. The justification from the board perspective was that the TMC might find itself responsible for any accident to an ailing employee that might occur in the process of rehearsal or performance. However, when Elmer presented a letter from his own doctor that assured the reader of his capacity to carry out his responsibilities, it was treated with some suspicion. Apparently the board was receiving less optimistic medical information from elsewhere.

The next steps in the process were seen to be both cruel and unusual. The board initiated a meeting to present the proposals the board deemed fair and equitable and the final offer was delivered just a few weeks after the initial surgery. On the holiday weekend in May 1997, when all of Elmer's friends and advisors were away and with Elmer suffering from the presence of more than a dozen clamps in his head following surgery, TMC President Irene Bailey and long-time board member Tom Laurie arrived at Quail Hill Farm armed with an agreement that would provide a further year's salary on the assumption that Elmer would accept all the other provisions — the conducting of only the first concert presentation of the 1997–98 season, before which a birthday dinner celebration would take place, the mentorship arrangements with his successor, and the conducting of a millennium concert all included. Elmer was virtually helpless: he needed money to survive but had no interest in the birthday celebrations or in mentoring a successor or in returning occasionally as a guest conductor. Financial exigencies demanded he sign off — and with no one at his side but Jessie, Elmer's career as conductor of the TMC was terminated. He accepted the financial element of the proposal and, seeing no alternative path, signed the documents. With understandable rage and bitterness, Jessie ushered Irene Bailey and Tom Laurie out of the house, and then collapsed beside Elmer in the four-poster bed on which he lay.

Elmer and Jessie, supported by their daughter, Buffy, had agreed to be present at the next TMC rehearsal when Irene Bailey would inform the choir of Elmer's appointment as conductor emeritus, a role that signalled the end of Elmer's role as the TMC's artistic director. In choral circles it became a night to remember. When the president's announcement reached the ears of choir members, many unaware of all the machinations that had been transpiring thought that Elmer's approval was to be taken for granted and he was being appropriately celebrated. The words "conductor emeritus" evinced confused applause. It was at that point Elmer interrupted Irene Bailey's announcement with a shout: "Don't applaud — I'm being dumped." That new information elicited interjections of "Shame!" and hearty expletives from some choir members that revealed their surprise and horror. After Buffy intervened and expressed the extent of her wounded heart that her father was being so treated, she, Elmer, and Jessie left. A number of choir members followed them out the door and Roger Hobbs, who had been warned of what might transpire, took over the rehearsal. It was now clear that the entire world would know of the sordid events that had led to Elmer's departure in this his last year of life.

Elmer refused to speak to anyone but his friends and colleagues who had soon gathered round. In particular the board and members of the Elmer Iseler Singers were immediately informed of the latest state of negotiations. The latter were of course very much threatened by the fact that their role as the professional core in the TMC was now in jeopardy. There were other issues that demanded attention.

In June of 1997, Elmer's colleagues, honorary EIS patron Vern Heinrichs and prominent former EIS board member John Bird, took on the responsibility of negotiating on Elmer's behalf. Irene Bailey and Tom Laurie continued to represent the board of the TMC. There was, however, no initial agreement on what outcome any such process might elicit. Heinrichs and Bird assumed that the process allowed a revisiting of all the disputed elements of the separation and that Elmer might be given a three-year contract that would continue his leadership with the presence of a mutually agreed upon artistic advisory committee that would allow for Elmer's involvement in decision making but would dispel any fears of Elmer's domination. In fact, by the end, Heinrichs had achieved Elmer's agreement that he would determine the choral program only for concerts he would conduct, reduced in number until the year 2000 when he would celebrate the millennium by conducting a very special TMC performance. That concert would end the entire affair and Elmer would be gone!

What were called "intensive negotiating meetings" were initiated and conducted between the four participants — Bird and Heinrichs for Elmer and his Elmer Iseler Singers, Bailey and Laurie from the TMC board. From the ninth to the sixteenth of June 1997 the discussions went on and on. In the early stages, it appeared that all the areas of confrontation and disagreement were to be covered and Bird and Heinrichs believed that progress was being made. All the participants were extremely busy but the pace of the meetings was initially breathtaking in seeking agreements. However, it became evident that the TMC representatives were impatient to reach an agreement that would resolve all the issues and allow steps that they regarded as essential to be taken. First on the list was the relationship with the Toronto Symphony Orchestra. A choir with a professional core was the basis of this partnership — a contract with the TSO was awaiting signature that included this provision. In forcing Elmer's resignation as conductor, the TMC was really "firing" the entire complement of the Elmer Iseler Singers.

Members of the boards of the TMC and EIS met at one point, and in the meeting Irene Bailey asked whether the Singers would remain as the core of the TMC if Elmer was not rehired. John Fenton, the EIS treasurer, was adamant. "Not a chance," he replied. A letter from George Pennie, the chair of the EIS board, informed the TMC board that unless Elmer was hired for the next three-year period, the Singers would not be available. (The year 2000 was a culmination point that even Elmer had now accepted.) There was deep anxiety in TMC ranks about what that meant, in artistic terms but also, more important to board members, the implications that it had for the TSO relationship and the TMC budget. Throughout these months, the unresolved situation was particularly brutal for the Singers whose salaries were obviously at risk. "A terrible period" sums up EIS board member John Fenton's memory of this period.

On June 19, 1997, the TMC board met, and it was reported to that body that the Elora Festival Singers, the only other sizeable professional chamber choir in the Toronto region (and indeed in Ontario), had been approached to see if its chorus would work with the TMC over the next two years.[5] June 24 saw a further meeting and an agreement on the solution to the TMC's professional core dilemma was reached — the Elora Singers under Noel Edison would become the professional core. However, a letter from Vern Heinrichs to Tom Laurie[6] on the June 23 assured the recipient of his commitment to continuing the negotiation process between the Toronto Mendelssohn Choir and Elmer Iseler. In Heinrichs's letter, it was clear that he had perceived that all the negotiators had, by June 16, reached some level of agreement on the need to reach a decision that would "allow the TMC Board and Elmer Iseler to move forward in an orderly fashion."[7] It must be noted that this missive had been mailed four days after the TMC had approached the Elora Festival Singers. It is apparent that Heinrichs was writing under the assumption that there had been no closing down of the negotiations and that both John Bird and Vern Heinrichs were proceeding on the basis that these discussions would eventually find a common ground for the continuance of Elmer's relationship as conductor of the TMC over the succeeding three years.

Referring to a memorandum of understanding that Iseler had signed and was open for TMC board acceptance, the Heinrichs letter continued, "It is also important to confirm that we are continuing to negotiate in good faith on the points that give the TMC Board concern." It was clear that Laurie and Heinrichs were keeping in touch by telephone of necessity because Heinrichs had been forced to return to the United Kingdom and Irene Bailey had indicated that her work made further time in continuing negotiation quite impossible. Nor did the June 23 letter reveal that Heinrichs and Bird had any notion that the TMC board was carrying on negotiations with the Elora Festival Singers board.

The one sticking point was obviously Elmer's desire to have control over artistic direction during the entire three years until, in 2000, he conducted the millennium concert. However, Heinrichs had convinced Elmer that this was not possible to achieve within the context of TMC's determination to "move on." Heinrichs could report Elmer's willingness to "relinquish all programme and artistic direction over ALL concerts that he does not conduct."[8] It led Heinrichs to believe that a memorandum could be prepared that resolved the differences between the TMC and

Elmer and that, as well, an artistic advisory committee would be created, with names offered by both sides and a process included that would enable all to feel comfortable with the membership and presumably with the kind of advice presented on artistic direction.

The letter sent to Tom Laurie received a reply dated June 25, not from Laurie, but from TMC chair Irene Bailey. In her view, the main concerns of the TMC had not been laid to rest, and that, indeed, the memorandum "prepared by yourself and Dr. Iseler and possibly others unknown to us, completely ignores our basic premise on which 8–10 hours of intensive discussion took place between yourself, John Bird, Tom Laurie and myself." Her conclusion was that "It is clear from your letter and the Memorandum from Dr. Iseler that nothing less than re-instatement as Conductor, but conducting fewer concerts, was going to satisfy."[9] Was institutional survival sufficient reason for the TMC board decision to carry on negotiations with the Elora board while still appearing to be working on a compromise that would satisfy Elmer? Rumours were in the air that Elmer was making overtures to the TSO that he could provide an alternative to the TMC that would serve the orchestra's needs, no doubt fuelled by Elmer's threat he would "destroy the TMC" as some claimed he had the Festival Singers some twenty years before. However, there is no evidence that Elmer was moving on that threat, indeed, in his physical condition there was no assurance he could carry through on such a strategy.

The letter brought to an end any further negotiations. The TMC board sent Dr. Iseler a letter informing him that his signed memorandum of agreement would be declined. The issue of the need to have the Elmer Iseler Singers as the core of the TMC had been decided when the Singers board had insisted that the Singers' contracts would be conditional on Dr. Iseler's reinstatement — a condition the TMC board had rejected. (The unsigned contract with the TSO that demanded the presence of a professional core obviously weighed heavily on the minds of the TMC leadership.)

Vern Heinrichs was informed by Irene Bailey's letter that the negotiations had ended. "We did negotiate in good faith with yourself and John Bird. However, regrettably, it seems that much of what we said was

not heard. I am sorry we have not been successful," Bailey concluded.[10]
It was only later that Heinrichs and Bird discovered that in the latter
stages of the negotiation of Elmer's continuing presence and transition
over a three-year period, the TMC board had been in negotiations with
the Elora Festival Singers board. Once again, Elmer and his colleagues
had every reason to be bitter and disillusioned about the values and
behaviours of individuals devoted to the transforming impact of great
choral music, while at the same time there were TMC board members
who were convinced they were saving Canada's primary conveyor of
choral excellence.

Certainly the negotiations were made more complicated by the terrible
state of Elmer's health, and one would have thought that knowledge of this
factor might have diverted the worst features of his enforced departure.
(It was, in fact, the first confrontation of this nature that had taken place
over thirty-three years.) Though the contract with the TSO (along with
an assurance that the TMC could provide outstanding performance)
was crucial, there is no evidence that the TMC was being pressured to
secure an immediate decision on that point. (It is unexplainably tragic
that certain crucial documents for this period mysteriously disappeared
from the files of the TMC.) Certainly by the spring of 1997, there was a
general realization in the TMC board and beyond that Elmer would soon
be dead. In the end, it was not the question of whether Elmer should
retire or be forced to do so that devastated the choral community from
coast to coast. It was, as William Littler put it, the feeling that Elmer was
being kicked while he was down and that a man with a half-century of
unique contribution to the choral art deserved much better.

The longer term implications of these events were serious. Although
there was a search for a new conductor, these circumstances had
undermined any perception of seriousness regarding the outcome. Robert
Cooper, who had by this time conducted the Toronto Mendelssohn Youth
Choir for over two decades, was seen by many as the crown prince who
had leaped into the breach and conquered the Bach B Minor Mass to
great acclaim when Elmer's health made his appearance impossible in the
winter of 1997. The whole situation brought deep suspicion upon any
process for seeking a successor. Cooper's path was blocked, it seemed, by

the single TMC criterion of having a professional choir to present to the TSO as its professional core. As well, Cooper had made his feelings of support for Elmer quite plain and public. Within a few more months and after a sabbatical, he was no longer the conductor of the Mendelssohn Youth Choir.

The impact on the Ontario choral community was extraordinary. It was rent in two, with the vast majority of choristers and conductors lining up with Elmer, who they knew was near death. The normal warm, congenial atmosphere at choral events of celebration and mourning that have been part of the choral culture, the opportunities for mutual support of great causes, were permeated by a bitterness that has not entirely dissipated through all these intervening years. It remains a searing event of monumental tragedy in the memories of hundreds of choristers and choral enthusiasts.

Meanwhile, the circumstances that surrounded Elmer's death distorted the manner in which his life work was viewed. There should have been months of quiet triumph, an opportunity for revelling in the success of his pursuit and capture of a vision of what his country was capable of doing. The flood of cards and letters he received did not dwell on the disasters of spring 1997 but on the glorious events of the previous half-century. Fortunately, his rebirth as a University of Toronto adjunct professor, his honorary degree, and his knowledge of the presence of a chair occupied by a distinguished choral academic, along with a national choral conducting scholarship program that would now bear his name in the Faculty of Music, were now satisfying realities. This most certainly provided Elmer with some sense that his friends and colleagues had not abandoned or forgotten him and that his contributions were being widely recognized.

However, the circumstances of his severance with the TMC coloured the very nature of the assessment his life's work received upon the occasion of his death. Too often, along with an account of his contributions were the comments about his being "difficult," as though there was some fatal flaw that every journalist had to identify and explain. Less was said about the fact that in his tenure with both the Festival Singers and the TMC Elmer had outlasted a host of TSO conductors and an army of choral conductors across the entire nation. Being "difficult" scarcely explained the phenomenon of the long tenures of thirty-three years, twenty-four years, and twenty years of extraordinary success in the three choral enterprises to which he had given his life — the Toronto Mendelssohn Choir, the Festival Singers, and the Elmer Iseler Singers, the latter still in place and thrilling crowds into the new millennium.

Elmer's very last days of March and early April of 1998 were particularly hard. He so much wanted to spare both Jessie and Buffy waiting upon him hour by hour. At one point he found them weeping nearby and jokingly invited them to include him in their moments of despair. Every time he could, he would tell them something he thought funny. Buffy looks back on those dark winter days wondrously filled and fun. Elmer loved to laugh — he was an admirer of all the American-based comics — Red Skelton, Bill Cosby, Carol Burnett, Jackie Gleason, indeed the whole array of humorists who dominated television programming in the last decades of the twentieth century. And laughing was an activity he insisted upon throughout those last days!

The full impact of the cancer inevitably affected Elmer's capacity to speak. Richard Shibley came by, took his hand, and was moved to tears. Unable to express his farewell, Elmer pressed his finger into Shibley's palm in the rhythm of the first bar of Beethoven's Fifth Symphony. It was Elmer's final contribution to a lifelong argument about who was the greatest composer — Shibley's Beethoven or Elmer's beloved J.S. Bach.

Just a few days before Elmer died, he experienced a sublime moment of joy. The frogs returning to his nearby wetland began to sing, a sound that Elmer had welcomed every spring for three decades at Quail Hill Farm. Their song rang out and brought a smile — only this time it would be nature's farewell to a man who never lost his wonder of the sound and beauty of the world around him.

On the day of his passing, there were a number of strange events. John and Dolores Bird were driving north past Quail Hill Farm in the early afternoon. They returned south a couple of hours later, knocked on the front door — and were taken aback by Jessie's question, "How did you know?" Elmer had died just a couple of hours before — at the very moment of the Birds' initial sighting of the familiar Iseler homestead that afternoon. In minutes, John Bird was helping by telephoning the Elmer Iseler Singers roster to inform them of Elmer's passing.

Just four days later, in the Cathedral Church of St. James, Toronto, a "Service of Love and Remembrance" took place. Even with the short notice, the church was packed with twelve hundred worshippers, filling every seat and lining the walls of the magnificent sanctuary. Jessie, with the help of Lydia Adams and Giles Bryant, had spent hours preparing what was the most moving musical and spoken tribute to a man who had given himself so completely and so passionately to those around him. (How ironic that a man accused of an enormous ego had done nothing to prepare for his own memorial service except request that Bryant play an appropriate Bach organ selection. He left it all to Jessie, who began her planning with Elmer's famous rendition of a familiar children's Christmas hymn, "Away in a Manger.")

There were sixteen clergy in attendance, led by the Very Reverend Douglas A. Stout, the dean of Toronto, but the two clerics who had perhaps spent more time talking to Elmer in recent years had been the Reverends Lillian Perigoe and Bill Kervin, both incumbent ministers of Lawrence Park Community Church where the Elmer Iseler Singers had rehearsed weekly and occasionally performed throughout the choir's presence in that building over the previous two decades.

Bill Kervin remembers the cathedral procession on that day and in spite of the presence of all members of the Iseler and Balsillie family, the image of Jessie, clad in black, walking down the aisle alone. She had decided, in spite of all entreaties to accept the support of a brother, son, or daughter, or one of a host of close personal friends, to walk down the long aisle of the sanctuary alone. On that day, she wanted to be seen as she now felt she was — truly alone.

The music of Willan, Bach, Vaughan Williams, Croft, and Taverner filled the cathedral, sung, of course, by the Elmer Iseler Singers, recovering from an all-night vigil at St. Mary Magdalene's, organized and staffed by Elmer's "Northview kids." People present were overwhelmed by the words, but it was the singing of the hymns that proved most memorable. It seemed as though every singer that Elmer had touched was there that day and formed a chorus that sang "Love Divine, All Loves Excelling,"

"A Mighty Fortress Is Our God," "Ye Watchers and Ye Holy Ones," and "Praise, My Soul, The King of Heaven" as these great hymns had never been sung before.

There were speakers who had been a part of Elmer's life and spoke intensely about their knowledge of his career. Richard Shibley provided an account of his relationship in those early years in Port Colborne. Jean Ashworth Bartle had known Elmer as a mentor; as a conductor of the Toronto Mendelssohn Choir in which she sang for seventeen years; as a close colleague of her husband, Don Bartle, who had sung with him for some forty years; and, most of all, as an inspiration in her own career as the conductor of the Toronto Children's Chorus, who were also present at that service along with Elmer's own Singers. In a voice breaking with her sorrow, Jean stressed his artistic contribution to the choral life of a nation and brought to the congregation's attention the response of the choral musical giants with international reputations who had worked with Elmer over so many years.

The singing of Elmer's own anthem, "King of Glory, King of Peace," by his Singers was the moment of truth for many who yearned for some hope that the Iseler sound and the Iseler repertoire would not be gone forever. Perhaps the most emotional moments came from the description of Elmer as the paragon family figure by David Balsillie and, even more, Margaret McCoy's reading of daughter Buffy's poem in celebration of Elmer's love for his granddaughter Vanessa. It spoke of the sacred moments when Elmer carried his granddaughter in his arms to show her "the sun, the moon and the starry universe" and "the red wing blackbirds," and of the joy "when [my] loved ones hold me tight" with the precept that "laughter, nature and music fall in behind love, the best gift of all." Elmer was "her guardian angel now," Buffy told her three-year-old that afternoon. It was followed by Elmer's arrangement of "Away in a Manger" sung by the Toronto Children's Chorus, and there were few dry eyes in the cathedral.

At the graveside in Caledon East, the Elmer Iseler Singers sang Elmer to the next stage of the divine plan he had so intensely celebrated. The particular piece selected was one that the EIS had performed to great acclaim in Salt Lake City at the meeting of the American Choral

Above: Great friends John Peter Lee Roberts and Elmer Iseler looking over plans at the 1988 Olympics in Calgary. John brought Igor Stravinsky to Toronto to work with the Festival Singers in the 1960s while he was head of music at CBC Radio.

Below: A happy gathering at Quail Hill Farm with special friends. Jessie and Elmer, Frieda and Vern Heinrichs, and Dolores and John Bird.

Elmer and Jessie loving life on a merry-go-round in upper New York State.

Photo by Jessie Iseler Bride.

Who's in charge: Elmer or Jessie? Loved having fun! Ocean City Beach Patrol, New Jersey shore.

Above: Elmer Iseler, Jessie Iseler, and Lydia Adams before a gala concert at the International Choral Kathaumixw, Powell River, British Columbia.

Below: Always full of love and support: brother and sister-in-law David and Darlow Balsillie.

Elmer Iseler Singers with honorary patrons Vern and Elfrienda Heinrichs at 88 Elm Avenue for Strawberries and Champagne, circa early 1990s.

Courtesy of the Toronto Mendelssohn Choir.

Above: Always ready for fun. Elmer entertains in a Santa outfit and conducts the Toronto Mendelssohn Choir with a candy cane baton during a recording session at Roy Thomson Hall, March 30, 1992.

Below: Elmer Iseler with Mary McKellar Couttes after a National Youth Choir concert in St. Thomas Anglican Church, St. Catharines, circa 1992. Mary's father, J.O. McKellar supported Elmer through the University of Toronto.

Photo by J. Iseler.

National Youth Choir, with Elmer Iseler, conductor, and Lydia Adams, pianist (wearing a purple sweater), in May 1992.

Above: Best friends Elmer Iseler and Sir David Willcocks celebrate at a reception at the Heinrichses' home in Toronto.

Below: Vern and Elfrieda Heinrichs host Elmer, Sir David Willcocks, Jessie, and Canadian composer and dear friend Srul Irving Glick following a performance of Srul's music.

Above: CBC host Howard Dyck interviews conductor Elmer Iseler, librettist Robertson Davies, and composer Derek Holman about *Jezebel*, an oratorio commissioned by the 1993 Toronto International Choral Festival. The world premiere performance took place at Roy Thomson Hall, Toronto, with the Toronto Symphony Orchestra, the Toronto Mendelssohn Choir, and soloists conducted by Elmer Iseler.

Below: The three musketeers! John Bird, T.L. Roy, and Elmer Iseler, 1993.

Photo by Jessie Iseler.

Elmer, a legendary photographer, at Niagara Falls circa 1992. Elmer's camera was never far from his music briefcase!

Above: Elmer and Jessie celebrate Elmer's honorary doctorate from York University, June 15, 1994.

Below: Elmer and Jessie in Yellowknife, Northwest Territories, dogsledding on Great Slave Lake following a concert with the Elmer Iseler Singers in 1996.

Above: Tireless in their dedication and support towards the Toronto Mendelssohn Choir and Elmer's work with the choir: Roger Hobbs, Patti Tompkins, J. Stuart Stephen, John B. Lawson, Jack Brook, Hans Schade, Suzanne Bradshaw, Andrew Davis, and Elmer with Lois Marshall.

Below: Great family friends and former students of Elmer's, Margaret and Leslie McCoy, with son Tim (now in the NAC orchestra), celebrating with Elmer following a performance at Roy Thompson Hall.

Above: Elmer's lifelong friend, famed Canadian contralto Maureen Forrester, shared in performing for the launch of the annual fundraiser for Covenant House at Toronto City Hall.

Below: Internationally renowned conductors (left to right) Tonu Kaljuste, Doreen Rao, Howard Dyck, Elmer Iseler, Jean Ashworth Bartle, Lydia Adams, Stefan Parkman, and Robert Cooper at St. Paul's Anglican Church, Toronto, June 1997, preparing for a concert presented by Soundstreams Canada.

Photo by Maura McGroarty.

Above: Nearing the end of a career that spanned five decades, Elmer Iseler conducts workshops in St. John's, Newfoundland, at Festival 500, July 1997.

Below: Elmer Iseler with good friend and colleague Helmuth Rilling following a Bach B Minor Mass performance with the Toronto Mendelssohn Choir and Toronto Symphony.

Photo by J. Iseler.

Above: Dean David Beach, Vern and Elfrieda Heinrichs, University of Toronto President Rob Prichard, Jessie Iseler, Doreen Rao, and Elmer Iseler at the announcement of the Elmer Iseler National Graduate Fellowships gratiously donated by Vern and Elfriend Heinrichs to the Faculty of Music, University of Toronto, 1997.

Below: Vern and Elfrieda Heinrichs toast Elmer Iseler at 88 Elm Avenue on the announcement of the Elmer Iseler scholarships at the Faculty of Music, University of Toronto, in September 1997.

Photo by Michael Hudson.

Above: A friendship for life: Richard Shibley gives one of four eulogies at St. James Cathedral for Elmer Iseler. April 7, 1998.

Below: The legacy continues: Jessie Iseler, John Bride, Jessie Iseler Bride, Vanessa Bride, Juzzelle ("Zellie") Bride, and Lydia Adams. Photo taken before a tribute concert for John Charles Bird in Toronto, 2007.

Photo by C. Nelles.

Directors Association, Canadian composer Sid Robinovich's "Prayer Before Sleep." David King, an EIS chorister and conducting colleague of Elmer's, describes the last moment with some emotion: "There could not have been a more appropriate selection. Though Jewish, it contributed to the ecumenical spirit of the whole occasion. It was a calm, quiet musical moment but as the piece ended there was a 'swoosh,' as a completely unexplainable breeze blew through the cemetery. It was quite moving ... as though Elmer's spirit was taking its leave."[11]

Son Noel expressed both his love and his sorrow in a typically practical fashion. He had been present throughout the night's vigil and had wrapped Elmer in a blanket "to keep him warm." Then, as his last act of love, he ensured that Elmer's fishing rod was placed by his side in the coffin and remained after all the mourners had left to assist the cemetery workers in filling in his father's grave.

There were countless other moments of joy and sadness but there was most of all the realization that Toronto, Ontario, and Canada would never be the same from that afternoon. The "difficult" Elmer was forgotten in the realization that a great human being had passed on, one who had made a unique contribution to those who had ears to listen and the wisdom to understand what his Singers were expressing.

Perhaps the last words belong to Robert Cooper. "Elmer Iseler was the single greatest influence on the maturation of both the Canadian choral conductor and the Canadian choral art."[12] He was now gone.

Chapter 15

The Legacy

IN THESE DAYS OF THE COMINGS AND GOINGS of prime ministers and presidents we hear a great deal about the importance of leaving a legacy. It is a part of the human condition to fear that death represents oblivion and each one of us harbours the hope that through the things we have done, the individuals we have influenced, the memory of our presence by family and friends, there will be some residue of our lives that will remain when our time has come to depart this earth. There is little doubt that the diminution of any widespread belief in the hope of eternal life has increased humankind's concern about the evidence of something left behind after death has erased an individual's presence on the planet.

Elmer had certainly accumulated a monumental legacy by the time he had reached his middle years. He had created Canada's finest chamber choir, the Festival Singers, and had toured it, with unparalleled success, across Canada, into the United States, and through eastern and western Europe. He had restored the reputation of the Toronto Mendelssohn Choir and had taken that chorus to new heights of musical excellence and then toured this ensemble to major choral venues in the United States, the United Kingdom, and Europe. By the late 1970s, he had created a second outstanding chamber choir, the Elmer Iseler Singers, and had toured it to warm accolades across the North American continent and to both Europe and the Far East. In all these exploits his choirs had received the acclaim of critics and audiences alike and Canada's reputation as a choral nation had been enhanced.

Elmer had been responsible for commissioning, largely through the resources of the CBC, an extraordinary spectrum of fine contemporary choral music by Canadian composers. The impact of that commitment had been substantial, providing other ensembles with Canadian works as a significant fraction of their repertoire. His own choirs had sung the repertoire again and again, not only at concerts in Canada, but around the world. Even more important, conductors such as Jon Washburn in Vancouver, Lydia Adams and Robert Cooper in Toronto, and Gerry Fagan in London, Ontario, had emulated Iseler's example and even today Canada's major music makers are engaged in writing for voices as well as for orchestras and smaller instrumental ensembles. His influence on the paramount capacity of the human voice has spilled out into the genre of opera, with Wayne Strongman energizing the creation of Canadian works through his Tapestry New Opera Works process in Toronto, in part encouraging the emergence of Canadian composers as well as vocalists who have reached opera stages both in Canada and abroad.

Elmer had spurred on the movement to establish his chamber choirs as professional ensembles with quality singers prepared to spend their lives enhancing the choral art and joining him in his efforts to encourage broader efforts to improve choral music presentation across the country. By the 1990s there existed in Canada a splendid array of fine choirs, a few of them professional, and a significant bevy of capable conductors leading a large number of choristers who had, through his influence, experienced what quality choral music could achieve.

Elmer's international reputation was evident by the responses to his death of the major figures in the world of choral music. Jean Ashworth Bartle contacted them about Elmer's demise as she prepared to participate in his memorial service. Dale Warland, a celebrated American choral conductor, had been inspired by Elmer to create his Dale Warland Singers, a professional choir of considerable accomplishment. He wrote, "What a giant! What an inspiration! What a friend! Elmer's contribution to choral music was enormous. His influence, without question, will circle the globe for generations to come ... A bit of this man's fire and zest for life will always burn in my heart and in my music. He touched me deeply."

Sir David Willcocks in the United Kingdom echoed his American colleague and described Elmer as "a charismatic figure who excited performers and audience," and in a personal letter to Elmer spoke to him of all those "whose lives had been enriched by your music-making."

However, it was Robert Shaw, retired conductor of the Atlanta Symphony Orchestra Chorus, the pre-eminent figure in choral music in the United States for several decades, who in his eulogy at St. James Cathedral best described Elmer's universal impact abroad beyond Canada's borders:

> Elmer Iseler was, for this century and the world of choral music, both star and morning sun. His thorough musicological study, his technical mastery of choral crafts, his devotion to a composer's language, his commitment to new voices and forms, and his passion to share the joys of music making with even the "least of us," have reached beyond our continent to the whole world of music-lovers.

Major publications of worldwide significance recorded the significance of his work. The *Choral World News* published the news of his death:

> In a career that spanned five decades, Dr. Iseler was pivotal to the development of choral music in Canada ... Under his baton Dr. Iseler's choirs have achieved international status for their technical brilliance and artistic versatility ... He has, in the estimation of many of his peers, conductors and professional musicians in Canada and abroad, created a vibrant world-class choral infrastructure in Canada.

The *Choral Journal*, the official publication of the American Choral Directors Association, printed a tribute that recorded the highlights of his career, attributing his reputation to the fact that "he achieved a sound and a technique in choral singing that were unmatched in Canada" but emphasized his role in encouraging choral music creativity:

He initiated and established a tradition of performances
of Canadian compositions, fostering that goal as one of
his priorities. He also consolidated the place of Canadian compositions by commissioning Canadian composers and premiering their works. Subsequently, he ensured
their communication and dissemination through publication in the Elmer Iseler Series, through radio broadcasts and recordings. Whether in the educational forum,
in the concert hall, or in the recording studio, his role as
communicator was unique and unparalleled in Canada.

However, the tributes that Elmer would have enjoyed most were
presented through the pages of *Anacrusis*, the publication of the Association
of Canadian Choral Conductors, in its Spring-Summer 1998 issue. His
contributions were dutifully enumerated but the most moving comment
came from Diane Loomer, a Vancouver choral conductor, who expressed
her memories in a very personal comment:

> There are three things I'll always remember about Elmer:
> 1) his insatiable curiosity, 2) his uninhibited wonder at the
> earth and its people, and 3) the joy of play The image?
> He and Jessie in my little convertible, top down, driving
> off to Whistler Mountain with their hair flying in the
> breeze, laughing and singing their cares away to the sky.
> He never failed to move people in one way or another,
> and I believe his first concern was to always serve the
> music. I will miss him.

A more restrained and formal but unsigned assessment of Elmer's
role in the same publication emphasized the fact that "many of us had
experiences in working with Elmer that were unforgettable in bringing
about professional and artistic growth. He was instrumental in helping
so many young conductors develop to their full potential, and to a large
extent, the vibrancy of Canada's choral scene now is due to the teaching,
mentoring and touring that Elmer and his choirs did for so many years."

It was more than just another formal accolade by Canadian conductors for a fallen colleague just days after his death. In a letter to Jessie, an attendee at the Association of Canadian Choral Conductors conference in Halifax just after Elmer's demise commented, "I was struck by the part that people all over the conference talked of how Elmer helped them. This you can easily imagine, but what struck me was the depth of their feelings and the sincerity of their comments." They departed the conference "more resolved to continue to teach and inspire their choirs just as he did for us."

Was Elmer universally loved and respected? Hardly. There was throughout his career a "Let's Hate Elmer" movement that feasted on the fact that he seemed to regularly receive comparatively generous financial treatment by the Canada Council and Ontario Arts Council. That he was favoured by the CBC's artistic leadership, for both broadcast opportunities and commissioning funds, was a widespread belief. Elmer's lack of easy geniality, his assumed "arrogance" as he strode to the podium, his reluctance to speak to his colleagues about his own understandable fears and insecurities, all fed the envy of a considerable number of figures in the choral community. Elmer was very much a visible target for some forty-five years. In moments of resentment over his broad public recognition in awards and honorary degrees, Elmer's critics were loath to concede that he had ceaselessly advocated on behalf of the appropriate funding of all choral music throughout these years and that his relentless perseverance along with the quality of his own choristers' performance had been a determining factor that had finally allowed choral music to be accepted and celebrated in the country he loved so deeply.

No account of Elmer's legacy could be complete without the comments of both Jon Washburn and Wayne Riddell. They were the two comparable figures as professional choral conductors, the first in Vancouver, the second in Montreal, who were both inspired to create chamber choirs like Elmer's Festival Singers in the decades after the founding of that extraordinary ensemble.

Jon Washburn could be described as the Elmer Iseler of the West Coast of Canada. His Vancouver Chamber Choir broadcasts coast to coast, records extensively, and tours the nation and beyond. He credits several concerts and workshops by the Festival Singers at the University of British Columbia and Simon Fraser University in the late 1960s as the moment of truth leading to his decision to create a similar choir with the same standards of singing and similar aspirations to performing a contemporary repertoire. He, like Elmer, turned his attention in the early years to recording and broadcasting. "Elmer made a tremendous difference to choral music in Canada. His presence and performance was a treasure particularly in the 1960s and 1970s. While he was touring in the Vancouver area I followed him from concert to concert for nearly a week, mesmerized by the incredible sound of his Singers. I decided that creating such music at that high level was what I wanted to do."

Jon worked regularly with Elmer on Canada Council juries for over a decade, making decisions about how that body would best support the burgeoning choral activity of the 1980s and 1990s, and also found ways to co-operate with him on choral projects that involved all three professional choirs, the Tudor Singers in Montreal, the Vancouver Chamber Choir, and Toronto's Festival Singers — even though several thousands of miles apart. Was Elmer a saint without either ego or survival instinct in the reality of diminishing resources for choir work? "Hardly," Jon asserts with warmth and generosity of spirit, acknowledging that one doesn't build a professional choral ensemble without having certain qualities of strength, determination, and competitiveness. Elmer's attitude could be dismissive and distant if his own work seemed at risk — a normal reaction, even in dealing with the apostles who had sat at his knee but a few years before.[1]

Wayne Riddell's response to a question about Elmer's role in the musical life of the nation was immediate and enthusiastic: "Elmer was the pioneer of Canadian choral music, establishing the first professional choir and ensuring standards of performance that were the benchmarks for all of us who followed. Perhaps his greatest contribution was the prominence he gave to contemporary music, particularly that of Canadian composers. That was his real art — the interpretation of the work of an R. Murray Schafer, giving his composition life and exciting exposure." Wayne, like Jon Washburn, spent many hours with Elmer adjudicating and evaluating the work of choirs seeking support from a Canada Council with dwindling resources.

Riddell continues: "Elmer's influence has been massive. The TMC had, in the 1960s, a choral conductor's workshop program and I, along with ten other conductors from across the nation, spent a week under Elmer's supervision." The creation of the Tudor Singers came from that experience. "Later the TMC gave up the program and the Canada Council supported its shift to Montreal and for a couple of years Elmer and I gave it together." They became colleagues and a close friendship developed between the Riddells and the Iselers that included fellowship in each other's homes and a relationship that went far beyond the demands of choral activity and a series of joint projects that engaged their attention.

Riddell concedes that there were areas of competitive confrontation. "Elmer's genius as a conductor was instinctive rather than learned and this put off many colleagues." He had in his subconscious a pure choral sound that he was determined his choirs should produce. Riddell, working in the province of Quebec and under appropriate pressure to sing a French-language repertoire, found that his choristers had to achieve a greater variety of colour and this meant building sound beyond that demanded by Elmer's circumstances. Nevertheless, the quality that Elmer expected from his choristers remained a beacon in the minds of all the conductors he encountered.[2]

In these incredible months of late 1997 and early 1998 during which Elmer alternated between being bedridden and immobilized and yet capable of miraculously reviving briefly for rehearsals and performances on the podium of the TMC or the EIS and on occasion reaching yet another height of splendid music making — letters, faxes, emails, cards, and telephone calls flooded the Quail Hill Farm. His treatment by a handful of members on the TMC board; the triumph of particular concerts, whether in Roy Thomson Hall with the TMC or in Newfoundland with his EIS; his appearance as an adjunct professor at the University of Toronto; the announcement of the national choral conducting scholarships in his name and subsequently the awarding of an honorary degree — all aroused hundreds of former choristers, conductors, composers, and former students to make contact and express their memories of his contribution to their careers and their lives.

The letters were invariably addressed to both Elmer and Jessie, and after April 3, 1998, the flood of mail continued to come to Jessie. These missives almost universally recognized the extent to which Jessie was now part of that legacy, though none could be sure of the role she would now play. The comments often expressed the reflection that without Jessie there would have been no such career. The final months of her nursing Elmer during his physical frailty seemed nothing more than an extension of more than four decades of serving his every physical, intellectual, and spiritual need.

In the final days of his life it was these eclectic contacts with fellow Canadian citizens from across the expanse of his country that most thrilled him, coming from every corner of the land, all aware of his life's work but moved by him individually in many different ways. One poignant personal letter came from a New Brunswick woman who had been a member of the TMC for nine years: "Mendelssohn was my 'life line' when my marriage was falling apart. I had a newborn baby girl, a two year old son, and my husband didn't love me anymore … those Monday nights were like a transformation that sustained me through the week … I thank God for Elmer's presence in my life." Jessie laughs about a piece of doggerel that Elmer enjoyed. It ran "Meet your Mate in Mendelssohn," and this particular writer fortunately did find her new spouse at a TMC event.

Though history will emphasize the great performances of the towering choral masterpieces, for many, many singers, his rehearsals stand out as memories to cherish, choreographed with care and precision to create dramatic experiences week after week of tough choral expectations. There were memories of Elmer's relentless determination to secure the sound, the musical phrase that would enhance the text. For the dozens, perhaps hundreds, of conductors who participated in the workshops that were held across the continent over several decades, the quality of these rehearsals may well be his major legacy.

Especially, Elmer and Jessie appreciated all the letters from composers: from John Beckwith and Lou Applebaum, from Victor Davies and his mate, Lori, from Srul Irving Glick, Harry Somers, and many others. Ruth Watson Henderson, who stated on every appropriate occasion, "I learned everything I know about composition from watching Elmer," included in her missive a composition she had written in his honour that is now a respected addition to the choral repertoire. In every case composers emphasized Elmer's role in their careers. They reflected Beckwith's simple "I owe a lot to you both. What can I say but warm thanks?" In his citation for Elmer Iseler's University of Toronto honorary degree, Dean David Beach quoted composer Derek Holman's assessment of Elmer's career: "Dr. Iseler is unquestionably one of the most distinguished musicians in Canada, and the greatest choral conductor this country has known. He has set and maintained standards of excellence in choral performance to which all other musicians in this field have sought to emulate."

Elmer, in his last months, recognized the significance of leaving a legacy through his renewed contact with the University of Toronto. He had abandoned his short-lived academic career at the university in the mid-1960s, but miraculously, as he faced the end of his life, an opportune connection was achieved at his alma mater that would remain as a singular reminder of his role in the choral life of this nation. This return to the University of Toronto revolved around choral conductor and academic colleague Doreen Rao, Dean of the Faculty of Music David Beach, and the initiatives of music enthusiasts and philanthropists Vern and Elfrieda Heinrichs.

It was in the early 1980s that Doreen Rao first came to Toronto with her Glen Ellyn Children's Choir in order to participate in a concert with Jean Ashworth Bartle's Toronto Children's Chorus. A return concert, with Bartle's ensemble visiting Chicago, cemented a friendship that became a base for Rao's future permanent move to Toronto, Canada. She had been a protegé of the famous Margaret Hillis, the conductor of the Chicago Symphony Chorus, and was working with that ensemble as well as conducting her Glen Ellyn Children's Choir and teaching at Roosevelt University. She had met Elmer Iseler at various festivals and had found him somewhat aloof, exhibiting all those paternal autocratic behaviours she had already encountered in other conductors and found quite unattractive. She later came to realize that "shy" and "insecure" were better adjectives to describe Elmer's demeanour, but that came only after she arrived in Toronto in 1988 as a result of University of Toronto Dean Carl Morey's invitation to direct the Music Faculty's choral program, conduct the university's choirs, and accept an associate professorship in the field of music education. In an effort to reach out to students, alumnae, and the wider community, Rao immediately established a University of Toronto Symphony Chorus, whose rehearsal schedule aroused the ire of local choir directors, including Elmer, as it conflicted with the scheduled rehearsal times of already established choirs. Her immediate rocking of the stable vessel of choral work in Toronto was not broadly appreciated.

It was not until the early 1990s that Rao became involved with Elmer in a concert program to honour the centennial of Sir Ernest MacMillan's birth. It was then that she came to understand that Elmer was really "Sir Ernest's successor as Canada's pre-eminent choral conductor and music educator." She saw, for the first time, Elmer's passion for the choral art, indeed it was "as a teacher that I fell in love with him."[3] By 1994, Rao had named her major university choir the MacMillan Singers and had initiated a concert to "Celebrate the Legacy," naming Elmer, choral composer Derek Holman, and Toronto Board of Education music educator James Maben as the honorees who had made contributions to the well-being of the choral art in the city she now lived in.

At this point, the tensions around Rao's arrival on the Toronto scene began to dissipate. Early in that same year, she had invited Elmer to take classes with her students and he brought his Elmer Iseler Singers to assist him in the process. The sessions went well. When Rao wished to take a research sabbatical in the 1995–96 academic year, Elmer took over her teaching role, and when she returned for the 1996–97 academic session, they were close friends. Indeed, in a rare example of trust and confidence, Elmer participated in a three-choir concert that included the Elmer Iseler Singers, Rao's MacMillan Singers, and Noel Edison's Elora Festival Singers at St. Patrick's Church in downtown Toronto. Elmer invited both Rao and Edison to share the conducting of the three choirs in varied elements of the evening's program.

It was early in that year of 1997 that there was a general sense that Elmer's health was failing, and this realization was even more apparent when Rao, conductor Bramwell Tovey,[4] Gerry Fagan, and Elmer and his Singers were all invited to Newfoundland in that summer to participate in the aforementioned Festival 500, the celebration of the anniversary of Europe's discovery of the island half a millennium before. Elmer was still recovering from his surgery and his confrontation with Irene Bailey and Tom Laurie and was aware that back in Toronto Vern Heinrichs and John Bird were still in negotiations with the TMC in regard to his future as conductor of the TMC and the role of his Singers as members of the TMC and its professional core.

Indeed, it was in Newfoundland that Lydia Adams received the phone call from Elfrieda Heinrichs that informed her that not only was it now official that Elmer was no longer to be employed by the TMC as conductor but the role of his Elmer Iseler Singers as the professional core had also ended. Lydia informed Jessie and Elmer. The Singers were informed of the TMC decision at Newfoundland's Gander Airport before departure for Toronto so that they would not discover their fate from the newspapers on their arrival back home.[5] Vern Heinrichs was at Pearson Airport to greet the Singers, answer their questions, and with the choir-in-residence concept in his mind, to assure them they would not suffer financially as a result of the TMC intransigence. (The University of Toronto's Elmer Iseler Professional Choir-in-Residence program was funded by a number of parties in the first year, then by the Heinrichs for the total ten-year duration.)

Rao, recognizing that Elmer was failing and that the surgery had not been entirely successful, had realized that Elmer needed a tangible vote of confidence in the midst of this crisis and had already arranged for him to be a member of the Music Faculty in 1996 and for the 1997–98 academic year. In that role he was teaching choral conducting and enjoying his time with students of the Music Faculty, even though his discomfort was obvious. It was in these months that the Heinrichs initiated a program of Elmer Iseler National Scholarships in Choral Conducting for students enrolled in such a program and through their generosity established a permanent Elmer Iseler Chair in Conducting at the University of Toronto's Faculty of Music. Although the arrangements for the chair were not completed until after his death, he was made aware that such an honour would be a guaranteed recognition of his contribution to the art of choral music.

As a symbol of what would become the Iseler legacy, an afternoon concert that included Lydia Adams's Amadeus Choir, Rao's MacMillan

Singers, and the Elmer Iseler Singers took place in October 1997. It was the last time that Elmer was to mount the podium in a formal concert setting. All the university administrative and academic leaders, the conductor and officers of the Toronto Symphony, as well as a stellar representation of the choral community were gathered at St. Basil's Church on the University of Toronto's campus to experience this last hurrah. It was at the reception following the concert at the Heinrichs home (over the years a venue for countless evenings of song mounted to financially assist one choral ensemble or another) that University President Rob Prichard announced the creation of a scholarship program in Elmer's name for students enrolled in the University of Toronto's choral program. It was a gala occasion.

These scholarships recognized the pressure placed on the University of Toronto's Faculty of Music to be in competition for gifted vocal students with every other such institution in the world. The Heinrichs' contribution, matched by the university and the Ontario government, gave the Music Faculty an opportunity to make scholarships available for the study of choral music to a number of its students. This assistance could not provide as generous support as the more affluent American music schools could offer, but nonetheless nothing could have assisted the future of Canadian choral music more effectively. In spite of the sparse resources of the past, the Music Faculty and its splendid teachers and coaches had, over the years, graduated the most extraordinary array of singers. They were already gracing the stages of the world's opera houses and concert and recital halls. The Heinrichs' support for scholarship funds given in Elmer's name ensured that the opportunities for many young Canadians would be even brighter in the future. For a musician who had never lost sight of young people, from his New Hamburg days to the sessions in Doreen Rao's classes, it could not have been a more appropriate legacy.

The new focus on choral scholarships would also include the Elmer Iseler Singers as a professional choir-in-residence in the University of Toronto as an essential aspect of the program. The Heinrichs family had ensured that Elmer's name and contribution would be recognized by generations of future choral scholars and conductors in the most direct way possible — through a link with the performance of choral music at its finest.

The awful year 1997 ended with the sweet taste of recognition from the Royal Conservatory. On December 9, Elmer received a letter from its president, Dr. Peter Simon, asking him to accept a diploma *honoris causa* (Fellowship of the Royal Conservatory of Music), "in recognition of the extraordinary contribution you have made over several decades in enriching the lives of millions of Canadians through music." Recognizing the serious surgery that might lie ahead for Elmer as well as the long and difficult recovery, Simon invited him to the ceremony in January but offered as well to award the diploma at a private ceremony.

In speaking of a legacy, one cannot forget the precious memories included in the nearly fifty recordings of the Festival Singers, the Elmer Iseler Singers, and the Toronto Mendelssohn Choir that are now a part of the ongoing history of choral music in Canada. It is fortunate that recordings and CDs have a long life and are to be found in the collections of many Canadians and in music libraries of universities and in the Canadian Music Centre. Nevertheless, the presence of these records and discs is a valuable advantage for those who wish to hear the most authentic sound of his Singers at the time when the recording was created. The last complete recording that Elmer was able to produce with his beloved Singers was *Noel*, released in October 1998. Those who have heard the entire Iseler collection are convinced it is one of the best!

A tragedy in the matter of providing a lasting record of Elmer's conducting genius is the fact that technological change has been brutal in terms of the retention of musical reproduction. The obsession with the latest version that encourages recording companies to withdraw the distribution and marketing of fine recordings just a few years after their production deprives average music lovers of the opportunity to build their own archives of great recording achievements. The fact that Canada does not have a strong classical recording industry merely exacerbates these problems. Nevertheless, with the CBC, the Canadian Music Centre, and Earl Rosen's Marquis Records producing discs these sounds still remain to whet the ears of music enthusiasts, particularly choral devotees in the academic institutions devoted to retaining these treasures of the choral art of the past.

Very early in the life of the Festival Singers, while Elmer was building the extraordinary spectrum of Canadian works commissioned largely, but not completely, by the CBC, his close friend John Bird came up with a plan for the choice and publication of quality music for choirs across Canada and beyond. Bird was on his way to becoming the CEO of Gordon V. Thompson Music Publishing Company. Bird had an intimate professional relationship with Elmer, and realizing his impeccable good taste and wide knowledge of appropriate repertoire for choral forces, he interested Elmer in becoming the individual who would choose a spectrum of selections that could be marketed to conductors both in Canada and in other English-speaking countries. It was a brilliant move. Choristers and conductors heard his Festival Singers and then after 1979 his Elmer Iseler Singers perform pieces and were delighted to know that there was the Festival Singers of Canada Choral Series, which later became the Elmer Iseler Singers Choral Series, catalogue of selections in which they could find and order printed sheet music that they could take back to their own choirs. With more than three hundred selections, some 90 percent written or arranged by Canadian composers and musicians, the series became a resource for the entire choral community.

This initiative had a side effect. Bird realized that if Elmer could take his Singers on tours not only to perform but also to provide workshops that emphasized the repertoire to be found in the Elmer Iseler Choral Series list, he could sell sheet music and make a decent profit on the interchange. It worked perfectly again and again. John Bird can be given some of the credit for the enormous commitment that Elmer developed to both touring and workshopping across the continent and even in foreign countries. The Gordon V. Thompson Music Publishing Company found that after the Festival Singers, or later the Iseler Singers, had been on the road through parts of Canada or other countries, the orders for music came pouring in. Over many years, Elmer's involvement in the sheet music promotion changed the repertoire of many choirs who depended on his wisdom and good taste.

Unfortunately, the Gordon V. Thompson Music Publishing Company became part of the American conglomerate Warner/Chappell of Florida, and with the death of John Bird in 2006, the chief overseer of the series, even in retirement, disappeared. Recently, Alfred Music publishers in California took over responsibility for the series. Fortunately, Leslie

Music, a Canadian enterprise based in Oakville, Ontario, has agreed to publish music dropped by Alfred Music, ensuring these selections are now available to Canadian choirs. Efforts to restore the entire Elmer Iseler series to Canadian control has become an objective of those who wish to retain this resource for Canadian conductors and choristers.[6]

In little over a month after Elmer's demise, the Elmer Iseler Singers, who had played such a major role during the events that followed his death, provided a concert that was titled "Dr. Elmer Iseler, A Tribute." The Singers were conducted by the choir's now interim director (soon to be made permanent), Lydia Adams. She was joined by artists who had worked closely with Elmer — the Canadian Brass, James Campbell, Mary Lou Fallis, Maureen Forrester, Lawrence Cherney, and Moshe Hammer. It had been originally advertised in the Elmer Iseler Singers brochure as a seventieth birthday celebration of its founder but now it was being presented just a month after his death. The program began with a hymn — "We gather together to ask the Lord's Blessing" — and included Bach, Brahms, Schubert and Henderson, Glick, and the Taverner *Hallelujah*. The concert was an assurance that there was now a commitment to carry on Elmer's work as a presenter of the greatest choral music at the highest standard. There could not have been a decision that would have pleased Elmer more. The quality of sound, the precision, and the articulation of the text of the tribute concert proved that, with Elmer's encouragement, the board of the Elmer Iseler Singers had made the right choice in seeing Lydia Adams as Elmer's successor.

Lydia Adams was more than just appropriate and capable: she was exactly the leader whose musicality and knowledge of the Iseler quality of performance was needed to bring confidence and stability to a chorus that had shared the tragedy of Elmer's situation since the spring of 1997. However there were board members with a long history with the EIS who worried that she did not have the aggressive personality that was demanded by a professional chorus. Don Kramer, who had been on the EIS board for many years, was concerned that in spite of her ability and commitment, her reticence and humble demeanour would make her an uncomfortable recipient of Elmer's mantle. He was delighted to be proven mistaken.[7] He was eventually joined by all the doubters who soon realized that their anxiety was unwarranted. As Jessie observes, "The cohesiveness and spirit of the Board of Directors of the EIS and Lydia's incredible musicianship is a wonderful example of support for Elmer's artistic vision and lifetime legacy."

It was a courageous decision that the board and Iseler family had taken to carry on the work of the Elmer Iseler Singers. The ensemble's name was retained and thus the past was honoured — but would a future be possible without Elmer's presence? Many said no. However, the last decade has revealed the strength and determination of conductor Lydia Adams and manager Jessie Iseler, along with able and committed Singers, a few of whom have remained from the earliest days. The decision to remain a valued asset to the country's choral spectrum has been a vote of confidence in Elmer's dream. Without Jessie's enthusiastic involvement, the Elmer Iseler Singers could never have carried on.

As Elmer lay dying in the early spring of 1998, Elfrieda Heinrichs and Nancy Thomson jointly wrote a letter in support of a nomination for a Royal Bank Award for Canadian Achievement for the Iselers:

> A cohering thread of Elmer and Jessie's conjoint career has been a celebratory zeal, commitment, and shared vision for excellence which has directed their lives, and given expression to their music-making. To speak of Canadian choral music is to speak of Elmer and Jessie Iseler. They have become an institution. They have managed to fuse a passion for music, and a passion for Canada, and direct them toward the "common good." Together, in communities across the breadth of Canada, Elmer and Jessie Iseler have inspired ordinary Canadians, who never thought themselves able to "make music," to achieve a standard of performance which is legendary.

The nomination was not successful but that in no way diminishes the truth of the perception that there were two leading players in the Iseler family drama.

Yet the Singers wisely forsook the role and function of a museum to honour the great conductor. Lydia Adams is clear on that point:

> There is a great joy in performing with this group who bears his name. In order to keep the group vibrant, Jessie and I agreed that the chorus had to not so much carry on in his footsteps, but to make our own as well. Music is a genuine life force, reflective of all the joys and sorrows we feel and experience throughout our lives. We felt the compulsion for keeping the choir alive — the true need for another positive voice to demonstrate the beauty possible in the world — to inspire composers to give voice to Canadian writers and composers.[8]

The chorus has continued to commission an extraordinary number of new works, has maintained the commitment to touring and singing across the country, and has aspired to improve the quality of its performance. Lydia has not been ground down by her role as bearer of the sacred task. The choristers sing for her because they trust her musicality and her integrity. She had watched both Elmer Iseler and David Willcocks for many years and learned how to achieve that loyalty and that focus on great music. Choral music is a genre of performance that reveals like no other the fake and the counterfeit, and in Lydia the Singers discovered that they had found the real goods.[9]

There were countless choirs across Canada who dedicated the last concert of their 1997–98 season to Elmer Iseler. One would expect the Toronto Children's Chorus to be on that long list but others soon joined. David Christiani, the conductor of the St. Lambert Choral Society, had been moved by Elmer, and the first St. Lambert concert program after his death included an account of his feeling of loss: "It was Elmer who inspired that love in me and in thousands of colleagues and singers worldwide. Since Elmer first touched my life in 1967 there has not been one day when I have been unaware of his influence as a choral musician."[10]

Even the Toronto Mendelssohn Choir, in the fall of 1998, gave a tribute presentation to its recently departed conductor. John Lawson, who had joined the choir in 1963, had been its president in 1963 for six years, and became the chairman of its board for a further ten years, was the designated speaker. In words that must have made some former TMC board members cringe, Lawson concluded,

> There is no question that Elmer Iseler was one of the greatest musicians Canada has ever produced. His influence at home and abroad was enormous. His legacy speaks for itself. He was a man of passion. For me the greatest experience of all, which I will always cherish, was to receive during a performance with all the voices going full tilt, a smile from Elmer, eye to eye contact, like a shaft of sunlight, a beam of pure joy, a direct pipeline, I felt, to the mighty Creator of us all.[11]

It seemed that April and May 1998 in Canada resonated with the sound of voices expressing their remembrance of Elmer in songs of praise. Colleagues, composers, conductors, and choristers all had their own personal reasons for despair, but there was a collective understanding that went beyond the individual response that sustained this chorus. For one thing it was an appropriate realization and a statement of intense appreciation for Elmer's 1990s personal crusade to restore funding of choral music by the Canada Council. Those excursions to Ottawa had, indeed, convinced the major national arts granting agency that this was an activity deserving of support, and this realization, not even known or recognized by most of Elmer's colleagues, was a major bequest to his colleagues that Elmer had left behind.

The Elmer Iseler Singers have become a part of an initiative to gather strength from a "Creative Trust" aimed at securing working capital for the mid-size Toronto artistic enterprises, those that are in many ways the most vulnerable to changing circumstances. The major symphony orchestras and opera companies and the large theatre festival operations have the size and presence to attract both government and private support. The small performing arts organizations have the flexibility and financial manoeuvrability to avoid crisis. But the mid-size choirs, like the Elmer

Iseler Singers, and theatre companies, like the Tarragon in Toronto, have to compete with the "biggies" and are disadvantaged in so doing. Elmer went through his career life trying to establish and maintain a professional choir that could perform at a quality level matching the splendid repertoire to be sung, both ancient and contemporary. The Elmer Iseler Singers' commitment to the Creative Trust partnership over a six-year period seeks to assure the success of the EIS and similar-sized arts organizations in following their vision and in developing sustainability.[12]

Elmer's career, its triumphs but particularly its tragedies, was a lesson to every choral conductor and to every board member. Behind the efforts to establish some level of financial stability, the Creative Trust is attempting to bring greater clarity to the relationship between a board of directors and the artistic leadership. It is very much about power, vision, and the choral enterprise. For a variety of reasons, the artists are the most vulnerable to inappropriate behaviour on the part of those who are participating. The requirement for wisdom and patience is monumental. The methods for selecting and orienting board members must be as carefully discerned and followed as they are for choosing singers in a choral ensemble that wishes to remain both stable and exciting.

In the cases of both the Festival Singers and the TMC, disruption was caused by the underlying financial stress created by inadequate funding from stretched and indigent government granting councils whose lack of financial response to the choral music community failed to inspire support from the private sector and had thereby brought Elmer's work to an end. The choral community has learned to avoid these pitfalls and has sought to make these circumstances less likely for other choirs, other choir boards, other administrative officers, and other conductors in the future.

In many ways, the functioning of the choral enterprise corresponds to human society in miniature. Every choir has a culture and that culture is merely the sum of its stories of past and present and the tales it tells of its future expectations. These stories were contained in both the text and sound that Elmer loved and passed on to both his singers and his audiences. The human species lives by these stories, and the compositions that filled Elmer's programs spoke of the land, the ocean shores, the struggles for national survival and well-being, the leadership in making a world of peace and justice. All were significant elements in the texts of the repertoire that filled his concerts. His understanding of the world emerging in the new millennium was one that stressed interdependence and horizontal realities included in a cultural view that made the choral art an integral element of his neighbourhood, his municipality, his province, and his nation's cultural expression.

Elmer was in a lifelong tension with a society that was dominated by a philosophy and an ideology that rewarded successful competition and confrontation, celebrated ambition and greed, and was willing to accept the presence of death-dealing violence, massive weaponry, and destructive conflict that has been the inevitable result of these propensities. His intense Lutheran faith had emerged from such a society but included elements of a very different world view, one that stressed common goals, communal outlook, shared responses, and an inclusive search for love and inspiration — all attributes of the values expressed by the choral art at its best. There are those who would argue that only these values can save the human species from its ultimate destruction, probably to be measured in decades rather than centuries.

Such values emerge from an understanding and appreciation of the earth as a welcoming home, the only one yet discovered in a vast universe only to be comprehended, in greater part, in latter years of research and discovery. Elmer's love of nature, whether on land, on water, or in flight, his preoccupations with growing food for his family's consumption, his searching of the skies with his telescopes, were not mere amusements or hobbies. Indeed, his appreciation of light, space, and form, especially to be found in his celebration of the human body in his photography, were all part of his personal search for a new heaven and a new earth.

There is always irony in the dissonance created by the need for leadership that within democratic institutions appears to include a measure of individual dominance in order to comprehend and take action to resolve the complex affairs of humankind. For Elmer it was the essential reality of a vision that demanded his control of the efforts of his singers, not only in the context of the performance of a great work but in the inclusive policies and style of their ongoing commitment to the choral art. The inequality of the conductor-chorister relationship displayed the inevitable irony of all human interactions that seek to discover the values and behaviours that will allow the species to survive in a very different world than the power-mad society that has existed through so many centuries. We make war in order to create peace, we kill and maim fellow creatures in order to give them freedom, and we expect direction and control of artistic activities that will enhance democratic values. Elmer, and the society of which he was a part, has never been able to square that circle.

Perhaps the most compelling feature of Elmer's lifestyle, that which most clearly reflected his inarticulate philosophy, was his intense love for Jessie, her family, his children, and those friends who were close to him and could be trusted at every turn. The communal style and functioning of the Iseler-Balsillie household was in itself a study in positive human interaction in a civil society. Music, in, for example, the form of a requiem Mass, expresses the human need for divine compassion, and Elmer assuredly found this element of his faith in supportive relationships with those who shared this vision.

Elmer rarely spoke of his theological leanings in his mature years. Rather he lived a life that exhibited daily his innermost commitments. He saw an old order that was obviously unsustainable. The clash of civilizations that has been identified as the next threat to continued life on the planet could be seen emerging in his latter years. The implications of this confrontation were more devastating than the wars between nations that had filled the previous centuries. With modern weaponry of mass destruction, the survival of his beloved creation was becoming perilously unlikely. The extent of the planet's deterioration also contrasted with Elmer's experience of the natural beauty of his life at Quail Hill Farm. His extraordinary balance of music, agriculture, astronomy, and travel, along with his nurturing of personal and particularly family relationships, wove a tapestry that exhibited to the world the lifestyle he wished could be the lot of humankind.

Elmer Iseler was an extraordinary man — as a musician, as a conductor, as an educator, as an advocate, as a visionary, as Jessie's lover and husband, as a world citizen. For all who knew him, his career was a celebration of life at its fullest. He would have agreed with Kenneth Graham, who wrote in his foreword to *The Wind in the Willows*, "The most priceless possession of the human race is the wonder of the world." Elmer exhibited that wonder in everything he did — he never lost it amidst the most tragic circumstances, and he bequeathed it to Jessie and his children, to Lydia Adams and every chorister who followed his hands and eye, to every person whether singer or listener who shared his love of the human voice and the music it has inspired. Elmer saw in choral musical expression the grace of a Creator who extended to the human species the creativity to ensure its survival along with a capacity to love and bring into being a compassionate world.

Appendix I
Port Colborne

ELMER ISELER NEVER PERCEIVED HIMSELF AS A victim of a community whose air, water, and soil were contaminated. There is no proof of a direct connection between the state of the environment in Port Colborne, where Elmer was born and raised, and the early demise of all four children of Theo and Lydia Iseler. Indeed, the neighbourhood in which the Iselers lived was not specifically identified as polluted or unsafe for children. However, the impact of the environmental factors on human health is being recognized and demands the attention of any biographer confronted by the reality of the unexplainable deaths of his subject and all his siblings.

Indeed, over much of the twentieth century, the connection between human health and the increasingly contaminated environment of many North American communities has been a simmering issue. Though the full consequences of industrialization and, in particular, the increasing number of chemicals that the Second World War and its aftermath unleashed on an unsuspecting society did not occur until later in the 1900s, the beginning of this issue can be traced back to the late 1800s. It certainly attracted the attention of the citizens of Port Colborne in the last decades of the twentieth century and on into the twenty-first.

Only a few weeks after the author began work on this volume, a news story on Port Colborne appeared in the *Globe and Mail* carrying the headline, "Court okays suit against INCO. Landmark ruling paves way for Ontario's first class action on environmental issue" (Martin Mittelstaedt, *Globe and Mail*, November 19, 2006, p. 9).

The Ontario Court of Appeal had decided that the $750-million class action against both INCO and the Province of Ontario could go ahead, thereby overturning two lower court rulings that had dismissed the case. Understandably, the evidence of lower property values on houses built on contaminated land was considerably easier to prove than the seemingly inappropriate number of cancer victims who had died as a result of that same polluted environment. It was the latest explosion in a long struggle for justice. Originally, the issue had revolved around a suspicion that there was a higher than average rate of deaths from cancer in Port Colborne. Many citizens came to believe that this state of affairs could be linked to the fact that INCO had been raining emissions from its smoke stack upon the people of this community for most of a century.

The issue came to involve both federal and provincial governments. There were conflicts between levels of government and suspicions of cover-up. An assessment of the Port Colborne situation by the Ontario provincial government in 1997 had to be withdrawn, revised, and further updated. One ongoing problem with the data was the fact that the population studied numbered only eighteen thousand — not the hundred thousand necessary to give legitimacy to the survey results. The report revealed there was no evidence of higher levels of "adverse human health effects than anticipated as a result of exposure to nickel, copper, cobalt in soils in the Port Colborne area." However, it was clear that initiatives to "remediate the affected lands were to be strongly supported by the Regional Niagara Public Health Department" ("Assessment of Potential Health Risks of Reported Soil Levels of Nickel, Copper, and Cobalt in Port Colborne and Vicinity," January 2000). The report was not universally received with any confidence that it was the last word.

Further controversy arose from the fact that the Province of Ontario was content to accept North American standards (essentially those of the United States) while the federal government took the position that World Health Organization standards should be attained. As Eric Gillespie, the lawyer representing Port Colborne citizens, stated, "The U.S. standard doesn't take into account nickel's potential cancer-causing properties when inhaled." The Province responded that it was under no obligation to use international standards. Further delay and confusion came in

March 2000 when the Province had to withdraw a further assessment after calculation errors were found.

In 2001, the controversy reached another level of confrontation when Dr. Mark Richardson, former head of Health Canada's Air and Waste Section and a risk assessment expert, revealed in an article that "the studies relied on by the [Ontario] Ministry of the Environment and public health officials cannot be used to say that anyone in Port Colborne is safe." It became clear that it was not nickel but nickel oxide that was the high-risk contaminant — it was, in fact, a group 1 carcinogen. Dr. Richardson could proclaim that "the wrong methods had been used" to assess the danger. Citizens were left perturbed by the observation of one unnamed Ministry of the Environment official who publicly stated, "There's something going on … There's areas where every single household has someone sick, every single family, some member has something — cancers, rashes, leukemia" (Press Release, "Port Colborne Community launches 750 million dollar action lawsuit against INCO and the Province," March 27, 2001).

In the 1950s, Rachel Carson wrote the incomparable *Silent Spring*, a stunning account of the effects of the chemical revolution and how emissions of the industrial and agricultural process could be undermining the health of citizens in North America. It was an alarm bell, but little happened to restrain the poisoning of the atmosphere and ultimately the water and earth upon which humans depended. Her book was followed in the late 1990s by Sandra Steingraber's *Living Downstream: An Ecologist Looks at Cancer and the Environment* (Don Mills, Ont.: Addison-Wesley, 1997). The book is a sequel to Carson's groundbreaking examination of the effect of a "contaminated environment." Steingraber was herself diagnosed with cancer in her twenties, even though her family had recognized the danger of living in an area of the state of Illinois, where industrialization had erupted with extraordinary power during and after the Second World War. She had survived.

The industrial development around Port Colborne had taken place at the end of the First World War with the establishment of the International Nickel Company (INCO). The arrival of Theodore and his wife took place within a decade. Steingraber, in her account, records the long time lapse between the recognition of the problem of industrial emissions and the appearance of possible unhealthy effects on the citizens upon whom these emissions had descended.

Even more obvious, connections between known carcinogenic substances and human use were not given formal recognition for decades. For example, it was thirty-three years before the announcement of a concern about the hazard of tobacco smoke by the United States surgeon general became a source of government regulation. There was suspicion of deleterious effects from the spraying of DDT in the 1940s but it lost its recognition as a harmless product only in 1972 in the United States. These time lapses occurred in Canada as well. Into the mix of a lack of complete and reliable research comes the corporate resistance that must be dealt with — at some political cost.

In the case of the Port Colborne, the reasons for the lack of immediate attention to the obvious fact that INCO was polluting the air, land, and water are similar to those at work in Normandale, the Illinois home of Sandra Steingraber. The Iseler family spent their childhood and teenage years in a deeply contaminated environment, but how does one amass reliable evidence in a small community of eighteen thousand people, many of whom are and have been on the move? Being close to the Canadian-American border made it even more difficult, as the contaminants could come from the emissions of industries situated in another country, even if there had been an established connection with cancer deaths. Steingraber's statement that "I have been protected from a proven danger by those who have the courage to act on partial evidence" could have been the expectation of every Iseler child, but it was not.

Finding reliable statistics, or any statistics at all, that proved deteriorating health among the citizens of a community was frustrating when only large numbers count. An entire street may have a plethora of cancer victims, but this may also be the result of circumstances that have nothing to do with the presence of smoke from a local industrial chimney stack.

Invariably, acting on their concern becomes the responsibility of a group of citizens who harass local government and heath authorities. But they do so in the shadow of the reality that action taken to reduce the risks can have negative results on the employment possibilities of both themselves and their neighbours. Regulation may cause the loss of jobs, may lose tax revenues for the municipality, may indeed end the presence of a much wanted industrial development. Lack of evidence becomes an argument for silence, the silence identified in Carson's *Silent Spring*. The book "can be read as an exploration of how one kind of silence breeds another, how secrecies of government beget a weirdly quiet and lifeless world." Citizens of Port Colborne, aware of so many cancer victims in their neighbourhoods, questioned officials at various levels for many years and the silence was deafening. There were even suspicions, like those of people in Steingraber's Normandale, that there were others who knew more than they were telling, a sense of the "hushed complicity of many individual scientists who were aware of, if not directly involved in documenting the hazards created by chemical assaults on the natural world."

In this effort to identify the evidence of environmental health hazard, complexity is the name of the game. As Steingraber puts it, "Science loves order, simplicity, the manipulation of a single variable against a background of constancy. The tools of science do not work well when everything is changing all at once." Nevertheless, the struggle goes on, as it did in Port Colborne — long after the Iselers were no longer part of the community.

All this contemporary controversy speaks to a serious reality. Elmer Iseler grew up in a community now perceived as seriously polluted by emissions that were dangerous to the health and well-being of its inhabitants. The full impact of environmental factors and their effect on the human body has not been fully ascertained. How long the poisons of the air and land of Port Colborne worked in his body and affected his performance and behaviour will never be known. However, we do know that Elmer Iseler's untimely death in 1998 was the result of a cancerous brain tumour.

Elmer Iseler Chronology

1927	Born October 14 to the Reverend Theodore and Lydia Iseler in Port Colborne, Ontario
1940	Graduates from Elm Street Public School, Port Colborne
1945	Graduates from Port Colborne High School with senior matriculation and enrols in first-year arts at Waterloo College
1947	Marries Gertrude (Trudie) Mosig
1950	Graduates with a Bachelor of Music from the Faculty of Music, University of Toronto
1950–51	Conducts the University of Toronto Symphony and the All-Varsity Mixed Chorus
1951	Appointed Assistant Conductor, Toronto Mendelssohn Choir (TMC)
1952	Graduates with teaching certificate from the Ontario College of Education
1952	Appointed to the staff of York Memorial Collegiate Institute (YMCI)
1952	Meets Jessie Balsillie, YMCI orchestra cellist
1954	Participates in the founding of the Festival Singers
1955	Festival Singers appear at the Stratford Shakespearian Festival
1957	Appointed Head of Music, Northview Heights Collegiate Institute
1960	Collapses physically and mentally and is hospitalized for several months
1961	Returns to position as Head of Music at Northview Heights

1961	Divorce proceedings involving Trudie Iseler conclude; marries Jessie Balsillie
1962	Returns as permanent Conductor of the Festival Singers
1962	Prepares Festival Singers to perform and record the works of Igor Stravinsky
1964	Takes Festival Singers to Carnegie Hall for a concert of Stravinsky's music along with the New York Philharmonic to perform under the composer's baton
1964	Appointed Conductor of the TMC
1965	Appointed Adjunct Professor (lecturing in choral music) at the Faculty of Music, University of Toronto
1965	Takes the TMC to Boston to perform at the 150th Anniversary of the Handel and Haydn Society
1967	Establishes the Festival Singers as the professional core of the TMC
1967	Resigns adjunct professorship from the Faculty of Music, University of Toronto
1967	Takes Festival Singers to Montreal to perform at Expo '67 in the Canadian Pavilion TMC performs at Expo '67 at Gala Performance, Place Des Artes, Montreal
1967	Recognized as Waterloo College's Canadian Centennial Most Distinguished Alumni
1967	Takes the Festival Singers to Washington, D.C., to perform in the Lighting of the National Christmas Tree Ceremony on the White House lawn
1968	Establishes the Festival Singers as the first professional choir in Canada
1968	Becomes editor of the Festival Singers of Canada Choral Series
1968	Suffers from a serious phlebitis attack in his legs
1968	Receives the Canada Centennial Medal
1971	Receives Honorary LL.D. from Dalhousie University
1971	Takes the Festival Singers to the U.K. and Europe
1972	Takes the TMC on tour of Europe and the U.K.
1972	Receives Honorary LL.D. from Brock University

1973	Receives Gold Civic Award of Merit, City of Toronto
1973	Receives Silver Medal, Societé d'Encouragement et d'Education de Paris
1975	Receives Citation from the Canadian Music Council for unique contribution to Canadian choral music
1975	Appointed an Officer of the Order of Canada
1976	Conducts the TMC at the Montreal Olympics
1976	Takes the TMC to the Kennedy Center to perform as part of the U.S.A. Bicentennial celebrations
1977	Takes the Festival Singers on second tour of Europe: Paris, London, and eastern Europe
1978	Forced to resign as Conductor of the Festival Singers
1978	Founds the Elmer Iseler Singers (EIS)
1980	Takes the TMC on tour of Europe and U.K.
1981	Takes the EIS on tour of the U.S.A.
1984	Elmer Iseler Day proclaimed in the City of Toronto on November 2
1984	Receives the first Association of Canadian Choral Conductors Honorary Life Membership
1984	Conducts the EIS at the Toronto International Festival of the Arts
1985	Receives the Grand Prix du Disque from the Canadian Music Centre
1985	Receives Honorary LL.D. from Wilfrid Laurier University
1985	Invited to be lecturer and presenter on "North American Contemporary Music" at the first World Congress on Choral Music Travels to Vienna, Austria, accompanied by the EIS
1988	Takes the EIS to sing at the Calgary Winter Olympics
1989	Celebrates twenty-five years as Conductor of the TMC
1989	Conducts the EIS at the Toronto International Choral Festival
1990	Receives the Distinguished Service Award from the Ontario Choral Federation on its twenty-fifth anniversary
1992	Prepares and conducts the National Youth Choir
1994	Receives Honorary LL.D. from York University
1994	Participates in the hundredth anniversary of the TMC as its Conductor for an unprecedented thirty years

1995	Receives the Order of Ontario
1996	Prepares and conducts the Ontario Youth Choir
1997	Undergoes operation for removal of cancerous brain tumour
1997	Receives Timothy Eaton Centre Twentieth Anniversary Award
1997	Asked to resign as Conductor of the TMC
1997	Appointed Adjunct Professor of Choral Music, Faculty of Music, University of Toronto
1997	Elmer's EIS becomes the choir-in-residence at the Faculty of Music, University of Toronto
1998	The Elmer Iseler National Scholarships in Choral Conducting is established by the Heinrichs Foundation at the Faculty of Music, University of Toronto
1998	The Elmer Iseler Chair in Conducting in the Faculty of Music, University of Toronto, is established by the Heinrichs Foundation
1998	Honoured by the Royal Conservatory of Music
1998	Receives Honorary LL.D. from the University of Toronto
1998	Dies, April 3, at his home in the Caledon Hills surrounded by family and friends
2000	Northview Heights Auditorium named the Elmer Iseler Auditorium in his honour
2000	Elmer Iseler is honoured by the Council for the Town of Caledon as the Caledon Walk of Fame recipient for the year 2000, at the Trailway Pavillion on the Trans Canada Trail in Caledon East

Plaque dedication by Mayor Carol Seglins and Rev. Jim Ball.

Notes

Preface

1. Keith MacMillan, when quoted by music critic William Littler on his
   designation of Elmer as "exasperating" some years later on the occasion of
   Iseler's "firing" as conductor of the Festival Singers, wrote a letter to the
   editor of the *Toronto Star* in support for his friend, indicating that "the search
   for perfection is incompatible with tranquility" and that Iseler was "a choral
   conductor without like in this country and among the few in the world."

Chapter 1

1. Malinsky Memorial Archives. I am indebted to Carol Nagel, archivist, for
   details of the career of the Reverend Theodore Iseler.
2. Jessie Iseler, interview by author, 2 March 2006. The other reason for his
   enthusiasm for shorter trips to nearer destinations was that he wanted his
   beloved Jessie nearby at all times, and where possible, his two children, all
   in the family car playing word games and telling stories. But there was the
   reality of discomfort about air travel that edged him, both consciously and
   unconsciously, away from a life on planes and in airports and it can be traced
   back to these early years.
3. Trudie Cochrane, interview by author, May 15, 2006. Trudie Cochrane was
   Elmer's first wife. She was one of five daughters of Reverend Richard Mosig
   and his wife, Melinda, both serving the congregation of Trinity Lutheran
   Church in New Hamburg. Four daughters, Gertrude, Rosemary, Frieda,

and Gretel, were to sing in Elmer's New Hamburg Youth Choir. The oldest, Elsa, in training as a nurse, had departed before Elmer's association with the church, but the whole family was to play an important role in Elmer's life.

4. Ted Moroney, interview by author, 13 February 2006. Ted is an outstanding accompanist for the Orpheus Choir, the Bell'Arte Singers, and the Opera in Concert Chorus, all of Toronto. He was the first winner of the Leslie Bell Choral Conducting Competition and has played a major role in the choral life of Toronto as both an organist and choir leader.

5. Jessie Iseler found these comments in the introductory paragraphs of a speech in Elmer's handwriting and passed it on to the author. It is undated, and there is no indication the speech was ever delivered. Iseler Papers, Quail Hill Farm, Caledon, Ontario.

6. See Appendix I: Port Colborne.

Chapter 2

1. Richard Shibley, interview by author, 23 November 2005. Richard Shibley, QC, became one of Ontario's most prestigious lawyers. He was a founding partner of Shibley, Righton & McCutcheon, a prestigious Toronto law firm. Richard has been retained by many of the leading corporations in Canada. Over nearly a half-century of legal practice he has argued cases before all levels of the Ontario and federal court system, including the Supreme Court of Canada. However, Richard also served on the boards of Elmer's Festival Singers and the Elmer Iseler Singers. Throughout his life Elmer regarded Richard as a close friend, adviser, and confidant.

2. *Ibid.*

3. *Ibid.*

4. Mary Coutts (née McKellar), interview by author, 19 January 2006. Mary had to give up her study of the violin when she proceeded from Port Colborne High School to the University of Toronto as she had no place to practise. However, after some interruption in her academic career to serve as a driver with the Red Cross until the end of the war, Mary returned to her studies and graduated from the University of Toronto with a degree in English language and literature and then proceeded to a degree in social work. In the 1950s, she was invited by Elmer to join the Festival Singers Board of Directors. She remained a supporter of Elmer's vision throughout his life.

5. *Ibid.* Captain McKellar's charity was essential to Elmer's future. However, the Captain was equally important as an example of the humanistic characteristics and love of learning that Elmer wished to emulate. The Captain was, for example, the initiator of a passion for astronomy that Elmer never forsook over his entire life. Any visitor to Quail Hill Farm would find a telescope pointed towards the skies, holding its place on a verandah with a range of bird feeders that exposed one of his other great enthusiasms.

6. Jessie Iseler, interview by author, 17 November 2006.

7. Margaret McCoy, interview by author, 24 November 2005.

8. Jessie Iseler, interview by author, 17 November 2006.

Chapter 3

1. Richard Shibley, interview by author, 23 November 2005.

2. Elmer arrived at Waterloo College at precisely the right time. In 1929, the college had been nearly bankrupt and had been forced to mount a campaign to raise $150,000. The Lutheran community was generous, and within a month $120,000 had been pledged. The college was ready for an increase in numbers when veterans returned in the late 1940s, and by 1946 a major expansion was planned. By 1952, the college had collected $400,000, and by 1960 the college had become part of Waterloo Lutheran University. Within another dozen years, full recognition as a provincial university and full funding for its programs were accorded when, in 1973, the name of the institution was changed to Wilfrid Laurier University. Elmer was considered a distinguished alumnus of WLU and received that citation in Canada's Centennial Year, 1967.

3. Trudie Cochrane, interview by author, 15 May 2006. I am indebted to Mr. Paul Fischer and George Pennie, who put me in touch with those who knew something of Elmer's Waterloo College and New Hamburg days. Their assistance was crucial in examining a little-known aspect of Elmer's career.

4. Trudie Cochrane, letter to Elmer Iseler, 6 February 1998, Iseler Papers.

5. Dr. Delton Glebe, interview by author, 31 May 2006. Dr. Glebe, a distinguished faculty member at Wilfrid Laurier University with degrees from Boston University and the University of Chicago, was a colleague of Dr. Leupold and remembers Elmer Iseler well. Of the latter he commented, "He seemed to be walking around on his tiptoes expressing his delight and bursting with energy and enthusiasm."

6. Gertrude Leupold, interview by author, 29 May 2006.

7. In 1968 Dr. Ulrich Leupold eventually became the principal of the Waterloo Lutheran Seminary. Helmut Kallman in the *Encyclopedia of Canadian Music* (Toronto: University of Toronto Press, 1992) states that he was "one of the first trained musicologists to settle in Canada ... a specialist in Lutheran church music." He wrote and published extensively in the fields of theology and music. By 1960 he was president of the Canadian Society of Biblical Studies and in 1965 he became the chairman of the Committee on Music of the Lutheran Church of America's Commission on Worship.

8. Gertrude Leupold, interview by author, 29 May 2006.

9. *Ibid.*

10. Charles and Ann Cooley, "Waterloo Roots," *The Canadian Lutheran* 13, 4 (May 1998).

11. Richard Shibley, interview by author, 23 November 2005.

12. Ezra Schabas, *There's Music in These Walls* (Toronto: The Dundurn Group, 2005).

13. Trudie Cochrane, interview by author, 15 May 2006.

14. John Bird, interview by author, 31 October 2005. Though John Bird was born in India, he came to Canada at an early age with a father hired by the Canadian National Railway to start a brass band in Stratford, Ontario. John played in his band but moved towards music publication, eventually becoming the CEO of Gordon V. Thompson Music Company. He thought playing in the university orchestra would improve his chances of connecting with students who would eventually become clients as they moved on into music teaching and performance. He became Elmer's closest friend and most valued advisor.

    It was appropriate that the Elmer Iseler Singers opened their 2007–08 choral year with a tribute performance to John's life and contribution in the light of his death only a few months before.

    It was in the percussion section of the University of Toronto Symphony Orchestra that Elmer encountered and befriended Helmut Kallman, perhaps Canada's most prolific writer on music in Canada and a major figure in the production of the *Encyclopedia of Canadian Music*.

15. Giles Bryant had come from England at the end of the war. He was a fully trained singer with a fascination for the pipe organ. He had followed his teacher, Frederick Geoghegan, to Canada when his father, an employee of the T. Eaton Company but based as a representative in England, had secured him a job in the same company in Canada. Geoghegan, by this time an

accompanist for Elmer's Festival Singers, introduced Giles to Elmer and within a week of his arrival in Canada in 1959 he had become a member of this now famous ensemble. He continues to have a prestigious career as a highly prized organist and choirmaster in Ontario and far beyond. Over many years, he became what he proudly refers to as the Iseler "family organist," playing at the funerals of Elmer and Jessie's parents, and ultimately at the funeral of Elmer himself.

16. Howard Cable, interview by author, 17 August 2006. Cable conducted his first radio broadcast in 1942 at the age of twenty-one. He has been an extraordinary bridge between the world of serious and popular music. His list of "clients" include the top performers in both the U.S. and Canada.

17. *Ibid.*

Chapter 4

1. Brad Ratzlaff is the music director at Toronto's Trinity–St. Paul's United Church. For some years, both he and his wife, Carol Woodward Ratzlaff, sang in the Elmer Iseler Singers. Indeed, they met, courted and decided to marry while Singers. They were united in the presence of the choir and took their honeymoon with the Singers on tour. Carol is an outstanding arts educator who teaches everything she believes about the arts and their influence on young people. Both are involved with a program of choral music for young people called Viva Youth Singers.

2. Ken Thomson, interview by author, 15 November 2005. Thomson himself became a teacher in the same mould and worked in Ontario secondary school classrooms for four decades.

3. Margaret McCoy, interview by author, 24 November 2005. Margaret moved to Ottawa in 1973 and joined the Ottawa Choral Society. She ultimately served as that organization's vice-president, president, and administrator. The leadership she brought to these tasks was extraordinarily effective. She is as well the mother of a family that includes a son who plays a bass in the Metropolitan Opera Orchestra, one who plays cello in the National Arts Centre Orchestra, and another who is an accomplished vocal soloist.

4. Ken Dyck forsook music for accountancy and business studies. However, his experience with spirituality-based music led him to work for organizations like World Vision and, today, with Feed the Children.

5. Trudie Cochrane, interview by author, 15 May 2006.

6. Jessie Iseler, interview by author, 8 February 2006.

7. Elmer Iseler, letter to Colonel Singleton, no date, Iseler Papers. Elmer's respect for Colonel Singleton was boundless. Not a man to write letters of admiration, Elmer nonetheless penned a note at the end of the first year that displayed his opinion of Singleton's administrative genius:

> Dear Jim.
> I have never written to any of my previous bosses on any account. However this time I feel it a necessary thing. I want to thank you for the most enjoyable year of teaching I have had. Many things contributed to this enjoyment but the main one (and this may be a surprise to you, knowing my sloppy nature) was that I felt part of a system with a completely efficient administrator. I was surprised to feel at the end of last September that I was in a collegiate which had been in existence for twenty years (rather than one opened just 30 days before) such was the smoothness of its running. Such a smoothness is a morale booster of great weight…
>
> I'm planning a revue-type show this coming year and have permission from Howard Cable to use some of his original music in our show….

8. North York was a particularly advantaged municipality in the Toronto orbit, as the city's new subway system would bring about the building of thousands of homes to house the burgeoning population produced by immigration from Europe, the Caribbean, and Asia. As well the baby boom after the Second World War was particularly intense in Canada, increasing the nation's population figures more dramatically than in any other country on earth. The results of all this fecundity was felt by the North York educational system in particular.

9. Jean McKay (née Burkholder), interview by author, 13 February 2006. Jean took a degree in English and philosophy at the University of Western Ontario and became a professional writer, but she continued to play in community orchestras. She became the spokesperson for the "Northview kids." Her description of the preparation for the Beethoven work is inspired:

... morning after morning, Carol Hope, Carol Godfrey and Sue Canton working on that triplet passage from the Beethoven Violin Concerto ... the luster, the flush in all three of their faces, from the concentration, and the embarrassment of having to play it alone. Carol Godfrey was a bundle of nerves, she clenched her teeth, her anxiety infecting the rest of us, and we all held our breath when she played. On the days when Sue hadn't practiced, her excuses were works of pure genius. Eventually they all got it and it started to ripple out and sound like music. We heaved a collective sigh and went on to the next hard bit. I've played with a lot of cellists since, but never with any I've loved more.

McKay became a valued Iseler family friend — a babysitter for Elmer and Jessie's son, Noel, at music camps. Her brother Rollin Burkholder sang in the Festival Singers.

10. John Bird, interview by author, 31 October 2005.

11. David Smith, interview by author, 6 February 2006. David Smith had also graduated with a Bachelor of Music degree and had played in the University of Toronto Symphony Orchestra with Elmer as a colleague and a year later under his leadership as conductor. He remained at Northview Heights as head of music upon Elmer's withdrawal from teaching in 1964. After a further time at Mackenzie Secondary School, he went to the Faculty of Education and the Music Faculty at Queen's University, where over the ensuing decades he influenced hundreds of students who were to be music teachers in Ontario classrooms.

12. Nancy Thomson (née Fockler), interview by author, 28 November 2005. One day, realizing the depth of her ignorance, Elmer adopted the role of instructor to student in an interaction that began by his asking, "What is your favourite symphony." Nancy blurted out "Beethoven's Fifth" — it was the only classical orchestral composition she had ever consciously heard. Elmer took her to the piano and proceeded to play the entire symphony, bar after bar, stopping every few moments to deconstruct the music to show how the themes were repeated and how the rhythm became the focus of the entire composition. This experience changed her whole understanding about music and its possible role in her life. Elmer was sufficiently impressed

with her music intelligence that he insisted she audition for the Festival Singers. Nancy protested that she had a weak voice. She auditioned and Elmer realized that her assessment had been correct. He then asked her if she would like to join the board of the Singers. Eventually she did so, finally becoming the board chair. Unfortunately in the mid-1970s she had to accompany her husband to Vancouver and was forced to resign.

13. Susan Silverburg and Barbara Myers, interview by author, 10 February 2006. These two students regarded Elmer as a third parent. They were at the centre of the group called the "Northview kids" that had such an impact on Elmer's eventual reassessment of his teaching career.

14. Jean McKay, Address, Toronto District School Board's "Iseler Dedication," May 1999, Iseler Papers.

15. Linda Sword, interview by author, 26 March 2006.

16. Pat Hartman, interview by author, 16 March 2006. Pat Hartman sang at Toronto's St. George's Anglican Church under Lloyd Bradshaw and went on to sing in the Bach Elgar Choir in Hamilton, Ontario.

Chapter 5

1. Trudie Cochrane, interview by author, 15 May 2006.

2. Elizabeth Elliott, interview by author, 20 October 2005. These were experienced choristers. For example, Gordon Wry had been associated with Benjamin Britten, Peter Pears, and the Aldeburgh Festival in the United Kingdom. Joan Eaton had known Elmer at the University of Toronto, where she had received her Bachelor of Music, had sung in the Leslie Bell Singers, and realized she had the intelligence and voice to sing professionally.

3. The name "Festival Singers" remained in place for twenty-four years, until the demise of the choir in 1978–79 concert season. A minor change in the formal name of the ensemble took place in the 1960s to more accurately designate its home base, and the ensemble was known as the "Festival Singers of Toronto," but eventually, as it became a chorus that sang at international festivals, it had to adopt the name "Festival Singers of Canada." There were those even at this time who thought the ensemble should be called "The Elmer Iseler Singers," so dominant was Elmer's leadership in these early years. Elmer, however, was enamoured with the original designation and gave in reluctantly to its loss even after the Festival Singers ensemble, having

bankrupted itself in his absence, were disappearing from the choral scene. All his friends and associates were determined that its successor should be called the Elmer Iseler Singers.

4. Giles Bryant, interview by author, 24 March 2006.

5. John Kraglund, *Globe and Mail*, 11 December 1962.

6. Don Bartle, interview by author, 30 September 2005.

7. *Ibid.*

8. John Kraglund, review of Festival Singers concert, *Globe and Mail*, 13 December 1960.

9. John Kraglund, *Globe and Mail*, 28 February 1962.

10. John Kraglund, *Globe and Mail*, 1 December 1962. Former student Margaret McCoy describes a rehearsal when Elmer had actually split his shirt when his angry gyrations proved too violent for the clothes he was wearing. Margaret stresses that such behaviour only happened when "students were not prepared or properly focused." However, some students did leave this "tyrant who expected too much" (Margaret McCoy, interview by author, 24 November 2005).

11. John Kraglund, *Globe and Mail*, 1 December 1962. This conversion was not to be total, as many choristers discovered in the years to come! There was observable improvement in his temperament day after day, but in times of trial he could still be most deprecatory. Jessie had much to do with the state of Elmer's morale and sense of well-being and restrained him at his most intemperate moments. Even at its worst, his anger seemed mercurial and dependent on several factors — the state of his health being a particular one.

12. Giles Bryant, interview by author, 24 March 2006.

13. Alex Jozefacki, interview by author, 13 February 2007. Jozefacki had a special relationship with Elmer. Although a chorister until the age of twelve, he had become a professional brass player and then had returned to the excitement of singing. As well, he had taken on the responsibility for the sound and lighting needs, particularly on tour, when before a concert he found himself removing tapestries in ancient venues where they had seemingly hung there for centuries.

14. Don Bartle, interview by author, 30 September 2005. At the outset of the Festival Singers Elmer had been uncomfortable with even the romantics, to say nothing of contemporary composers, except, of course, the works of his beloved Healey Willan. However, he came to love the exciting experience of introducing compositions to the world for the first time.

Chapter 6

1. Don Bartle, interview by author, 30 September 2005.
2. John Beckwith, *Toronto Daily Star*, 11 April 1962.
3. John Beckwith, *Toronto Daily Star*, 26 May 1962.
4. George Kidd, review, *Toronto Telegram*, 31 December 1967.
5. John Kraglund, *Globe and Mail*, 15 March 1963.
6. Udo Kasemets, *Maclean's Magazine*, 24 August 1963.
7. W.J. Pitcher, review, *Stratford Record*, 17 August 1964.
8. Ralph Thomas, *Toronto Daily Star*, 17 August 1964.
9. By the mid-1960s Elmer had added Stravinsky's name as a patron to those of Glenn Gould, Sir Ernest MacMillan, Healey Willan, Oscar Shumsky, Tom Patterson, and Robert Craft.
10. Professor Fred Graham, interview by author, 14 February 2006. Dr. Fred Graham has played a major role in the area of church music in Canada. A splendid organist and choirmaster at the cathedral in Halifax, he was paramount in the formation of the Institute for Choral Music at Antigonish. He moved to Ontario and gave extraordinary leadership in the creation of Voices United, the new hymnary of the United Church of Canada. He is now at Emmanuel College as both an administrator and a faculty member. His wife, Melva, is a fine organist and choir leader in Toronto and has given extraordinary leadership to Choirs Ontario, formerly the Ontario Choral Federation.
11. William Littler, *Toronto Daily Star*, 17 November 1966.
12. Ibid., *Toronto Daily Star*, 28 November 1966.
13. Earl Werstine, *Galt Reporter*, 7 November 1966.
14. For example, R. Murray Schafer's *Epitaph for Moonlight* had become a regular selection for Iseler's choirs and was played dozens of times both in Canada and abroad.
15. Eric McLean, *Montreal Star*, 5 July 1967.
16. Ted Bond, *Kingston Whig-Standard*, 5 October 1967.
17. Robert Missen, interview by author, 29 March 2006. Robert Missen was a close colleague of both Elmer and particularly of Jessie after she took over the management of the Elmer Iseler Singers in the late 1970s. Missen became an arts entrepreneur while continuing his work as a distinguished tenor soloist. He speaks in some awe of Elmer's ears as an acoustician. Elmer, Missen claims, achieved his reputation after studying sound in the Hart House swimming pool at the University of Toronto!

18. One of Elmer's Northview Heights students recounts the day that Elmer arrived at her parents' home bereft of shoes. He had picked up a hitchhiker, discovered he had no footwear, and had given the unfortunate man his own shoes. In order to conduct the concert that afternoon he had to borrow his student's father's shoes. On another occasion, just before a concert, a couple turned up at Elmer's dressing room, frantic to have their car rescued from a snowdrift outside the hall. Elmer proceeded to help push the car to safety before rushing back to appear on stage a few minutes later. These stories abound among family and friends who counted him their colleague.

Chapter 7

1. Ezra Schabas and Keith Bissell, Report to the Ontario Arts Council on Music Education, 1968.
2. Kenneth Winters, *Toronto Telegram*, 8 December 1969.
3. Kenneth Winters, *Toronto Telegram*, 23 February 1970.
4. Peter Goddard, *Toronto Telegram*, 2 November 1970.
5. Festival Singers, Fall 1971 tour brochure, Iseler Papers.
6. *Ibid.*
7. Ronald Chickton, *Time Magazine*, 14 June 1971.
8. Festival Singers, Fall 1971 tour brochure, Iseler Papers.
9. *Ibid.*
10. *Ibid.*
11. Sid Adelman, *Toronto Telegram*, 17 July 1971. In this interview, Elmer expressed his appreciation to a CBC he regarded more positively than most of his colleagues: "I read about the CBC as a monster but I don't know it as such." He saw only the producers who had assisted him from the beginning — Geoffrey Waddington, Terrence Gibbs, John Reeves, John Peter Lee Roberts, James Kent, and Carl Little, along with the other CBC colleagues who had been his allies.
12. David Murray, *Financial Times* (London), no date, Iseler Papers.
13. Barbara Kaempfert Weitbrecht, *General-Anzeiger* (Bonn, Germany), 1971, Iseler Papers.
14. Robert Richard, *Ottawa Citizen*, 23 December 1977.
15. John Fenton, interview by author, 5 September 2006. John Fenton, a prominent accountant, had joined the Festival Singers board in the early days. Elmer

had recognized his integrity, generosity, and talents and had groomed him to be treasurer as soon as the need for a board revealed itself. Fenton went on to play the same role with the Elmer Iseler Singers, being the conscience of that board on many occasions. He recognized the role the board should play and it was not to second-guess the artistic director in matters of repertoire and performance.

16. Malcolm Russell, letter to Elmer Iseler, 24 October 1972, Iseler Papers.

17. Mary Lou Fallis, interview by author, 27 November 2005. Mary Lou was preparing herself for an extraordinary career as a soprano soloist with an international reputation but with a versatility that allowed her to become Canada's most prestigious arts comedienne. Both she and her mother were Festival Singers but Mary Lou was "fired" as a result of her conflicting commitments to her own future in music presentation. Yet, as he lay dying Elmer was to receive a warm, supportive note from that "fired" soprano.

18. Minutes of a special meeting of the executive committee of the board of the Festival Singers of Canada, 15 December 1977, Iseler Papers.

19. Minutes of a meeting of the Festival Singers Board of Directors, 3 January 1978, Iseler Papers.

20. William Littler, "Why did Elmer Iseler get the old heave-ho?" *Toronto Daily Star*, May 1978.

21. Harry Somers, Letter to Editor, *Globe and Mail*, 29 June 1978.

22. Tom Brown, Letter to Editor, *Toronto Daily Star*, May 1978.

23. Boris Brott, Letter to Editor, *Globe and Mail*, May 1978.

24. John Reeves, Letter to Editor, *Globe and Mail*, May 1978.

25. Judith Young, interview by author, 18 January 2006.

26. Charles Tisdall, letter to Mrs. H. McCartney, 27 April 1979, Iseler Papers.

27. Malcolm Russell, interview by author, 8 February 2006.

28. Stephen Clarke, interview by author, 18 March 2006.

29. Elmer Iseler, handwritten note, 15 May 1979, Iseler Papers.

Chapter 8

1. Elmer Iseler, letter to John Bird, 28 January 1978, Iseler Papers. Elmer was to pen a heartfelt note of appreciation to John Bird for all of his support:

> Dear John,
> I go on from day to day thinking about how much you have

done for the Festival Singers, myself and therefore my family, over the years and it seems ridiculous not to have put my feeling of gratitude on paper more often.

The choir has just been through a great experience in their lives: whether or not they know it at the moment is beside the point, tours of other countries have to be mind-opening experiences and the Festival Singers have provided so many of these over the past ten years for the singers and myself that gratitude in itself seems a small thing, particularly towards someone such as yourself who has, on more than one occasion, kept the "glue" in the organization still sticking.

In the latest "crisis" I can only thank you for Jessie, the children and myself. I know that on occasion I have felt like throwing in the towel but as I get older I realize that I cannot "not conduct" or experience the lack of choral music for any length of time.

I hope to be writing letters of thanks over positive things for years to come. At any rate, without your help I could never have achieved what I have been able up to this time. I'm not yet near enough to my goals, therefore I am in need of your help as much as I have ever been.

Your friend,
Elmer

2. Minutes of the board of the Elmer Iseler Singers, 27 March 1980, Iseler Papers.
3. Helen M. Law, letter to Elmer Iseler, 21 March 1980, Iseler Papers.
4. John Kraglund, *Globe and Mail*, 14 March 1980.
5. Edward Weins, interview by author, 4 October 2006.
6. Lydia Adams, written submission to author, 11 September 2006.
7. Douglas Dunsmore, "Douglas Dunsmore," in *In Their Own Words: Canadian Choral Conductors*, ed. Holly Higgins Jonas (Toronto: Dundurn Press, 2001), 80.
8. Susan Knight, "Susan Knight," in *In Their Own Words*, 157.
9. Bill Gilday, "Bill Gilday," in *In Their Own Words*, 118. While in Yellowknife, Gilday arranged for Elmer to take a dogsled ride on Yellowknife Bay: "I'll never forget the sight of Elmer, perched like a king on the back of a sled, full of life and waving at a roaring Twin Otter that flew low over our heads under a

deep blue sky." The team of huskies was owned by Christine Milani, a former student of Elmer's at Northview Heights, another example of the devoted young people who were a part of his entourage wherever he visited.

10. Don James, "Don James," in *In Their Own Words*, 138.

11. Jessie Iseler, Submission to Zelda Heller, Music Officer of the Ontario Arts Council, 7 May 1980, p. 1, Iseler Papers:

> The year has been full of exciting diversity, from the sounds of Bach, with Andrew Davis at the organ, for two capacity audiences at the Church of Our Lady of Sorrows, to the student and family Christmas concerts at the Granite Club and Hart House, again full to the rafters. It was a Fall of music to remember. In Prince George the Indians in the front row brought tears to our eyes. The Western tour was so good in many ways, an artistic triumph, 13 concerts in 17 days, many sold out houses, wonderful togetherness and also a time for reflection and restoration through the magnificent beauty of the Canadian landscape. Our souls have been refreshed.
>
> As of late the wonderful colours of sound and the "Limericks" in the Harry Somers premiere for the Guelph Spring Festival put the audience in a perpetual state of laughter. The impact of packed St. Peter's Basilica in London, Ontario, after the audience had lined up for their seats and the beautiful music ringing from the Canadian Brass and our choir made us feel as though we were back in Europe. The CBC rehearsal sessions have had such a public response that all five will be repeated in August. It has all been so worthwhile and rewarding.

12. Minutes of a meeting of the board of the Elmer Iseler Singers, 29 October 1981, Iseler Papers.

13. Patti Walker, unpublished manuscript of a memoir of her participation in the tour of the Elmer Iseler Singers tour of Korea, Hong Kong, and Taiwan, August 1988, Iseler Papers.

14. Kenneth DeLong, *Calgary Herald*, 25 January 1988.

15. Peter Mose, *Toronto Star*, 19 June 1989, sec. C, p. 5.

16. Harry Currie, *Kitchener-Waterloo Record*, no date (1992).

17. National Youth Choir concert program, 2–18 May 1998, Iseler Papers.

Chapter 9

1. The Toronto Mendelssohn Choir had been the main reason for Toronto's reputation as a great choral centre in the early years of the twentieth century. Although the city had been graced with four major choral societies devoted to the performance of great compositions for the human voice, along with a number of choirs, only the TMC had survived into the century. There had been in the mid-nineteenth century the Toronto Philharmonic Society (serving orchestral as well as choral interests), the Toronto Vocal Music Society, the Metropolitan Choral Society, and the Musical Union. Of all this activity, the TMC remained, now almost as a symbol rather than a representation of Toronto's history of devotion to this genre of music making (*Encyclopedia of Music in Canada* [Toronto: University of Toronto Press, 1992]).

2. Udo Kasemets, *Toronto Daily Star*, 14 November 1962.

3. John Beckwith, *Toronto Daily Star*, 25 March 1964.

4. Elmer Iseler, letter "From the Conductor" to the TMC Executive Committee, dated Monday, 27 January 1969, Iseler Papers, indicated how important the audition process was to Elmer's transformation of the choir:

> As a result of the auditions last spring, the women's sections are exceptionally strong. This fall and winter I have followed the principle of auditioning new members whenever a vacancy has occurred.
>
> I wish to thank you in mid-season for our finest musical efforts in memory. And for at least the women of the Choir (the men, too, are performing admirably!) I want to announce that I am content with the membership, both in quality and number and find no necessity for auditions in the spring.

5. Lee Willingham, "A Community of Voices" (doctoral thesis, University of Toronto/Ontario Institute for Studies in Education, 2001).

6. *Ibid.*, 167.

7. *Ibid.*, 171–72.

8. *Ibid.*, 173.

9. *Ibid.*, 177.

10. *Ibid.*, 181–82.

11. John Kraglund, *Globe and Mail*, 10 November 1964.

12. John Kraglund, *Globe and Mail*, 31 December 1964.

13. John Beckwith, *Toronto Daily Star*, 10 November 1964.

14. George Kidd, *Toronto Telegram*, 14 April 1965.

15. John Beckwith, *Toronto Daily Star*, 14 April 1965.

16. Michael Steinberg, *Boston Globe*, 1 November 1965.

Chapter 10

1. During the 1960s, the author lived with his family of wife and four children in the small Ontario city of Peterborough, very much a largely white Anglo-Saxon enclave off the main concentration of industrial development that, after the Second World War, had been directed along the Macdonald-Cartier Freeway, the 401. The 1965–67 years were a revelation as Les Feux Follets and a barrage of Canadian artists appeared with orchestras and as individual performers in the Memorial Centre, the local ice rink. It was a convincing argument for an investment in the artistic community as the leading force in any effort to enhance a unity that would retain the qualities of those people who were now a part of the nation whose centennial was being celebrated.

2. Kenneth Winters, *Toronto Telegram*, 6 April 1966.

3. Kenneth Winters, *Toronto Telegram*, 16 November 1967.

4. William Littler, *Toronto Daily Star*, 28 August 1967. Littler was prepared to concede of Elmer's presentation of the work almost a year later in Massey Hall that "Iseler is gaining on the Bach B Minor Mass ... when, if ever, some Torontonian does scale the summit, my money says it will be the man who led last night's assault. Iseler's interpretation hasn't solved all the problems but he holds the score firmly in his grasp."

5. Elmer Iseler, handwritten note to the Mendelssohn Choir, April 1986, Iseler Papers.

6. Ron Hambleton, *Toronto Daily Star*, 18 December 1968.

7. James Kent, letter to John Lawson, president of the Toronto Mendelssohn Choir, no date, Iseler Papers.

8. Karel Ancerl, handwritten note to Elmer Iseler, 27 November 1969, Iseler Papers.

9. John Kraglund, *Globe and Mail*, 11 February 1970.

10. Kenneth Winters, *Toronto Telegram*, 11 February 1970.

11. Elmer Iseler, note to members of the Toronto Mendelssohn Choir, February 1970, Iseler Papers.
12. John Kraglund, *Globe and Mail*, 13 May 1970.
13. William Littler, *Toronto Daily Star*, 8 April 1971.
14. Ernest Bradbury, *Yorkshire Post*, 11 August 1972.
15. Andrew Porter, *Financial Times* (London), 24 August 1972.

Chapter 11

1. John Kraglund, *Globe and Mail*, 13 April 1973.
2. Harry Chusid, *Toronto Daily Star*, 6 November 1973.
3. Lauretta Thistle, *The Ottawa Citizen*, 25 October 1974. The concert was an enormous success. She observed, "It almost passes belief, in fact, that Mr. Iseler has elicited so many of the virtues of his small professional choir, the Festival Singers. He is a conductor to be cherished." She was outdistanced in her flattery by the *Ottawa Journal's* Ruth Francis, whose review headline proclaimed "Elmer Iseler in a stunning performance — an almost-perfect choir."
4. William Littler, *Toronto Star*, 29 October 1977.
5. Fred Graham, interview by author, 14 February 2006.
6. Victor Feldbrill, interview by author, 21 October 2005.
7. Eugene Watts, interview by author, 22 December 2006. Reaching out to the audience was, in Watts view, the caring for the audience by ensuring the best acoustics were available and resulted in Elmer's actions which could include, in one case, the removal of previously untouched tapestries from a ninth-century church in Lucerne, Switzerland.
8. John Reeves, interview by author, 27 January 2006.
9. Doreen Rao, interview by author, 1 September 2006.

Chapter 12

1. R.N.H., *Harrogate Herald*, 13 August 1980.
2. Het Volk, Ghent, 16 August 1980, in "The Toronto Mendelssohn Choir on Tour, August 1980," released by the TMC upon their return to Canada. TMC Archives.
3. Vers L'Avenir, 19 August 1980, in "The Toronto Mendelssohn Choir on Tour."

4. William Littler, "In Europe with the Toronto Mendelssohn Choir," *Toronto Star*, 19 August 1980.

5. Keith Aswell, *Edmonton Journal*, 22 August 1980.

6. Littler, "In Europe with the Toronto Mendelssohn Choir."

7. Jessie Iseler, interview by author, 18 July 2007. At one point in Elmer's crusade to restore choral funding an extraordinary drama was played out in the Canada Council offices in Ottawa. The confrontation at the table was between Canada Council chair Ms. Donna Scott and Canada Council CEO and author Roch Carrière and Elmer Iseler and choir manager Jessie Iseler. Before discussion opened, Elmer placed a suitcase on the table. Removing several issues of *Flare*, a magazine that Donna Scott had edited, he announced, "I have read these issues and I know who you are!" He then placed a pile of Roch Carrière's books before him and told the illustrious author, "I have read all your books and I know who you are. Now do both of you know who I am and why I am here to see a restoration of choral music funding by the Canada Council?" The line was ultimately restored to the budget allocations of the Canada Council and Scott and Carrière became Iseler friends and supporters.

8. As it turned out, some two decades later, the interior of Roy Thomson Hall had to be totally redesigned and reconstructed using wood interior decoration to replace the cement surfaces, and the reflectors and small tubes at the summit of the auditorium's dome had to be torn out. The sound was improved exponentially, but Elmer was no longer on the podium to appreciate the impact of the renovation.

9. There are those who would say that the symphony orchestra as a performing entity was and is still threatened by the same pressure. But there is much more opportunity for flexibility open to an orchestra in terms of the variety of instruments, an easier connection to the music of other countries and cultures, compared to the narrower historical legacy provided by the English and European tradition in choral music for large SATB oratorio choirs.

10. Ruth Watson Henderson, interview by author, 15 March 2006.

11. Actually, in 1988, Elmer received a blow well below the belt, one that revealed the extent to which the performing artist is at risk. In the fall of 1988, Michael Tumelty, critic for the *Glasgow Herald* accompanied the Scottish Symphony Orchestra on tour in North America. Elmer Iseler was conducting concerts in Toronto and Kitchener. For some unexplainable reason, he inappropriately attended Elmer's rehearsal and wrote a savage column that questioned every aspect of Elmer's conducting of the orchestra:

"his beating is wishy-washy ... Lots of curvaceous, evocative, manual gesture but not a lot of help to 70 orchestral players and over 100 singers ... too emotionally indulgent ... He quivered and shivered ... he flushed and rushed." On and on it went and yet Tumelty had to concede that the actual performance of the TMC was "superb, whatever else I've said about their mentor." *Glasgow Herald*, 2 November 1988.

12. A note, in Elmer's handwriting, found by Jessie amidst her personal papers. December 2006.

13. The irony of the author's membership is that he had spent almost his entire career, not in the private, but in the public sector, thus adding to the imbalance and the resulting incapacity of the TMC to fundraise effectively even more apparent. This merely demonstrates that boards have a tendency to appoint like-minded people with backgrounds not unlike those already represented by the existing membership rather than individuals who might assist the institution to cope with changing times.

14. The author put his attention to the affairs of the Toronto Mendelssohn Youth Choir, an extraordinary chorus of young people, initially under the leadership of Gerald Fagan but after a year under the baton of Robert Cooper. He and Elmer were one on the role of the TMYC, but though the board continued to allow the continued presence of the Youth Choir, there was little effort to provide adequate financing or administrative support for the enterprise. Elmer attempted to use Cooper's choral forces as often as it was possible in regular TMC concerts. Yet it was plain that there were some TMC choristers who resented the presence of such a splendid chorus of young people and complained of the cost at great length.

Chapter 13

1. Robert Cooper, interview by author, 27 September 2006.
2. Patricia Davies, *Globe and Mail*, 22 June 1983.
3. Elmer claimed to William Littler in an article describing the impact of his forced resignation from the leadership of the Festival Singers that he was a "deeply religious man" and expected to be judged on the basis of how well he had made use of his talents. It led him to believe that he must form another such choir.
4. Jessie Iseler, interview by author, 1 August 2006.

5. **Wilder** Penfield III, *Toronto Sun*, 26 November 1984. Elmer was also a vora-
    cious reader. Elmer claimed he read a book a week in order to keep himself
    vital and abreast of the thinking of writers of the literature of the day.

6. Noel developed a range of practical skills. Mary Coutts (née McKellar) and
    John Coutts speak in tones of appreciation of his carpentry skill. He built
    a verandah for them in St. Catharines and it was a work of art. The same
    attention to detail that characterized Elmer's attitude to choral performance
    was present in Noel's building projects.

    When David Balsillie purchased land in Copp Bay just a short distance
    from Jessie and Elmer's cottage, Noel was one of those who brought the logs
    from a disassembled Scarborough house and, in ten days, reconstructed the
    building on the Copp Bay shore.

7. Mr. Rose, Mayfield Secondary School, note to Buffy Iseler, undated, Iseler
    Papers.

8. Buffy Iseler, letter to her parents, undated, quoted by Elmer in handwritten
    notes for a speech. Iseler Papers.

9. Edwina Carson, interview by author, 2 June 2006. Carson was, during the
    1980s, Niki Goldschmidt's assistant for the Guelph Spring Festival and saw
    Jessie's role in action. The festival program did not contain a full biography of
    Elmer's career but rather a terse "professional" outline. Jessie realized that is
    was insufficient to satisfy Elmer's determination to expose the complete role
    of a choral conductor's life and insisted on an insert that would expand the
    program's account. On a Sunday morning before an afternoon performance
    Jessie's insistence led the festival staff to make use of the University of
    Guelph's reproduction services to supply the necessary copies.

10. Jessie Iseler, interview by author, 7 August 2006. Some years later, realizing
    that Elmer had no plumbing skills, the "boys" (all the husbands with plumbing
    skills on Copp Bay) informed Elmer, "By tonight Jessie will have running
    water." They purchased the necessary water lines, sink, and equipment, drilled
    through the floor, and installed a water system. It is an example of the close
    warm, special relationship of those fortunate to be part of this community.

    It was Jessie who, in the late 1980s, upgraded Elmer's water transport on
    Copp Bay by buying him a twenty-foot launch, named the "Sinful Jubilee," an
    extravagance to celebrate Elmer's twenty-five years as conductor of the TMC.

11. Paul Singleton, interview by author, 7 August 2006. Singleton was a board
    member of the Elmer Iseler Singers and a continuing supporter of Elmer
    from the 1970s. He understood the role of the board: to ensure the financial

health of the choir, warning the artistic director when there was no money to carry out overly ambitious projects, but leaving it to that figure to decide how to shift his policies to accommodate the monetary shortfall. He also recognized the enormous courage it took to be constantly challenging the Singers, board members, and audiences with unfamiliar and in some cases dissonant music. He reacted to any idea that Elmer could be expected to be present at a fundraising event before a performance when his entire focus had to be on preparing his mind to address the music he would conduct later in the evening. That he was often alone in his concern made him realize how little many board members understood the process they were overseeing.

12. Barbara Singleton, interview by author, 7 August 2006.

13. Martie Strayer Russel and Philip Russel, interview by author, 7 August 2006. Martie and Philip were among the Copp Bay people who came to the Iseler Singers and TMC concerts. After one gala occasion after which many parties had been organized in well-to-do homes, Martie was amazed that Elmer chose to come to a modest gathering of Copp Bay neighbours and spend the rest of the evening in their company. Philip, attending a Christmas program at the Granite Club that included a short singalong, found the key of "The First Noel" too high — and dropped an octave on the second verse. Elmer's first comment to him was "I heard that," and Philip discovered the extraordinary power of Elmer Iseler's ears.

   The Severn River–Copp Bay family included a vast range of cottagers — the Scheetzes, Irwins, Strayers, Smiths, Chants, Barks, Bedfords, Marshalls, Hallidays, Singletons, Jolliffes, Balsillies, Singers, Watermans, Goodwins, Pagets, Fitzpatricks, Clewes, Buchlers, Hollings, and Rouges. The importance of this gathering of support can be seen by the fact that Jim and Paul Singleton, Max Holling, and Gordon Marshall were all chairs of the Festival Singers board during the early building years of this choir. An extraordinary group of people!

   Major support figures beyond Copp Bay was the Mantei family, who lived in upper New York State but who not only joined Elmer and Jessie in fishing expeditions to the Iseler homestead in Quebec but also brought carloads of people from New York State to Elmer's concerts in Toronto.

Chapter 14

1. Edward Wiens, interview by author, 2 October 2006. A Festival Singer who

joined Elmer as a chorister in his Elmer Iseler Singers, Wiens was brought up in rural Saskatchewan and attended a Mennonite College in Winnipeg. In 1971, after further education, he came to Toronto, sang under Lloyd Bradshaw, and joined Elmer when the Festival Singers began afternoon rehearsals. He remembers the first concert and being terrified by the demanding music of Igor Stravinsky but was placed with Gordon Wry on his one side and Giles Bryant on the other. Wiens is still a chorister in the Elmer Iseler Singers and regarded Elmer's death as the loss of a very close friend.

2.   Peter Fisher, interview by author, 10 October 2005. Another singer who faced the same questions about Elmer's health in these last days was Peter Fisher, who, over some years, sang with Wayne Riddell's Tudor Singers, Elmer's Iseler Singers, and Noel Edison's Elora Singers. Peter is reluctant to dwell on comparisons but states, in reference to Elmer, that he never encountered a choral conductor who more clearly understood the architecture of every musical composition he encountered. His wife and partner, Jo-Anne Bentley, a mezzo-soprano soloist and a member of the University of Toronto Music Faculty, states that she attended an Iseler concert at the University of British Columbia and "was blown away and decided that it was in such elegant performance that I wished to use my voice."

3.   Lawrence Cherney, email to author, 3 December 2006.

4.   Irene Bailey, interview by author, 16 May 2006. Irene Bailey had no choral experience but had been recruited to lead the 100th Anniversary Celebration Committee of the Toronto Mendelssohn Choir a few years before. Her arrival on the board came at a time when there was a need for more corporate representation and particularly more women from the business world on the boards of arts organizations. She, in turn, brought colleagues from her community. It was a perfect case of inevitable tension around values and priorities. It was Irene's view that she had been brought on to assist in the celebration of an anniversary and had remained to assure the financial health of the TMC as a first priority.

Elmer had worked for decades within the limitations of inadequate financial support, sometimes donating his conductor's fee back when things were particularly difficult, but often delaying the cashing of his own remuneration cheque until there were sufficient funds in the choir bank account. However, he did insist that his professional choir members be paid in full and on time!

It was ironic that although both were possessed with the fear of financial ruin, Elmer and Irene Bailey found no common ground. It was Irene Bailey's view that only Elmer's retirement would initiate a solution to the TMC's monetary recovery.

5. Noel Edison had indicated that the TMC had not inquired about his availability as a conductor, but whether his Elora Festival singers were available. "They did not want me, they wanted my choir" was his sense of the situation. His efforts to bridge the gap by visiting an Elmer who was by then totally bedridden were considered untimely. The TMC ultimately signed a two-year contract with both the Elora Singers and Noel Edison. Both remain in place over a decade after the events of the spring of 1997.

6. The letter in question was addressed to Tom Laurie, vice-president of the RBC Dominion Securities Inc., as Irene Bailey had indicated she could devote no more time to the process and had to focus on her business responsibilities. Iseler Papers.

7. Vern Heinrichs, letter to Tom Laurie, 23 June 1997, Iseler Papers.

8. *Ibid.*

9. Irene Bailey, letter to Vern Heinrichs, 25 June 1997, Iseler Papers.

10. *Ibid.*

11. David King, interview by author, 19 October 2006. David King was one of the first members of Elmer's newly created Elmer Iseler Singers. However, he went on to become a choral conductor in his own right. He took his training at the Faculty of Music, University of Western Ontario, and became involved in music theatre, eventually becoming a professional singer. He has led the Canadian Brass All Star Choir but he is the founder and conductor of the ensemble All the King's Voices. He is an active teacher of vocal technique, sight singing, and musical theatre.

12. Robert Cooper, interviews by author, 27 September 2006 and 30 November 2006. Cooper was born in Ottawa. He sang in choirs in both elementary school (in particular, a Gilbert and Sullivan production in Grade 8) and secondary school. His full commitment to choral music came as a result of a year in England where he attended choral concerts at the Royal Festival Hall, Albert Hall, and other venues. He went on to graduate from the music program at the University of Western Ontario, where he became involved in conducting musicals and choral events in and around London, Ontario. He spent two years on a Canada Council Grant studying in Germany with Helmuth Rilling. On returning to Canada, he joined the CBC, eventually becoming the executive producer, opera and choral music at the CBC and conductor of the Toronto Mendelssohn Youth Choir, the Opera in Concert

Chorus, and Chorus Niagara. Recently, he has become artistic director of the Orpheus Choir of Toronto. He is recognized as a leading choral conductor and clinician and in 2003 received an honorary degree from Brock University and was appointed a Member of the Order of Canada.

Chapter 15

1. Jon Washburn, interview by author, 22 June 2007. Washburn continues to conduct his Vancouver Chamber Choir nearly forty years after its founding by him in 1971. His contribution to Canadian choral music is prodigious, including thirty recordings and hundreds of radio broadcasts and thousands of concert performances. His choir has commissioned and given premiere performances of more than 265 new choral works, including those by 85 Canadian composers. His Vancouver Chamber Choir has been honoured as the Canadian Ensemble of the Year by the Canadian Music Council and given the prestigious Margaret Hillis Award by Chorus America.

2. Wayne Riddell, interview by author, 26 June 2007. Riddell founded his Tudor Singers in Montreal in the 1970s and for decades provided a level of excellence that could be called legendary. He continues to teach and conduct, though the Tudor Singers no longer perform. In spite of ill health, his knowledge and professional expertise are in constant demand. When, in 2007, the eightieth birthday of Canadian composer John Beckwith was celebrated by a gala concert of his music, it was Wayne Riddell who was called upon to conduct the special chorus in an evening of his music.

3. Doreen Rao, interview by author, 1 September 2006.

4. Bramwell Tovey, a distinguished conductor in both the United Kingdom and Canada, was so outraged by the treatment Elmer had suffered that he refused to honour a contractual arrangement he had made to conduct a TMC concert. In a letter to Jessie on Elmer's death, Tovey described his first experience of seeing Elmer conduct the National Youth Choir in 1992. "I was absolutely staggered by his control of these young voices. In Schafer's work (*Epitaph for Moonlight*) the descending pyramids need to be so carefully balanced, so rhythmically poised, as well as perfectly in tune ... He was in control of the music, not just the technical aspects but in control of the heart of it. No performer can achieve more than that" (Bramwell Tovey, letter to Jessie Iseler, April 1998, Iseler Papers).

5. Lydia Adams, interview by author, 11 September 2006. Lydia Adams first heard the Festival Singers while she was a student at Mount Allison University. She was thunderstruck! She now knew she wanted to work with this man, Elmer Iseler. Before leaving for the United Kingdom to continue her studies with David Willcocks, she wrote a letter to Elmer Iseler indicating her determination to be a part of his world. She finally became the Elmer Iseler Singers' pianist and was accepted as Elmer's successor when cancer struck him down.

6. *Ibid.*

7. Don Kramer, interview by author, 11 September 2006. Dr. Kramer, by profession a dentist, has been an active chorister in Toronto for some decades. He received his enthusiasm for choral music from his mother, who, as a citizen of Langenburg, Saskatchewan, was an avid CBC listener. He joined the McGill Male Chorus while at university, but after some time in the United States, came to Toronto to establish himself professionally and joined, one by one, the Cantabile Singers, the Classical Singers, and the Orpheus Choir of Toronto. He continues to sing in the latter ensemble, under Robert Cooper's direction. It was John Fenton who, in 1982, convinced him to join the EIS board.

8. Lydia Adams, interview by author, 11 September 2006.

9. *Ibid.*

10. David Christiani, St. Lambert Choral Society 1997–98 Programme, Iseler Papers.

11. John Lawson, Address on the occasion of the November 4 TMC Tribute to Elmer Iseler, Iseler Papers.

12. Lydia Adams, interview by author, 11 September 2006.

Index